Charles Ives in the Mirror

MUSIC IN AMERICAN LIFE

*A list of books in the series appears
at the end of this book.*

Charles Ives in the Mirror

*American Histories
of an Iconic Composer*

DAVID C. PAUL

UNIVERSITY OF ILLINOIS PRESS

Urbana, Chicago, and Springfield

Publication of this book was supported by AMS 75 PAYS
Endowment of the American Musicology Society, funded
in part by the National Endowment for the Humanities and
the Andrew W. Mellon Foundation, and by a grant from the
Henry and Edna Binkele Classical Music Fund.

The Library of Congress cataloged the cloth edition as follows:
Paul, David C., 1973– author.
Charles Ives in the mirror : American histories
of an iconic composer / David C. Paul.
pages cm. — (Music in American life)
Includes bibliographical references and index.
ISBN 978-0-252-03749-8 (cloth : alk. paper)
ISBN 978-0-252-09469-9 (e-book)
1. Ives, Charles, 1874–1954—Appreciation—History.
2. Musicology—United States—History—20th century.
I. Title.
ML410.I94P38   2013
780.92—dc23   2012035258

PAPERBACK ISBN 978-0-252-08051-7

To Winnie

Contents

Acknowledgments

It has been just under a decade since I first set out to explore Ives's "after-lives," a term I am borrowing (and creatively misreading) from Walter Benjamin's well-known essay about the task of a translator. In that period, I have had many Virgils and one Beatrice to guide me along the way.

First to the Virgils. I cannot imagine a better apprenticeship than the one I received at the hands of Richard Taruskin, Mary Ann Smart, and the other stellar faculty at Berkeley, where I completed my PhD. I am just as much indebted to the cohort of graduate students who were my colleagues there. Two of them deserve special mention: Michael Markham for reading a draft version of chapter 4 and saving me from an embarrassingly infelicitous turn of phrase or two, and Noel Verzosa for doing some last-minute digging in the Library of Congress. I spent several of my graduate-student years in Seattle, where I found a second home among the graduate students of the University of Washington. Lincoln Ballard, Timothy Kinsella, Gwynne Khuner-Brown, Rachel Mundy, and Glynn Olive welcomed me into their informal dissertation workshop and read early versions of chapters two and three.

The second half of the book is the product of my years as an assistant professor at the University of California, Santa Barbara, where I have accumulated many more debts. I am blessed with two wonderful musicology colleagues, Stefanie Tcharos and Derek Katz, who have been invaluable as mentors and the most trusted of friends. I have also enjoyed the support of Patricia Hall, Timothy Cooley, Ruth Hellier-Tinoco, and David Novak, whose different disciplinary perspectives have led to many stimulating conversations. My graduate students too, have been a vital source for engaging discussion. I am especially grateful to Anita Ip, who did some quick translation work, and Michael Joiner, who tracked down a few errant pieces of information for me while he was conducting his own research at Yale. Crucial to the career of any assistant professor is the network of supportive colleagues who volunteer their services as peer readers. Here again, I have been very lucky. Tim Freeze, Derek Katz, Gwynne Khuner-Brown, Michael Markham, and Drew Massey all read drafts and offered suggestions about parts of the manuscript. I look forward to returning the favor. My thanks also to Carol Oja for helping me secure an image of Henry Cowell.

The last three chapters of this book would have been impossible without the generosity of the Ives community. They have welcomed me into their midst without reservation, whatever misgivings they might have felt about becoming a part of my narrative. J. Peter Burkholder, Gayle Sherwood Magee, Vivian Perlis, Larry Starr, Geoffrey Block, Judith Tick, Clayton Henderson, Robert Morgan, and Philip Lambert all agreed to interviews or responded to my lengthy email inquiries. Peter Burkholder, in particular, has been extraordinarily helpful, reading two chapters of the book and offering useful feedback. For me, he is the model of scholarly propriety and magnanimity. Gerald Soliday, though not a member of the Ives community, agreed to be interviewed about his friend and colleague Frank Rossiter, whose death deprived us of a transformative Ives scholar. Two additional members of the Ives community, Michael Broyles and David Nicholls, served as readers for the entire manuscript when it was submitted to the University of Illinois Press. Their enthusiastic comments and insightful advice helped sustain me through the final stages of completing this book.

Institutional support has also been crucial to my project. Capable staff at several libraries helped me make my way through archival material. They include the New York Public Library, where George Boziwick and his colleagues in the Music Division have been generous with time and energy; the Irving S. Gilmore Music Library at Yale University, where Richard Boursy and Emily Ferrigno have fielded many requests; the Library of Congress; and the Rare Book and Manuscript Library at the University of Pennsylvania. The American Musicological Society provided crucial financial support in the form an AMS 50 fellowship when I was a graduate student, and it has come to my aid yet again through a publication subvention. The *Journal of the American Musicological Society* also served as the first venue for portions of chapters two and three. I have benefited from a Hellman Fellowship, which funded a research trip in the fall of 2009 and other sundry costs associated with this book. UCSB provided me with a quarter of sabbatical relief from my teaching duties, which allowed me to complete large portions of the manuscript. Of course, without the efforts expended by the personnel at the University of Illinois Press, all this would have been for naught. I am particularly grateful to Senior Acquisitions Editor Laurie Matheson, who solicited the manuscript in the first place and guided me through the initial stages of the publishing process; Assistant Managing Editor Jennifer S. Clark, who oversaw production; and copyeditor Nancy Albright, whose discerning eye caught many things mine missed. The index was expertly constructed by Janyne Ste Marie.

Finally, I turn to the people closest to me. My parents, Anne and Reg Paul, and sister, Beth, have always supported me. The rich memories of our family life—summer holidays, the bustling festivities of Christmas, bicycle rides along the Bow River, quiet Sunday afternoons immersed in books—are the threads from which my strongest affinities for Charles Ives are woven.

But the person for whom I reserve my deepest and most heartfelt thanks is my wife Winnie Cai, my Beatrice. Unlike poor Dante, whose intimacy with Beatrice could never trespass beyond the bounds of poetry, I, throughout my exploration of Ives's afterlives, have had Winnie's real companionship. She was there when I wrote the first words of this book, and she is here now, as I write these last words, her support never once faltering along the way. Her unfailing optimism has tempered my pessimism; her wise pragmatism has channeled my ambitions toward grand, but realizable, ends; her foresight has saved me countless times from the chaos wrought by procrastination. My life would be much poorer for the absence of Winnie and her love—and as for this book, it wouldn't exist.

Charles Ives in the Mirror

Introduction

Charles Edward Ives is a stolid New England name. For those who know it, it is likely to conjure up images of a man in old age, bearded, clutching a cane, perhaps his bald pate exposed, but more likely hidden beneath a dilapidated old hat. In photographs, when he looks at the camera directly, there is mischief in his eyes that belies his years; more typically, though, he stares off into some middle-distance, lost in thought. The name might also prompt recollections of a life lived unusually. Of a wealthy executive in the insurance industry who pursued composition as an avocation, cramming music making into the spare moments afforded him in the evenings and on weekends. Of the man as composer, enduring years of withering criticism and ridicule before winning autumnal fame, but by then a sexagenarian whose muse had long since departed. And then there is the music: symphonies, string quartets, sonatas, and songs through which process a cavalcade of musical Americana. Old fiddle tunes and fraternity songs, solemn hymns and exuberant marches—they are all there, often enveloped in a nostalgic aureole, sonic sepia memories of boyhood summers in a small town long ago.

It is a name that has prompted some of the most extravagant encomiums from American musicians. "Charles Ives," Leonard Bernstein famously declared in 1958, "has been said over and over to be our greatest, our first really great composer; our pride and our passion; our Washington, Lincoln, and Jefferson of music."[1] At the time, Ives still drew enough criticism to make this hyperbole. But in another sense, though not quite the one Bernstein intended, his comparison between Ives and the patriarchal figures of American history was fitting then and remains so today. Ives has been the subject of mythologies as varied as those that have accumulated around our founding fathers and best-remembered presidents. And like Washington, Lincoln, and Jefferson, the stories told about Ives are bound up in deep convictions about what it means to be American. Already by the late fifties, Ives had been variously portrayed as an American pioneer of musical modernism, an ethnographically inclined composer who had discovered the richness of American folk music, and a symbol of American freedom. Since Bernstein's pronouncement, Ives has taken on other guises: a victim of sociosexual mores of Gilded Age American culture; a composer steeped in the European classical-music tradition but approaching it from an American vantage; the patriarch of a line of maverick composers; and, in the grand tradition of American hucksterism and snake-oil salesmen, the perpetrator of one of the greatest musical hoaxes of all times. Hero, victim, villain—Ives has been all these things, sometimes singly, sometimes simultaneously.

The changing images of Ives across the twentieth and twenty-first centuries, the faces of an American music icon, are the subject of this book. In the pages that follow, my focus is not the historical Ives but the way he has been imagined by the critics, composers, performers, and scholars who have been moved to speak or write about him. Many of them are marquee names of American classical-music history themselves—Bernstein, Henry Cowell, Aaron Copland, Elliott Carter—while others are not so well known. Whether they are remembered today or not, these men and women imbued their ideas about Ives with something of themselves and their experiences—especially their experiences as Americans. Thus the history of Ives's reception is not simply a series of portraits of an unusual composer, it is also a series of mirrors that reflect the way Americans have viewed themselves. It is the restive, fractured story of nation in miniature.

. . .

The reception of Ives has been an abiding preoccupation almost as far back as there is serious writing about him. Biographers in particular have felt obliged to trace the trajectory from anonymity to canonicity that distinguishes the last third of his life, when he was no longer active as a composer. Indeed, the first full biography, Henry and Sidney Cowell's *Charles Ives and His Music* (1955), includes a chapter devoted to the subject and is surely one of the earliest reception studies in musical scholarship. But while biographers have frequently charted the vicissitudes in Ives's reputation, the imperatives of the genre in which they work are constraining. The spotlight can never rove far from the central subject—Ives—and, as a result, the advocates and detractors that have shaped conversations about him are necessarily confined to supporting roles. A proper reception history, as I have tried to supply with this book, makes them the principals.

The Cowells set the precedent for the approach that has been most common in Ives scholarship. Their reception chapter is essentially a list of successful premieres annotated by quotations of critical accolades drawn from the popular and scholarly press. The image they project is one of gradually expanding celebrity that is true as far as it goes, but it belies the complex factors contributing to Ives's popularity, assumes that the discourse about him has been singular, and effaces the individuality of the interlocutors who have participated over the years. Of the seven Ives biographies in the English language, only two depart from Cowellian precedent. The earliest of the pair, Frank R. Rossiter's *Charles Ives and His America* (1975), is notable for the space it devotes to examining the American avant-garde of the late twenties and early thirties, where discourse about Ives first thrived. According to Rossiter, this is the context for the crystallization of the eight tropes of what he calls the "Ives legend":

- Precedence as a musical pioneer
- Preeminence as a fundamentally *American* composer
- Self-chosen isolation from the professional world of music
- The disgraceful neglect of his music
- His discovery by the younger composers of the early 1930s
- The slow recognition of his music
- The certainty that music lovers of the future would finally understand and vindicate him
- The flagellation of American culture (past and present) for neglecting him[2]

This is a thorough inventory of ideas in circulation about Ives by the thirties. However, Rossiter tends to treat his "Ives legend" as a static entity, as if all subsequent commentators recycled the same material without variation or transformation. The most recent biography, Gayle Sherwood Magee's *Charles Ives Reconsidered* (2008), offers a more dynamic view of Ives's early reception, and one in which the composer himself played a proactive role. Magee's Ives is the perennial salesman, packaging and repackaging his music until he hit upon a winning combination. But Magee, like the other biographers, leaves the narrative at 1954, the year Ives died, and ventures only tentatively into the posthumous period. Understandably, the obligations of the biographer become murky after he or she has narrated the death of the subject. The problem is that Ives has been reimagined several times over in the decades since.

The pull of biography is centripetal, toward the composer, and this too is the tendency of most other modes of scholarship, whether they are concerned with issues of formal construction, hermeneutics, aesthetics, or cultural context. Reception, by contrast, pushes outward centrifugally. This is what made it so controversial when it first became the prerogative of a group of German literary theorists in the sixties. The Konstanz School, as they are sometimes called, challenged the regnant essentialist view of literary works, with Hans Robert Jauss leading the charge. In an influential 1967 essay, Jauss postulated, "the quality and rank of a literary work result neither from the biographical or historical conditions of its origin, nor from its place in the sequence of the development of a genre alone, but rather from the criteria of influence, reception, and posthumous fame, criteria that are more difficult to grasp."[3] Although it would take American musicologists some fifteen years before they began to explore the implications of this postulate for the history of music, a handful of their German colleagues responded more immediately. Among them was Carl Dahlhaus, who worried that Jauss and his cadre opened the door to relativism, that they granted legitimacy to any interpretation of a work, whether its source was the composer, a critic, or whomever happened to be sitting in the left-center aisle seat of the third row during a concert. How was the music historian to arbitrate between interpretations that could be as numerous as there were listeners?[4] This is a problem that every subsequent reception historian has had to resolve, and it is much discussed in the burgeoning recent literature on the subject.[5]

My solution is to invoke what literary theorist Stanley Fish calls "interpretive communities," or to use an alternate locution deployed by intellectual historian David Hollinger, "communities of discourse."[6] The crucial idea here is that no interpretive act takes place in a vacuum. It is instead constrained by the "practices and assumptions" that the interpreter shares with other people.[7] Or, to put it in different terms, interpretations of Ives are the product of particular habits of thought, artistic philosophies, political agendas, or scholarly paradigms that arise from social interactions and are sustained by institutions. Thus, in this book, I place as much priority on mapping the interpretive communities in which people have spoken about Ives as I do to unpacking their ideas. It is my conviction that the richness of Ives's reception stems in large part from the wide variety of such communities: the denizens of modernist salons and readership of politically passionate "little magazines" of the twenties and thirties; the audiences that filled major concert halls and the consumers of high-circulation newspapers of the post–World War II period; the proponents and organizers of the cultural diplomacy programs run by the U.S. Information Agency (USIA) during the Cold War; and, since the late sixties, the professoriate of several academic disciplines.

The topographies of interpretive communities are not flat and undifferentiated since not all members carry equal sway—some voices always speak louder and with greater effect than others. This being the case, I pay particular attention to issues of agency (how an idea transfers from one person to another) and constituency (the nature and size of the audience to which a person speaks). The voices I privilege are the ones that have had the most impact in shaping the various conversations about Ives. Practically, this has meant omitting the contributions of some perceptive Ivesians, for it is not the quality of ideas that is the criterion for inclusion, but how widely disseminated they have become. As a further limitation, I have confined my attention to American discourse about Ives, glancing occasionally at Europe, and not at all at other parts of the globe. Within these bounds, I have tried to be comprehensive, though I too am subject to the biases of my own community of discourse and have likely overlooked things that will seem salient to others. Some speculations about how I locate my voice in the discussion can be found in the postscript.

· · ·

For the most part, this book is organized chronologically, but some of its chapters do overlap when the subject matter has seemed to me to demand it. The first chapter, which is concerned with Ives's own self-promotional activities, spans the period from 1920 to 1934. Its point of departure is an analysis of *Essays Before a Sonata*, which Ives published as a prose prolegomenon to his Piano Sonata No. 2, "Concord, Mass., 1840–60" in 1920, and it concludes with a discussion of the unpublished autobiographical *Memos*, which dates from the early thirties and constitutes his last substantial writings. The second chapter jumps back to 1927, a year that marks the beginning of Henry Cowell's protracted engagement with Ives and his music. Cowell is the dominant figure in both the second and third chapters, which together take my narrative to 1965, but there are a number of other men and women who jostle for attention, their stories and ideas being crucial to this period that witnessed Ives's initiation to the classical pantheon—Cowell's wife Sidney, pianist John Kirkpatrick, and celebrity conductors Leonard Bernstein and Leopold Stokowski to name a few. The fourth chapter is the first of two that cover the same twenty-year span, centered on the 1974 centenary celebrations of Ives's birth. During this period, scholars from a variety of disciplines—history, musicology, English literature—superseded the composers and performers who had formerly been Ives's most vocal proponents. It witnessed discourse about Ives take root in academia. Chapter four focuses on the impact of scholars who worked under the "American Studies" rubric, while in chapter five, musicologists move to the footlights. The final chapter picks up where the fifth left off, exploring how Ives has been affected by the dramatic transformations American musicology has undergone over the last twenty-five years. Finally, I double back to the thirties, to trace the international and multidecade voyage of a narrative that casts Ives as the patriarch of a line of American maverick composers—a narrative that now, at the beginning of the twenty-first century, has become integral to his portrayal in concert halls across the United States.

Covering nearly a century, the sweep of this book is broad, and the locales it visits are many and varied, from the bohemian enclaves of the Bay Area to the most prestigious concert halls of the United States, from the makeshift offices of a New Orleans arts magazine to the lecture halls and libraries of Ivy League universities. My protagonists, the inhabitants of these spaces, are diverse too, as are the stories they tell. But what links them all, aside from a fascination with Ives, is an abiding preoccupation with the nature of American experience. Ives and his music have served as a prism, refracting the rhetoric of the nationalist, the passions of the patriot, the ruminations of the discontent, and the grievances of the outcast.

Conservative Transcendentalist
or Modernist Firebrand?
Ives and His First Publics, 1921–1934

Early in 1921, several hundred Americans were puzzled to discover an unsolicited package in their mail that contained a pair of books.[1] The larger of the two was bound in dark red cloth, and on the cover, framed by horizontal double lines, gilt lettering with a curlicued "M" and "E" lent a modest decorative touch. Roughly twelve inches in height, its size was typical for a volume of music, which the title, "Second Pianoforte Sonata," declared it to be. There was also a subtitle, "Concord, Mass., 1840–60," and for it the largest lettering on the sparse front cover had been reserved—larger even than for the name of the composer, Charles E. Ives (Figure 1.1). The second, smaller book, entitled *Essays Before a Sonata*, contained only prose, but it was attributed to the same Mr. Ives.

The name was unfamiliar to all but a few of the recipients. Perhaps some of them thought they had received the books as targets of a marketing strategy devised by the ingenious minds of the rapidly growing advertising industry. They would not have been far off the mark, for Mr. Ives, composer and author, was also responsible for some of the most successful advertising copy ever written in the insurance business. Moreover, it was his motivational ideas and sales methods that were the standard equipment of a small army of door-to-door salesmen, who worked for the successful New York–based firm of Ives and Myrick, a subsidiary of the Mutual Life Insurance Company. Though there were many New Yorkers who received the two books, none of them (excepting personal acquaintances) realized it was that Ives. This *was* a pitch for a product, but one that was more intangible than an insurance policy; it was a bid for musical recognition on the part of a businessman who devoted his spare time to composing.

Those who read through the smaller book of essays would have encountered familiar ideas expressed in tortured prose. Ives had a predilection for parenthetical

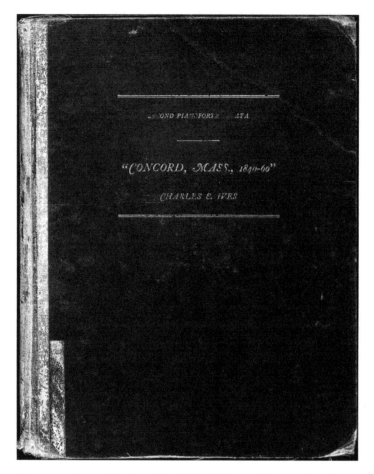

Figure 1.1. Cover of Ives's self-published "Concord" Sonata (1920).
Courtesy Eda Kuhn Loeb Music Library of the Harvard College Library.

asides, oracular pronouncements, and an aversion to footnotes, though he laced his text with literary and scholarly references. The subjects of the essays were mid-nineteenth-century American literary worthies who had lived in Concord, Massachusetts—Ralph Waldo Emerson, Nathaniel Hawthorne, Bronson and Louisa May Alcott, and Henry Thoreau. Every educated American had learned to venerate these writers as the foundational and foremost figures of American letters, and Ives in *Essays* added his voice of assent.

Unfortunately for Ives, the conventional opinions about Emerson and his circle conveyed in *Essays* were a poor match for the unorthodox music of the "Concord" Sonata. The work is comprised of four movements, each bearing the name of one of the Concordians (two of them in the case of the third movement, "The Alcotts"), and each purportedly giving musical expression to the corresponding essay in the prose volume. At times, the music is fabulously difficult, posing challenges to even the most accomplished pianist, and it often spills into three staves (occasionally even four), the intricacies defying the customary piano-score pair. There are long passages that dispense with the rhythmic reassurances of the bar line, a section in which the composer called for a heavy board to be laid across the keys of the piano to create tone clusters; shocking dissonances; and, almost as startling, moments of utter diatonic simplicity. Few people had seen anything like it.

And so, with this mismatched pair of vanity publications, Ives began a long journey from margin to center; over the course of the next forty years, this obscure, enigmatic figure would come to be seen as the great patriarch of American music. In 1921, this outcome could hardly have been predicted, for the self-publication venture seemed a failure—and an expensive one at that. The reviews were dismissive, if not outright derisive, though the "Concord" Sonata did manage to win Ives a few early devotees, most of them denizens of the scattered modernist enclaves across the United States. It was a poor return on a substantial investment.

Nonetheless, good businessman that he was, Ives fostered the loyalty of his handful of admirers, just as he encouraged his agents to pursue any opening to secure a sale. Generally speaking, these first Ivesians placed a premium on technical innovation and expressed little interest in the putative literary content of the sonata. Accordingly, the composer's tactics of self-promotion shifted. By the early thirties, when his diabetic condition necessitated that he scale back his activities, Ives no longer enveloped his music with the literary aura of Concord. Instead, he staked his claim as the inventor of musical techniques that were on the cutting edge of musical modernism. This was the first of many transformations Ives would undergo as a public persona, and the only one in which he, as his own advocate, would play a substantial role.

Imagining Concord: *Essays Before a Sonata* and Its Literary Context

The work of completing the "Concord" Sonata from copious draft manuscripts and the writing of *Essays Before a Sonata* were done in Asheville, North Carolina, where Ives and his wife Harmony stayed for eight weeks, early in 1919. The previous October, Ives had suffered a breakdown that was psychosomatic in nature, though incipient diabetes may have played a role. In the medical argot of the day, neurasthenia would have been the diagnosis, a nervous disease that mental health specialists regarded as having reached epidemic proportions among overworked businessmen.[2]

Ives fit the bill. For just under a decade, he and his business partner Julian Myrick had led their firm from success to success, becoming rich men in the process. At the same time, in the evenings and on weekends, Ives avidly pursued his avocation as a composer. When the United States joined the First World War, his schedule became even more hectic as he sought outlets for his patriotic fervor. Ives launched a second hobby as a political pamphleteer, threw himself into the Liberty Bond drive, and even attempted to enlist in the Red Cross, with intentions of driving an ambulance in France (he failed the medical exam). The pace was frenetic, unsustainable, and on October 1st, after a contentious meeting of the Liberty Bond Committee in New York, his health gave out.[3] During the long period of convalescence that followed, the Iveses took the standard prescription meted out to neurasthenics: a "rest cure." They traveled to the picturesque town of Asheville nestled at the confluence of two rivers in the Blue Ridge Mountains, the home of one of Harmony's sisters. But while there, Ives did little resting. Instead, freed of his business commitments, he devoted his time to preparing for the biggest gambit he would ever attempt to get his music noticed.

Ives never explained the inception of the blind mailing campaign nor the decision to make the "Concord" Sonata the lynchpin, but given his reputation in the insurance industry for successful sales strategies, it is reasonable to assume that he gave these matters considerable thought. Over the years, Ives had made numerous overtures to the broader musical world. He had importuned friends who were music professionals for opinions about his works, hired copyists to generate clean parts and performers to play through them, and, on one notable occasion in 1910, secured a reading of his First Symphony by the conductor Walter Damrosch and the New York Symphony Society.[4] Those efforts had met with noncommittal shrugs at best and vehement rejection at worst. Ives would later recount the story of a concert violinist who floundered through the opening of his First Violin Sonata and gave up in disgust, declaring, "When you get awfully indigestible food in your stomach that distresses you, you can get rid of it, but I cannot get those horrible sounds out of my ears."[5] It is a measure of Ives's temerity that he would attempt an end-run around the professional musicians like this violinist, who had responded so poorly to his music, and make a direct appeal to the musical public. For this is surely what he was trying to do when he distributed his vanity publications to individuals whose names he had assembled from membership and subscription lists of major music organizations and magazines.[6]

As to why he chose the "Concord" Sonata, there were practical considerations. His output consisted of several symphonies and string quartets, but choosing a work in one of those genres made little sense since most of the recipients would have neither the means to render it nor the ability to hear it in their inner ear. Songs were a viable possibility, and indeed, in 1922, Ives would issue a third self-published volume containing a selection of 114 of his songs. But a piano sonata had the obvious advantage of requiring a single player, and, recording technology still being relatively new, most musical Americans possessed some skill at the keyboard. By the time Ives departed for Asheville, he had substantial drafts for two piano sonatas, but the second one had more obvious appeal: it was programmatically associated with the writers who were, by near unanimous agreement, the most important canonical figures of American literature.[7] Ralph Waldo Emerson, in particular, enjoyed a posthumous celebrity that had proven enormously lucrative for publishers and helped make the small town of Concord, Massachusetts, where he had lived alongside the other literary worthies celebrated in Ives's sonata, a tourist destination.[8] The name *Concord* was one to conjure with, and Ives knew it.

It is unclear precisely when Ives's affinity for the mid-nineteenth-century Concordians developed. Later, his proponents would claim that the Ives family had been steeped in the writings of Emerson, Thoreau, and their associates for generations, and that Ives imbibed the transcendentalist views that had been Concord's special issue early on, just as he did the sounds of amateur music making in his hometown of Danbury, Connecticut. But the evidence is thin. More likely, Ives's first real engagement with Emerson and his circle came in college, when, as a student at Yale University, he took an American literature course taught by the well-known pedagogue William Lyon Phelps. Even then, the Concordians do not appear as a regular presence in his correspondence or as a musical inspiration until after his marriage to Harmony Twichell, a minister's daughter who had a strong literary bent.[9]

That said, Ives cannot have been wholly oblivious to the Concordians growing up, for the process of hagiography that enshrined them in American literary history coincided with his formative years. When Emerson died in 1882, eight years after Ives's birth, eulogies poured forth, praising him as an American spiritual seer whose luminous personality, perhaps even more than the profundity of his thought, had exerted an ennobling influence on those who had read his writings or heard him lecture.[10] Nor did the flood of encomiums abate, for over the subsequent two decades, leading up to the centennial of his birth in 1903, Emerson's celebrity grew enormously, and along with it, that of the writers who had been in his orbit.

Several interrelated factors propelled this process of canonization. Most significant was the expansion of print culture in the late nineteenth century, facilitated by the development of more efficient and inexpensive methods of paper making. Shrewd New York and Chicago publishing houses produced reprints of works by Emerson and his contemporaries in library series that were affordable even for Americans of limited means. At the same time, and partly in response to the expanded profile the Concordians enjoyed through mass print culture, a secondary literature of short essays, longer commentaries, and biographies proliferated. Finally, the American literature courses that began to appear in public schools, colleges, and universities in the 1880s made national heroes of this coterie.[11] Ives, in taking such a course at Yale, underwent a rite of passage experienced by many of his contemporaries, but one that had not existed a generation earlier.

The advent of American literature courses typifies the self-reflexivity of the late nineteenth century, when Americans, confronted by rapid changes—mass immigration, the escalation of industrialization, and a growing role on the world stage—raised questions of national identity. Studying the literary past was one way of finding answers—or rather, inculcating in American youth a particular set of socially sanctioned answers. Textbooks from the time period reveal a startling regularity to the narratives then advanced in high school and college literature courses. As literary historian Nina Baym has shown, the common factor is a trials-to-triumph trajectory in which a definitively American literature arises from Puritan roots but attains its full flower through the secularizing tendencies of Unitarianism and the élan of transcendentalism. The pivotal figure in these textbooks, the great redeemer of American letters is always the same: Ralph Waldo Emerson.[12]

Exemplary is *Initial Studies in American Letters*, authored by Yale English professor Henry A. Beers, first published in 1887, reissued in 1891, and revised in 1895 (by which time, Ives was a sophomore). The first three chapters of the book span 1607 to 1837 and are mostly spent enumerating the shortcomings of early American writers. By and large, Beers viewed this period as having more historical than literary significance, and what little Americans produced that could be called belletristic fell far short of the mark set by contemporary English authors. But in 1837, Emerson delivered his Phi Beta Kappa address at Harvard, "The American Scholar," and inaugurated the "one movement in the history of the American mind which has given to literature a group of writers having coherence enough to merit the name of a school." Besides Emerson, there was Bronson Alcott, Margaret Fuller, Henry Thoreau, and Nathaniel Hawthorne—all denizens of Concord at one time or another, and, excepting Hawthorne, all committed transcendentalists. Typically, Beers did not regard the Concord coterie as the unexpected yield of previously barren soils. Rather, he explained, "the movement was but a new avatar of the old Puritan spirit," a spirit that Unitarianism had quickened by softening the "traditional prejudice . . . against the ornamental side of life." Also typical were the traits Beers assigned to the individual authors belonging to the school. Emerson, for example, was the seer, the man of principled and poetic abstractions, who could be hard to understand, sometimes contradictory, but always the dispenser of truths. Hawthorne, on the other hand, was the consummate artist, whose style though at first "stilted and bookish . . . gradually acquired an exquisite perfection, and is as well worth study as that of any prose classic in the English tongue."[13] Consulting other textbooks of this period—Henry S. Pancoast's *An Introduction to American Literature* (1898) say, or William P. Trent's *A History of American Literature, 1607–1865* (1903)—one finds much the same narrative and similar critical assessments of the members of the American literary pantheon.[14]

In a brief prefatory note, Ives explained that *Essays* and the "Concord" Sonata were together "an attempt to present (one person's) impression of the spirit of transcendentalism that is associated in the minds of many with Concord, Mass., of over a half century ago."[15] The acknowledgment of subjectivity in the parentheses—Ives's insertion, not mine—is misleading, for what he presented was not just his impression but one that he shared with the majority of Americans who had studied the Concordians in high school or college literature courses. It was an impression garnered from textbooks and classroom instruction by the likes of Beers, Pancoast, and Trent, who recycled the same narrative of American literary history. Thus, from the standpoint of the reception of Emerson, Hawthorne, the Alcotts, and Thoreau, the content of *Essays* is wholly unremarkable—and, as it would turn out, a bit dated.

Because the turn-of-the-century consensus made Emerson the central figure of the Concord milieu, and because Emerson had become a flashpoint for debate by the time *Essays* was written, it is worth taking a closer look at Ives's assessment of the writer. His Emerson essay is divided into three sections, the first dealing with the "substance" of the Concordian's accomplishment, the general content of his prose writings, poems, and lectures, apart from specific examples.[16] In this section, Ives drew the curtain on an Emerson garbed in the raiment in which he was customarily portrayed: "Though a great poet and prophet, he is greater, possibly, as an invader of the unknown,—America's deepest explorer of spiritual immensities." And, in keeping with past precedent, Ives traced the standard lineage of the Concord sage. Generations of Emerson's forebears had prepared the way, he explained, their "mental and spiritual muscles" hardened by the rigors of Puritanism. To a great extent, theirs was a religion "based . . . on a search for the unknowable, limited only by the dogma of its theology . . . while Emerson's transcendentalism was based on the wider search for the unknowable, unlimited in any way or by anything except the vast bounds of innate goodness." Freedom from the shackles of dogma had come through the agency of Unitarians, who "fought for the dignity of human nature" against "arbitrary revelation."[17] Like a dutiful undergraduate, Ives was hitting all the marks as he reiterated received opinion. Indeed, his former professor, William Lyon Phelps, enthused over *Essays* after he received the volume and encouraged Ives to send a copy to none other than Henry A. Beers. "He will *love* it," Phelps predicted, "I'll guarantee that."[18] There is no record of whether Ives followed through, but Phelps was probably right about how Beers would have responded.

In the second section of the essay, Ives turned to the question of "manner," the means by which Emerson expressed himself, and admitted that there was sometimes a lack of coherence in the prose. This too was a typical assessment, something Ives acknowledged by citing Thomas Carlyle, whose correspondence with Emerson was first published in 1883 and then reissued in many subsequent editions.[19] Though Ives was not specific, he probably had in mind an 1844 letter in which Carlyle chided his American colleague for sentences that did not "rightly stick to their foregoers and their followers."[20] Besides Carlyle, Ives could have mustered any number of more recent critics who repeated the same opinion. He might, for example, have turned to Beers, who opined, "The sentence was [Emerson's] unit in composition. His lectures seem to begin anywhere and to end anywhere and to resemble strings of exquisitely polished sayings rather than continuous discourses."[21] Ives's own formulation closely resembles Beers's, though the logic is inverted: "Emerson wrote by sentences or phrases, rather than by logical sequence. His underlying plan of work seems based on the large unity of a series of particular aspects of a subject, rather than on the continuity of its expression."[22] Here, Ives presented a solution to the problem of Emerson's prose by appealing to higher unities, a standard tactic for late-nineteenth-century commentators.

One of the most influential of such commentators was Oliver Wendell Holmes, who deployed this tactic in his 1884 biography of Emerson. Holmes, a Bostonian who had many ties to the Concord milieu, was so intent on portraying Emerson as existing on an elevated plane of thought that he more or less neglected the writer's engagement with contemporary reform movements, the abolitionist cause in particular.[23] Ives referenced Holmes's biography in *Essays*, and its influence can be detected in several places, notably the assertion that for Emerson "slavery was *not* a social or political or an economic question, nor even one of morals or ethics, but one of universal spiritual freedom only."[24] Here was an Emerson whose thought was so lofty it impinged only incidentally on the workaday world.

In Holmes's biography and other contemporaneous writings, the tendency of explaining away the quirks of Emerson's prose by appealing to abstraction often went hand in hand with panegyrics to his character. Sure enough, Ives devoted the third and final part of his essay to just such a tribute. Emerson's character, he asserted, "has much to do with his power upon us. It is directly at the root of his substance, and affects his manner only indirectly."[25] This was a view that had been repeated so often that it was a cliché by the beginning of the twentieth century. Time and again, as literary historian Charles E. Mitchell notes, commentators asserted that it was Emerson's "nobility of mind and purity of spirit," his "timeless qualities of character and temperament" that would secure his reputation for posterity, not anything found specifically in his writings.[26] One anecdote that was particularly shopworn from its circulation among Emerson apologists concerned a washerwoman who liked to attend Emerson's lectures not because she understood what he said but because "he looks as though he thought everybody was as good as he was."[27] Although it is impossible to determine where Ives encountered this anecdote—he might even have come across it in the original source, Edward Waldo Emerson's *Emerson in Concord* (1899)—he could not resist using it himself.[28]

What should be imminently clear by now is the extent to which *Essays Before a Sonata* was enmeshed in turn-of-the-century ideas about the Concord cohort. When Ives came by these ideas is unclear, the documentation not being sufficient to make a precise determination. Likely, he absorbed some of them in his American literature course with Phelps, for which he received one of the few respectable grades on his college transcript.[29] But he might also have become newly acquainted with parts of the standard cant about the Concordians through the extensive reading he did in and around his Asheville sojourn, as he wrote *Essays*. Whatever the case, the content of Ives's prose volume would have been comfortably familiar to the men and women who received copies of *Essays*. Not so the music of the piano sonata.

"Emerson" begins with an aggressive wedge-shape gesture, prying open musical space. From a neutral B natural, lying near the center of the keyboard, the left hand thunders down in octaves into the lower register, mirrored by an ascent in the right hand, as the dissonances pile up. Doubtlessly, this gesture alienated most of those who sat down at the piano bench to read through the sonata in 1921. Perceptive players persisting long enough to get some bearing in the forbidding musical landscape might have noticed a motive that appears several times on the first page of the score: three accented notes on the same pitch, followed by a fourth, longer note, a third lower. Once perceived, it is readily recognizable as the principle motive of Beethoven's Fifth Symphony, which Ives described as an "oracle," containing "in those four notes one of Beethoven's greatest messages."[30] It symbolized for Ives the soul of humanity knocking on the door of the divine mysteries—a door unlatched by transcendentalism. For many of the composer's contemporaries, however, the act of studding the perplexing, cacophonous contours of that first page with one of music's most venerated motives would have seemed irreverent, like painting a moustache on the Mona Lisa.

The opening moments of "Emerson" set the precedent for much that is to come, both in the movement itself and those that follow. There are passages that are more meditative, that glory less in astringent or boisterous dissonances, but for the most part they show just as much unconcern for conventional harmonies—or, for that matter, the metrical niceties of regular bar lines. The most notable exception is "The Alcotts," which contains large swaths of music evocative of the sounds that issued from the parlor piano of the Alcott home in Concord, simple Scotch airs and hymns coexisting with transcriptions of Beethoven's Fifth.

Two motives from the beginning of Emerson also permeate the sonata: the ascending three notes of the initial wedge gesture, each a whole tone apart, capped by a falling fifth, and the Beethovenian "oracle." In the freewheeling rhapsodic second movement, the first motive appears amid a chromatic swirl of passagework at the beginning. The second motive is held in reserve, and nearly a third of Ives's homage to Hawthorne whirls by before the oracle aggressively shoulders its way into the musical foreground. Thereafter, the two motives loom in and out of focus as parts of a bewilderingly kaleidoscopic array of original and borrowed music. Adding to the peculiarity of the movement is a section featuring high-register tone clusters, which, according to Ives's instructions, are to be played using a wooden board. In "The Alcotts," the motives become incipits for the two parts of a melody that serves as main thematic material. Full statements of the melody occur only twice in the movement, once on either side of a disarmingly intimate middle section, redolent of sentimental nineteenth-century parlor songs. The final movement, "Thoreau," is the most introverted, lacking the warm tonal harmonies of "The Alcotts," the rhythmical whimsy of "Hawthorne," and the gregarious virtuosic outbursts of "Emerson." An attentive listener might spot allusions to the first motive in a passage at the midpoint, where segments of the whole-tone scale figure prominently. But for the most part, Ives concerns himself with other motivic material. At the very end of the movement, the melody from "The Alcotts" returns, assigned to a flute—if one happens to be at hand. According to the programmatic description Ives supplied, this is Thoreau, who was a flautist, meditatively playing at day's end on Walden Pond.[31]

Insurance agents at Ives and Myrick were taught to be hard-nosed and systematic rather than casual and opportunistic when dealing with prospective clients.[32] It is hard to imagine that Ives, who devised the aggressive strategies for his agents, did not seek to press any advantage he could find in disseminating his own, admittedly unusual, music. It seems probable then that Ives hoped the orthodox substance of the "Concord" Sonata, as expressed in *Essays*, might compensate for its extraordinary manner. It was a reasonable strategy, but it assumed that opinions about Emerson and his circle had remained static in the two decades since the beginning of the twentieth century. While this might have been true for the general public, it was not the case in the contentious and growing arena of American cultural criticism.

Concord Under Fire: A Literary Debate and Its Consequence

During the 1910s, the writings of the Concord coterie served as important points of reference in a debate about the nature and direction of American Society. The combatants gravitated toward two poles. On one side, so-called "New Humanists" made grim prognostications about the prospects for the United States and called for the cultivation of a self-restraint guided by the wisdom of the past. The most publicly visible representatives of this perspective were Irving Babbitt, a professor of French literature at Harvard University; Paul Elmer More, who worked as a journalist at the time but would take a position at Princeton University in 1921; and Stuart Sherman, an English professor at the University of Illinois. On the other side was a circle of younger intellectuals who did not enjoy university appointments but supplied the articulate voice of bohemian Greenwich Village—Van Wyck Brooks, Randolph Bourne, James Oppenheim, Waldo Frank, and Paul Rosenfeld. They saw little to commend in the American past, but in the artists of their own generation, anticipated a cultural maturity that would bear a distinctively American imprimatur, genuine as anything that issued from the much older cultures of Europe. It was a debate that would prove archetypal for the twentieth century, aligning members of an established older generation against representatives of a youthful counterculture.

The disputants published their views in forums large and small—full-length books, staid, long-running magazines, including *Atlantic Monthly* and the *Nation*, and their mass circulation imitators like *McClure's* and *Cosmopolitan*, as well as so-called "little magazines," which were long on passionate opinion but short on subscribers. Accordingly, the debate provides a window on vibrant, early-twentieth-century American print culture, with its characteristic mingling of political and literary content. This culture was sustained by a broad base of upper- and middle-class Americans whose upbringing and education compelled them to regard conversation with the arts as a moral imperative and not simply a source of pleasure. American literature courses of the sort Ives took at Yale, for example, were premised on the idea that a familiarity with the country's literary past would instill patriotism.[33] Such courses formed just a small part of the humanities battery, which, in universities and colleges across the country, was fixed in the bedrock conviction that good art was morally salubrious. When, in 1908, Harmony Twichell wrote to her future husband Charles Ives, imagining a married life in which reading played an important role, she was articulating values widely shared by the members of her class. "We must plan to have times for leisure of thought & we must try & read a lot, the best books—we can live with the noblest people that have lived that way."[34] Here, Harmony echoed Matthew Arnold's influential definition of culture, "the best that has been thought and said."[35] The magazines and books consumed by people like Charles and Harmony Ives took Arnold's definition as dictum and offered reading material that laced entertainment with virtue. With an audience so minded, the stakes of literary criticism were high, and in the case of the debate between the New Humanists and Greenwich Village intellectuals, nothing less than the future of the United States hung in the balance.

Irving Babbitt, in his various writings, stridently articulated the New Humanist position. The United States, Babbitt maintained, rested on deeply flawed philosophical principles owing to the deleterious influences of Jean Jacque Rousseau and Francis Bacon: first, belief in the uncorrupted nature of instinct, and second, faith in science.[36] In *Rousseau and Romanticism* (1919), Babbitt attacked the first of these, arguing that the celebration of "natural man" ignored the innate human capacity for depravity. There was ample historical testimony to the violence that followed when people gave free reign to their emotions, and there was no reason to think that the instinct unfettered today would produce better results.[37] The worship of science added to the problem, for it provided the instinct with no moral guidance, instead facilitating the pursuit of its desires by the most efficient means. Lacking in the United States was a fixed moral order, a standard against which individuals could measure their own behavior and its impact on others around them. A moral order would also show up the lie of equality, revealing that not all men and women were born equal, as Americans liked to believe. The nature of intellectual pursuits in the United States was enough to show the lack of the discernment on the part of the majority. "What must one think of a country," Babbitt would ask in his 1924 book *Democracy and Leadership*, "whose most popular orator is W. J. Bryan, whose favorite actor is Charlie Chaplin, whose most widely read novelist is Harold Bell Wright, whose best-known evangelist is Billy Sunday, and whose representative journalist is William Randolph Hearst? . . . As 'Punch' remarked, the United States is not a country but a picnic."[38]

New Humanists, who regarded Matthew Arnold as their Victorian progenitor, were convinced that the works of the Western literary canon should serve as a source of moral authority, that encounters with great literature were crucial to the formation of "character."[39] According to contemporaneous usage, the latter term had to do with the cultivation of moral rectitude, the calibration of an inner compass that would guide the individual in his or her life pursuits. Cultural historian Joan Shelley Rubin observes that character "denoted integrity, balance, and restraint, traits which well served the needs of an economy dependent on diligent producers."[40] In other words, for New Humanists, the development of character required an authority external to the self: the canon. And this was the source of their beef with the transcendentalists.

The central premise of transcendentalism is that the human soul is a fragment of God, and the mind of God, the oversoul, serves as the substratum of human thought. The corollary to this belief is that all peoples of the world are linked by inborn divinity. "We," Emerson had written, "are the photometers, are the irritable gold-leaf and tinfoil that measure the accumulations of the subtle element. We know the authentic effects of the true fire through every one of its million disguises."[41] To which Babbitt was inclined to ask, just whom did Emerson include in this "we"? In his 1912 book, *The Masters of Modern French Criticism*, he averred, "Granting that man is a photometer or measure of light, it is yet absurd to add, as Emerson at times comes dangerously near doing, that this ideal measure exists unimpaired in the ordinary untrained individual." Especially objectionable to Babbitt was Emerson's belief that intuition and instinct are the means through which the oversoul is reached. According to the transcendentalist writers, it was up to the individual to scrape off the encrustations of tradition in order for the intuition to fulfill its function of interfacing with the inborn divine. For Babbitt, this was nothing more than the perpetuation of Rousseau's harmful ideas about the uncorrupted nature of instinct:

> Emerson is thus one with Rousseau in denying intrinsic evil in human nature. His main weakness, as it seems to me, from which all his other weaknesses derive, is that like Wordsworth and so many other Rousseauists, he thus "averts his ken from half of human fate." This attitude towards the problem of perversity is so contrary to the ascertained facts, so opposed to all hard and clear and honest thinking, that it may compromise gravely in the long run the reputations of all those who have taken it.[42]

Much the same argument can be found in the writings of Paul Elmer More and Stuart Sherman, though the latter was much more willing to grant Emerson the benefit of the doubt.[43] Ultimately then, the premises of transcendentalism were antithetical to New Humanism, which called for a society grounded in tradition, the character of its people formed by an engagement with the great canonical works.

It is not possible to determine the extent to which Ives was familiar with the work of the New Humanists, though in his Emerson essay he does mockingly allude to Babbitt's *Rousseau and Romanticism*.[44] What is clear, however, is that Ives would have run afoul of the New Humanists—had they been aware of him—over the source of moral authority, for in this he stood with the transcendentalists. "Is it not," Ives asked, "[Emerson's] courageous universalism that gives conviction to his prophecy and that makes his symphonies of revelation begin and end with nothing but the strength and beauty of innate goodness in man, in Nature and in God, the greatest and most inspiring theme of Concord Transcendental Philosophy, as we hear it."[45] Ives went further, making Emerson's assertion about intuition the central tenet of his own faith in the "majority." In Ives's view, the economic, political, and social decisions of the general populace were directly linked to the oversoul, the transcendent manifest in the prosaic world. The workings of the universal mind could be discerned through statistical analysis, in the "divine law of averages" that was at the center of Ives's work as an insurance actuary.[46] In opposition to the majority, Ives cast the "hog-mind of the few," individuals who insisted on foisting their own particular view on others and typically pursued positions of leadership to achieve that end. Citing some of the progressive developments of his time—labor federation and suffrage extension—Ives argued that the influence of the minority was crumbling. "But the day of leaders, as such, is gradually closing—the people are beginning to lead themselves—the public store of reason is slowly being opened—the common universal mind and the common over-soul is slowly but inevitably coming into its own."[47] This was an image of the future from which Babbitt, More, and Sherman would have recoiled.

As far as his view of the Concord circle of writers was concerned, Ives also shared little with a group of younger critics based in Greenwich Village, almost literally around the corner from his New York home. The members of this group were, in the teens, embarking upon careers that would play a major role in shaping American culture over the next three decades. Calling themselves "Young America," they were committed to a project of national revitalization, exhorting the writers, artists, and composers of their own generation to cultivate a genuine American voice. Insistently forward-looking and sympathetic to modernist currents, the Young Americans regarded the past dubiously; their writings codified the list of grievances against American culture that animated the Greenwich Village rebellion of the teens.

Literary critic Van Wyck Brooks, who was responsible for the rubric "Young America," provided the group with the cultural critique that served as its foundation. Brooks, a former student of Irving Babbitt, shared his teacher's abhorrence of American culture. But his response was not to retreat to the Arnoldian realm of ideals—in fact, he believed that American intellectuals had failed precisely because they had pursued such a course. In his most influential essay, *America's Coming-of-Age* (1915), Brooks diagnosed American culture as suffering from a debilitating bifurcation, a division between the mutually coexisting but exclusive realms of lowbrow and highbrow. "In everything," he complained, "one finds this frank acceptance of twin values which are not expected to have anything in common: on the one hand, a quite unclouded, quite unhypocritical assumption of transcendent theory ('high ideals'), on the other a simultaneous acceptance of catchpenny realities. Between university ethics and business ethics, between American culture and American humor, between Good Government and Tammany, between academic pedantry and pavement slang, there is no community, no genial middle ground." Repeating a line of reasoning he had advanced in his first book, *The Wine of the Puritans* (1908), Brooks traced this problem back to the peculiarities of the Puritan mindset. The first New England settlers arrived with a fully formed culture that emphasized the eternal over the quotidian. But to wrest a living from the wilderness of the New World required practicality, economy, and intensive labor. As a result, a rift developed between theory and practice: "The eternal issues the Puritans felt so keenly, the practical issues they experienced so monotonously threw almost no light on one another." For Brooks, this rift was epitomized by the antithetical characters of Jonathan Edwards, with his intellect "like the Matterhorn, steep, icy, and pinnacled," and Benjamin Franklin, whose practical advice filled *Poor Richard's Almanac.* "Desiccated culture at one end," Brooks wrote, "and stark utility at the other have created a deadlock in the American mind, and all our life drifts chaotically between the two extremes."[48]

From Jonathan Edwards, the ethereal flame of idealism passed to the transcendentalists, who were equally incapable of creating a vital link between theory and practice. Emerson, as Brooks viewed him, "never lingers in the bodily world, he is always busy to be off again; and if he takes two or three paces on the earth they only serve to warm him for a fresh aëriel adventure." Perceiving in everything and everyone the trace of the oversoul, Emerson moved quickly to the abstract realm, dissolving difference in his search for the overarching commonality. As evidence, Brooks cited Emerson's proclivity for lumping canonical figures together to support whatever argument he was trying to make—in one notable instance, Plato, the apostle Paul, Plutarch, Augustine, Spinoza, Chapman, Beaumont, and Fletcher.[49] The image of these men "arm in arm" was ludicrous, scoffed Brooks, the lamentable consequence of stripping away the particularities of each man's life. Emerson simply regarded the members of this motley as "exceptionally fine manifestations of the Over-Soul." As a result, "philosophy like death had leveled them and had, as entirely, removed them from the region of terrestrial society, literature and art."[50]

The transcendentalist preoccupation with the abstract also had moral consequences in the eyes of Brooks and his Young America colleagues. Waldo Frank, echoing Brooks's thesis in his *Our America* (1919), suggested that Emerson "presented a path to 'poetry and spirit' so splendidly remote from crass reality that it could in no way lead to it. If the pursuit of beauty took one to these chill Emersonian heavens, why then of course the earth was safe for the pursuit of money."[51] The rampant materialism of American society had been vouchsafed by an idealism that made no demands on what ends one pursued in the real world.

Born after 1885, the Young Americans viewed the canons and manners of the Gilded Age bourgeois—what George Santayana famously called the "genteel tradition"—as moribund. Included in this judgment was the ideal of "character" so prized by nineteenth-century moralists.[52] In *America's Coming-of-Age*, Brooks offered a prescription for achieving a new vitality that displaced "character" as the measure of the man (or woman). He called for a "focal center" to American life, an "object of living," or, as he put it most tellingly, a "social ideal." Strongly influenced by William Morris and the English Arts and Crafts movement, he envisioned an America in which industrial-corporate society had been overturned, the hierarchies of business and factory life abandoned, the individual fulfilled by active civic engagement, and the arts restored to the center of life.[53] Brooks did not limn his "social ideal" further, but he did describe the process through which its particulars were to be uncovered. The material from which a new American identity would be forged was already present, "a thousand potential currents and cross-currents" awaiting discovery in the lives and principles of the multiple peoples inhabiting the United States. Uncovering these currents was to be the business of critical discourse—itself a social process that would require its participants to abandon the primacy of individualism. "To leave behind the old Yankee self-assertion and self-sufficiency, to work together, think together, feel together, to believe so fervently in the quality of standards that we delight in prostrating our work and our thoughts before them—all that is certainly in the right direction."[54] Randolph Bourne echoed Brooks's call for a new "social ideal" in the peroration to his most influential essay "Trans-National America": "All our idealism must be those of future social goals in which all can participate, the good life of personality lived in the environment of the Beloved Community."[55] A communitarian ethos lay at the heart of the Young Americans' project of cultural renovation.[56]

Ives's political screed, "The Majority," written at roughly the same time as *Essays Before a Sonata*, contained its own vision of a beloved community. Instead of turning forward, his social ideal lay in the mythological American past, in the New England village, where major political decisions were made through the institution of the town meeting.[57] In Ives's imagination, such meetings brought together men as equals in order to discuss the best direction for the community. Each was granted his say—"every man for himself" as Ives put it—and a consensus was reached through reasoned argument.[58] Ultimately, force of character would win the day; the best men, guided by an inner rectitude that partook of the divine moral order, would convince their fellows of the wisdom of their words. Ives's town meeting was an assemblage of individuals whose sense of self derived from within, a marked contrast with the "Beloved Community" of Brooks and Bourne in which identity was defined by social relationships.

None of the Young America critics are named in *Essays Before a Sonata*, and it is questionable whether Ives was aware of their existence. In his writings, there are no references to *Seven Arts*, the short-lived magazine (1916–1917) that served as the organ for Brooks and his confreres. Ives did, at some point, become a sub-scriber to the *New Republic*, which began publication in 1914, and, in its early days, included Randolph Bourne among its contributors.[59] Ives's unawareness is unfortunate, for the influential critics at the heart of the Greenwich Village rebel-lion would likely have been sympathetic to the venturesome nature of his music and might have sped up its dissemination. Then again, there was a significant barrier to his acceptance in that milieu, because the position he staked out in *Es-says* was every bit as unpalatable to the Young Americans as the New Humanists, though for different reasons. One wonders whether Ives, had he known that the critical reputation of the Emersonian cohort was waning in literary circles both progressive and conservative, would still have pinned his hopes for musical rec-ognition on the "Concord" Sonata.

First Inroads: Ives among the Modernists

Soon after the distribution of *Essays* and "Concord," Ives began to hear back from the recipients. There were many polite thank-you notes for the unexpected vol-umes and generally positive comments about *Essays*, with William Lyon Phelps, Ives's former Yale professor, sounding an especially enthusiastic note.[60] The so-nata, however, was another matter. Puzzlement was a common reaction, and many of the respondents conceded that the work was too "modern" for their tastes. Walter Goldstein of New Orleans admitted, "With the exception of the orthodox passages in the 'Alcott' movement, to me the sonata seems to be expressed in the Schoenberg-Scriabin-Ornstein idiom, the musicality of which is not yet compre-hensible to me."[61] Ives scrawled an ornery reply on the back of Goldstein's letter: "Dear Goldy: Ain't never heard nor seen any of the music—not even a god damn Note,—of Schoenberg—Scriabin—or Ornstein."[62] Composer Charles Wakefield Cadman, one of the more celebrated personages to receive *Essays* and "Concord," sent what Ives biographer Jan Swafford aptly describes as "an elegantly vicious letter."[63] Cadman pilloried "Concord" in a manner reminiscent of the expostula-tions of the violinist who had been flummoxed by the first violin sonata. "I 'get' *nothing* [from the music]," he wrote, "but a disordered sea of sound and form, and hurting my ears, much the same, I imagine, as a very blatant cornet would hurt the ears of a canine friend."[64] To this Ives offered no repartee, but he must surely have been hurt.

For the most part, there was also little comfort to be had from the published reviews that started to appear in the summer of 1921. Again, the most common reaction was incomprehension, a typical sampling of which is the assessment offered by a Denver critic: "I must say that I do not understand [Ives's] form of art—even tho I have a great sympathy with the 'moderns'—and that I consider his motives of a joking nature and that he must not be taken too seriously—not even slightly seriously." There were also some critics who saw fit to mete out derision. In *Musical America*, a widely read music magazine, the sonata was declared "the most startling conglomeration of meaningless notes that we have ever seen." All told, this response did not augur well for Ives's musical future, and certainly none of the critics who received the sonata, much less Ives himself, could have predicted his later success. In hindsight though, it is possible to see the beginnings of his transformation into an American icon in the one review that offered the slightest measure of cautious praise: "Mr. Ives' sonata is a piece of work sincerely done, and if a failure, a rather splendid one."[65]

Few people read this assessment for it appeared in the *Double Dealer*, a magazine with a paltry budget and low circulation, its "office" a loft on the edge of the Latin Quarter in New Orleans that had been loaned to the editor by a generous uncle.[66] The *Double Dealer* served as the organ for modernist-minded artists and critics of New Orleans, playing much the same role as the *Seven Arts* had for the Young Americans of Greenwich Village several years earlier. And like the *Seven Arts*, it was a relatively short-lived affair, exploding onto the scene with great élan in January 1921 only to disappear five years later. By the end of its run, the *Double Dealer* could claim two distinctions: it had printed the first published work by Ernest Hemingway and the first extensive review of the music of Charles Ives.

The author of the review was Henry Bellamann, a music educator and poet loosely affiliated with modernist enclaves in both New Orleans and Chicago (Figure 1.2). At the time Ives mailed out his sonata and companion apologia, Bellamann was living in Columbia, South Carolina, where he served as piano instructor and dean of the School of Fine Arts at Chicora College. In his spare time, he wrote poetry and occasional pieces of musical criticism, both of which reveal the modernist inclinations he had picked up in Paris, where he completed musical studies with Charles Marie Widor. Bellamann would move to New York in 1924, serving as chairman of the Examining Board at the Institute of Musical Arts (later renamed the Julliard School of Music); visiting professor at Vassar College; and, beginning in 1931, dean of the Curtis Institute of Music. But for all this, he remained a reluctant musical pedagogue, aspiring instead to a career as a writer. In 1940, his third novel, *King's Row*, launched his literary celebrity and at last provided him with the financial security to pursue his activities as a writer full time.

Formative for Bellamann's ideas about art generally, and Ives's music specifically, was one of the most talked about musical treatises in European modernist circles during the 1910s, *Sketch of a New Esthetic of Music* (1907) by the Italian composer Ferruccio Busoni. In the treatise, Busoni sought to resolve the nineteenth-century controversy between the proponents of "absolute" and "program" music

Figure 1.2. Henry Bellamann,
Ives's first promoter, 1904.
Courtesy Kingdom of
Callaway Historical Society.

by appealing to Goethe's doctrine of organicism: "Every [musical] motive—so it seems to me—contains, like a seed, its life-germ within itself. From the different plant-seeds grow different families of plants, dissimilar in form, foliage, blossom, fruit, growth and color."[67] From this Busoni derived two corollaries. First, music must remain in its own realm and follow its own natural consequences, a prescription with which advocates of absolute music would readily agree. The imposition of verbal programs—the travails of Tasso or the antics of Don Quixote, for example—could only result in misshapen progeny. Second, Busoni condemned conventional form and insisted that each motive should naturally give rise to its own unique structure, a view consistent with that of the program music faction. In addition, he granted music the capacity to mean: "Let music be naught else than nature mirrored by and reflected from the human breast."[68] Thus, while music may not narrate the life of a hero (or antihero, as in the case of Don Quixote) it dealt with things interior, with the moods of the soul. As it turns out, it was not so much Busoni's compromise solution that sparked discussion among musical modernists as the possible avenues of technical development he envisioned. Conventional notions of what constituted a legitimate musical motive were too limited, he argued, and thus existing musical flora were more homogenous than they naturally might be. It was the system of equal temperament that was to blame because it limited the pitches available to composers. Abandon the system, Busoni advised, and embrace the full spectrum of sound.

The extent to which Bellamann had absorbed Busoni's ideas is apparent in an article he wrote for *Musical Quarterly* that postdates his review of the "Concord" Sonata but is worth considering for the light it sheds on his general aesthetic outlook. Titled "Notes on the New Aesthetic of Poetry and Music," an obvious homage to the Italian composer's treatise, it began with a criticism of the mindless pursuit of stylistic novelty, something to which Bellamann felt modernist artists were prone. While some of them "fasten decorations of a fantastic harmony" to traditional forms, others pour "the old wine of conventional musical speech into the new bottles of unfamiliar form." It was not "fantastic harmony" or "unfamiliar form" that was irksome but their usage simply for the sake of sounding new. For Bellamann, the quality of a work, modern or otherwise, was dependent upon the artist's fealty to the original impetus of the piece, what he referred to as "pure idea." In a passage that is clearly derivative of Busoni, down to its metaphorical excess, he wrote,

> Pure idea is unique—however slight. Its form—"its ultimate and unique form"—
> lies within itself as a plant lies in seed. Its ultimate exact foliation is predestined
> in conception. Tradition, background and technique are but soil and sunshine.
> Everything should fall away (be weeded out) before the solitary growth of the idea.
> The freedom, the genuine freedom, which implies *freedom from even the author's
> preconceptions*, involves simultaneous creation of a special aesthetic [his italics].

In the case of music, the "fetish of tonality" had shackled composers and prevented "pure idea" from achieving its full realization. The remedy he suggested was straight from Busoni: abandoning equal temperament. After all, Bellamann reasoned, "[the scale] is an arbitrary selection of points fixed in the midst of countless other points." Turning to modern poetry, Bellamann commended the Imagist poets for already having taken steps in the right direction: "The Imagist[s] accomplished a much needed task of housecleaning in throwing out the ancient clutter of outworn poetic formulae. . . . The sum of their achievement was the creation of a technique that fitted the body of contemporary thought and feeling like a perfect garment."[69]

Bellamann was personally acquainted with the Chicago-based Imagists, having submitted some of his own verses to *Poetry*, the magazine that served as their organ, in 1920. Harriet Monroe, the magazine's editor, was duly impressed and struck up a friendship with Bellamann, providing him with an entrée into a circle that included Amy Lowell, Carl Sandburg, and Ezra Pound.[70] In contrast to the "Young Americans" of New York, the focus of this Chicago cohort of modernist poets was aesthetics. The Imagist credo, spelled out in Lowell's preface to an anthology of their poetry, was the presentation of "hard and clear" images freed of the strictures of traditional form.[71] Like Busoni, the Chicagoites were raising a hue and cry for an art that developed organically from its basic materials, without the artificial confinement of convention. Their agenda lacked the kind of communitarian social ideals that motivated a Van Wyck Brooks or a Randolph Bourne. The past figured prominently in the thinking of both groups, but whereas for the Young Americans it stood as a witness to the insubstantiality of American culture, for the aesthetically inclined Imagists, it was only a threat insofar as modern artists remained slavishly beholden to it. Bellamann, approaching the music of Ives with the dual equipage of Busonian and Imagist aesthetics, lacked the prejudice against the history of American arts and letters that was the chief characteristic of Ives's closest modernist neighbors. For Bellamann, the names Emerson, Hawthorne, Alcott, and Thoreau were not emblematic of the shortcomings of American culture.

This, however, did not automatically mean Bellamann would embrace the "Concord" Sonata when he discovered it on his doorstep. Indeed, as evidenced by the equivocation in his *Double Dealer* review, the sonata was an awkward fit to the Busoni-derived precepts that governed his aesthetic sensibilities. Particularly troubling was the musical idiom, Bellamann's discussion of it being equal parts admiration and bewilderment. On the one hand, the sonata lacked the kind of organic unity that Busoni had insisted upon. "Indeed there is no unity of idea in the sense that one part grows out of the another. One feels only a psychic kind of connection that might in this case reasonably be called a musical logic." On the other hand, the composer had thrown convention to the wind and followed his own course—a course independent even of other moderns. "[The score] reveals music unlike anything one has seen before—a broad, strong and original style with no recognizable derivations from Debussy, Strauss or Strawinsky." Thus the piece was not simply a matter of filling out a conventional form with new sound, Bellamann's chief objection to the output of other musical modernists. Everything about Ives's score seemed new: its disregard for the conventions of musical notation, the unprecedented technical challenges it presented to the performer, and its sprawling outer movements, which sometimes ambled and sometimes hurtled through sonic space, tracing unfamiliar trajectories. "Certainly," Bellamann concluded, "it must be considered in a class by itself. Conceived independently of any instrumental idiom, it must be regarded as an essay of lofty thought and feeling expressed in musical notation. One arises from a reading of it with much, much more of satisfaction than dissatisfaction. Its loftiness of purpose is evident; its moments of achievement elevating and greatly beautiful."[72]

To invoke an Ivesian dichotomy, Bellamann's initial attraction to the music had more to do with manner than substance. It was the newness of it all that engaged him, and even though he described the "Concord" Sonata as "an essay of lofty thought and feeling," he had little to say about the subject of the "essay," namely the transcendentalists. Ultimately, then, it was the unusual qualities of Ives's music that spurred Bellamann to become the composer's earliest visible partisan, and, in the process, initiated a lifelong friendship. Over the course of the next decade and a half, before devoting himself to a career as a novelist, Bellamann would write and speak publicly about Ives on multiple occasions. Notably, the "Concord" Sonata figured in the lecture tour Bellamann embarked upon late in 1921, which took him to Columbia, Atlanta, and New Orleans in the company of pianist Le-onore Purcell, who supplied musical illustrations. Just how much of the sonata Purcell performed is unclear. But it is an irony, given Ives's discomfort with what he perceived as the overly feminized character of American music culture, that the first real audience for his sonata was comprised, according to Bellamann's wife, of "little old white-haired Southern ladies, painfully genteel."[73] Unfortunately, no record exists of how these audiences responded. Ives, for his part, supported Bellamann's artistic endeavors, doing what he could to find publishers for the writer's poems and setting two of them to music.[74]

The preoccupation with manner, the stylistic particulars of an idiom, was characteristic of another early Ives supporter, the French pianist E. Robert Schmitz. An ardent champion of new music, Schmitz had settled in the United States in the late teens, founding the Franco-American Musical Society in 1920 (later renamed Pro Musica) with the mandate of promoting new works by French and American composers. Schmitz's base of operations was New York, and his presence there along with the success of the Franco-American Society attest to the concurrent emergence of a New York avant-garde focused on technical innovation alongside the socially conscious Young Americans. In fact, some members of the Young America milieu actively supported the newly emergent aesthetic modernism, exploring the role it might play in the beloved community of their imaginations. Paul Rosenfeld, for one, served on the board of the Franco-American Society.

It is not clear how Schmitz, who was not among the recipients of the "Concord" Sonata, met Ives in 1923, although there is an apocryphal story about their acquaintance being a matter of happenstance. Supposedly, Schmitz came to Ives and Myrick looking to purchase an insurance policy, and in the course of his conversation with Ives, discovered that they shared a mutual passion for music. Since Ives left the actual business of selling life insurance to others, preferring to remain behind the scenes dreaming up marketing stratagems, this story seems unlikely. However they met, their shared devotion to things musical was real enough.[75]

By the midtwenties, Schmitz had become fascinated with the possibilities of quarter-tone music, picking up on a general vogue among musical modernists that had been spurred by Busoni's *Sketch of a New Esthetic of Music*. Ives found the pianist's quarter-tone enthusiasms infectious, heredity and nostalgia having made him prone to such things. The composer had fond memories of his father, a small-town bandmaster and perennial musical tinkerer, "rigg[ing] up a contrivance to stretch 24 or more violin strings and tun[ing] them up to suit the dictates of [his] own curiosity."[76] Schmitz managed to persuade the composer to write a set of three pieces making use of quarter-tones, and two of them were performed as part of a Franco-American Society concert on February 14, 1925.

Just as he had done when preparing the "Concord" Sonata for its public unveiling, Ives penned an apologia for his *Three Quarter-Tone Pieces*, this one published in the *Franco-American Musical Society Bulletin*. *Essays* and "Some 'Quarter-Tone' Impressions," as the new apologia was entitled, are a study in contrasts. While the former was almost entirely given over to substance—Ives's thoughts on the transcendentalists—the latter was focused on manner, the technical nitty-gritty of assembling a coherent music language that incorporated quarter tones. Ives did manage to slip in a few references to Hawthorne, but he seems to have recognized that the people who greeted his music with the most enthusiasm were not much interested in the American literary past.

The quarter-tone concerts did not provoke a surge of interest in Ives, and the critics who attended were underwhelmed by the whole affair.[77] But the event, coupled with Ives's decision to join the board of directors for the Franco-American Society the following season, served to strengthen his connections with the avant-garde. Parenthetically, it is also worth noting that Ives's involvement in the administration of the society was far more than advisory. It was his financial largesse that kept it afloat at several precarious junctures.[78] This was a pattern of generous patronage and self-advocacy that would persist throughout the rest of his life. Ives's promoters, no matter the capacity in which they worked—whether editing, publishing, or performing his music, or lecturing and writing about it— were remunerated for their efforts.[79]

Early in 1927, the society (now called Pro Musica) sponsored a performance of the first two movements of Ives's Fourth Symphony, with Eugene Goosens conducting a reduced New York Philharmonic Orchestra. Henry Bellamann, who had moved to New York by this time, wrote the program notes and an accompanying article for the society's journal. As in his earlier review, Bellamann drew attention to the stylistic innovations of Ives's music, introducing a new subsidiary theme. "Charles Ives grew up with a conviction gained from his father, that only a fraction of the means of musical expression had been utilized. Unusual chord structures, exotic scales, polytonality, atonality, harmonic rhythm and the like were familiar matters to him long before they appeared as bugaboos in musical aesthetics."[80] In 1921, not knowing the dates of completion for Ives's scores, Bellamann had simply claimed that the style of "Concord" seemed wholly independent of the music of Debussy, Strauss, or Stravinsky. Now, better acquainted with Ives's oeuvre and actively involved in a musical circle that placed a premium on novel technique, he was making a much stronger assertion: Ives had set precedents, exploring musical innovations long before those who claimed credit for them. Bellamann was himself setting a precedent, for his assertion would appear close to the beginning of virtually every piece of writing produced about Ives from the late twenties onward.

Bellamann would set another precedent for Ives's reception when he presented an explanation for the double life of the composer. This was the subject of his last article about Ives, published in 1933 in the *Musical Quarterly*. The journal catered to an avid constituency of musical devotees, the sort of people who might be expected to recognize the name Ives even if they had not yet heard his music. The crux of Bellamann's article was that the realms of business and art were not mutually exclusive, contrary to popular opinion. Invoking the composer's modernist reputation, he explained, "Mr. Ives' business success was founded on the same sort of daring experiment, together with an interest and confidence in human nature, that characterizes his music." Then, letting Ives speak himself, Bellamann quoted a lengthy meditation on the venturesome nature of the business community. "It is my impression," Ives mused, "that there is more open-mindedness and willingness to examine carefully the premises underlying a new or unfamiliar thing, before condemning it, in the world of business than in the world of music." In any case, the "fabric of existence weaves itself whole" and to conclude that an artist could find little inspiring in the insurance industry was narrow-minded. There are traces here of Ives's transcendentalist commitments, and, after the Second World War, advocates of the composer would capitalize on this facet of the article. But what is most characteristic of Ives's reception at the moment Bellamann wrote it was the emphasis on exploring "new or unfamiliar things."[81]

If, on the whole, interest in Ives centered on matters of style and technique, there was a small group of early enthusiasts on the fringe of the modernist movement who did engage with the "substance" of his music. Two of them had been recipients of the "Concord" Sonata when Ives first sent out copies in 1920: organist and composer T. Carl Whitmer, who lived in Pittsburgh, and aspiring critic Clifton Joseph Furness, who was then studying at Northwestern University. Though not acquainted, both men were devoted to the music of Scriabin, and, equally important, its mystical underpinnings in theosophy. Furness, when he moved to New York after completing his studies, sparked an enthusiasm for Ives's music in a Scriabinist-theosophist salon led by pianist Katherine Heyman. Transcendentalism was a natural draw for Whitmer, Furness, and Heyman because it shared much with the expansive mysticism of theosophy: both aimed to reconnect the individual with inborn divinity, both stressed intuition as the primary agent, and both drew heavily on Eastern religion, particularly Hinduism.[82]

Despite being among Ives's earliest devotees, the collection of Scriabinists had little impact on the reception of the composer. Even within the small world of critics and musicians interested in the musical avant-garde, they lacked the kind of constituency that could facilitate the dissemination of their ideas. Moreover, in the few instances in which they aired their views on Ives publicly, they proved to be poor advocates, too beclouded by mysticism. Consider Furness's cryptic remarks about Ives in a 1926 article: "[T]his music of the soul, inwardly apprehended, brings into conscious action the Will nature, the highest of the threefold activity of the human spirit."[83] Slightly more comprehensible (but just as eccentric) are Whitmer's comments in a review of the second movement of Ives's Second Symphony: "Ives has cast aside, as altogether unworthy, all prettiness of effects and gets down to the bottom of elemental man—of you with your superficial self lifted away. You are now primitive in force and not sophisticated. This innerness plus machinery of the man-from-Mars makes great music."[84] From the standpoint of the reception history of Ives, the main significance of Furness and Heyman was that they introduced the composer's music to Elliott Carter and John Kirkpatrick, two men who would exert considerable influence beginning in the late thirties.

In 1922, Ives distributed a third vanity publication, this one consisting of 114 songs he had composed over the course of his career. It begins with "Majority," a song that is every bit as forbidding as anything found in the "Concord" Sonata. The visual impress of the thick black-key and white-key clusters notated on the first page would have been enough to make most musical conservatives blanch. This gleeful provocation is belied by the eclectic nature of 114 Songs, the contents of which contain something to suit all tastes. Alongside more recondite experiments like "Majority," there are sentimental ballads for the parlor, imitation lieder, rollicking numbers reminiscent of Stephen Foster in minstrel mode, and even a cowboy song.

In the postface to his collection, Ives explained that he had not produced it for money, fame, or love, but that he had "merely cleaned house. All that is left is out on the clothes line; but it's good for a man's vanity to have the neighbors see *him*—on the clothes line."[85] The tone of studied indifference, with a dram of puritanical moralizing, was, in all likelihood, there to protect the composer against rejection. 114 Songs was another bid for recognition, and Ives clearly hoped that recipients of the volume would sort through his musical laundry, choosing those things they liked for themselves. It represents yet another tactic in a protracted campaign of self-promotion. Whereas the "Concord" Sonata was an attempt to supply the public with a piece that expressed widely shared beliefs about the Concord writers, in *114 Songs*, Ives offered prospective listeners with a range of options, both in substance and manner.

Although reviews of *114 Songs* were similar in tenor to those of the sonata, in a larger sense, as Gayle Sherwood Magee has noted, the volume enjoyed a warmer if less noisy reception than its predecessor.[86] Soon after Ives began distributing the 1500 copies he ordered from the printer, a baritone named George S. Madden performed two of the more conservative songs on a New York recital. Two years later, in 1924, Madden added another pair of Ives songs to his repertoire, his selections now coming from the experimental offerings in *114 Songs*. The performances provoked no outcry from the critical fraternity, and for this reason have attracted comparatively little attention from later Ivesians. But Madden deserves the credit for initiating the process by which Ives's songs eased their way into the concert repertory—a process that would be overshadowed by the clamorous discourse about his bigger, venturesome instrumental works.

It may well be the case that *114 Songs* did more for Ives's long-term reputation than anything else he published in the twenties and thirties. It was, after all, the most widely distributed of his early publications. In addition to the initial run of 1500 copies, Ives had to print 500 more of a shorter volume, *50 Songs*, after word got out that he would furnish a volume to anybody who requested one (the *New York Sun* and *Musical Digest* both announced that he was giving his songbook away for free).[87] True, most of the requesters were prompted by curiosity, but undoubtedly some of the songs wended their way into the hearts of those who acquired them. Certainly, the letters of thanks Ives received indicate that the songs were explored with pleasure and interest in a variety of different forums, from private read-throughs at home to performances in amateur music clubs.[88] Unfortunately, after these initial letters, the historical record goes dry.

A Composer's Envoi

In the end, despite the ambition Ives demonstrated in planning and executing his massive mail campaigns—the distribution of *Essays*, the "Concord" Sonata, and, subsequently, *114 Songs*—his attempts to manipulate his public reputation proved to be more reactive than proactive. Ives's involvement with the Franco-American Society made it clear that the facet of his oeuvre that attracted most attention was its deployment of novel techniques: the dissonances, microtonal experiments, spatial effects, and unusual schemes for pitch organization. Accordingly, the works he produced in the early twenties foregrounded such devices, displaying what Magee describes as "a consciously modernist style."[89] At the same time, as he fielded inquiries about his life and musical education, he projected a persona consistent with the image of the composerly pioneer Bellamann depicted in his Fourth Symphony commentary. That persona, manifest already in Ives's essay about the quarter-tone pieces, is overwhelmingly present in his two final prose writings.

The first, tellingly titled "Music and Its Future," was published as a "Conductors Note" for a 1929 partial score of the Fourth Symphony and then as a separate essay in 1933. The subject again is musical experiment, though this time, instead of quarter-tones, Ives expounded on the antiphonal benefits arising from the unorthodox distribution of the players in a musical ensemble—offstage, in another room, down the block, across a lake. Emerson and Thoreau do make cameo appearances, and toward the end of the essay, Ives solemnly intones an Arnoldian conviction about the best music making, "itself a part with the finer things that humanity does and dreams of" (most modernists would have rolled their eyes at this genteel chestnut). But on the whole, technical matters are his main preoccupation. Notably absent are the names of previous composers who explored spatial effects—Ives might have pointed to Mozart's *Don Giovanni* or one of Mahler's symphonies, for example—as if the issue had never been broached before. In fact, the only real music Ives discusses is remembered from his childhood experiences, when a small-town bandmaster arranged the members of his ensemble in several groups around the town square to play a hymn, "Jerusalem the Golden." Though he is not named, that bandmaster is transparently Ives's father George. Implicitly, this gesture of filial piety credited George for the inception of techniques that his son would take up in some of his most-celebrated "modernist" output. At the same time, it deflected attention away from the Western European classical-music tradition, implying that the titular future of music would grow from roots sunk in American soil.[90]

This was a tactic that Ives pursued more aggressively and explicitly in his final extensive prose work. Admittedly, to call it a work is a bit misleading, for unlike the other writings I have discussed, *Memos*, as Ives referred to it, was never completed. It is really an autobiographical scrapbook, accumulated piecemeal over the course of some three years in the early thirties, with a vague overarching structure.[91] Moreover, *Memos* was not published until 1972, and then only in a somewhat baroque edition thickly overlaid with scholarly commentary. As a consequence, its influence on Ives's reception was indirect, mediated mostly by the persons of Henry and Sidney Cowell, who were permitted to use *Memos* for their 1955 book, *Charles Ives and His Music*. Ives himself declared of *Memos*, "This is not for publication, but anybody who can read can read it."[92] Given the content though, it is clear that he had some distinct anybodies in mind. *Memos* is, as Magee observes, "another extended sales pitch directed at a specific audience for a specific purpose."[93] That audience was comprised of modernists.

There are many striking—even disturbing—things about *Memos*. The vitriol Ives spilled in its pages is legendary, his vituperations being directed against the musical establishment for its treatment of unusual music—his own, mostly, but also that of other modernist composers. The text is thick with invective that now reads as misogynistic and homophobic, Ives taking every opportunity to attack the "commercial pansies," "nice Lizzies," and "ladybirds" whom he regarded as dominating and emasculating American culture, musical and otherwise.[94] (Issues of gender as they pertain to Ives's reception will be taken up in chapters 4 and 6.) But this invective distracts from the real abiding preoccupations of *Memos*: precedence and independence. Indeed, safeguarding his claims to both was the immediate impetus for writing.

By the early thirties, Ives's modest celebrity among modernists had expanded enough that his devotees had begun to introduce his music in other countries (it helped that he was willing to fund such enterprises). The details will have to wait until the next chapter, but for my purposes here, it suffices to mention a duo of Paris concerts that took place in June 1931. The programs featured the works of several American modernists, including Ives's *Three Places in New England*. Though, on balance, the response was more positive than Ives was accustomed to receiving, several of the reviewers suggested that he had been influenced by such European modernist composers as Arnold Schoenberg, Igor Stravinsky, and Paul Hindemith. For Ives, this was galling, and he determined to set the record straight. "All of the music that I have written," he proclaimed at the beginning of what would become *Memos*, "with the exception of about a dozen or fifteen songs, was completed before I had seen or heard any of the music of the European composers."[95] Musicologists have since determined that this is a misrepresentation, for Ives engaged in considerably more compositional activity in the twenties, when he was most certainly familiar with the names Schoenberg and Stravinsky, than a paltry "dozen or fifteen songs."[96] By this time, however, his reputation was so bound up with claims to priority for technical innovations that any suggestion of influence threatened to impeach his modernist credentials.

In *Memos*, Ives used two kinds of evidence to vouch for his compositional precedence and independence. The first, and most straightforward, is a catalogue of his works, itemizing the dates of composition and describing any unusual techniques contained therein. A typical, if brief example, is the entry for the song "Tarrant Moss," which Ives dated to 1902 and described as "a rough song, some chords of bare 5ths, ending in keys of C major and F♯ major together."[97] In this entry, Ives made a bid on the patent for bitonality, its usual claimant, Igor Stravinsky, having not composed the ballet *Petrushka* with its famous passage superimposing C major and F♯ major, until 1910. As I discuss in chapter 6, many of the dates Ives supplied have since proven to be spurious. The second kind of evidence is subtler and has more to do with insinuation than concrete facts. *Memos* is strewn with reminiscences pertaining to Ives's musical education, and what is notable about them is the way they skew toward the informal experimentalism of his bandmaster father and away from his formal training at Yale.[98]

The warm glow of nostalgia suffuses Ives's many anecdotes about the guidance he received from his father while growing up in small-town Danbury. To take just one of many examples, Ives recounted how, as a young boy, he would thump out snare and bass drum band parts on the piano, using clusters of notes played by the fist or flat of the hand. "Father didn't object to all of this," he recollected, "if it was done with some musical sense—that is, if I would make some effort to find out what was going on, with some reason." This is typical of the way George is depicted in *Memos*: open-minded, encouraging, and ever committed to putting what might seem to be musical tomfoolery in the service of higher objectives. In his role as town bandmaster, George emerges as a benevolent leader of musical life in Danbury, not only bearing with good humor the quirks of the amateur music making over which he presided, but seeing in it profound and genuine expressions of feeling. A passage from *Memos*, oft-quoted in the Ives literature, purports to record George's response after he was asked how he could stand the raucous, off-tune singing of the town mason: "Watch him closely and reverently, look into his face and hear the music of the ages. Don't pay too much attention to the sounds—for if you do, you may miss the music. You won't get a wild heroic ride to heaven on pretty little sounds."[99]

The outsize presence of George in *Memos*, along with his milieu of small-town amateur musicians, minimizes the import of Ives's more formal musical educa-tion. As an undergraduate at Yale, Ives spent two years studying counterpoint, instrumentation, and composition with Horatio Parker, then one of the most prominent American composers. But in *Memos*, Ives claimed that much of what he did in university was a revision of material he had covered with his father. Thus, the impression one gets is that Ives endured his musical studies at Yale with good humor and Parker with equanimity (though occasionally chiding his student for musical eccentricities), and that ultimately neither of them benefited much from the experience.

It is hardly surprising that Ives should seek to distance himself from Parker. After all, the prerogative of all modernists was to stand in opposition to the es-tablishment—and Parker, as a prominent music professor, was nothing if not a man of the establishment. Ives was careful to retain a respectful tone when writing about his erstwhile teacher, but even the gentle criticism he essayed—that Par-ker was "governed too much by the German rule"—is telling.[100] If there was one defining characteristic of the major American musical institutions against which the modernists were in revolt, it was an allegiance to the European classical music tradition. Ives was well-versed in this tradition, thanks to Parker's tutelage at Yale, but given the aesthetic commitments of his devotees, it was in his interest not to draw attention to the fact. Fortunately, he could claim an alternative pedigree in his bandmaster father and the amateur musical life of postbellum Danbury.

Ives had not always been so dismissive of his time with Parker. In fact, for several years after his graduation in 1898, when he was still working part-time as a church organist and contemplating his prospects for a more extensive career as a professional musician, he had regularly touted himself as a Parker student. Moreover, Ives may have been attempting to emulate a crucial event in his former professor's career when, in 1902, he organized the premiere of his cantata *The Celestial Country*. As it turns out, Parker had launched his musical celebrity with a cantata *Hora Novissima*, its premiere helping him secure the Yale professorship.[101] Unfortunately, the reception of *The Celestial Country* was lukewarm, and it failed to achieve for Ives what *Hora Novissima* had done for Parker. Shortly after the premiere, Ives resigned from his post as organist at Manhattan's Central Presbyterian Church, thereby ending a successful fledgling career as a church musician and severing his ties to the professional musical world. It was not until 1910 that he would resume his efforts to find an audience, a process that involved a good deal of trial and even more error.

By 1931, when Ives began writing *Memos*, he had repackaged his music multiple times. He had solicited readings of his scores from professional musicians and widely disseminated the vanity publication of the "Concord" Sonata, which linked him to the foremost figures of the American literary canon. Another volume, *114 Songs*, had followed, a grab-bag collection drawn from all stages of his career and offering something to the gamut of musical expectations. But what Ives learned through his efforts was that his music attracted the most attention from modernists, and it was to them that he addressed *Memos*. There are distortions and misrepresentations aplenty in this autobiographical scrapbook, but to accuse Ives of engaging in a protracted campaign of misinformation would be to go too far. Instead, he was responding to his own reception, mirroring the public persona that his devotees had created for him.

Physically, Ives was a shadow of his former self, ill health preventing him from sustaining the active role he had played in promoting his music during the teens and twenties. He had stopped composing in 1929, and though he would live until 1954, the last twenty-five years of his life were spent mostly as a recluse in his country home in Redding, Connecticut. The growing public discourse about Ives was dominated by other voices, and the one that resounded most loudly belonged to a sunny bohemian from California named Henry Cowell.

2

Songs of Our Fathers

The Advocacy of Henry Cowell and the Appeal of the American Past, 1927–1947

Contemporary photographs show a young man dressed in an oversized tailcoat and pinstripe pants, his hair slightly longer than fashionable, earnestly pounding away at a grand piano with his fists and forearms or clawing with equal aplomb at the instrument's innards. This was Henry Cowell at the zenith of his musical celebrity during the 1920s (Figure 2.1). Throughout the decade and into the early thirties, Cowell conducted a highly visible career as a concert pianist who performed his own works, attracting headlines around the world for the unusual way—brutal, in the estimation of some critics—in which he coaxed sounds from the piano. Undoubtedly, there was an element of the Barnumesque to his tours, but Cowell was also motivated by an insatiable curiosity about sound, a desire, as he later memorably put it, to live "in the whole world of music."[1] That world was brilliantly populous, where the Asian musics Cowell heard as a child in the Bay Area coexisted with the Amerindian music he discovered on scratchy field recordings as a university student; where the folk-infused idiom of Béla Bartók coexisted with the howl of a banshee, created by sliding a fingernail along a piano string; where the distant roar of an old Irish god resounded in the thunder of low-register tone clusters. Cowell was the most ecumenical of modernists. However, he did tend to view his world of music through lenses colored by American nationalism, a tincture that infused his activities as an impresario and critic much more than his performances or compositions. Ultimately, this proved to be more important than the flamboyant pianism that garnered him so much attention at the time; one of his most lasting legacies would be the advocacy work he did on behalf of Ives.

Cowell's ideas about Ives were not static, though they are conveniently grouped into two periods: those produced prior to the sentence he served at San Quentin

Figure 2.1. Henry Cowell poses for reporters in 1924.
Courtesy Musical America Archives.

State Prison for a 1936 conviction on a morals charge, and those produced after his release in 1940. It is the writings of the earlier period that are my first concern in this chapter. They are animated by the belief that the distinctiveness of Ives's music, the quality that made it definitively American, arose from a fealty to the idiosyncratic practices of amateur, small-town musicians. Ives, for Cowell, was a music ethnographer, and his greatest innovations sprang directly from his childhood experience of music in postbellum Danbury.

By the late thirties, when Cowell's imprisonment temporarily silenced his voice, the culture of places like Danbury was attracting attention from a large subset of American artists and intellectuals. The Concord writers of the nineteenth century, who had not fared so well in the early days of the American modernist movement, became the subject of a new vogue, and studies of Emerson, Thoreau, and their associates multiplied. This phenomenon is my second concern, for it provided the context in which Ives's views on the transcendentalists, expressed in *Essays Before a Sonata*, found receptive ears at last, and a new strain of Ivesian criticism emerged that placed the "Concord" Sonata at the center of his oeuvre.

New England Gets Its Musical Due:
Ives as Ethnographer

Cowell first became aware of Ives after the 1925 Pro Musica concerts featuring *Three Quarter-Tone Pieces* caused a minor stir in New York.[2] At that time, however, Cowell's interest was not sufficiently piqued to prompt him to seek personal contact. The two men became acquainted in 1927, when Cowell sent out a prospectus to members of the musical community seeking subscribers for a journal devoted to the publication of scores by American composers. When the first issue of *New Music Quarterly* arrived featuring Carl Ruggles's *Men and Mountains*, nearly half of the subscriptions were canceled; Ives, who had originally purchased two, bought twenty-five more.[3] This gesture spurred a grateful Cowell to meet his benefactor face to face in late February of 1928. That summer, Cowell published an article entitled "Four Little Known Modern Composers" in an obscure, short-lived arts magazine. Ives was among the quartet of "little-knowns," and the article, though only a scant two and a half pages, with little more than a quarter of it devoted to Ives, marked the onset of Cowell's protracted promotion campaign on behalf of the Connecticut composer.[4] This article supplied the basic fund of ideas about Ives that Cowell would draw upon until 1936, when his activities were abruptly curtailed after he was imprisoned. In this period, from 1928 to 1936, Cowell produced a regular stream of articles on Ives, which were published in forums ranging from "little magazines"—the *New Freeman* and *Modern Music*—to large circulation dailies like the *San Francisco Examiner*.

Because of its brevity, Cowell's first article on Ives is not the best place to explore his early conception of the composer. A much more developed version of the same ideas can be found in a 1932 article he wrote for *Modern Music*, his contribution to the journal's ongoing series of studies devoted to American composers. As his point of departure, Cowell wrote about the failure of past composers to capture the essence of American folk music:

> Many before Ives have tried to utilize American folk material; men like Stephen Foster practically composed folk songs. But much of their product took on a banal European flavor because they invariably altered the original rhythms (often fascinatingly irregular) to fit the current European modes in meter and note-length. All those slight deviations of pitch in the musical scale of the American village folk, wrought out of deepest ecstasy, were "arranged" for the conventional European major or minor tuning. Worst of all, a school-book, hymn-like four-part harmonization was imposed on everything. The original life and fire of the music were completely squeezed out.[5]

There followed a list of some of the musical idiosyncrasies one might encounter in rural New England and that would likely be "squeezed out" in transcription: a village band, some of its members rushing, some lagging, and some out of tune; the "slips and slides" of a country fiddler, whose "slightly off pitch tones . . . could loosely be called 'quarter tones'"; and the "nebulous pitch" of a church congregation, vaguely centered on the "supposed notes of the tune." Far from being mistakes, these were the earmarks of American "folk" authenticity. As Cowell pointed out elsewhere, much of the music could be traced back to England, but what made it local was the way it was performed.[6]

Where composers of the past had failed, in Cowell's estimation, Ives had succeeded, realizing that genuine American art music must be rooted in local performance practice, in the nooks and crannies of New England's musical vernacular. Cowell credited Ives's father with having spurred this important realization. George E. Ives, the local bandmaster, had encouraged his son to listen with open ears and to experiment. But what in the father had been a predilection for acoustic tinkering grew in the son into a comprehensive musical empiricism. "Inspired by a feeling rooted in the spirit of [local] music," wrote Cowell, "he raised his whole musical structure from the ground up. It was impossible for him to confine himself in the scale, harmony and rhythm systems of cultivated Europe. A new and broader musical architecture was essential, a scheme of things permitting the use of all that is to be found in American folk music."[7] Cowell went on to describe how aspects of the "new musical architecture" were indebted to particular elements of the New England sound world. The great independence of line, which Cowell called "full polyphony," was linked to Ives's experience of hearing two marching bands pass while traveling in opposite directions and playing different works. His complex rhythms, though unprecedented on paper, were associated with the performances of folk musicians. Similarly, the use of quarter tones was related to the unconventional tunings of country fiddlers: "He does not write down approximate tones of our scale, but attempts to transcribe the exact shades of pitch."[8] Thus, in Cowell's view, the music of Ives grew out of an attempt to re-create the New England sound world as accurately as possible, discarding European conventions where they proved a hindrance. As a result, Ives got a jump on European modernists like Schoenberg and Stravinsky, anticipating many of the innovations for which they would become famous.

Cowell was not quite willing to leave Ives as a New England musical ethnographer because, he noted, "[h]is music finally travels far from its folk origins toward symphonic works of length and complexity." However, no matter the distance traveled, Ives granted the performer a central place in his music, not just as source of inspiration but also as cocreator. As a sort of corollary to his thesis about Ives's attentiveness to local performance practice, Cowell suggested that the composer granted leeway to performers of his works such that they could develop their own authentic rendering. "Ives gives the performer unusual latitude. If the performer is great, Ives believes, he will add creative fire to the composer's; new and unexpected beauties will be born and the work will increase and flourish with each rendition."[9] In short, the performer was much more than a mouthpiece for the oracular voice of the composer.

All of the articles on Ives that Cowell penned between 1928 and 1936 vary the same two themes that I have drawn out in his *Modern Music* article: first, that Ives's American authenticity, as well as his stylistic innovations, stemmed from the faithful replication of what Cowell called "folk material"; second, that the creativity of the performer played an integral role in realizing the works of the composer. Together, these two themes convey a fundamentally social image of Ives, crediting him with an attentiveness to performance practice unprecedented in American music history.

The portrait of Ives as creative ethnographer was an outgrowth of ideas that Cowell first aired publicly in an article entitled "Moravian Music," published early in the summer of 1927. In this article, Cowell described his revelatory musical experiences in the Moravian backcountry, which he briefly visited during a 1926 tour of Europe. The folk music encountered on the excursion was, he enthused, "of a wild beauty utterly removed from the customary conventionalized harmonization of folk themes." It included "many effects we have considered to be of recent invention in 'modern' music, many things not to be found in any known music new or old, and above all, a method of procedure of its own." Cowell was surprised that Czech composers he met were only vaguely aware of this music, especially since he believed it could serve as the foundation for a new art music. The article concluded with a challenge and prophecy:

> When a Czechish composer comes along who realizes that in the writing of his national music it is false to borrow the harmony, scales and rhythms of conventional acceptance, and that an entirely new set of musical values and a new art music may result from the building of a structure from the ground up based on the Folk conception of music, not only in the theme, but in all particulars, he may create a style which will set the world by the ears.[10]

If "American" is substituted for "Czechish" in the preceding quotation, one arrives at a synopsis of the achievement Cowell subsequently credited to Ives. Clearly, folk performance practice and its possibilities were already on Cowell's mind over a year prior to his first substantive explorations of the Ivesian oeuvre.

An interest in folk music—though not the particulars of its performance—can be traced even further back in Cowell's published writings to 1925. That year he proclaimed the "value of eclecticism" in the British journal *Sackbut* and expressed his dismay at the limited tastes of his musical contemporaries:

> It is curious how seldom I find anyone who can share my sincere enthusiasm for such different composers as Bach, Wagner, and Schönberg; or who admires both our own simple folk tunes and also Chinese opera; or who follows me in my conviction that Palestrina is neither far enough back to go in appreciation of the old, nor Ruggles far enough forward in appreciation of the new.[11]

Beyond a general admiration, this passage reveals nothing about Cowell's engagement with "our own simple folk tunes." But even that much was unusual when considered against the backdrop of perceptions of folk music in America at the time.

Anthropologists, Folklorists, and Musical Modernists: Folk Music through Different Lenses

By the midtwenties, folk music had been at the center of two discourses in the United States. University-based scholars were the main interlocutors in the first of these, although their discussions increasingly attracted amateur enthusiasts from outside academe. These scholars were motivated by a desire to preserve oral traditions, capturing and codifying whatever they could before it was lost in the dawning age of mass media. Composers, music critics, and interested members of the musical public sustained the second discourse. Creation, not preservation, was their principal concern, for they regarded folk music as a repository to be drawn upon in the creation of a definitively "American" art-music idiom. Although both discourses produced ideas that may have been suggestive to Cowell, neither yielded a direct precedent to the line of argument he advanced in his articles about Moravian music and Ives.

The closest American kin to the ethnographic Ives of Cowell's imagination were the anthropologists who had studied the music of indigenous cultures. Scholars such as Franz Boas, Frances Densmore, and Alice Cunningham Fletcher had wrestled with issues pertaining to performance practice as they sought the most effective means of transcribing music heard in the field.[12] The distinctiveness of Amerindian music, so clearly outside the traditions of Western European musical culture, prompted them to stretch and augment standard musical notation to accommodate the sounds they heard. For example, Densmore's studies of Amerindian music, which were published under the auspices of the Smithsonian Institution, made use of frequent time changes, complicated rhythms, and a collection of symbols to indicate where pitch and rhythm fell outside the limits of conventional notation.[13]

At the time Cowell began writing about Ives, he was aware of the ethnographic work that had been produced by Densmore and her colleagues. In a 1927 article, he mentioned the Smithsonian Institution studies in conjunction with his own composerly frustrations about "our inadequate notation." He felt, however, that the solutions posited by the anthropologists fell short of the mark:

> Those interested in collecting native Indian music or writing down any sort of oriental music have had the greatest difficulty in even suggesting the original by means of notation. The printed examples of Indian music published by the Smithsonian Institute [*sic*] if sung purely as written, by one who has never heard Indians, become conventional tunes, no different in type from thousands of our own. An Indian would not recognize them. The yells changing to a tone, the tones which develop into wild cries, the curious wavering sounds, in other words, all that is typically Indian and therefore of interest to preserve, is carefully omitted, as it cannot be put down.[14]

Here, Cowell made no suggestions about the creative potential of the "wild cries" and "curious wavering sounds," a contrast with his comments in the Moravian music article, published two months later.

Credit for Cowell's familiarity with the actual sound of Amerindian music, along with his awareness of ethnographic studies, is almost certainly owed to Charles Seeger. Nearly ten years earlier, when Cowell was Seeger's most promising student at the University of California at Berkeley, Seeger had discovered the collection of wax cylinder recordings of Amerindian music stored in the anthropology department. Widely read, he also knew some of the work of his anthropologist colleagues Robert Lowie and Alfred Kroeber, both former students of Boas and scholars of Amerindian culture.[15] It seems likely that Seeger would have shared this discovery with his prize pupil, whose musical interests he knew to be wide-ranging. Moreover, a reference to Seeger toward the end of Cowell's article on the inadequacies of notation suggests that teacher and student had similar concerns. Seeger, Cowell reported, has developed a "remarkable system" of notation that would give composers (and presumably ethnographers also) an unprecedented degree of precision.[16] At the time, however, Seeger had no interest in the potential of Anglo-American folk music for composers and thus cannot have been the spur to Cowell's conception of Ives.[17]

The care anthropologists took in investigating the music of the indigenous peoples was not carried over by their folklorist colleagues who plied their trade closer to home. The scholars who studied folklore among Anglo-Americans—the material most relevant to Cowell's argument about Ives—tended to be the products of English departments, and they were mostly concerned with philological matters pertaining to folk-song texts. For these scholars, Harvard English professor Francis James Child had set the bar. In his five-volume study, *The English and Scottish Popular Ballads* (1883–1898), Child published the texts (without music) of what he thought were the earliest English-language ballads, along with their known variants. The notable absence of "American" from the title of his study, even though numerous sources of American provenance were consulted, is indicative of his conclusion that only variants were to be found in the United States, not originals. Thus, as English literature scholar Gene Bluestein observes, "Child's work seemed to offer overwhelming evidence that American balladry was but a pale reflection of the British ballad tradition."[18]

Child's ideas proved to be persistent. Critic Paul Rosenfeld, three decades later, dismissed "American folk music" in his landmark survey, *An Hour with American Music* (1929). No such thing existed, Rosenfeld claimed, and what was labeled American folk music was in fact "traceable to extra-American conditions." With the exception of Amerindians, all Americans were immigrants and had arrived in the New World with a fully formed culture. In consequence, the United States had bypassed "the stage of civilization that is productive of folksongs."[19] At the time, Rosenfeld was the best-respected music critic sympathetic to modernism and an acquaintance of Cowell's.

In the years following the publication of *The English and Scottish Popular Ballads*, several scholars widened the narrow limitations of folk authenticity imposed by Child. Most notably, John Lomax, also a Harvard product, demonstrated that a body of American folk song did in fact exist.[20] But Lomax was still beholden to the precedent set by Child: his 1910 anthology *Cowboy Songs and Other Frontier Ballads* contained very little music. (Incidentally, this anthology supplied Ives with the text for his song "Charlie Rutlage.") By the late teens and early twenties, there was a growing vogue for "old songs" across the country, fueled in equal parts by nostalgia for a preindustrial age and a sense that preservation was urgently required before this material was drowned out by the sounds of the modern world.[21] Professional folklorists and amateur enthusiasts joined the enterprise launched by Lomax, collecting material believed to be of American provenance. In the preface to a collection of folk songs from the Kentucky Mountains, Josephine McGill observed: "Plainly folk-song is having a real awakening, and interest in it is no longer to be merely scientific or literary and confined to the new."[22] But neither professional folklorists nor amateur enthusiasts showed much interest in folk performance practice and, consequently, seem an unlikely stimulus for the ethnographic conception of Ives.

Art-music discourse does not yield any direct precedents to Cowell's vision of Ives either. Folk music had, of course, been a major preoccupation in the latter half of the nineteenth century, when composers who were not of Austrian or German stock sought a place for themselves in a musical mainstream dominated by a Teutonic canon. A folk tune used as basic thematic material, but worked over with the standard procedures of the Austro-German symphonist, was one way of signaling difference. Tourist nationalism, as musicologist Richard Taruskin has called it, was the result—a bit of spice injected into a familiar idiom.[23] It was just this approach that Antonín Dvořák advocated during his three-year stint at the National Conservatory in New York, where, beginning in 1892, he had been charged with the task of fostering an American school of composition. Close to the beginning of his stay, Dvořák was introduced to the plantation songs and spirituals of African Americans, which struck him as the perfect source for a specifically American idiom. "I am now satisfied," he announced in a newspaper interview, "that the future music of this country must be founded upon what are called negro melodies. . . . There is nothing in the whole range of composition that cannot be supplied with themes from this source."[24]

A few composers followed the spirit of Dvořák's injunction, though not quite its letter. In her *"Gaelic"* Symphony (1897), Amy Beach drew on the stock of Anglo-Irish folk tunes that were popular in New England—far more representative of the American musical culture she was familiar with than plantation songs. Other composers turned instead to the music of Amerindians, most notably Arthur Farwell and Charles Wakefield Cadman, the latter achieving a major success with his *Four American Indian Songs* (1907–1908) and an opera, *Shanewis (The Robin Woman)* (1918). By the twenties, however, when Ives was beginning to make a name for himself among the avant-garde, the so-called Indianist movement had largely run its course.

Other composers were not so happy with Dvořákian prescriptions. Edward MacDowell, lecturing at Columbia University some ten years after Dvořák's pronouncement, declared:

> So-called Russian, Bohemian, or any other purely national music has no place in art, for its characteristics may be duplicated by anyone who takes the fancy to do so. . . . [B]efore a people can find a musical writer to echo its genius it must first possess men who truly represent it—that is to say, men who, being part of the people, love the country for itself: men who put into their music what the nation has put into its life; and in the case of America it needs above all, both on the part of the public and on the part of the writer, absolute freedom from the restraint that an almost unlimited deference to European thought and prejudice has imposed upon us. Masquerading in the so-called nationalism of Negro clothes cut in Bohemia will not help us. What we must arrive at is the youthful optimistic vitality and the undaunted tenacity of spirit that characterizes the American man.[25]

As this passage reveals, MacDowell also hoped for the emergence of a distinctly American music; he simply regarded the appropriation of folk song as an inadequate and superficial approach. For MacDowell, whether a piece could be considered American or not hinged primarily upon the character of the composer. If he or she possessed the virtues that were distinctive of the American genius, "optimistic vitality" and an "undaunted tenacity of spirit" for example, then the resulting music would bear an American imprimatur.

During the twenties, several writers explored the issue of American-ness in connection with Ives before Cowell, and they did so with reference to the viewpoints of either Dvořák or MacDowell. Ives himself launched the discussion, touching briefly on the issue in *Essays Before a Sonata*. Without naming Dvořák but with the Bohemian's views clearly in mind, he dismissed the use of "negro melodies" to create an American idiom. Ives, however, did not opt for MacDowell's viewpoint for he believed there had been an "overinsistence upon the national in art." In keeping with his transcendentalist framework, he thought it a waste of time to devote oneself to creating a national idiom; it was far more important to pursue one's own interests: "[I]f a man finds that the cadences of an Apache war-dance come nearest to the soul . . . let him assimilate whatever he finds highest of the Indian ideal so that he can use it with the cadences, fervently, transcendentally, inevitably, furiously." Committed to the idea of an oversoul that linked all humanity, Ives had little time for the concept of national genius intrinsic to the views of both Dvořák and MacDowell. But he did regard the ideals upon which the United States had been founded as coming closer than any other nation to universal truth.[26]

Ives's views on American musical identity were not embraced by the handful of critics who dealt with his music in the twenties. Henry Bellamann, in his 1921 review of the "Concord" Sonata, advanced a position that was indebted to MacDowell. Adding his voice to the chorus of Dvořák critics, he wrote, "No serious musical mind can be interested in the *applique* of Indian or negro characteristics." Art music is "the universal voice of thought and feeling on a high plane," and if it took on local shading—a rhythm, harmony, or melodic contour suggestive of a particular place—it was a matter of little consequence. But, Bellamann was quick to add, "any effort which goes deeper into some mode of thought or manner of living essentially and exclusively American must interest as a movement in the direction of artistic integrity." Thus, like MacDowell, he was desirous of seeing specifically American virtues translated into the universal language of music.[27]

As Bellamann familiarized himself with the music of Ives, he became convinced that the composer had accomplished just such translation. An observation he had made about the "Emerson" movement of the "Concord" Sonata served as the point of departure for a comprehensive theory about the significance of Ives. "The beauty of this division of the work," Bellamann had written in his review, "is severe and difficult. It is a beauty of high and remote things. It is austere. It is informed with the stark and ascetic beauty of lonely and alien reaches of human imagination."[28] In all Bellamann's subsequent writings about Ives, descriptions of the music's austerity run like a leitmotif. He seized upon this quality because it furnished him with the means of linking Ives to a "mode of thought or manner of living" that was exclusively American, namely New England Puritanism. Consider the following excerpt from his 1927 program notes for the Fourth Symphony: "[The music] is of New England—the New England of granitic Puritanism—and reflects a strangely introspective and profoundly philosophic temperament. . . . Almost it would seem that the New England spirit of the forefathers had come incredibly into an adequate artistic expression." Puritan virtues, Bellamann maintained, guarded Ives against "any concession to sensual externals," keeping the music tightly focused: "It is bound into technical unity by the most extraordinary mastery of material that is often crabbed and fractious." Ives's use of hymns in the symphony was a masterstroke since they had been the Puritan's "only expression in art medium," and all of the "repressed humanity of those rock-bound souls was poured into fervent renditions of [hymns]." To put it another way, the fervency of Puritan hymn-singing reflected a manner of living exclusive to the United States, and, by Bellamann's standards, this meant it was worthy of being projected into the universal realm of art music. Bellamann hoped that his theory would serve as the basis for further study of Ives's music. But, other than foregrounding the issue of Ives's American-ness, the connection with New England Puritanism he posited was largely ignored.[29]

One other pre-Cowell Ives critic, independent of Bellamann, also wrote about the composer's New England heritage. During the twenties, Winthrop P. Tryon, music critic for the *Christian Science Monitor*, devoted several articles to Ives, including an editorial entitled "Folk Song and Hymn Tunes of America." The piece, published in November 1924, was written several months after Tryon's first exposure to the music of Ives, the premiere of the Second Violin Sonata.[30] Based on that performance, he had come to the conclusion that Ives was pursuing the Dvořákian stratagem but instead of using "negro melody" had turned to the largely ignored repertoire of New England hymns. Tryon was noncommittal as to whether such an approach produced "the true national thing or not," but he did feel that it had the salutary effect of broadening "the phrase, 'American folk song,' which, as far as instrumental music is concerned has signified chiefly Indian and Negro melody."[31] Three years later, reviewing a Pro Musica concert that featured movements from the Fourth Symphony, Tryon encouraged his readers to rethink their prejudices against the "unmusical Puritans." Ives had demonstrated that New England hymnody was a rich vein, largely unmined, and Tryon suggested musicologists "pause in their rummagings Wagnerian and make further inquiries Masonian" (Here, Tryon had in mind Lowell Mason, a nineteenth-century composer, educator, and promoter of American hymnody.)[32] The upshot was that the United States—or rather Anglo-Americans—had produced a vital folk-music tradition that demanded attention.

At the time, few writers would have agreed with Tryon. A new generation of composers had emerged, and preoccupations with rural folk (whatever their ethnicity) were replaced by preoccupations with modern urban spaces, stylistic innovation, and cosmopolitan culture. In 1927, Copland was leaving behind the jazz inflections of his Piano Concerto (1926) for the more austere sound world of Symphonic Ode (1927–1929). Edgard Varèse's *Arcana* (1927) was successfully premiered in Philadelphia under Leopold Stokowski, adding to the reputation of a composer who was then the most famous musical modernist in the United States.[33] That year also witnessed the less successful but much-talked-about premiere of *Ballet mécanique* (1925), by George Antheil. A glance at the index for *Modern Music*, the organ of the League of Composers and primary forum for musical modernism in the United States, reveals comparatively few entries for folk music during the twenties and early thirties.[34]

Again, then, as is in the case of the discourse of American folklorists, the music-specific discourse of composers and critics during the twenties yielded no precursor to the ethnographically oriented Ives. For the roots of Cowell's conception of Ives (and Moravian music, for that matter) it is necessary to look elsewhere. First to John Varian, an obscure poet who belonged to a West Coast theosophical community, and to whom Cowell owed his interest in folk music. And second, to Béla Bartók, to whom he owed an anthropological framework that explained how the latent potentialities in folk music could be translated into an art-music idiom.

Hidden Treasure: Cowell's Folk-Music Awakening

Cowell was still a teenager when he first met John Varian, a charismatic eccentric who lived in Palo Alto, not far from the cabin on the outskirts of Menlo Park that Cowell shared with his mother. A theosophist, Varian melded science and mysticism into a potent amalgam that, as musicologist Steven Johnson has demonstrated, made a lasting imprint on Cowell and his music. In the big, often impracticable ideas of Varian (among them a "harmonious speaking cave" made of concrete and modeled on the human vocal mechanism) can be found the roots of the inventive spirit that informed Cowell's *New Musical Resources* (1930). In addition to a shared interest in acoustics and metaphysics, the friendship of Cowell and Varian rested on a sense of shared heritage. Varian's pride in his native Ireland provided Cowell with a way to explore an aspect of his background that had been lost when his mother and Irish father separated. By the time Varian met Cowell in the early teens, he had been in the United States for many years, but his attachment to Ireland remained strong. He assiduously fostered connections with the people he had left behind upon emigrating, and in his poetry and plays, elements of Irish and Celtic mythology were blended with theosophy. Some of this material Cowell set to music, leaving a trail of titles in his work list evocative of things Celtic—*The Tides of Manaunaun*, *The Voice of Lir*, and *The Trumpet of Angus Og*. Varian also cultivated Cowell's interest in Irish folk music, at one point lending him a collection of ancient Irish tunes. The enthusiasm this engendered proved to be long-lived: twenty years later, after visiting Ireland himself, Cowell wrote to Varian recounting the wonderful experience he had had meeting folk musicians, studying their musical practices, and even buying several instruments for his own collection.[35]

That same trip prompted Cowell to publish an article in *Modern Music*, exploring the potentialities he discerned in Irish folk music for the modern composer. Entitled "Hidden Irish Treasure" and appearing in the May-June issue for 1929, it was one of the few early essays on folk music to appear in the journal. "In this age of great harmonic development," Cowell began, "it may prove valuable to observe certain little known modes of melodic usage. A special style of unfamiliar conception, not to mention actual tunes, may offer the composer the basis of a new and individual music." Although this idea is reminiscent of the advice dispensed by Dvořák during the 1890s, Cowell had something quite different in mind. First, he was not issuing a prescription for the development of a national art. Rather, in keeping with his earlier plea for eclecticism, he was suggesting that unfamiliar music, whatever its origin, might have a beneficial effect on the creative, open-minded composer. Second, Cowell was relatively uninterested in using Irish melodies as a source for thematic material. What was foremost on his mind was the inspiration that could be drawn from the way in which folk musicians performed. Although Irish tunes had been sung all over the world, upon "hearing the tunes sung in the old style, . . . [one realizes that] the written form in which one has previously encountered them is the merest indication, a skeleton on which to hang the flesh and blood of the real melodies." Traditional notation tended to leave out the very things that make a musical style individual.[36]

This is the same argument Cowell advanced in the context of his discussion of Moravian music and Ives; but, unlike his earlier work, "Hidden Irish Treasure" drops a significant hint about the origins of his position on folk-music practice. Cowell concludes his discussion by citing the example of a composer who had followed just the course he had in mind, but with another body of folk music:

> Béla Bartók has shown us how to convey the essence of a people's music by building up a type of harmonization which amalgamates the characteristic features and sets them off, a sort of harmony perhaps unsuited to any other purpose. He has

done this very successfully for his native Hungarian music. Whoever approaches Irish material with as much insight will find a wealth of splendid material and unfathomed resources leading in unexplored directions.[37]

During his 1923 European tour, Cowell had met Bartók in London and a relationship of mutual respect developed between the two men.[38] When, four years later, Bartók arrived in the United States for his first tour of North America, Cowell arranged accommodations in New York, securing a room in the home of his friend and sometime patron Blanche Walton.[39] Walton's home was also where Cowell stayed during his frequent visits to New York, one of which happened to coincide with Bartók's brief sojourn. In a letter to his father and stepmother, Cowell wrote, "Bartók is here, and we are all enjoying him tremendously—it is interesting to have so distinguished a man in the family, and to have him so fine to get along with!"[40] Unfortunately, there is no record of the discussions that took place between Cowell and Bartók during this visit. But Cowell's writings dating from after the winter of 1927–1928 clearly bear the imprint of Bartókian thought, an indication of the nature of the exchange between the two men.

Several years earlier, Bartók had published a synopsis of his ideas in English under the title "The Relation of Folksong to the Development of the Art Music of Our Time."[41] It appeared in the same British journal in which Cowell published his 1925 essay championing eclectic music tastes. Bartók recounted how the research of musical folklorists "drew the attention of certain musicians to the genuine peasant music, and with astonishment they found that they had come upon a natural treasure-store of surpassing abundance." But, he insisted, with an authority that he could justifiably claim as a practiced ethnographer, the essence of "genuine peasant music" eluded traditional notation: "The harsh characters [musical notes] cannot possibly render the subtler shades of rhythm, or intonation, of sound transitions, in a word all the pulsing life of peasant music."[42] The "treasure-store of surpassing abundance" lay in the performance practice of peasant musicians and, in order to have access to it, composers needed to hear the music firsthand.

Bartók was equally insistent on another point: composers did not have to devote themselves exclusively to the folk music of a particular country. "It would be stupid," he stated bluntly, "to force a selection for exterior reasons such as a wrongly conceived patriotism." (This viewpoint Cowell implicitly acknowledged by presenting his "Irish treasure" as free for the taking, whether the taker was Irish or not.) What Bartók was censuring was the nationalistically motivated pursuit of a fundamental essence in folk culture. To his mind, the origins of the primitive music of a people were as inscrutable as the origins of speech. Even if the original body of folk music could be isolated, it was not the sum total of a people's musical authenticity:

Through various causes foreign melodies . . . are disseminated among the people in question, and in the process of their dissemination, local variants arise—first through small changes, later from an accumulation of more important deviations from the original form. By reason of the peasants' innate conservatism the foreign melodies are ornamented with the idiosyncrasies of the existing musical style of the country into which they have been imported, or they may be completely transformed by the same means.[43]

Whether he read this passage or gleaned its content through conversation with Bartók, Cowell must have been struck by its pertinence to the American situation.

The phenomenon Bartók described was known among anthropologists as *diffusion*. It had been at the center of a heated debate at the turn of the century about the mechanism of cultural development. An older school of anthropological thought, propounded by the likes of E. B. Tylor, Herbert Spencer, and Lewis H. Morgan, held that cultures functioned much as did organisms, manifesting specific characteristics at each stage of evolutionary growth. Thus the appearance of totemism, for example, could be expected at a certain point in the development track, each culture "independently inventing" it.[44] A paradigm in which the peoples of the world were imagined to have developed independently and in comparative isolation precluded any claim that "American culture" was a coherent, distinct entity. As a nation of immigrants, the United States was a mixture of cultures at different stages of development, and so beyond the bounds of anthropological discourse—though the marginalized indigenous peoples of North America were not. By contrast, diffusionists held that contact between different societies was the principal agent of change, one group passing a particular element or set of elements along to another. Franz Boas was the foremost advocate of diffusion, his position having developed in the course of fieldwork among the Amerindian tribes of the Pacific Northwest. Boas's 1898 summary of his work on tribal mythologies is a clear antecedent to Bartók's observations about folk music. "The mythologies of the various tribes as we find them now are not organic growths, but have gradually developed and obtained their present form by the accretions of foreign material. . . . [This material was] adapted and changed in form according to the genius of the people who borrowed it."[45] Bartók, it should be noted, added contradicting provisos to the diffusionist framework, declaring some syntheses authentic and others inauthentic—notably those that involved urban-gypsy music.

According to Romantic orthodoxy, a genuinely national art could derive only from an autochthonous folk; but according to Boas (and Bartók), the practices of any particular "folk" included a significant amount of borrowed material. To speak of a pure national essence was entirely wrong-headed. With diffusion recognized as the rule and not the exception, the United States could be seen as representing an extreme manifestation of the process. Americans also possessed culture, and while its greater part might be indebted to a mixture of European sources, it was no less significant. The culture of a German villager was heterogeneous, as was that of a New Yorker. From this perspective, contentions of the sort Paul Rosenfeld advanced about the lack of indigenous folk music in the United States were baseless. The ground was cleared for Cowell to claim that "Charles E. Ives is the father of indigenous American music, and at the same time one of the freshest and most experimental composers today."[46] American folk music had become the root of a specifically American art music.

In 1930, two years after first portraying Ives as an American ethnographer, Cowell was appointed to the faculty of the New School for Social Research, bringing him into a milieu where cutting-edge social theory, including Boasian anthropology, figured prominently. Seeger joined him the following year. This new context may well have served to nurture the ideas Cowell had first gleaned from Bartók.[47] Although a range of perspectives was represented in the faculty, it is possible to discern certain consistent strains of thought that together comprise something that might be called a "house paradigm."[48] The prevailing epistemology at the New School was instrumentalism, a close cousin of Boasian anthropology. Knowledge, for the instrumentalist, was context-dependent and not absolute. Thus what was "instrumental" to one group of people at one particular place and time may not be applicable to another group at another place and time. This was consistent with Boas's dual contentions: first that there is no single track along which all societies naturally evolved; second, that every culture is fluid, adopting and refashioning elements from other peoples according to its own demands.

Boas was never officially part of the New School's teaching staff (he was tenured at Columbia), but he did give lectures there from time to time, as did one of his most famous students, Margaret Mead. Also, the New School could boast the presence of another Boas student who was on the faculty, Alexander Goldenweiser. It was Goldenweiser's vision of a reference work for the social sciences that was the impetus behind the sole publication in which the names Boas and Cowell can be linked directly. In *The Encyclopaedia of the Social Sciences* (EOSS), its multiple volumes published between 1930 and 1935, Boas supplied the article on anthropology and Cowell coauthored the article on music with Charles Seeger and Helen H. Roberts, yet another Boas student. The director of the New School, Alvin S. Johnson, served as associate editor for the encyclopedia and ensured that it was consistent with the instrumentalist perspective.[49] Of course, it would be too much to conclude that a direct exchange took place between Cowell and Boas on the basis of the fact that they both contributed to the EOSS. Moreover, despite Cowell's employment at the New School, his correspondence bears no trace of the vibrant discourse about the social sciences that was taking place there. If he attended the lectures of Boas, Mead, or Goldenweiser, he did not see fit to commit his impressions to paper.

Spreading the Gospel: The Influence of Henry Cowell

The amount of energy Cowell expended on Ives's behalf is astounding, dwarfing the efforts of the many other individuals who enabled the reticent Ives to move from anonymity to canonicity. In addition to penning hundreds of pages of prose—chock-full of encomiums—he found other ways to promote the composer. His *New Music Quarterly*, launched in 1927 and devoted to the publication of scores by avant-garde American composers, featured numerous compositions of Ives. When a series of recordings was issued to complement the quarterly, Ives's works were among the offerings.[50] Assuming the role of impresario, Cowell also saw to it that Ives was represented on concert programs sponsored by the San Francisco–based New Music Society and the New York–based Pan-American Association of Composers. Cowell's interest in Ives's music was genuine enough, but his motivations for promoting the composer were not solely altruistic. He received major financial returns on his investment, Ives's deep pocketbook allowing him to keep *New Music Quarterly* afloat, hire musicians for concerts, and meet the administrative costs of the various organizations to which he belonged.[51] Fortunately for Ives, Cowell's enthusiasm and ideas proved infectious.

In 1928, Cowell introduced Ives to Nicolas Slonimsky, who was pursuing a fledgling career as a conductor in Boston.[52] Slonimsky solicited a score from the composer and was given *Three Places in New England*, which he premiered in New York on January 10, 1931. Follow-up performances were given in Boston (January 25), New York (February 7), and Havana (March 18). Upon Slonimsky's return from Cuba, arrangements were made for two Paris performances to take place later that year under the auspices of the Pan-American Association of Composers: Cowell did the organizing, Slonimsky the conducting, and Ives paid the bills. *Three Places in New England* was not the only work featured on the Paris concerts, but it was especially well received. The Parisian critics waxed eloquent, one of them exclaiming, "Ives is not imitative, he has something to say. He is a musical artist-painter, if such an expression may be used, an impressionist not without a mixture of naïve realism; his art is at times awkward and raw, but in him there is real power and true invention, thematically and rhythmically speaking, which does not follow either the fashion or authorities. Ives is perhaps, the only one among the American composers whose art is truly national—in this he has something in common with Walt Whitman."[53] The tour proved so successful that Slonimsky, Ives, and Cowell organized another for the following year—again with

Ives footing the bill. Though this one was more extensive, with performances in Paris, Berlin, and Budapest, reviews proved to be more mixed.

Beyond piquing Slonimsky's interest, Cowell exerted an influence on several writers who tackled the subject of Ives in the early thirties. Bernard Herrmann, who had become an Ives devotee after stumbling across the privately printed music of the composer as a high school student, essentially echoed Cowellian cant.[54] "Ives's modernism," he asserted in a survey article from 1932, "is the result of his observation of town and country. . . . And the early reproducing of these perceptions brought about a highly complex and dissonant musical style."[55] Arthur Berger, though not so ardent an Ives fan as Herrmann, made a similar observation at a preview talk for a 1933 Pan-American concert:

> No one before him [Ives] has given such genuine and sincere expression to American music, simply because no one with equal musical ability has been so deeply moved by this native heritage. Though [the songs of which this heritage is comprised] are to a large extent of English derivation, the manner in which they are performed is distinctly American. Ives' success where others have failed is due to the fact that he captures the peculiar quirks of performance, the slips and slides of the country fiddler, for instance.[56]

Herrmann and Berger were both members of a short-lived organization modeled on Les Six, with Aaron Copland functioning as mentor. They dubbed themselves the Young Composer's Group and, beginning in 1932, met regularly at Copland's loft for almost a year and half. The topics of discussion encompassed music, aesthetics, and politics, and the name of Ives was frequently invoked. Herrmann and Jerome Moross, another member of the group, were responsible for cajoling their avuncular mentor into investigating *114 Songs*, Copland having displayed little interest in Ives in the past.[57]

The most dramatic Ives conversion of the period was that of critic Paul Rosenfeld, and again, Cowell played an integral part. Rosenfeld had been in attendance at the 1927 Pro Musica Concert that featured two movements from Ives's Fourth Symphony but came away unimpressed. In an omnibus review of several New York concerts, he dispatched the work briskly: "[T]he prelude and second movement of a symphony for orchestra and pianos by Charles E. Ives besides being literary are badly orchestrated as though Schumann had done the instrumentation, doubling all the parts."[58] Reports from Europe about the positive reception that greeted Slonimsky's Ives performances in 1931 caused him to rethink his position.

Despite a strong nationalist streak, Rosenfeld always had an eye toward European culture, treating it as the yardstick against which the products of American artists were to be measured. Musicologist Carol J. Oja rightly observes that for Rosenfeld, American modernism had to "conform to long-established European standards at the same time as it found its own distinctive manifestations."[59] What Rosenfeld desired was an American voice that could claim parity with those issuing from Europe; and European critics, responding to Slonimsky's concerts, had discerned just such a voice in Ives. Rosenfeld was chastened, having failed to recognize the significance of the composer himself. Fortunately, he had an excuse handy. Shortly after his conversion, he explained that "spirited young musicians" had been the first to embrace Ives, but that their admiration had been "esoteric" and resulted in few performances. As a result, "to the public of amateurs [Rosenfeld always referred to himself as such] both his place and figure perforce remained vague and indeterminable."[60] In short, the neglect Ives suffered at the hands of music professionals was the reason why Rosenfeld had failed to discern the presence of such an important American voice. In excusing himself, Rosenfeld supplied another theme that would become standard in Ives commentary.

Rosenfeld began to make amends for his oversight in a review of a concert that took place in May of 1932 and included seven songs by Ives. These songs, he enthused, "revealed the presence of a great *lieder* writer in the ranks of American music. A deeply sentient New Englander, somewhat of the type of Robert Frost, Ives has expressed his deep wise feeling of life in songs of perfect design and original color and with characteristic touches."[61] Over the course of the next four years, two full-length articles on Ives issued from Rosenfeld's pen, one published in the *New Republic* and another in his 1936 book *Discoveries of a Music Critic*. In the earlier article, Rosenfeld dubbed Ives "the pioneer of atonality," falling into line with the composer's earliest modernist advocates and their focus on innovation and precedence. As an explanation, he tentatively advanced Cowell's anthropology-derived thesis: "It is even possible that Ives's early espousal of the principles of atonality and polytonality is due to the strongly imitative inclination of his eminent talent. . . . [I]t appears that it was while listening to the humorous musical distortions of church organists, village bands and itinerant fiddlers, that his imagination was actually touched by dissonant idiom."[62] The speculative tone suggests that Rosenfeld was not entirely convinced. But, by the time he wrote his second Ives article, in 1936, he had fully digested Cowell's thesis:

> [Ives] very early began observing that the melodic, harmonic, and rhythmic distortions of traditional music—frequently of English origin—produced under the stress of excitement by church organists, village bands, country fiddlers, frequently initiated forms truer to their feelings and to the essences and ideas they apprehend than the more regular performances. The untuned organ, the choir soulfully soaring "off key," an organist excitedly striking the "false" notes in his musical élan, the members of a rural orchestra embroidering individually on the rhythms and wildly playing simultaneously in different tonalities, the clashing bands at Fourth

of July celebrations, were actually initiating living forms certainly possessive of a freedom the cut and dried originals did not have, and of truth of their own.[63]

Only seven years earlier, Rosenfeld had denied the existence of American folk music altogether in his book *An Hour with American Music*. Now, he was attributing Ives's accomplishment to the perception of "living forms" in folk performance practice.

It was not simply the cogency of Cowell's argument that caused Rosenfeld to revise his position. As an alumnus of the Greenwich Village Young America milieu, where progressivism had been the rule, Rosenfeld spent the teens and twenties looking optimistically forward, toward the horizon, where he expected a genuine American voice to appear at any moment. Over the years, he had heralded the arrival of a variety of American musical messiahs, ranging from Leo Ornstein to Roger Sessions. But, in each case, after a flush of ebullient prose, his hopes faded, and he turned once more to the horizon. By the thirties, Rosenfeld tired of the cycle; a new pessimism set in, his health declined, and, after the stock market crash, he found himself in a precarious financial position. Critic Edmund Wilson, in a tribute essay to Rosenfeld, captured something of the disillusionment of the moment: "The times had not brought to fulfillment that creative and enlightened era of which they [the Young Americans] had seemed to be witnessing the dawn when the *Seven Arts* was founded: totalitarian states and class pressures were closing down on the artistic elite."[64] In this dark mood, Rosenfeld's progressivism wavered and he found himself drawn to Oswald Spengler's apocalyptic historical treatise, *The Decline of the West*.

Rosenfeld was not alone, for Spengler enjoyed a vogue in the thirties, offering as he did a compelling counternarrative to the typical meliorism of contemporaneous world histories. Instead of perpetual progress, Spengler described a twofold process in which "culture" gave way to "civilization," a dichotomy he borrowed from Nietzsche.[65] As Rosenfeld's friend Lewis Mumford put it in a commentary on *The Decline of the West*, in the "culture" stage, "[all] life is bound up with a common soil and a deep intuitive sense of the importance of blood, race and caste." The second stage, "civilization," begins when the so-called "actors of history" (the small minority of people who change things rather than those who "merely live") reach a consciousness that transcends instinctive life. Suddenly, they become aware of the "cultural idea" that is at the root of the society to which they belong. But this moment of transcendence also marks the beginning of decline, for once the "actors" have reached consciousness, they are less inclined to remain entangled in the web of connections that culture has woven about them. They become cosmopolitan, urbanized, and devitalized as their roots are severed. Mumford explained, "to succeed in terms of civilization, one must be hard: what remained of life, if one could call it life, belonged to the engineer, the business man, the soldier. Life, in short, was to reassert itself as brutality: the sole energy left centered on destruction."[66]

Rosenfeld explicitly invoked Spenglerian theory in an article entitled "The Nazis and 'Die Meistersinger.'" As a longtime advocate of nationalistic art, he had been outraged by an order the Nazi government issued shortly after it came to power, requiring the Berlin Opera to perform *Die Meistersinger*. "To those of us eager to see American artists, by musical or poetic means, project a symbol of the national idea as magnificent as the symbol of the German superindividual entity constituted by Wagner's comic masterpiece, this latter revelation brought an additional shock." Rosenfeld could not stomach the implicit message: that the Nazis and Wagner were of the same transcendent moment, German national identity achieving its mature political and cultural forms. Freely adapting Spengler, Rosenfeld wrote, "All nationalistic art is expressive of the national superindividual entity at the moment that entity offers to form itself freely in the union of individuals—a formation inevitably flowing from the inner liberty of the individual." For Rosenfeld, *Die Meistersinger* was a masterwork because it affirmed the democratic moment in German history. The fascists had made the mistake of thinking themselves at the apex of the culture-civilization trajectory alongside Wagner; in actuality they belonged to the period of decline.[67]

Rosenfeld was mindful of his own failure to discover an American composer who had given voice to the "national superindividual entity." Perhaps he too was on the wrong side of history and had missed the American apex. In this frame of mind, Cowell's theory about Ives held considerable appeal, even if it did contradict assertions Rosenfeld had made about American folk music in the past. Spengler's "actors of history" possessed the ability to perceive the characteristics integral to their culture, things that had previously been a matter of instinct. Ives's achievement, as Cowell portrayed it, was just this: he had identified the idiosyncrasies of folk performers that were distinctively American and had made them the basis of an art music. In short, Rosenfeld's essays about Ives from the early- to midthirties were the product of a confluence between the mystical pseudohistory of Spengler and Boasian anthropological theory, the latter drawn not directly from its source but from Cowell (who in turn got it from Bartók).

But this confluence was not sustainable; Spengler's culture-civilization trajectory was fundamentally at odds with the multiple-tracked cultural development pictured by Boas. By the end of the thirties, Rosenfeld still retained the idea that Ives had developed "his idiom from the germs of the current folk songs and hymn tunes,"[68] but made no mention of performance practice. He also continued to conceive the appearance of Ives as marking a moment of cultural epiphany, but jettisoned Spengler's thesis that such epiphanies inevitably marked the onset of decline. As of about 1939, his pessimism seems to have been ameliorated and there was even talk of a book about Ives to be jointly authored with Elliott Carter, a project left tantalizing unrealized at the time of the critic's death in 1946.[69]

Although unique in its particulars, the respect Rosenfeld developed for Ives during the early thirties does illustrate two broader trends. First, it reveals the extent to which the efforts of Henry Cowell were responsible for propelling Ives into the spotlight and conditioning the way in which the composer was received. The concerts Cowell organized and the articles he wrote played a crucial role in Rosenfeld's rethinking of Ives, even if Spenglerian broodings were the principal reason for his receptivity. Second, Rosenfeld's interest in Ives is indicative of a wide-scale rethinking of the past on the part of American intellectuals. Rosenfeld was only one of many writers whose disillusionment with the present led to a new appreciation for the cultural figures of earlier times.

The decade bore witness to a rehabilitation of the New England transcendentalists who, once shunned by the most vocal constituency of modernists, now found the unlikeliest of champions in Van Wyck Brooks. The new interest in Emerson and other members of the Concord cohort was fortunate for Ives, who had long held the transcendentalists in high regard. In 1921, Ives's hope that the "Concord" Sonata would secure him a sympathetic audience had been misplaced; by 1939, however, anything to do with the literary figures of the so-called "American Renaissance" could be counted upon to attract attention. Indeed it was the burgeoning interest in transcendentalism that bolstered Ives's profile in the late thirties, which had begun to sag after Cowell was incarcerated at San Quentin.[70]

Finding a "Usable Past"

In 1918, Van Wyck Brooks, one of the foremost voices of the Greenwich Village intelligentsia, completed an essay that called for a rewriting of the history of American literature. The memorable title, "On Creating a Usable Past," introduced a rubric that has since been borrowed so often it has become cliché. Brooks launched in with an attack on professors of literature, whom he accused of cudgeling present-day writers with the example of the past. Academia, he explained, had accommodated itself to the "exigencies of the commercial mind," and, consequently, its denizens could not but be the stalwart defenders of business. Since the literature being produced by a younger generation (Brooks probably had Sherwood Anderson foremost in mind) was critical of the rampant commercialism of American life, the professors set out to quash it: "There is in their note an almost pathological vindictiveness when they compare the 'poetasters of today' with certain august figures of the age of pioneering who have long since fallen into oblivion in the minds of men and women of the world." As far as business interests were concerned, the history of American literature as told by academicians was a safely irrelevant thing. But it deprived younger writers, leaving them floating in a void "because the past that survives in the common mind of the present is a past without living value." Brooks went on to ask "is this the only possible past? If we need another past so badly, is it inconceivable that we might discover one, that we might even invent one?"[71]

A "usable past," Brooks suggested, could be created by sifting through the detritus of history and discovering things useful to the creation of national culture. The search was not for hidden masterpieces; it was for "tendencies," for creative impulses that suggested great potential but had been thwarted. At the same time, it was necessary to examine the conditions that had led to their demise, for, armed with an understanding of the destructive forces, preventive measures could be taken so that their second growth would be more fruitful.[72]

In practice, as Brooks biographer James Hoopes notes, the critic tended to focus on the latter part of his program.[73] Witness the line of questions Brooks proposed for exploration at the end of his essay: "Why did Ambrose Bierce go wrong? Why did Stephen Crane fail to acclimatize the modern method in American fiction twenty years ago? What became of Herman Melville?"[74] Consider also his subsequent book, *The Ordeal of Mark Twain* (1920), which reached the sort of grim conclusion that was typical of Brooks's criticism at the time: Twain, he determined, had fallen victim to the pecuniary preoccupations of the Gilded Age, sacrificed his artistic potential, and ended up using humor as a cathartic outlet for his dissatisfaction.[75] Failure, not possibility was Brooks's emphasis—an indication of how hard he found it to relinquish his own prejudiced view of the American past, hopelessly bifurcated into highbrow and lowbrow spheres.

During the twenties, a handful of people took Brooks's lead and busied themselves with the task of creating a usable past, achieving mixed results. One of them was Aaron Copland, who may not have known Brooks personally but became acquainted with his ideas shortly after returning to New York from Europe in 1924. Paul Rosenfeld furnished Copland with an entrée into a milieu in which such veterans of the prewar Greenwich Village revolt as Waldo Frank and Alfred Steiglitz mingled with young up-and-comers like Edmund Wilson and Lewis Mumford. Copland absorbed the "Young America" spirit in this milieu, seeing himself as playing an important role in a vanguard intent on improving the cultural life of the United States. "They were all aware," he recollected in his autobiography, "that music lagged behind the other arts, and they took it for granted that I, as the contemporary composer among them, would do something about the situation. I thought of myself as involved in their movement and instinctively felt part of a 'school.'"[76] Motivated by the nationalist ideals of his "school," Copland set about exploring the musical past of the United States in the hopes of discovering the constituent elements of an American voice. As he would later recollect, he was in search of "a music that would speak of universal things in a vernacular of American speech rhythms."[77]

Copland biographer Howard Pollack has pointed out that it is difficult to know the scope of this "search for musical ancestors" because Copland was consistently vague in describing it.[78] His most extensive discussion of the enterprise, a semi-autobiographical lecture delivered at Harvard in 1952, doubled as a history of American music prior to the modern movement. Consequently, it is not clear whether his critical assessments of such figures as John Knowles Paine, George Chadwick, Arthur Foote, and Horatio Parker were the product of his midtwenties research or more recent work. Whatever the case, Copland's opinions about these composers bear a suspicious resemblance to those Rosenfeld advanced in his various books and articles.[79] It is clear that Copland came up empty-handed, abandoned the past, and turned to jazz instead for the desired American imprimatur.

It is also clear that Copland's studies did not turn up the name Charles Ives. Long after the fact, Copland would muse, "There we were in the twenties searching for a composer from the older generation with an 'American sound,' and here was Charles Ives composing this incredible music—totally unknown to us."[80] According to Pollack, Copland did not discover Ives until 1929, when Henry Cowell published the second movement of the Fourth Symphony in *New Music Quarterly*. Even then, it would take the promptings of Bernard Herrmann, Jerome Moross, and the other members of the Young Composer's Group to provoke serious engagement.

While Brooks and Copland focused on the negative forces that hindered American talent, Lewis Mumford launched his quest for a "usable past" with more positive results. Mumford had been an avid reader of *Seven Arts*, which Brooks coedited during its brief run in the teens, and, in the twenties, Mumford made the personal acquaintance of Brooks through their mutual involvement in yet another short-lived magazine, the *Freeman*. Galvanized by Brooks's ideas, Mumford wrote the first architectural history of the United States, *Sticks and Stones* (1924), which he later described as "using architecture as an index of our civilization." In the book, he sought elements in the past that might be fused with the modern to create an American garden city, an environment more conducive to the "beloved community" dreamed of by Young America than the inhospitable cityscapes of the time. In *The Golden Day* (1926), Mumford's next project and a book he viewed as a companion to its predecessor, he used "imaginative literature" as a gauge of American culture. Again, the intent was to find tendencies in the past that might profitably be pursued in the present.[81]

The terrain of American letters had been crossed multiple times by Brooks, although he kept circling back to his point of departure. Mumford's excursion into the same territory yielded different results. The sweep of *The Golden Day* was much broader than any of Brooks's works, for Mumford regarded the flaws of American culture as symptoms of a general decline in western civilization. He argued that the reformation and enlightenment had dissolved the organic connections of the medieval period: Catholic ritual and ornament gave way to "the bare abstraction of the printed word," myth yielded to scientific principle. Romanticism was a desperate attempt to resurrect the passing order, and it was the cry "back to nature" that propelled the nineteenth-century pioneer into the "primitive and undefiled" wilds of North America. But the men and women who pushed into the West lacked the residue of organic culture that lingered in Europe: "uninfluenced by peasant habits or the ideas of an old culture, the work of the miner, woodman, and hunter [the main professions of the pioneer] led to unmitigated destruction and pillage. What happened was just the reverse of the old barbarian invasions, which turned Goths and Vandals into Romans. The movement into backwoods America turned the European into a barbarian." The rapacious pioneer set the precedent, making "the path of a dehumanized industrialism in America as smooth as a concrete road."[82]

Though there are resemblances to the pessimistic narrative Brooks traced in his criticism, Mumford's work differs in leveling the blame for the impoverished nature of American culture on the pioneer, not the puritan. This crucial difference made Mumford's foray into the literary past far more productive because it allowed him to consider in new light the nineteenth-century writers who lived far from the destructive frontier. There had been a golden day, he maintained, a short period of autumnal growth before the West was gripped by the winter of the machine age, and five writers basked in its glow: Emerson, Thoreau, Whitman, Melville, and Hawthorne. Not all of these men were associated with the transcendentalist movement, but Mumford linked them together, believing each man, in his own particular way, had pursued the precedent set by Emerson, the "morning star."[83]

Emerson's doctrine of "self-reliance" was the key to the flourishing culture of New England in the antebellum years. "Self-reliance" referred to the ability to push beyond institutions, to interrogate a habit, ritual, or mode of thought for oneself and determine how it could be made meaningful in the context of one's own experiences. This was not the raucous individualism of the pioneer, for it did not mean exchanging the past for barbarism. Instead it meant circumspect consideration of the past, something that could be facilitated by New England's unique position: distant from Europe, where habits of thought were still so deeply ingrained their presence escaped notice of even the most perceptive European, yet close enough to Europe for the value of its cultural legacy to be sensed. The "great activity of the Golden Day" was to "prefigure in the imagination a culture which should grow out of and refine the experiences the transplanted European encountered on the new soil, mingling the social heritage of the past with the experience of the present." More than this, in the position of being aware of, but not beholden to, the European past, the New Englander could also submit other pasts to scrutiny. "Emerson," Mumford explained, "divested everything of its associations, and seized it afresh, to make what associations it could with the life he had lived and the experience he had assimilated. As a result, each part of the past came to him on equal terms: Buddha had perhaps as much to give as Christ: Hafiz could teach him as much as Shakespeare or Dante." In short, Mumford credited Emerson with doing exactly what Van Wyck Brooks advised three quarters of a century later: creating a usable past.[84]

The golden day faded to the night of the Civil War, which Mumford characterized as a "struggle between two forms of servitude, the slave and the machine."[85] The machine won and, in the postbellum period, theory and practice separated: on the one hand, the newly rich and leisured collected the artworks of Europe without a mind to their bearing on everyday life; on the other, the philosophy of pragmatism was ascendant, spiritual ideals cast aside, and expediency enthroned. American literature suffered accordingly. But Mumford, despite this reversion to Brooksian tropes for the Gilded Age, had gleaned more from the past than the negative lessons about stifling American culture that were the stuff of a book like *The Ordeal of Mark Twain*. He had seen something of positive value in the transcendentalist movement, where Brooks and other writers in the Young America cohort had seen only airy abstraction. Brooks acknowledged and affirmed this aspect of Mumford's book in an ecstatic letter: "*The Golden Day* seems to me the culmination of the whole critical movement in this country during the past ten years. . . . In your glowing appreciation of the *golden* age you have done the *positive* thing which the rest of us have mostly left out."[86]

That Brooks should be so receptive to the usable past quarried by Mumford is not as surprising as it might at first seem. Roughly at the same time as Mumford was working on *The Golden Day*, Brooks had, independently, begun writing a book about Emerson. The motivation behind the project was a desire to find a more encouraging subject than the failed talents of the Gilded Age. Initially, he contemplated Poe and Hawthorne, but settled on Emerson after a perusal of the *Journals* caused what he later described as a "religious experience."[87] It was the discovery that he and Mumford were both writing about the same literary coterie that brought them closer together. Although Brooks's *Life of Emerson* was not published until 1931, it was more or less finished by 1926, too soon for *The Golden*

Day to have made its impact.[88] In contrast to Mumford's luminous optimism about the transcendentalist period, Brooks failed in his book to wrestle Emerson to the ground. As James Hoopes points out, Brooks devoted so much of his attention to the otherworldly preoccupations of Emerson that the transcendentalist once again floated off into highbrow irrelevance.[89] Dissatisfied with his own efforts, Brooks was delighted to find that Mumford's *The Golden Day* fulfilled the goal that had eluded him.

During the period in which Brooks was working on *The Life of Emerson*, he also read some of the manuscript for V. L. Parrington's *Main Currents of American Thought* (1927–1930) and recommended it for publication to Harcourt. This multivolume intellectual history of the United States, the first written by a professional historian, lingered over the transcendentalists and, like Mumford's work, cast them in a positive light. Parrington, according to historian Charles Capper, was "the first modern scholar to link together his leading Transcendentalists—Emerson, Thoreau, Parker, and Fuller—by seeing them, again for the first time, not as philosophical or literary figures, but as radical social and political critics."[90] As portrayed in *Main Currents of American Thought*, the transcendentalists were very much engaged with the real world and not lost in idle, abstract speculation. Thus Parrington added to the growing body of evidence against Brook's negative characterization of the American past in general, and the coterie of Concord writers in particular.

When, after a period of illness, Brooks set out once more in search of an American usable past, he did so animated by the ideas of Mumford and Parrington.[91] His new project was an epic five-volume literary history of the United States, the first volume of which was published in 1936. Entitled *The Flowering of New England*, it was a lovingly detailed study of the transcendentalist period, obviously indebted to *The Golden Day* but even more celebratory than Mumford's book. At last, Brooks pinned Emerson and his fellow transcendentalists to the ground, identifying them with a short-lived but genuine national culture that thrived in the middle decades of the nineteenth century. The elegiac tone of the book was a striking departure from the acerbic tincture that colors much of his earlier prose. Brook's concluding remarks about the New England writers are representative:

> The breadth of their conscious horizon, the healthy objectivity of their minds, their absorption in large preoccupations, historical, political, religious, together with a literary feeling, a blend of the traditional and the local, that gave the local wider currency while it brought the traditional home to men's business and bosoms. They filled the New England scene with associations and set it, as it were, in three dimensions, creating the visible foreground it had never possessed. They helped to make their countrypeople conscious of the great world-movements of thought

and feeling in which they played parts side by side with the intellectual leaders of the older countries. In their scholarship, their social thought, their moral passion, their artistic feeling, they spoke for the universal republic of letters, giving their own province a form and body in the consciousness of the world.[92]

Beyond the shift in tone, it is worth noting the recycling of Mumford's two key ideas: the blending of local experience and tradition in the work of the transcendentalists, and the "healthy objectivity" of their intellects as they explored the full spectrum of world movements. This passage also posits the transcendentalists as a resolution to the division of American culture into two solitudes—theory and practice—that had long preoccupied Brooks. The Concord cohort may have ranged widely in their philosophical ventures, but they remained grounded in the local, and, whatever abstractions they discovered, they made tangible for ordinary people. If only briefly, antebellum New England had witnessed theory and practice merge into a genial middle ground.

The Flowering of New England was generally well received by the critics, although in private some had reservations about the sentimental, uncritical tone. It also proved to be popular with the general public, becoming a best seller and winning the Pulitzer Prize for history in 1937. The book arrived at a time when economic depression and the rise of fascism in Europe prompted Americans to look at their preindustrial history with renewed appreciation. Critic Malcolm Cowley noted in his review of *The Flowering of New England* for the *New Republic*, "[Many Americans are] turning back to the great past in order to see the real nature of the traditions that we are trying to save, and in order to gain new strength for the struggles ahead."[93] Artists and critics who had been attracted by the radical left in the early thirties, drifted back toward the center. There was a felt need for unity founded on the conviction shared by liberals and radicals alike that fascism presented a grave threat. Notably, the tenor of the pronouncements made by the Communist Party in the United States (Cowley being a prominent member) began to shift from strident declarations of proletarian revolution to a more anodyne nationalist and nostalgic populism.

The transcendentalists fared well in this climate. Brooks's *The Flowering of New England* was certainly the most popular book on the Emersonian cohort of the thirties, for it appealed to intellectuals and lay readers alike. But there were numerous other books as well. Several of the transcendentalists were subjects of what intellectual historian Charles Capper has characterized as "middlebrow" biographies, "breezy and sentimental" in style and "directed at the mushrooming market for uplifting, American-centered" narratives.[94] Works of this sort included Odell Shepard's *Pedlar's Progress: The Life of Bronson Alcott* (1937), Henry Seidel Canby's *Henry David Thoreau* (1939), Mason Wade's *Margaret Fuller: Whetstone of Genius* (1940), and Madeline B. Stern's *The Life of Margaret Fuller* (1942). Signaling the beginning of a serious engagement on the part of academe with antebellum American writers, Harvard professor F. O. Matthiessen published his massive study *American Renaissance* in 1941. Matthiessen's book centered on five authors—Emerson, Thoreau, Hawthorne, Melville, and Whitman—the same pantheon (minus Poe) that basked in the sunshine of Mumford's golden day.[95] Though he was unsympathetic to transcendentalism, what Matthiessen accomplished was to treat the work of his subjects with the same kind of seriousness that had previously been reserved for the canonical works of English literature. Moreover, he brought to bear the techniques of "New Criticism" that were just beginning their ascendance in the literature departments of American universities.[96] Thus, despite his skepticism, Matthiessen contributed to the growing interest in the Concord writers. By 1950, intellectual historian Perry Miller could speak of a "florescence of historical scholarship over the last generation" around the transcendentalist movement.[97] More than usable, Emerson and the Concord coterie had become central to conceptions of the American past. Ives stood to gain from this development.

"Concord" at Last

When, in 1920, Ives published the "Concord" Sonata, hoping it would be the vehicle that would carry him from artistic seclusion to public light, only a small handful of theosophists—Katherine Heyman, Clifton J. Furness, and T. Carl Whitmer—engaged with the "substance" of the sonata. As mentioned in chapter 1, they discovered many resonances between transcendentalism and their own metaphysics. Though the members of this group proved ineffective in conveying their ideas to a larger public, they did win a few individual converts. In the midtwenties, Heyman left New York for Paris, partly funded by Ives, and it was there, amid the circle of occultists and ultramodernists, that she met a young American pianist named John Kirkpatrick. Heyman showed Kirkpatrick her copy of the "Concord" Sonata, and, spurred by an interest in American composers, he wrote to Ives requesting a copy for himself in 1927. At the time—and for some time afterward—Kirkpatrick was also absorbed in theosophy, and it is reasonable to infer that part of the sonata's attraction was its connection to transcendentalism.[98] After returning to the states, Kirkpatrick set about learning the various movements of the sonata, keeping Ives apprised of his progress. He began with "The Alcotts," which he first performed in 1933; moved to "Emerson," programming it on a 1936 recital attended by Ives's wife and daughter; and finally, by June 1938, had the entire work under his belt.[99] Kirkpatrick performed the complete sonata in two private recitals that year before giving it a proper debut at Town

Figure 2.2. Advertisement for John Kirkpatrick's concert featuring the "Concord" Sonata. January 20, 1939. Courtesy Yale University Irving S. Gilmore Music Library.

Hall in New York, on January 20, 1939 (Figure 2.2). Thus, the "Concord" Sonata had its second public unveiling, fortuitously coinciding with a renaissance of the transcendentalists.

By all accounts, Kirkpatrick's concert was not well attended—a small circle of devotees and a few of Ives's family members (minus Ives himself, who in typical fashion stayed home). But one of the attendees was Lawrence Gilman, the highly respected music critic for the *New York Herald Tribune*. Gilman had encountered the music of Ives once before, having reviewed the Pro Musica concert of 1927 featuring two movements from the Fourth Symphony. His comments then had been brief, but glowingly positive: "This music is as indubitably American in impulse and spiritual texture as the prose of Jonathan Edwards; and, like the writing of that true artist and true mystic, it has at times an irresistible veracity and strength, an uncorrupted sincerity. . . . It has, as Emerson said of Whitman, a long foreground." Why, after using such encomiums, Gilman should not have availed himself of the several opportunities over the next decade to hear more of Ives's music is something of a mystery. Perhaps it was a consequence of the practice of the major papers sending their second-string critics to review avant-garde concerts, which were, invariably, the only context in which Ives's music was performed. (The Pro Musica concert that Gilman reviewed was unusual for the celebrity presence of conductor Eugene Goosens, which may have accounted for the critic's attendance.) In any case, the references Gilman made to Edwards, Emerson, and Whitman in his Fourth Symphony review point toward an explanation for his decision to attend the performance of the "Concord" Sonata. Clearly, he had an interest in the literary past of the United States, and it is reasonable to suppose that the names Emerson, Hawthorne, Alcott, and Thoreau attracted his attention. Gilman was intrigued enough to request a copy of the score in advance of the performance, a measure he had not taken in the case of the Fourth Symphony.

On the whole, Gilman's review repeated the usual saws about Ives—his musical precedence and isolation—but what makes it notable, other than the renown of its author, is its explicit invocation of the transcendentalist revival. "This is an astonishing program indeed," the critic exclaimed, "a glimpse of the Flowering of New England a quarter century before Van Wyck Brooks produced his celebrated masterpiece." This was not mere name-dropping, for Gilman's discussion of the qualities that made the sonata American was informed by Brooks's criteria for a national voice. Probably referring to Edgar Varèse and Ernest Bloch, Gilman wrote, "The two distinguished composers who are sometimes said to have produced the best music written in America cannot be called Americans at all: they were born in Europe, and their music is about as 'American' in quality as the Mediterranean or the Quai d'Orsay." One needed roots in the United States and a feel for the unique qualities of the country, not a mature artistic voice formed elsewhere. Of course, this sort of conviction predated Brooks and had been an integral part of the debate about musical Americanness launched by Dvořák. More clearly derivative of the Brooksian critical perspective was Gilman's description of the reach of the "Concord" Sonata—a description that would become the most quoted passage of the review:

This sonata is exceptionally great music—it is, indeed, the greatest music composed by an American, and the most deeply and essentially American in impulse and implication. It is wide-ranging and capacious. It has passion, tenderness, humor, simplicity, homeliness. It has imaginative and spiritual vastness. It has wisdom and beauty and profundity, and a sense of the encompassing terror and splendor of human life and human destiny—a sense of those mysteries that are both human and divine.

Brooks had long criticized American culture for its division into highbrow and lowbrow spheres, calling for the cultivation of a mediating middle ground. And this seems to be exactly what Gilman was crediting Ives with having accomplished. Within the generous spread of its ambit, the sonata encompassed humor and terror, homeliness and spiritual vastness, simplicity and profundity. In short, it created a vital center, fusing American theory and practice.[100]

Ives scholars have justifiably stressed the significance of Gilman's review for the reception of the composer. In heralding an American messiah, Gilman sparked a flurry of interest on the part of other major publications. Olin Downes of the *New York Times*, who had not attended the Kirkpatrick concert, rushed to print a profile of Ives for the following weekend. (As Frank Rossiter points out, Downes was probably relieved to find that he had also given a positive review to the earlier Fourth Symphony concert. Thereafter, he habitually quoted from his Fourth symphony review as evidence of the part he too had played in discovering the great American composer.)[101] A month after the premiere, at Gilman's promptings, Kirkpatrick performed the "Concord" Sonata as part of an all-Ives concert to a full house. A flood of articles in 1939 heralded a banner year for Ives.[102] Gilman's partisanship also had repercussions beyond this sudden surge, for, in the forties and fifties, a large proportion of the major articles on Ives continued to cite his review as an important milestone.[103]

Besides Gilman's review, several articles about Ives written between 1939 and 1945 attest to the relationship between the composer's sudden renown and the renewed interest in Emerson and his fellow Concordians. *Time* magazine, for example, reporting on the Kirkpatrick concert, described the sonata as "a sort of musical equivalent to author Van Wyck Brooks' *The Flowering of New England.*"[104] A less obvious but nonetheless significant link can be found in the remarks of journalist Lucille Fletcher at the end of a lengthy profile on Ives she wrote for the *New Yorker*. (It was never published because Fletcher did not succeed in producing a draft that she and Ives could agree upon.) After describing Ives's life in some detail and, at the composer's insistence, reproducing passages from almost every positive review he had ever received, she wrote, "[Ives's] output has been enormous. Singlehanded[ly] he has summed up an age and spirit that is authentically American. Like the Concord folk, he has taken a portion of New England and made it universal. Somebody has called Charles Ives 'the last of the Transcendentalists.'"[105] It is not clear who that somebody was, but it might well have been Fletcher's then-fiancé, Bernard Herrmann, who wrote his own assessment of Ives. Here it is worth quoting at length:

> The strange neglect of Charles Ives at this time can be ascribed only to our musical apathy. The literary figures of New England's golden age, with whom Ives ranks in spirit, are coming alive again through the efforts of writers like Van Wyck Brooks and F. O. Matthiessen. But out of Ives's great body of works few pieces have been performed, and these only by adventurous singers and pianists. Our orchestras have almost entirely overlooked him. Even on the occasion of his seventieth birthday this year, not one conductor of a major symphonic group felt the need to present a work in his honor.
>
> In solitude, Ives's original mind and soaring imagination developed a technic of expression which owes nothing to Europe but is as daring as the innovations of Schönberg or Stravinsky. When Europe still considered Debussy a modernist, Ives was writing polytonal and atonal music, experimenting with multiple rhythms, acoustical juxtapositions and quarter-tones.[106]

All the themes present in Hermann's article—neglect, precedence, and American identity—would continue to appear in Ives criticism after the war.

The Problem of Freedom

After the 1939 premiere of the "Concord" Sonata, the balance on the ledger of Ives assessments swung decisively to the positive side, accolades outweighing criticisms. There would remain, however, an undercurrent of skepticism, which was given its most articulate voice by two influential modernist composers, Aaron Copland and Elliott Carter. Their reservations mingled with admiration and active advocacy, both men working in various capacities to expand the audience for Ives's music. The problem concerned technical facility, something they prized as alumni of Nadia Boulanger's studio in Paris, where consummate technique was one of the major emphases in the regimen for apprentice composers.

Copland, in a 1934 review of *114 Songs*, was the first to voice objections. The volume, he declared, was uneven in quality, due in no small part to the juxtaposition of popular music and "complex harmonies," an unhappy mixture in which coherence was sorely wanting. The problem stemmed from the peculiar nature of Ives's career, for he had been "cut off from the vitalizing contact of an audience." Public performance facilitated criticism, which in turn provided composers with the necessary information to hone their craft. Despite evidence of talent—a great deal of talent—Ives's failure to present his music before an audience that could serve as "stimulus and a brake" left him half formed as a composer, unable to develop an acute critical eye and ear. In a sense, Ives had too much freedom to follow his own whims wherever they might lead him, from simple-minded tunes whistled in the town square to complex chromatic experiments.[107]

Carter picked up this line of criticism in an infamous review of the "Concord" Sonata published in 1939. Unlike Copland, however, he had a personal history with Ives, and by drawing upon it, he raised serious doubts about the composer's reputation, something he would later come to regret. Carter was a teenager when he first met Ives, his high school music teacher Clifton Furness furnishing introductions in 1924. Through Furness, Carter also gained an entrée to the New York salon of pianist Katherine Ruth Heyman, where new music and theosophy mingled. Carter imbibed Ives along with the metaphysics, but disenchantment set in as he pursued more rigorous musical studies, first at Harvard and then under Boulanger in Paris. As Carter explained much later, "there was a mounting sense of frustration when I returned to Ives's music . . . because much of it seemed so disordered and even disorganized . . . it was nearly impossible to understand how or why much of it was put together as it was." For his part, Ives was decidedly unenthusiastic about the neoclassical idiom that Carter absorbed abroad.[108]

In his review of "Concord," Carter accused Ives of being indiscriminate, the recourse to quoting popular and folk music being particularly objectionable: "Behind all this confused texture there is a lack of logic which repeated hearings can never clarify. . . . The esthetic is naïve, often too naïve to express serious thoughts, frequently depending on quotation of well-known American tunes with little comment, possibly charming but certainly trivial." Again, the freedom with which Ives imported all manner of musical material into his compositions reflected an uncritical sensibility—it was not something to be celebrated. But Carter went further than Copland, whose criticisms centered on deficiencies of craft. Drawing on memories from his adolescent friendship with Ives, Carter recalled that the composer treated music with an "improvisational attitude." He remembered asking Ives why "every time he played ["Concord"] he did something different, sometimes changing the harmonies, the dynamic scheme, the degree of dissonance, the pace." Ives responded that the notation was merely intended to give "a general indication to the pianist who should, in his turn, recreate the work for himself." To Carter's mind, this left so much up to the performer that it amounted to an abdication of the responsibilities of a composer. Moreover, it undercut the claims of precedence that were so often advanced on Ives behalf. Carter opined,

The fuss that critics make about Ives' innovations is . . . greatly exaggerated, for he has rewritten his works so many times, adding dissonances and polyrhythms, that it is probably impossible to tell just at what date the works assumed the surprising form we know now. The accepted dates of publication are most likely those of the compositions in their final state. Anyhow the question is not important. Ives himself has said that he prefers people to judge his music not for when it was written but for what it is.[109]

Carter might have been right about this last point, but much of Ives's reputation in 1939 rested on the belief that a Connecticut Yankee had beaten Schoenberg and Stravinsky to the punch. Ives's commitment to freedom (in the sense of refusing to impose a fixed final form on his works) meant forfeiture in the modernist race to the patent office. Although Carter would revisit the music of Ives in the forties, reaching more positive conclusions, this damning memory became the center of a debate about Ives's precedence as a modernist that would not be resolved until the nineties (the details will have to wait until chapter 6).

In the meantime, doubts about Ives's craft persisted, typically following the precedent Copland set in faulting the indiscriminate usage of diverse musical materials (among the new voices articulating this view were two more Boulangerie alumni, Arthur Berger and Virgil Thomson).[110] But if Ives suffered from too much freedom in the view of his skeptics, the situation was precisely the opposite in a new strain of commentary conditioned by the political climate of the Cold War. In the fifties and sixties, Ives would undergo yet another transformation: from an American ethnographer, with an ear for local musical practice, to the archetype of the "autonomous man," an icon of freedom championed the world over.

3

Winning Hearts and Minds
Ives as Cold War Icon, 1947–1965

In 1950, sociologists David Riesman, Reuel Denney, and Nathan Glazer published a study of American culture with an enigmatic title: *The Lonely Crowd*. Though unflattering, depicting Americans as obsessed with the opinions of their neighbors, colleagues, and friends, the study resonated with the very people that it anatomized. Much to the surprise of its authors, *The Lonely Crowd* became one of those rarities of the publishing world: a best seller under a university press imprint. Accordingly, historians of the 1950s have treated the book as an important primary source, a snapshot of middle class culture and, at the same time, a window on the preoccupations of American intellectuals during the early Cold War period. *The Lonely Crowd* is also significant to scholars of American music. Outside of the context of a specifically musical text, it is the earliest source to drop the name Charles Ives in a casual manner, as if Ives's accomplishments were a matter of general public knowledge. The relevant passage, is, on the face of it, quite innocuous, comprised of two sentences that are unremarkable in their assertions about Ives. But this passage reveals that, as of 1950, the iconic status of Ives could be traded upon in a marketplace of ideas that extended well beyond the bounds of modernist musical circles.

Just five years earlier, Ives's celebrity had been much more narrowly circumscribed. Certainly he had achieved a measure of national recognition, that year, 1945, being nominated to the National Institute of Arts and Letters; however, he had made little headway in concert halls across the United States. One of the composer's youngest and most recent devotees, Lou Harrison, complained, "All Ives' larger works were written before 1920; it is now 1945 and not one of the major orchestra works has yet been played in full in America. Finished a quarter of a century ago and not yet done. We seem to be mighty slow, mighty slow."[1] In the ensuing half decade, Harrison would play a crucial role in pushing Ives from the modernist peripheries of the American musical world toward its center, his advocacy helping the composer secure the Pulitzer Prize in 1947 and attracting considerable press coverage in the process. But all of Harrison's efforts, and those of other Ives advocates, would have been for naught had the ideas in circulation about the composer not proved easy fodder for a broad sociopolitical discourse that involved many American intellectuals, including the authors of *The Lonely Crowd*.

In the period 1945–1965, Ives and his music were drawn into an urgent discussion about the nature of freedom—a discussion that transpired against the backdrop of the Cold War. Autonomy was the watchword for the interlocutors, and they saw it threatened on two fronts: first, by the totalitarian cultural policies of the Soviet Union; and, second, by mass culture, a fifth column that coaxed individuals to relinquish freedom for social conformity. Against such perils, the peculiarities of a life such as Ives's, which seemed to be lived entirely on his own terms, could be made exemplary of American ideals. Accordingly, his music was programmed on concerts designed to promote the artistic products of "cultural freedom," and the narrative of his life was recounted in journals and in lecture halls where it could advertise the benefits of individual autonomy as against social conformity. In this ideologically charged context, Ives's musical legacy was made a function of his commitment to transcendentalism, a philosophy that stressed independent self-realization. From the American musical ethnographer depicted in pre–World War II writings about the composer, particularly those of Henry Cowell, Ives was transformed into a Cold War icon, a champion of the liberating powers of individualism.

A Pulitzer Prize and Its Aftermath

In 1935, eighteen-year-old Californian Lou Harrison enrolled in the music program at the State College in San Francisco with aspirations of becoming a composer. Immersing himself in the musical life of the Bay Area, Harrison could not help but become aware of Henry Cowell, who still enjoyed the glow of lingering infamy left over from his days as an avant-garde concert pianist. When they met, Cowell recognized in Harrison a catholicity of musical taste that resembled his own and took the teenager on as a private student. Their lessons, along with the occasional concerts of the New Music Society, which Cowell oversaw, introduced Harrison to a wide range of repertoire, including the music of Charles Ives. Harrison was intrigued, and at the suggestion of Cowell, wrote to Ives in March 1936, politely requesting scores for his two piano sonatas. Ives obliged, sending copies of both works, and, several months later, a crate of photostat scores representing a substantial portion of his oeuvre—most of the chamber music, all of the songs, and a few orchestral works. For the next ten years, Harrison delved into this huge cache of music almost daily.[2]

In the forties, Harrison launched a campaign on Ives's behalf, a multipronged extension of Cowell's earlier efforts that included promotional essays, performances, and extensive editing work, preparing Ives's music for publication.[3] No part of this campaign would prove more significant than the coup Harrison scored by organizing the premiere of the Third Symphony, which took place on April 5th, 1946. Harrison conducted the work himself, having accepted the offer of the podium for half a concert with an ensemble that modestly called itself the New York Little Symphony. Rehearsal time was limited, and the players gave Harrison some trouble over his inexperience. But the concert was a success, receiving a positive review in the *New York Times* and, two weeks later, prompting a Sunday feature article that complained about how tardy the musical public had been in recognizing the composer.[4]

Although Ives had (more or less) completed the Third Symphony some three decades earlier, the fact that it received its premiere in 1946 made it eligible for the Pulitzer Prize in Music for 1947. That year the jury consisted of exactly one member: Chalmers Clifton, a composer-conductor who taught in the music department at Columbia University.[5] At the time, Ives was much on the minds of the faculty and students at Columbia. The Third Symphony premiere had taken place at the campus' MacMillin Theatre, and, as part of the university's annual festival of modern American music, Elliot Carter had helped organize an all-Ives concert that featured the premieres of *The Unanswered Question*, *Central Park in the Dark*, and the Second String Quartet. Clifton's awareness of Ives may have had further stimulation through the person of Henry Cowell, who served with him on the Pulitzer jury the previous year. In any case, Clifton awarded the prize to Ives's symphony.

As recorded by a local newspaper interviewer, Ives's public response to winning the Pulitzer was wholly consistent with his antiestablishment reputation: "Prizes are the badges of mediocrity," he harrumphed. In privacy at home, he hung the Pulitzer Board certificate on the wall, recognizing that it not only affirmed his abilities but would also stimulate further interest in his music.[6] Indeed, the prize was a watershed that marked a transformation of his relationship with the broader public. The methods Ives had previously used to disseminate his music—occasional publications in noncommercial enterprises like *New Music Quarterly* or manuscript photostats mailed directly to interested parties—no longer proved feasible. By the end of the forties, Ives was signing contracts with commercial publishers, which ensured his scores much wider distribution.[7] Ives's music also began to attract the attention of high-profile performers and ensembles: E. Power

Biggs played *Variations on 'America'* in 1948; the same year, the Boston Symphony, conducted by Richard Burgin, performed *Three Places in New England*; and, in 1951, Leonard Bernstein and the New York Philharmonic-Symphony gave the premiere of the Second Symphony. Finally, the Pulitzer led to a shift in venue for discourse about Ives. From the twenties to the midforties, outside the occasional review in a daily newspaper, articles about the composer were published in small-circulation "little magazines" like *Pro-Musica Quarterly*, *Modern Music*, *Trend*, and the *New Masses*. Now Ives was prominent enough to attract the attention of editors at larger publications, as evidenced by feature articles and reviews that appeared in the *Saturday Review of Literature*, *Harper's Magazine*, and the *New York Times Magazine*. Photographer W. Eugene Smith even managed to secure a portrait of the composer that was printed in *Life*, despite Ives's protestations over having his picture taken (Figure 3.1).[8]

None of these changes, however, resulted in an influx of new ideas. All of the themes sounded by the first generation of Ives devotees continued to figure prominently in the high-profile articles: his pioneering musical techniques, the neglect he suffered as an artist, his dedication to individualism, and his deep roots in the American subsoil. In *Harper's Magazine*, Paul Moor mingled the themes of innovation and neglect: "Ives' case is a pure and simple example of genius born in advance of its time and into a culture not ready for it, for even his early work was so far ahead of his contemporaries that performers and publishers were scared off." Moor also commented on the independent spirit of Ives in face of the conservatism of American musical institutions at the beginning of the century. "Some of his music he had tentatively shown around, but performers and publishers returned it, usually with a stifled giggle. Ives said to hell with them, and determined to continue composing as he pleased."[9] This, Moor explained, was the reason Ives abandoned a career in music and turned instead to business, where, incidentally, he found an environment more congenial to innovation. Howard Taubman, who was granted a rare interview with Ives, wrote about the composer's deep connection to New England in the *New York Times Magazine*, and in the process, dropped an allusion to Van Wyck Brooks's Pulitzer Prize winning literary history: "[In] his vast output of symphonies, choruses, songs and chamber music we have a living portrait of the land worthy to stand beside the literature of New England's flowering."[10]

If lacking in new ideas, the articles of Taubman and Moor are notable for the emphasis they placed on Ives's personality. In contrast to previous writers, Taubman and Moor fleshed out the "human interest" aspect, supplying their readers with a steady flow of personal information about the composer. Both writers gave detailed physical descriptions of Ives that were designed to capture something of the character of the man, and they discussed his social development, creating a

Figure 3.1 Portrait of Ives taken by W. Eugene Smith, ca. 1947.
Courtesy Yale University Irving S. Gilmore Music Library.
© The Heirs of W. Eugene Smith, Courtesy of Black Star Inc.

more full-blooded portrait. Taubman drew attention to the athletic activities Ives pursued in his younger days, suggesting that they were a by-product of George Ives's desire for his son to have a "many-sided" development.[11] Moor went further by describing Ives's adept negotiation of social situations. He noted that Ives "was gregarious and popular with his schoolmates, and was sometimes called upon for songs for special occasions." Moreover, during the postcollege period in which Ives settled into his schedule of working by day, he "was no drudge . . . for he would just as often go on a double date with one of [his roommates] . . .

or accompany the group as a whole whenever they decided to paint the town."[12] In short, despite Ives's reputation as a maverick, he was quite capable of fitting in—if he chose to do so.

Undoubtedly, the emphasis on biography and personality in the articles of Taubman and Moor was a function of their audience, which could not be expected to have the level of musical knowledge required to read specialist "little magazines" like *Pro-Musica Quarterly* and *Modern Music*. But in fleshing out the particulars of Ives's life, Taubman and Moor inadvertently created a portrait useful to writers who were concerned about the prospects of individual freedom in a world fraught by the tensions of the Cold War. Their Ives was individualistic without being misanthropic, accomplished in all his endeavors but modest about his success, intent on his own intellectual pursuits but not to the extent of alienating those around him. He was, in other words, a shining example of autonomy.

Lonely Crowds and a Festival in Paris

The groundwork for the Cold War–era discussion about individual freedom was laid in the thirties by the cohort of émigré intellectuals who fled fascism and landed on American shores. In exile, they looked back on their countries of origin and sought to explain the triumph of irrationality. At the New School for Social Research, Emil Lederer, Hans Staudinger, Max Ascoli and a number of other émigré scholars theorized about the origins of fascism, mingling such themes as class breakdown, mass culture, and alienation. Lederer notably expanded the concept of "totalitarianism" (first coined by Mussolini), applying it equally to fascism and communism, a usage that still obtains.[13] The justification for linking these two ideologies was that they offered the same antidote to the uncertainties of the modern world: freedom traded for comradeship, individuality traded for the reassurance of an external monolithic authority. While the émigré faculty at the New School mostly addressed their work to specialist audiences, other European intellectuals exiled in the United States sought a larger public. Especially influential was Erich Fromm, a psychoanalyst by training who was briefly associated with the Frankfurt School and whose book about fascism, *Escape from Freedom* (1941), was a best seller.

Fromm argued that the success of fascism could be attributed to its ability to fulfill psychological needs that had arisen in the wake of modernity. He explained that European history, as it had unfolded since the Reformation, had witnessed a long series of successes that gradually freed the individual from the bonds of clan and religion. This development was analogous to the "individuation" of a child, a process in which "growing strength and integration of [the child's] individual personality" was concomitant with the loss of "original identity with others," specifically the mother. It was crucial, Fromm asserted, that the child's ability to realize his or her individuality must keep pace with growing freedom; otherwise the loss of identity with mother would be experienced as profound aloneness. Metaphorically speaking, this had not happened in the course of European history. The old bonds had given the individual security, a sense of being rooted in "a structuralized whole in which he has an unquestionable place." As these bonds fell away, many people had been unable to develop their own individuality and were cast adrift without the skills to chart their own course through the shoals of the modern world. In Fromm's view, this had been especially true of the lower middle class, which was most adversely affected by the peaks and troughs of the industrialized economy. Desperate, the petite bourgeoisie launched themselves on a quest for new certainties, a flight from freedom that ultimately terminated in the nationalist mythologies that lay at the heart of fascism. Such a quest could end only in destructive failure. For Fromm, there was but "one possible, productive solution for the relationship of individualized man with the world: his active solidarity with all men and his spontaneous activity, love and work, which unite him again with the world, not by primary ties but as a free and independent individual."[14] This was autonomy, a concept Fromm would go on to explore in his subsequent book *Man for Himself* (1947).

Fromm's neo-Freudian approach made a strong impression on one of his students, David Riesman, who appropriated it for his own, equally successful book, *The Lonely Crowd*. Written in collaboration with Reuel Denney and Nathan Glazer, *The Lonely Crowd* provided some of the earliest fodder for the stereotype of the fifties as the "decade of consensus." Riesman, Denney, and Glazer described the dominant character type in modern society as *other-directed*, a term that referred to people whose sense of self depended upon the extent to which they remained in good standing with the crowd.[15] More often than not, given the pervasiveness of "other-direction," individuality was cast aside in the lonely quest for acceptance. "Tuned to the expectations and preferences of others," the authors explained, the "other-directed" man or woman was suited to an economy dominated by big corporations, where the emphasis was on conformity to company policy, not improvisation. What concerned Riesman, Denney, and Glazer was the relative scarcity of autonomous individuals, people "capable of conforming to the behavioral norms . . . [but] free to choose whether to conform or not." They suggested that autonomy might be cultivated by preserving leisure time for people's "real work": "the field into which, on the basis of their gifts, they would like to throw their emotional and creative energies." Ives, William Carlos Williams, and Henry David Thoreau were cited as examples of men who pursued just such a course, holding the destructive social forces of the workplace at bay by devoting their free time to artistic pursuits.[16]

The authors' differentiation between "real work" and the thing one does for money explains the peculiar quotation marks around "worked" and "played" in their brief reference to Ives: "Charles Ives 'worked' by heading an agency that sold half a billion dollars' worth of insurance, and he 'played' by composing some of the more significant, though least recognized, music that has been produced. Ives felt, and feels, not in the least guilty about the money he made or about the fact that he lived a 'normal' American life, rather than a Bohemian one."[17] The observation about Ives living a "normal" American life speaks to the authors' conviction that the denizens of "bohemia" were subject to a set of social expectations every bit as rigid as those encountered in a more conventional life. "Autonomy" meant self-awareness, not dogmatic nonconformity.[18] Ives the businessman-composer had forsworn the loneliness of crowds for the solace of individuality.

The name Charles Ives does not appear in any other published writings by the authors of *The Lonely Crowd*, which suggests that they had no more than a passing interest in him. The composer's inclusion in the book would seem to be a product of the post-Pulitzer publicity, given the close resemblance of the two-sentence sketch to the socially adjusted, independent Ives portrayed in the articles of Harold Taubman and Paul Moor.[19] If *The Lonely Crowd* supplied the only instance in which Ives's name figured in the larger sociopolitical discourse about autonomy, it would be little more than an intriguing footnote in the reception history of the composer. But this was not the case. Over the course of the next twenty years, Ives, treated as an exemplar of autonomy, would be deployed repeatedly to the front lines of ideological combat in the Cold War, the battle for hearts and minds then ranging around the world: in postcolonial nations choosing new forms of government; in the lecture halls and seminar rooms of Western Europe, where left-leaning intellectuals remained skeptical of American power; and in the arenas of art and sport, where proxy battles took place between athletes, musicians, writers, and artists from either side of the iron curtain. Two years after the publication of *The Lonely Crowd*, the music of Ives was presented as part of an arts festival in Paris that was held under the auspices of the Congress for Cultural Freedom (CCF). Ives was far from the focus of the festival offerings, but his inclusion was indicative of a growing awareness of his potential as a symbol for American individualism.

The Congress for Cultural Freedom was formed in reaction to covertly Soviet-sponsored "peace conferences," which were staged in Europe and the United States beginning in 1948. Through these conferences, the Cominform, the Soviet-led organization for coordinating communist activities around the world, sought to secure a commitment to peace from the Western intellectuals and artists who attended. Thus the names of major cultural figures would be co-opted to back Soviet complaints about the bellicosity of American foreign policy. The most infamous conference took place in March of 1949 at the Waldorf-Astoria in New York City and boasted a raft of major American artists and scientists among its attendees—Arthur Miller, Clifford Odets, Aaron Copland, Leonard Bernstein, and Albert Einstein, to name a few.[20] A contingent of anticommunist intellectuals led by philosopher Sidney Hook saw through the pretense. To be seduced by talk of peace was, in their view, to turn a blind eye to the violence the Soviet regime had visited on its own people and the threat it posed to the larger world. Unwilling to stand by while the Cominform duped gullible American celebrities, they became the driving force behind the CCF.

The new organization convened for the first time on June 26, 1950, in the Western sector of Berlin, a dramatic and aptly chosen setting since the German city had become a byword for Cold War hostilities. At the end of the meeting, a fourteen-point manifesto was unveiled, its central tenet a vigorous affirmation of individual autonomy: "We hold it to be self-evident that intellectual freedom is one of the inalienable rights of man . . . such freedom is defined first and foremost by his right to hold and express his own opinions, and particularly opinions which differ from those of his rulers. Deprived of the right to say 'no,' man becomes a slave."[21] Ironically, and unbeknown to most of the participants, the CIA provided funding to this and subsequent CCF activities.[22]

Beyond countering Soviet propaganda, the main goal of the CCF was to shunt European intellectuals off the middle road, where, in the name of even-handedness, all ideological options were considered with equal seriousness. Hook was especially irked by the unwillingness of many of his European colleagues to condemn "Communist totalitarianism" on the grounds that capitalism was equally flawed. Capitalism had its problems, he conceded, "[b]ut to conclude from this that Truman and what he represents is as bad as Stalin, or that the Marshall Plan is on all fours with the Cominform . . . is just as much the mark of political cretinism as to conclude that Roosevelt's America was as bad as Hitler's Germany."[23] By using "intellectual freedom" as a rallying point, it was the intention of the CCF to win over nonaligned European intellectuals in the cultural Cold War. The CCF agenda was not so much to secure a commitment to the United States (although that would certainly have been welcomed) but rather to foster anticommunism. As evidenced by the CCF's board of Honorary Chairmen, some of the most prominent Western thinkers were willing to sign themselves up for the cause: Bertrand Russell, Benedetto Croce, John Dewey, Karl Jaspers, and Jacque Maritain. The American affiliate of the CCF, called the American Committee for Cultural Freedom, was a veritable who's who of influential American thinkers at midcentury. On the roster were literary critics Lionel and Diana Trilling; sociologists David Riesman, Nathan Glazer, and Daniel Bell; historian Arthur Schlesinger Jr.; theologian Rheinold Niebuhr; and the philosophers Sidney Hook and James Burnham.[24]

The most conspicuous CCF-sponsored activities were arts festivals designed to show "the products of free minds in a free world," as secretary general Nicolas Nabokov put it.[25] The first festival, portentously titled *L'Oeuvre du XXe siècle*, took place in Paris in the spring of 1952 and featured concurrent series of symphonic and chamber music concerts. Nabokov, who was a composer by trade, chose the repertoire for the symphonic series, but the responsibility of programming the chamber series fell to Fred Goldbeck, a French critic and staunch advocate of the avant-garde.[26] The Hawthorne movement from Charles Ives's "Concord" Sonata appeared in the latter series, part of an eclectic, but comparatively tame, program that also included Double Variatione for Violoncello and Strings by Jean Françaix, "Five Variations" by Ralph Vaughan Williams, and *Socrate* by Eric Satie.

Likely, the inclusion of "Hawthorne" came at the behest of Nicolas Slonimsky, the man who had introduced Paris to Ives in 1932 by conducting the European premieres of two movements from *Set for Theatre Orchestra* and *The Fourth of July*. Slonimsky had gained anticommunist credentials by chronicling and criticizing the aesthetic dictates that the Soviet Union imposed on its composers.[27] His involvement in the Paris Festival is attested to by an essay he wrote for the program notes, prosaically titled "On American Music" and provocatively subtitled "The Declaration of the Independence of American Music."

Slonimsky made it abundantly clear why Ives figured in a festival devoted to "cultural freedom." "Throughout the entire 19th century," he explained, "American music, in both style and technique, was a province of German music." But, shortly after World War I, America declared its musical independence and the melodies, harmonies, and rhythms of the United States found their way into the works of "serious composers" such as Roy Harris, Aaron Copland, and Walter Piston. Charles Ives was the "prophetic precursor." He had anticipated the aesthetic autonomy of this younger generation of American composers, giving musical expression to the spirit of his country and, in the process, exploring polytonality and atonality at least ten years in advance of all other modernists.[28] Where, two years earlier, *The Lonely Crowd* emphasized the psychological payoff of autonomy, Slonimsky stressed its benefits to musical development. The message was clear: while American composers had remained beholden to the aesthetic creeds of other countries, their music languished. Freedom, prophetically portended by Charles Ives, was the precondition of artistic greatness. This too was the general message of the festival, a not too subtle condemnation of the Soviet government for the aesthetic dictates it forcibly imposed.

The decision to represent Ives by a movement from the "Concord" Sonata had a certain inevitability about it. Pianist John Kirkpatrick's performance of the piece in 1939 had been responsible for enlarging the reputation of the composer beyond a small circle of partisans. In 1948, Kirkpatrick recorded the "Concord" Sonata for Columbia, making it the first Ives piece to appear on a major (and thus widely available) label. Slonimsky reviewed the recording for the *Saturday Review of Literature*, and his comments reveal an additional motivation for putting the work on the CCF festival program. At the same time, they adumbrate a theme that would figure prominently in assessments of Ives from the midfifties onward.

Ever since Kirkpatrick made the "Concord" Sonata famous, the transcendentalist writers had been recognized as an important "indigenous" influence contributing to the American authenticity of Ives's oeuvre. But they served as only one influence among many others, including the popular music of Ives's youth, the musical experiments of his father, and, more broadly speaking, the sonic landscape of New England. Slonimsky departed from this precedent by making transcendentalism the root of Ives's aesthetic, the philosophy that organized his eclectic tastes and harnessed his inventive mind to a much larger purpose. "Much has been written," he noted, "about the prophetic use by Ives of the devices of polytonality, atonality, and polyrhythm [*sic*]. But these modern techniques are employed by Ives not as sophisticated enchantment of ultramodern music, but as a natural soul-extension to reach for the transcendental."[29]

In 1953, just over a year after the Paris festival, Slonimsky elaborated further what it meant to be "the musical transcendentalist among American composers." The context was a survey article published in *Américas*, one of the numerous "cultural exchange" magazines that flourished during the Cold War period. Slonimsky titled his article "Musical Rebel" and began with a description of the "Concord" Sonata that affirmed the centrality of the piece to his conception of Ives. Believing it to be emblematic, he fixated on one of Ives's aphoristic performance instructions in the score: "A metronome cannot measure Emerson's mind and oversoul, any more than the old Concord Steeple Bell could." Slonimsky continued, "In this observation lies the essence of every piece of music Ives wrote. To him music is a transcendental expression of the universal soul, not to be measured in materialistic terms of notes and tempo. But since Ives is an American, he looks at the universe from America. The subject of his work is American; their source of inspiration belongs to all mankind."[30]

The last two sentences of this quotation resonate with a famous passage from Emerson's oft-quoted address "The American Scholar" that enunciates a central precept of the transcendentalist creed. The scholar, Emerson had proclaimed, "learns that in going down into the secrets of his own mind he has descended into the secrets of all minds . . . the deeper he dives into his privatest, secretest presentiment, to his wonder he finds this is the most acceptable, most public, and universally true. The people delight in it; the better part of every man feels, this is my music; this is myself."[31] To access the universal, one had first to be an individual, to be autonomous. This was a maxim ripe for reconsideration by the proponents of "cultural freedom," and by making it applicable to Ives, Slonimsky had tapped a vein of ideas with enormous propagandistic potential.

The CCF festival in Paris set the precedent for putting Ives in service of American diplomatic interests. In the ensuing decades, he would serve repeatedly in this capacity, whether invoked by official cultural ambassadors with the sanction of the State Department, organizations like the CCF that had a less transparent connection to the American government, or private individuals. During the fifties and sixties, two of Ives's most prominent apologists, Henry Cowell and Leonard Bernstein, would embark on international tours under the auspices of the State Department, touting the composer and his music while abroad. But their efforts paled in comparison with the sustained project of promotion undertaken by the United States Information Agency (USIA), which was formed in 1953 to disseminate American propaganda around the world. In the midseventies, the music advisor for USIA, Daryl D. Dayton, gave a full account of the endeavor:

> For the past several years we have projected the image of Charles Ives, as the great American musical pioneer, the first American to work outside the European musical mainstream, the first to develop a truly American musical profile, in many countries in Latin America, Europe, Asia, the Orient and Africa. We have disseminated thousands of recordings and scores of Ives' music to libraries, music organizations, conservatories, composers and musicians in all areas of the world. We have sponsored distinguished lecturers, both American and foreign, in illustrated programs of Ives' music. We have held special "Charles Ives Music Weeks" in such cities as Lisbon, Sao Paulo, Athens, Mexico, D. F., Paris [and] Bucharest.[32]

Several of the international contributors to the 1974 Charles Ives Centennial Festival-Conference, discussed extensively in chapters 4 and 5, attested to the critical role Dayton and the USIA played in introducing them to the music of Ives.[33]

Undoubtedly there is a more extensive story to be told here about the role of cultural diplomacy in disseminating Ives around the globe.[34] That story is likely to be as involved as the more parochial one I am relating in this book, and so prudence dictates that I turn my attention homeward (though there will be a few further opportunities to look beyond the boundaries of the United States). As it turns out, the snapshot I have provided of Ives's international reception during the early Cold War period has a direct bearing on his fate at home. For here too the amalgam of Ives, transcendentalism, and autonomy that Slonimsky concocted proved potent. It was decanted in Henry and Sidney Cowell's *Charles Ives and His Music* (1955), which was the first book-length study of Ives and would remain the definitive source for two decades. The complicated genesis of the book requires some attention before I can assess its contents and influence.

Ives Transformed: The Collaboration
of Henry and Sidney Cowell

While many of Cowell's friends remained supportive in the wake of his 1936 sexual misconduct conviction, Charles Ives wrestled with the implications, confounded by his genteel moral values. Disgust was his first response, recorded by Harmony Ives in a letter to a friend: "I thought he [Cowell] was a man and he's really a g—d—sap."[35] A period of silence followed in which Cowell, having heard nothing from Ives, wrote several distressed letters to mutual acquaintances, hoping to glean any information he could about the man he regarded "same as a father."[36] Just over a year after the arrest, Ives's initial anger had abated and, unwilling to consign his friendship with Cowell to the dust heap, he sent a supportive letter. Undiscovered for decades, this letter is unusual for being in Ives's hand. He was hindered by cataracts and a palsied script and usually relied on his wife to serve as secretary—she read his correspondence, penned replies, and made judgment calls about what might provoke her famously excitable husband. Possibly, as musicologists Leta E. Miller and Rob Collins have suggested, the dwindling of communication to a lone letter, where previously exchanges had been frequent and regular, had more to do with Harmony's moral scruples.[37] She might well have decided to screen her husband from things having to do with Cowell and, as she euphemistically put it, his "Oscar Wilde practices."[38]

If not ruptured, the relationship between Cowell and the Iveses was certainly strained. This much is evidenced by the trickle of correspondence between Cowell and Harmony that dates from the year immediately following Cowell's release from prison in 1940. The tone of these letters is polite but impersonal, the subject restricted to business matters. The impetus for change came in September of 1941, when Cowell announced to Harmony, "I wish to tell you and Mr. Ives of my forthcoming marriage to Sidney Robertson, to take place very soon, probably before October. I am sure you will be happy for me over this event, to which I look forward with such intensity."[39]

Robertson was a folk-music scholar who met Cowell in the late twenties or early thirties, when she enrolled in a world-music course he frequently taught. Together with Cowell's stepmother, Olive, she had spearheaded the campaign to secure his release from prison and, ultimately, in 1942, a pardon from the Governor of California. Just when the pair became romantically involved is not clear, but the Iveses were certainly overjoyed by this development. In response to Cowell's announcement about his engagement, they sent a warm letter of congratulations and best wishes, signed by both Harmony and (in the shaky script he called "snake tracks") Charles.[40] For the Iveses, Cowell's marriage signaled the restoration of moral order; their reserve broke, and friendship was renewed (Figure 3.2).

Figure 3.2 Henry Cowell and Charles Ives reunited, ca. 1950. Courtesy
Yale University Irving S. Gilmore Music Library. Courtesy David and Sylvia
Teitelbaum Fund, Inc.

Over the next few years, the scope of Cowell's activities on behalf of Ives was
limited by the demands placed on him by his position in the Overseas Division
of the Office of War Information, which he worked for throughout most of the
period of American engagement in the Second World War. Among his many duties, Cowell was charged with the task of creating radio programs about American
music, the goal being to counter stereotypical depictions of America as uncul-
tured and materialistic. These programs furnished him with an otherwise rare
opportunity to tout Ives during this busy period of his life. By the fall of 1945,
however, with his government service obligations behind him, Cowell was ready
to concentrate his efforts and broached with Ives the possibility of writing the
composer's biography. The project did not immediately get under way, though
Ives, through his wife, responded positively with a typical offer of subvention.[41]
The real spur was Ives's Pulitzer Prize win in 1947, after which the publisher
Prentice Hall tendered a formal contract with Cowell for the book that would
eventually bear the title *Charles Ives and His Music*.

During the summer of 1947, Henry dutifully worked at the book, sending out inquiries to Ives's musical friends and supporters, sketching a general outline, and completing the draft of a section discussing Ives's music.[42] But he found his attempts to piece together the particulars of the composer's life frustrated by a "New Englander's personal reticence." Exasperated, Henry conscripted Sidney, and she found herself "gradually embroiled in Mr. Ives's search through his memory and his papers."[43] By the fall, Henry had become preoccupied with other matters, and the subject of the book dropped from his correspondence. As Sidney tells it, from then until June 1953, when the manuscript was finally ready for the publisher, the task of completing it was largely in her hands.[44]

The end result was a book written by two authors and comprising two parts: the first dealt with Ives's life and was mostly the work of Sidney; the second dealt with the composer's music and was mostly the work of Henry. The sense one gets from reading Sidney's account of the collaboration was that the second part was more or less complete by summer's end, 1947: "Henry wrote out his admirable section on Ives's music almost at once."[45] But, as I have shown elsewhere, Sidney's work on the book led to substantial alterations of the portion her husband had "finished."[46]

Early draft materials authored by Henry reveal that he was originally intending to present a more elaborate version of the ideas about Ives he had developed in the late twenties and early thirties: the composer as creative ethnographer, whose musical language was an outgrowth of the performance idiosyncrasies of American folk musicians and who would, besides, allow his performer considerable interpretive leeway. When Sidney took over the project, she set out to fulfill a different mandate. "I have confidence," she later asserted, explaining her approach, "that there is a certain consistency in any single life." Accordingly, when she set to work on the biography, Sidney sought to discover a unifying principle that would lend coherence to the narrative. In Ives, she faced the challenge of a wide-ranging and eclectic intellect, but ultimately it was transcendentalism that furnished her with the means of weaving a coherent fabric from the divergent threads of the composer's life.

In the published version of *Charles Ives and His Music*, much of the material Henry penned in the summer of 1947 was excised; Sidney's work, however, was retained with only minor alterations. As a result, while the importance of transcendentalism waxed from draft to published volume, the significance of folk-music practice to Ives's accomplishment waned. In the book, Ives was still credited with having been the first art-music composer to attend to and make use of the "American musical vernacular." However, of what the "American musical vernacular" was constituted was not detailed, save for the occasional mention of popular genres like the hymn and the march. Henry's description of the various sonic occurrences that had motivated a particular aspect of Ives's style—the two bands playing different pieces simultaneously, the nebulous pitch of church congregations, a lagging horn player—was also retained.[47] But the Bartók-derived idea that the essence of the American vernacular lay in these occurrences was discarded. Instead, they were depicted as exceptional and humorous musical events that set in motion the inventive mind of the composer.

New England philosophy served as the cornerstone of *Charles Ives and His Music*, something that was evident from the opening pages, where, following an epigraph drawn from Thoreau, transcendentalism was equated with the basic essence of the American spirit:

> Americans are . . . anxious to be themselves, to establish their relation to life and art straight from within. Such an attitude is far from being the expression of a personal romanticism. It is rather a spiritual concept which stems from the gospel preached by the Transcendentalists at Concord, who believed that man, nature, and God are one, and that truth and integrity are attainable by man only to the degree that he perceives his own identity with the creative forces of the universe, on which alone he may depend. This is a philosophy of the Ideal whose emphasis is on what could be, on the intuitively sensed possibility that is illimitable, rather than on what has been or what other people are.

Sidney showed that pursuit of the Ideal governed every aspect of Ives's life; "the intuitively sensed possibility" dictated his decisions in business and art. As an insurance man "his devotion to Emersonian doctrine led him to see, in the truths revealed by statistical averages, the expression of the Universal Mind, operating in the experience of many individuals." Similarly, Ives's various political ideas, especially his advocacy of direct democracy, were a result of his commitments to the Ideal. "What Ives was trying to do was to devise machinery for bringing to bear on the questions that most plague the average citizen . . . that Universal Mind, or Oversoul, declared by Emerson to be the source of all effective thought and action." The book even went so far as to suggest that Ives's dedication to establishing his relation to "life and art straight from within" had resulted in some of the inconsistencies in his musical output. "Most of his music was made in a state of fine creative excitement and satisfaction, for he believed that 'to speak adequately, he must speak wildly, with the flower of the mind, as Emerson has it,' 'abandoning himself to the nature of things and letting the tides roll through him.' Small wonder if even his most appreciative critics have found crudities and incongruities and awkwardness in the music."[48]

Why Sidney jettisoned the Bartókian interpretation of Ives that Henry had touted for so long is a matter open to speculation. Likely, her own experiences as an ethnographer led her to question her husband's assertions about Ives having "scientifically recorded" the musical practices around him. During the thirties, working for the Resettlement Administration under Charles Seeger, she had made some 150 recordings of folk music from all over the United States. In addition, in 1938 she had launched the California Folk Music Project under the joint auspices of the Library of Congress, the Works Progress Administration, and the University of California at Berkeley. The mandate was to create a collection of recordings that covered all the folk-music traditions in California.[49] Sidney was also acquainted with issues pertaining to transcription, having compiled *The Gold Rush Song Book* (1940) with Eleanora Black, and edited *American Folk Song and Folk Lore: A Regional Bibliography* (1942) with Alan Lomax. In short, Sidney had far more direct experience with American folk-music practice than Henry. Save for a few quirky incidents, such as the antiphonal mayhem of two bands playing different marches one against the other, she probably realized that it was inaccurate to credit Ives with having transcribed musical practice as it transpired around him.

Sidney's description of her work on *Charles Ives and His Music* presents a picture of solitary industry. Extracting, sifting, organizing—she pored over the facts of Ives's life until they revealed their inherent unity, as if no external motivation for the final image of the composer existed apart from her conviction as to "a certain consistency in any single life." Certainly, the evidence suggests that she got little help from Henry. But the Ives portrayed in the book was not sui generis; he was a composite of ideas that had accumulated from the midthirties to the early fifties. Sidney's awareness of the body of writing in which these ideas were to be found—reviews, articles, and the odd book—is attested to by the thorough bibliography that she compiled for *Charles Ives and His Music*. Her emphasis on transcendentalism had strong impetus from Ives himself, who made occasional reference to the Emerson cohort in his then unpublished *Memos*, which served as Sidney's principal source. Moreover, after John Kirkpatrick garnered rave reviews for performing the "Concord" Sonata in 1939, Ives and the transcendentalists became inextricably linked in the minds of the musical public. And, of course, a close friend of the Cowells, Nicolas Slonimsky, had set the precedent of making transcendentalism the interpretive frame for all of Ives's music, when he wrote about it under the auspices of the Congress for Cultural Freedom.

Transcendentalism, as I have suggested, was readily absorbed by the discourse about autonomy characteristic of the early Cold War period, and it should come as no surprise that autonomy figures as the other major theme in *Charles Ives and His Music*. "There were composers in New England before Charles Ives," it was pointed out early on in the book, "but none who questioned the value of European culture for America or who appreciated the music around him at home." This is similar to the assertion that Henry had made repeatedly in his earlier writings on Ives, but the focus had moved from the uniqueness of American folk music to the composer's act of independence. What was important about Ives was that his music heralded a rebellion against the imported European institutions that comprised the American musical establishment. That rebellion was abetted by Ives's decision to pursue a career in business, which, far from marking conformity to middle-class expectations, assured him the kind of artistic freedom he would not have had had he pursued music professionally. Similarly, in other parts of the narration of Ives's biography, the theme of autonomy was prevalent—albeit a more antisocial autonomy than that conceived by the authors of *The Lonely Crowd*. In his early postcollege days, as Ives set out in pursuit of his own artistic vision, he severed himself from outside influence: "on the whole he did little concert-going, since he found other people's music interfered with the music of his own that he was always carrying around in his head." In the business world too, he followed his own course, overturning marketing orthodoxies and developing his own method for selling insurance, which proved to be enormously successful. When, by the end of the forties, he had become a figure of some renown in the musical world, he refused to succumb to the demands of celebrity. "Ives was glad the music was liked, but he was unimpressed by all the to-do and he refused all requests from metropolitan and news-service reporters for interviews and pictures." From the beginning to the end of his life, Ives maintained his independence.[50]

As with transcendentalism, the theme of autonomy was also manifest in the part of the book devoted to Ives's music. "Ives's whole approach to his complex rhythms should be understood as an attempt to persuade players away from the straitjacket of regular beats, with which complete exactness is impossible anyhow, and to induce them to play with *rubato* in the involved places, with a freedom that creates the impression of a sidewalk crowded with individuals who moved forward with a variety of rhythmic tensions and muscular stresses that make constant slight changes of pace." Here are remnants of Henry's second major idea about Ives from his early writings, namely that he conceived the composer and performer as collaborative and creative equals. In the book, however, the rhythmic freedoms granted the performer are hedged in by qualifications designed to preserve the autonomy of the composer. Ives, the reader is told, did not write music "simply to sound well to the voice or the instrument." In his oeuvre, passages of "ideal" music could even be found where Ives aimed for something not realizable with normal instruments. An example from the Fourth Symphony was adduced: "The celesta is not normally audible above the trumpet, but Ives wishes the celesta tone-quality in the music, so he writes for an ideal celesta that *would* balance a loud trumpet, even though he knows perfectly well that it does not exist." The point was reinforced by a quotation drawn from Ives's *Essays Before a Sonata* that reduced the performer (or at least his or her instrument) to a hindrance. "My God! What has sound to do with music! . . . Why can't music go out the same way it comes in to a man, without having to crawl over a fence of sounds, thoraxes, catguts, wire, wood and brass. . . . The instrument!" Ives would broach no compromise when it came to the matter of his independence. "His isolation," the book explained, "increased his concentration upon the music of the Ideal, of the Transcendental, music that was to be uninhibited by the limitations of people and instruments, satisfying to the composer if unheard."[51]

Of all the passages in the book affirming Ives's autonomy and its linkage to his transcendentalist beliefs, a passage discussing the composer's maximum income scheme bore the strongest trace of the broad Cold War discourse about autonomy. The scheme, which evolved out of Ives's actuarial work, was simple enough: every individual would be guaranteed a minimum annual income ($900), which one could work to supplement up to a maximum ($7500); anything in excess of that amount would be redistributed to ensure that all would have the minimum. The book quoted Ives's own editorializing on the matter—"it has the good points of both the 'isms': capitalism and communism"—and, just in case the reader had missed it, went on to assert the independence of the idea from any particular ideology:

> It had nothing to do with any set of economic ideas as expounded by the various radical groups of the time. He [Ives] rejected socialism, syndicalism, communism, and anarchism as urgently as he did capitalism, for he felt they represented "minority thought" and that a solution acceptable to the Majority Mind lay elsewhere. He once undertook to read some much talked-of economic treatises, but they struck him as polemical, out to talk other men down rather than inquire for the truth; their insistence put them under suspicion and he discarded them.[52]

Here, Ives as portrayed by Sidney came closest to the autonomous man of *The Lonely Crowd*. That his ideas partook of any particular philosophy stemmed not from a desire to conform—as it would for the "other-directed" individual—but rather from what he himself deemed beneficial. And what was true for Ives's economic beliefs held true for his business dealings, political commitments, and artistic philosophy. Beyond describing Ives, Sidney was telegraphing an idea that lay at the heart of Riesman's book and the credo of the Congress for Cultural Freedom: autonomy was the prerequisite for truth, for the self-confidence to engage with a problem directly, and for the determination to work out its implications without recourse to the prescriptions of others.

This passage is also evocative of the suspicion of ideology that suffused much of the discourse about autonomy. I am using "ideology" in the sense that sociologist Daniel Bell defined and employed it in an influential series of essays published throughout the fifties, collected together in a single volume titled *The End of Ideology* (1960). His definition took the form of a memorable aphorism:

"Ideology is the conversion of ideas into social levers." It was the transformation of a particular utopian vision of the world—a collection of ideas—into a program of political action. In a passage reminiscent of the writings of Erich Fromm, Bell attributed the rise of ideology to the decline of religion in the nineteenth century. The empty space vacated by religious faith was filled by projects for restructuring the political landscape. Communism and fascism, the two faces of totalitarianism, were the twentieth-century archetypes of ideology, and both had visited unprecedented havoc on the world. It was ultimately the violence of communism and fascism that emptied ideology of its attractions in the Western world. "Few serious minds," wrote Bell, "believe any longer that one can set down 'blue-prints' and through 'social-engineering' bring about a new utopia of social harmony."[53] Thus the end of ideology—at least in the West. Here the basic parameters for successful society had been discovered—a welfare state, decentralized government, a system of mixed economy and of political pluralism—and it was no longer necessary to seek alternatives. But elsewhere, alarmingly, ideology persisted, its siren song issuing from Russia and China.

Of course, Ives was a veritable fount of theory, of what might be called utopian blueprints, from his vision of direct democracy to his maximum income plan. And, at least according to the postmodernist usage of the word "ideology"—any self-sustained set of a priori beliefs and values, not just those of our opponents—transcendentalism fits the bill. (Similarly, commitment to the set of parameters that Daniel Bell identifies with successful Western society—welfare state, decentralized government, etc.—could also be described from this perspective as ideology.) But in *Charles Ives and His Music*, transcendentalism was not considered to be of a piece with other isms, for it did not require the subversion of the self to the ideals of another. Instead, it demanded that one *discover* truth for and in oneself, experiment was its very essence, not following the dictates of fiat. As a result, the book described as empirical the process by which Ives arrived at his theories: "All his life he has been accustomed to carry forward some aspect of Emerson's or of Thoreau's thinking in terms of present problems, checking whatever conclusions he arrived at against what he has observed of 'science' and 'natural laws' operating in the insurance business, in music, and in Nature. If he could find a sufficient number of analogies in these various fields he was satisfied he was on the right track."[54] Significantly, the word "theory" is avoided in the book, "system," "scheme," and "idea" being the preferred words.

While the Ives portrayed in *Charles Ives and His Music* fits Bell's nonideological West, and—with some squinting, Riesman, Glazer, and Denney's definition of autonomy—there is no direct evidence to suggest that the Cowells were aware of the work of these writers. However, this lack of evidence does not reduce the resonances I have uncovered to happenstance. The ideas underpinning the work of Riesman, Glazer, Denney, and Bell enjoyed broad circulation at midcentury, and had become an integral part of the way Americans perceived their culture.

All these writers were high-profile members of what historian David A. Hollinger has called the "American liberal intelligentsia." Other thinkers Hollinger places in this cadre include Edmund Wilson, Lionel Trilling, Dwight Macdonald, Reinhold Niebuhr, and Sidney Hook. (A glance several pages back will reveal a significant overlap with the American membership of the CCF.) "So influential was this intelligentsia during the 1940s, 1950s, and 1960s," writes Hollinger, "that most Americans who thought of themselves as 'intellectuals' were either members of it, or part of its audience." These liberal writers set the intellectual status quo from positions in prominent university departments and in the pages of such magazines as the *New Republic*, *Partisan Review*, *Commentary*, and the *Nation*.[55] Historian Richard H. Pells, commenting about the same cohort of intellectuals, notes, "[T]heir ideas, reinforced by their multiple credentials, carried weight with other intellectuals, magazine and newspaper editors, academics, journalists, and segments of the general public. To the degree that one could measure the impact of their work, they provided what became the standard explanations of America's political ingenuity, economic success, and social stability in the 1950s."[56] Even if Henry and Sidney Cowell did not know the names Riesman, Glazer, Denney, Boorstin, or Bell, by dint of the pervasive influence of the liberal intelligentsia, the image of the United States as the bastion of autonomy, where men and women could thrive free of ideology, had become standard fare. Ives's life, as related by the Cowells, was a variation on a staple liberal apologia. It was a testimonial to the artistic freedoms that could be had in the United States.

As Nicolas Slonimsky had done before them, the Cowells realized that their conception of Ives could be turned to propagandistic purposes. Just prior to the publication of *Charles Ives and His Music*, the Cowells prepared an abridged version of the book for *Perspectives USA*, a journal published by the Ford Foundation.[57] This journal, like the activities of the CCF, was targeted at European intellectuals who remained ambivalent in the ideological Cold War, and, accordingly, it was printed in multiple languages: English, French, German, and Italian. Its express purpose was to counter stereotypes of American culture as materialistic and shallow, a mandate it proudly announced in the first issue: "It will be the main function of *Perspectives* to show that the spiritual and artistic elements in American life have not been sterile. . . . America, if judged merely by second-rate motion pictures, may appear to be a land of gilded barbarians; but America judged also by the poems of a Marianne Moore, the paintings of a Ben Shahn, the music of an Aaron Copland, or the outlook of a teacher like Jacques Barzun, becomes something different: a culture that exhibits an exciting and rounded vitality."[58] Working for OWI during the Second World War,

Henry Cowell had already put Ives and his music in service of such an agenda. It made sense to do so once again in the context of a new war, a Cold War, especially since the image of the composer that Sidney had developed played upon currently favored tropes of American identity: here was a man who by pursuing the archetypal American course—his own—had managed to arrive at musical innovations before Schoenberg and Stravinsky, Europe's modernist greats. Although space was limited, the Cowells chose to retain the passage on Ives's maximum income scheme, complete with its disavowal of any links between his ideas and a specific ideology. Ives owed nothing to socialism, nothing to syndicalism, nothing to anarchism, nothing to pure capitalism, and, above all, nothing to communism.

The care taken to cordon off Ivesian schemes from ideology has a darker subtext; it provided a definitive answer to the most notorious question of the early Cold War period: "Are you now, or have you ever been, a member of the Communist Party?" The writing of *Charles Ives and His Music*, roughly from 1947 to 1953, coincides with the apogee of the anticommunist crusade in the United States. It was a period marked by loyalty oaths, blacklists, and the inquiries of the House Committee on Un-American Activities (HUAC), all of which have come to be subsumed under the rubric McCarthyism, named for the Senator who made (and ultimately destroyed) his political career by red-baiting. Henry and Sidney had good reason to be sensitive to the inclement turn in the political climate. Federal investigations into the communist affiliations of prominent figures in the arts touched their lives directly.

Prior to his imprisonment in the thirties, Henry had been briefly associated with the so-called Composer's Collective, which met initially under the auspices of the Communist Pierre Degeyter Club in New York. The collective's objective was to provide musical support for the emergence of a united proletariat, and it had attracted a number of avant-garde composers eager to make their art more socially relevant. In addition to Henry himself, the more prominent members included Ruth Crawford Seeger, Charles Seeger, Aaron Copland, Elie Siegmeister, Hanns Eisler, and Marc Blitzstein.[59] The group was short-lived, its raison d'être obviated by the Popular Front and then swept aside as communism in the United States was undermined after 1936 by the Moscow trials and the Nazi-Soviet Pact.

During the McCarthy Era, the dalliance with the Left returned to haunt many of the former members of the collective, who found themselves the subjects of government investigations: Blitzstein testified before HUAC; Copland and Siegmeister testified before Senator McCarthy's Permanent Subcommittee on Investigations; Seeger was subjected to a grueling interview by the FBI; and Eisler was deported. Even Henry's friend Nicolas Slonimsky, who had not been involved in the Composer's Collective, was questioned for his possible communist affiliations.[60]

Henry escaped unscathed through the worst of it, perhaps because he had maintained a low profile after his release from prison. His reputation as a composer did not match Copland's, nor had he produced anything as overt in its political radicalism as Blitzstein's *The Cradle Will Rock*, and he did not occupy a position in an organization with government affiliations, as did Seeger (the Pan American Union). Nonetheless, he seized at the opportunity to clarify his political views on Edward R. Murrow's radio series "This I Believe":

> I used to be almost totally uninterested in politics: but it becomes increasingly clear to me that ethical individualism cannot flourish under radically extreme political conditions. Thus I abhor communism, under which individualism is impossible and expression of liberal thought is punishable; and I abhor its right wing counterpart. . . . My own belief is in a regard for individual rights according to the letter and spirit of the United States Constitution. This I fight for by creating music which I hope will reach and touch all who listen so that they will be thereby encouraged to behave according to their own highest possibilities. Unexpected inner response to the power of music dedicated to human integrity might reach dictators more easily than an atom bomb.[61]

Dick Higgins, compiler and editor of Henry's prose, suggests that the strength with which communism is disavowed here is indicative of the anxieties that beset American artists and intellectuals during the McCarthy era.[62] There is a clear determination on Henry's part to certify his own commitment to American ideals, to cast himself as a man who would broach no compromises on individual freedom. At the time Henry made this statement, Sidney was putting the finishing touches on a portrait that brought out just this quality of American authenticity in another man—Charles Ives.

Whether Sidney actually had the travails of Henry's friends in mind while working on *Charles Ives and His Music* will have to remain conjecture. Unfortunately, the Cowells' correspondence is almost completely devoid of any reference to political matters, even those that embroiled their closest friends. However, it is clear that Henry recognized the potential of the archetype that his wife had created in the book, for he began to use it as a post hoc rationalization for his own creative life. The image of Ives, so carefully stitched together by Sidney, would serve her husband as well: armor against anticommunist witch-hunters at home and an apologia for American culture abroad.

Shortly after the publication of *Charles Ives and His Music*, Henry embarked upon a new career as a cultural emissary. He was among the numerous artists and performers dispatched by the Department of State to sundry parts of the globe in an effort to convince the world of the cultural vitality of the United States. (Among the others were Dizzy Gillespie and the New York Philharmonic.) Two world tours would take him to some of the major theaters of conflict in the ideological Cold War, notably India and Iran. The Rockefeller Foundation and the U.S. State Department, longtime partners in the cultural Cold War, jointly sponsored the first tour, from 1956 to 1957; the second tour, in 1961, saw Henry in the role of John F. Kennedy's representative to the International Music Conference in Tehran and the East-West Music Encounter in Tokyo (the latter was sponsored by the CCF).[63]

At the International Music Conference, Henry gave a lecture detailing his musical philosophy and articulating some general principles about conditions conducive to composition. He relied heavily on the palette Sidney had used for Ives's portrait. Consider, for example, his rationalization for the musical eclecticism that had characterized much of his life: "It seemed natural for an American to stretch his mind beyond the limitations of European traditions, and to welcome the infinite variety and vitality of the human imagination as it has expressed itself in the music of the world. . . . The multiplicity of musical experience to which I subjected myself seemed to me to be a fact of modern life—useless to try to turn one's back on it." Henry went on to argue that the "unconscious side" of any composer's musical talent must be given free rein, pursuing whatever interested it in the vast array of the world's music. Impositions from outside—that is strictures on what the composer could and could not do—were fatal because they inhibited "the organic growth of the music, which depends . . . upon the free interplay of unconscious mental powers." Cowell cited the same lines of Emerson that Sidney had deployed in defense of the patchy quality of some of Ives's music: "To speak adequately one must speak wildly, with the flower of the mind, abandoning himself to the nature of things and letting the tides roll through him." The upshot was that freedom was crucial to the composer—freedom from tradition, freedom from political constraint, freedom even from the practical concerns of music making. Only then could the unconscious work its magic. "At that profound level," Cowell asserted at the conclusion of his talk, "everything the composer is or has been, all he has experienced or known or felt, will play its part. Only then will his music, however national, be *more* than national, so that he is able to speak freely, as man and artist, in personal accents of universal things."[64]

Spreading the Gospel (Again): The Influence of Henry and Sidney Cowell

The image of Ives that the Cowells presented in their book received additional reinforcement from music historian Gilbert Chase, whose landmark volume, *America's Music: From the Pilgrims to the Present*, was published the same year, 1955, and was also animated by the idea of autonomy. During the thirties, Chase had been a prolific music critic and sometimes encyclopedist, serving as associate editor of the *International Cyclopedia of Music and Musicians* (1938). He accepted an invitation to join the fledgling American Musicological Society, based in New York, and through the organization met Charles Seeger, who galvanized the interest in folk music that would be one of the defining features of his subsequent scholarly career. But if Seeger served as initial impetus, the formative influence for his intellectual framework was the work of folklorist Constance Rourke.[65] Like Béla Bartók and Henry Cowell, she was an early convert to the diffusionist model of culture, championed by anthropologist Franz Boas and his students. According to this model, a culture was not defined by tracing the origins of its raw materials; rather, it was the particulars of local practice applied to those materials that were its salient traits. Thus an English folk song or a German style of woodworking would become American by virtue of the alterations that came about through its usage on this continent. Given the heterogeneous nature of the American population and geography, one could also expect that the treatment of such materials would vary in different parts of the country, the end result being a vibrant plurality.[66] In *America's Music*, Chase followed the precedent set by Rourke in her posthumously published *The Roots of American Culture* (1942) by setting the plurality of American folk and popular culture in opposition to the "genteel tradition." Though by the fifties, this rubric usually referred to the canon and manners of the Gilded Age bourgeois, Chase deployed it as a blanket term. In his most specific application, it meant the European classical tradition and its American epigones, but more generally, he used it as a label for any force that threatened to homogenize. The genteel tradition stalks the pages of Chase's book, an insidious antagonist that threatens to undermine the multifaceted American folk. The history of American art music, as Chase recounted it, was a tragic story of voluntary slavery to the genteel tradition. Composer after composer fettered him or herself to the traditions of Europe, deaf to the vitality of the popular and folk music that had developed on American soil (and which Chase described with effervescent enthusiasm). All composers, that is, until Charles Ives.

The final and culminating chapter of the book is devoted to the "composer from Connecticut," as Chase, channeling Mark Twain, dubs Ives. It is only a slight exaggeration to say that the six hundred and fifty pages that precede this chapter serve as a massive upbeat to the dramatic unveiling of the composer:

> We can take almost the whole body of American folk and popular music, as we have traced it from the early psalmody and hymnody of New England, through the camp-meeting songs and revival spirituals, the blackface minstrel tunes, the melodies of Stephen Foster, the fiddle tunes and barn dance, the village church choirs, the patriotic songs and ragtime—and we can feel that all this has been

made into the substance of Ives's music, not imitated but assimilated, used as a musical heritage belonging to him by birthright. Thanks to his early background, to the decisive influence of his formative years, and to his utter independence of conventional musical standards Charles Ives, first and alone among American composers, was able to discern and to utilize the truly idiosyncratic and germinal elements of our folk and popular music

The genteel tradition meets its final match in Charles Ives. He stands as the great liberator of American art music, the composer who freed the United States from the dogma of conformists. To the hero he constructed, Chase was quick to declare his allegiances. "My own approach to America's music," he explained in his preface, "is not at all respectable—my bête noire is the genteel tradition, and I take my stand with that Connecticut Yankee, Charles Ives, whose most damning adjective is said to be 'nice.'"[67] Of course, by the midfifties, the long history of attacking genteelity in American letters, which stretched from George Santayana and Van Wyck Brooks to Constance Rourke, made Chase's position much more respectable than he was willing to admit.

The extravagant claim Chase made about Ives was an outgrowth of the argument Henry Cowell advanced relating the origins of the composer's idiom to folk performance practice. But Chase was not simply recycling old ideas from the late twenties and thirties—ideas, which, in any case, had receded into the background for their originator. In Chase's book, Ives the creative ethnographer, the American Bartók, was displayed in a different light. He represented American autonomy, the triumph of "human dignity, freedom, and justice" against the forces of conformity, a struggle Chase had chronicled in unprecedented detail.[68] *America's Music* was effectively an expansion of "The Declaration of the Independence of American Music" Nicolas Slonimsky had penned for the CCF Paris festival in 1952. But instead of casting Ives as a prophetic precursor as Slonimsky had done, Chase made him the culmination of American musical history. For this reason, he broke the chronological organization of his text by placing Ives at the end, after composers who were several generations younger—Henry Cowell, Virgil Thomson, Samuel Barber, and John Cage, to name only a few of them.

Chase's book was published too soon after the Cowells' *Charles Ives and His Music* to have been directly influenced. His image of Ives lacked the tight focus that the Cowells had achieved by placing transcendentalism in the foreground, and he did not make an explicit connection between transcendentalist philosophy and Ivesian autonomy. Nonetheless, Chase returned frequently enough to the subject of transcendentalism to suggest that it was formative in the composer's life. The passage with which he concludes the Ives chapter (and the book) is especially telling in this regard. Here, Chase inserted a quotation from Van Wyck Brooks's

The Flowering of New England—yet another testimony to the significance of that work to the reception of Ives. "Ironically enough, it was Boston and Cambridge that grew to be provincial, while the local and even parochial Concord mind, which had always been universal, proved also to be national." In the remaining two sentences of his book, Chase applied this assessment of the Emersonian cohort to Ives. The composer, he declared, "was local but never provincial. Like the ever-widening circles that appear when a stone is thrown into a pool of water, his music proceeds from the local to the regional, thence to the national, and finally to the universal." This is, of course, yet another formulation of the transcendentalist paradox. Just as the Cowells had argued, Chase maintained that the fierce independence of Ives had not resulted in musical solipsism, but in music that was universally significant.[69]

Throughout the remainder of the fifties and into the sixties, the idea that Ives's autonomy was a result of his devotion to transcendentalism spread, at first through the circle of the Cowells' musical acquaintances. An early trace of this process of dissemination is a 1956 two-part article published in *Etude* magazine, the work of John J. Becker, a composer who had been Cowell's Midwestern factotum. "Danbury," Becker pointed out, "was in the region where Emerson, Thoreau and Alcott had flourished a generation before, and had heightened and intensified the interest in the philosophy of Transcendentalism to such an extent that the area was literally steeped in it." Nourished by roots sunk into the transcendentalist soil of Danbury, Ives grew as a composer and looked obdurately forward. He ventured "into the business world to earn a living, in order to be free to follow his own ideas in his creative work."[70] Thus, Ives chose not to pursue the inviting and well-traveled road trod by his composerly contemporaries and forebears—a road that ran straight through Europe and made of its pilgrims unremarkable epigones. Ives's trailblazing had resulted in new methods, but this, for Becker, was not what made the composer's music significant. Instead, it was the spiritual element of Ives's music that seemed most compelling to Becker, himself a devout Catholic. Again, stressing the formative influence of transcendentalism, he opined, "[The] most important aspect [of Ives's music] is a deeply moving spirituality, a philosophical contemplation of God and man. Material methods become obsolete, but great thinking always remains, and deep spiritual thinking is the basis of his music."[71]

John Kirkpatrick agreed. The pianist delivered a preconcert talk at Tanglewood on Independence Day in 1958, before performing the "Concord" Sonata, a work that was responsible for his own measure of musical celebrity. He described Ives's music as an "enlivening contagion" that drew its listeners toward a transcendental awareness, toward a deeply sensed intuition of the linkage between each human being and the oversoul. It was the salve to global conflict, to what Kirkpatrick described as the "pure evil" that had manifest itself in the "the recent history of Hungary," a not so oblique reference to the violent suppression of the Hungarian Revolution in 1956 by the Soviets.[72] Three years later and several months after the construction of the Berlin Wall, Kirkpatrick ratcheted up the Cold War rhetoric to a fever pitch in another preconcert talk, this one titled "Ives, Transcendentalist in Music." It is worth quoting the peroration at length:

> Now, you all have been listening patiently to a talk about transcendentalism and about a piece of music [again, the "Concord" Sonata], and I wonder how many of you have been wondering what all this has to do with us, and with now, and with our problems and perils. For we are in real peril. War has been declared on this country, not in the old-fashioned, honorable way, but in the manner of a liar, and you probably have read that our defeat is confidently predicted for 1980. We face an enemy whom we know to be evil, but who commands a devotion and obedience to which we have never trained ourselves—or perhaps which our religion and our various churches have not quite evoked from us. . . . Their power is based largely on an absolute certainty that dialectical materialism is true. What I think we need most is a still stronger certainty that the world of the spirit is the real world. This you can't prove or even argue. Neither the senses nor logic are any use. Most of us know this only by hearsay. But the only way we can be absolutely certain of this is by our own intuitions. What Emerson's Transcendentalism does offer is an introduction to faith in one's own intuitions. It won't do our thinking for us. And it won't make us clairvoyant. But I am sure that Emerson would think he had lived and written in vain, if his readers did not receive some strengthening of faith that they too could glimpse and understand and know for a fact.[73]

Here, the political subtext of Henry and Sidney Cowell's *Charles Ives and His Music* is made blindingly explicit. The immediate motivation for this outburst was probably Kirkpatrick's absorption of the ideas of Frederic Schwarz, an evangelical Christian (as Kirkpatrick was), who sought to fuse faith and politics, prefiguring Jerry Falwell and the "Moral Majority" movement of the seventies. From his base of operations in Long Beach, California, Schwarz ran the Christian Anti-Communism Crusade, arranging speaking engagements across the country that would allow him to disseminate his message about what he perceived as a biblical imperative to combat communism. That imperative was spelled out in his facetiously titled book *You Can Trust the Communists*, which Kirkpatrick recommended to his lecture audience.[74] This would be the last time that Kirkpatrick publicly outfitted Ives as a Cold Warrior, armed with the wisdom of the transcendentalists, but he would continue to view the composer's aesthetics as being rooted in the writings of Emerson and the other members of the Concord coterie.

The same idea, sans apocalyptic overtones, found expression in the writings of Peter Yates, another friend of the Cowells and founder of an important series of new music concerts in Los Angeles. Beginning in the midforties, Yates authored several lengthy articles about Ives in the journal *Arts and Architecture*, but it was only in 1961 that transcendentalism moved to the foreground of his conception of the composer, a measure of the influence of the Cowells' book. In Yates's work, transcendentalism was again conceived as the spur to autonomy, and the life and music of Ives held up as a palpable example. Drawing on the language of Ives's "The Majority," Yates argued that transcendentalist philosophy infused the music with a message: it encouraged the listener to perceive "the masses" as comprising "individuals needing to be guided, to be directed, to be aroused, to be encouraged, not to be led."[75]

In 1962, a new edition of Ives's *Essays Before a Sonata* served to consolidate the link between autonomy and transcendentalism that the Cowells had threaded through their portrait of the composer. In his introductory note, editor Howard Boatwright, a friend of Kirkpatrick and yet another Cowell acquaintance, repeated what was rapidly becoming an orthodoxy: "The Sonata and Essays were the culmination of years of thought and work, and Concord and its 'divinities' were immersed in the ferment of Ives' creative activity from his student days onward." Boatwright credited Ives with two accomplishments: throwing off the "fetters of conventional techniques" and abandoning the "European-derived style of American composers at the time." This independence had its roots in the impact of "passages in Emerson" on "his receptive, imaginative, and ambitious mind." Boatwright continued, "If Emerson provided the philosophical support for Ives' artistic independence, Thoreau did likewise for his approach to the business of living." Ives was Concord come again, transcendentalism in its musical incarnation.[76]

Into the Mainstream

As the ideas of the Cowells percolated through the musical world, national and international, Ives's public profile grew exponentially. Between the years 1947, when the Third Symphony won the Pulitzer Prize, and 1965, when the Fourth Symphony was premiered, performances of Ives's music occurred with increasing frequency and a representative sampling of his output became available on major recording labels. And if Ives was not quite a staple of the concert hall by the end of this period, he had enough of a presence in the musical life of Americans, even those nominally interested in classical music, to merit the designation canonical.

There are several reasons that can be adduced to account for this dramatic transformation of Ives's fortunes. To begin with, advances in recording technol-

ogy—the LP in 1948 and stereophonic discs in 1957—made it possible to experience the music of Ives at home, replete with its characteristic antiphonal effects.
It helped that by the fifties, a number of Ives's devotees had attained positions of
power in the broadcast and recording industry. Goddard Lieberson, who, during
the thirties, had written enthusiastically about Ives in the communist magazine
New Masses, was now head of the classical music division at Columbia Records.
Oliver Daniel, another early Ives devotee, worked in the broadcasting division of
the same company. But the efforts of Lieberson and Daniel could not have borne
fruit without the availability of performance-ready scores. Until the midfifties, the
project of putting Ives's music into publishable form was a catch-as-catch-can
endeavor, sporadically sustained by different people—Henry Cowell and Lou
Harrison most notable among them. After 1955, when Ives's widow deposited
his manuscripts at Yale University, a more systematic attempt was made to put
the Ivesian oeuvre in order. The key figure was John Kirkpatrick, who finished
his *Temporary Mimeographed Catalogue* of the Ives manuscripts in 1960 and, in
1968, was named curator of the Ives Collection at Yale.

The ready accessibility of recordings and published scores, however, is not a
sufficient explanation for why the public responded positively. Since contemporary audiences and record consumers are not available for polling, the best one
can do is to examine the way in which Ives was portrayed by prominent musicians
and in the publicity that sustained them.

The place to begin is with Leonard Bernstein, who discovered Ives early in
his musical career and became one of the composer's most important proselytiz-
ers. Bernstein's first exposure to Ives seems to have come about as a result of his
friendship with Aaron Copland, whom he met in the late thirties. At the time,
Bernstein was a student at Harvard University. With a view to writing a senior
thesis on American music, he solicited advice from Copland about which composers to discuss. As he explained, "I will try to show that there is something
American in the newer music, which relies not on folk material but on a native
spirit."[77] In the end, this amounted to little more than a neo-Dvořákian argument about jazz music supplying the elements of a definitively American idiom.
The thesis included a few pages devoted to the "Concord" Sonata, identifying
"syncopative devices" that were indebted to "Negro rhythms," but Ives did not
then impress Bernstein. The sonata was "tiring, overlong, and a fierce challenge
to any pianist," he declared.[78]

Twelve years later, Bernstein had changed his mind. In the interim, he had
acquired and assiduously cultivated an enviable public profile as an American
eclectic who slipped easily between Broadway theaters and Carnegie Hall. Given
the attention that had redounded to Ives after being awarded the Pulitzer Prize
in 1947, particularly the notion that he was an audacious American pioneer, it is

not surprising that Bernstein took up the cause. On February 22, 1951, Bernstein gave the premiere of the Second Symphony, the first of many times he conducted the work in his lengthy career.

The critical response was generally positive, recycling the themes of Ives's reception that had been in circulation since the late twenties: innovation ("Ives was at least half a century ahead of his time"), independent-mindedness ("a work of definite individuality . . . full of interesting juxtapositions), and American identity ("by turns, rudely, tenderly, fantastically and cantankerously Yankee").[79] Transcendentalism was not mentioned in any of the reviews; Sidney Cowell was still hard at work on the book that would move New England philosophy to the foreground of Ives's reception. But at least one writer drew attention to the possibilities the symphony held out as a timely symbol of American culture. In a letter published in the *New York Times*, composer H. E. McMahan Jr. suggested that the freedom embodied in Ives's music could serve as an antidote to communism.[80]

Bernstein voiced his own thoughts about Ives and this particular symphony in October 1958. The concert occasioning his comments was significant in that it inaugurated his tenure as Music Director of the New York Philharmonic, a milestone that he, as the first native-born American to occupy such a prestigious post, underscored by programming American works throughout the 1958–59 season. His decision to launch what was to be a roughly chronological survey with Ives's Second Symphony suggests a rather truncated view of American musical history, but it is indicative of the extent to which Ives had come to be regarded as the great patriarch of American composers. During his preview talk, Bernstein dispensed an aphorism that has been quoted more often than anything else written about Ives, save perhaps Lawrence Gilman's 1939 encomiums to the "Concord" Sonata: "[Ives] has been said over and over to be our greatest, our first really great composer; our pride and our passion; our Washington, Lincoln, and Jefferson of music." Bernstein noted that much of the praise lavished on Ives rested on the idea that he had presaged twentieth-century techniques; however, this was not an accurate measure of the man. Instead, his "greatness" was to be sensed in those works, like the Second Symphony, that did not involve "such experimentation" but nonetheless succeeded "in carrying a strongly personal and original message." Ives lived at a time when being "a musician was then considered vaguely reprehensible," a time "when anything that was any good at all *had* to come from Europe." Despite this, he had the "brave resolve to be American, to write American music in the face of a diffident and uninterested world." The Second Symphony stood as testimony to this brave resolve, a "personal memoir" of the musical soundscape of Ives's youth, and while it borrowed European music—Beethoven, Brahms, Wagner—along with bits of Americana, it "all comes out Ivesian." For Bernstein then, as for many Ives advocates during the fifties and sixties, it was the expressive autonomy of the composer that vouchsafed his place in the American musical canon.[81]

Inadvertently, in the course of the talk, Bernstein also managed to offend Ives partisans and provide fodder for his detractors by describing the composer as a "primitive," the musical equivalent of Grandma Moses. Several reviewers roundly chastised him, pointing out that Ives had received an extensive musical education.[82] But such was Bernstein's influence that the "Grandma Moses" characterization remained in circulation for some time thereafter, a counterpoint to the more prominent theme of Ives as America's musical founding father. Also, although Bernstein prioritized expressive freedom, Sidney Cowell's thesis about the relationship between transcendentalism and autonomy did not figure at all in Bernstein's talk, and this despite the ready availability of *Charles Ives and His Music* by 1958.

Like the Cowells, Bernstein did realize that Ives could be deployed effectively to the frontlines of the cultural Cold War. In the summer of 1959, Bernstein and the New York Philharmonic embarked on a tour of Eastern Europe and the Soviet Union, arranged under President Eisenhower's Special International Program for Cultural Presentation. Five performances were given in Moscow in conjunction with the American National Exhibition, staged that summer by the U.S. Information Agency and site of the so-called "kitchen debate" between Nixon and Khrushchev.[83] Bernstein was well aware of the propagandistic mandate behind the tour, telling Max Frankel, the *New York Times* Moscow correspondent, that "the biggest single commodity Americans on tour here can sell is American freedom of expression in art."[84] For his most controversial program, Bernstein programmed two works by Igor Stravinsky, who had been a pariah in his homeland for decades, and Charles Ives's *The Unanswered Question*. The concert was a resounding success; such was the applause following the Ives piece that Bernstein repeated it. Only a Ministry of Culture apparatchik, assigned the thankless task of discrediting an effective piece of American propaganda, wrote negatively about the concert.[85]

After Bernstein began to use the bully pulpit of the conductor's podium to champion Ives, a number of his colleagues followed suit, including the aging Leopold Stokowski. Throughout his long career, Stokowski had displayed a shrewd and profitable ability to promote new music in a way calculated to attract maximum publicity: in the teens, he had given the American premiere of Mahler's Eighth Symphony, spurring a vogue that anticipated the post–World War II "Mahler revival"; in the twenties, he had championed the music of Varèse, making the French composer the matinee idol of modernism; and, in the thirties, he was the first major conductor to perform a work by Henry Cowell. It would have been peculiar if Stokowski had not noticed the ascendance of Ives in the musical firmament and thought about some way to capitalize on it.

Sure enough, in early 1939, shortly after Kirkpatrick's successful performances of the "Concord" Sonata, Stokowski queried critic Lawrence Gilman about the availability of Ives scores. Specifically, Stokowski was interested in the Fourth Symphony. Gilman explained that unfortunately the score was not in usable shape and suggested that instead the conductor might consider performing *Three Places in New England*, for which parts and a published score existed.[86] Stokowski wrote back, claiming, "I already know the score of Ives 'Three Places in New England.' I have played these in rehearsal and I think one or two of them in concerts. In any case, I know the score and like it."[87] Though this is evidence of Stokowski's early engagement with Ives, I have not been able to find anything to corroborate his assertion about performing *Three Places in New England*. In fact, his first performance of an Ives work, *The Unanswered Question*, seems not to have taken place until 1953, two years after Leonard Bernstein premiered the Second Symphony.[88]

Stokowski returned to his idea of premiering the Fourth Symphony in the mid-fifties, when, as the conductor of the Houston Symphony Orchestra, he hoped it would make for a suitably spectacular programming choice to open the 1956–57 season. The state of the manuscript score, however, remained much as it had been in the late thirties: the first and third movements were in fairly decent shape, the second movement had been published in Henry Cowell's *New Music Quarterly*, but the fourth movement was in absolute disarray and several pages had been misplaced. Again, Stokowski would have to wait; a performable version of the score took nearly nine more years to produce, with Henry Cowell and several others laboring over it in their spare time.[89]

When it was finally ready, Stokowski had left Houston and was directing the American Symphony Orchestra, a New York–based ensemble put together for the elderly conductor so that he could remain active in his profession without having to travel. Because of the unusual complexity of the Fourth Symphony, six extra rehearsals had to be scheduled, and the Rockefeller Foundation stepped in as deus ex machina to provide the necessary financial support. The lengthy and involved preparations were breathlessly chronicled in the press, whetting the public appetite for the premiere, which took place on April 26, 1965. The concert was sold out, and a recording of the Fourth, which Stokowski and his performing forces made within a week of the premiere, shot up the billboard charts when it was released later that year.

In contrast to the Second Symphony, which was relatively conventional in its harmonic language, the Fourth Symphony bristled with dissonance, antiphonal effects, and rhythmic complexities (except for the third movement). It was just the sort of work that fed the standard modernist cant about Ives having been ahead of his time. And this was the facet of the symphony that most attracted Stokowski, who explained his views in an essay included in the program notes for the concert:

> Ives' music is a self-portrait in sound, revealing his complex personality, and the many facets of his mind and imagination. It is sometimes based on New England folk and religious music, but foremost is his vision of the evolution of music so far ahead of his time and environment. . . . Ives' musical philosophy is complex, but is in no sense rhythmic or harmonic anarchy. In all his music there is a basic rhythmic pulsation and a controlling tonality. His Fourth Symphony is the most uncompromising expression of his revolutionary ideas in complex counterpoint, flexible melodic lines, polyrhythm, and polytonality.[90]

While Leonard Bernstein had stressed the freedom of expression evidenced in the music of Ives, Stokowski emphasized freedom of musical means, the technical innovations of the composer that had shown him to be a visionary.

By and large, however, published contemporary commentary tended more toward Bernstein's perspective than Stokowski's. Furthermore, it reveals that by 1965, the conception of the composer advanced by Henry and Sidney Cowell in *Charles Ives and His Music*—an icon of American autonomy, a transcendentalist who by diving into his own selfhood, arrived at the universal—had become the cant of the mainstream musical press. *New York Times* reviewer Harold C. Schonberg, who had listed Emerson and Thoreau among Ives's influences in earlier articles, but never as the foremost factor, supplied this description in a preview article on the day of the Fourth Symphony premiere: "A rugged individualist of a Yankee, something of an eccentric, a sturdy offshoot of Emerson, Thoreau and the transcendentalists, he stubbornly went his own way, waiting for taste to catch up with him."[91] The following day, in a review of the symphony, Schonberg declared that to understand the work "one must understand Ives the Yankee and his transcendentalism and, too, one must be steeped in the popular music of Ives's own day."[92] David Hall, in *HiFi/Stereo Review*, described the premiere of the Fourth Symphony as a "cultural turning point," and after having declared Ives a "visionary, deeply influenced by New England's transcendental philosophers," went on to observe that the final pages of the Symphony realized "the Emersonian-Thoreauvian transcendentalism that Ives was not able to make entirely clear with words in his *Essays Before a Sonata*."[93] But the most obvious signal that the autonomous, transcendentalist Ives had become lodged in the public imagination is a review of the Fourth Symphony published in *Newsweek* without a byline. Simply titled "The Transcendentalist," it included a description of the New England philosophy, quoting a passage from *Essays*: "If local color, national color, any color is a true pigment of the universal color, it is a divine quality." The reviewer, having praised the Fourth Symphony, added a final assessment. "[Ives's] transcendentalism was complete. He turned the sights and sounds of Danbury, Connecticut, on some hot fourth of July before the turn of the century, into everywhere, always."[94]

It is clear then that the Ives who shouldered his way into the canonical repertory in the fifties and sixties was the Cold War icon of American freedom of expression. Scores, recordings, and performances were, of course, the necessary material preconditions for the process of canonization, but they would likely have been ignored had Ives not served as a screen upon which American concertgoers could project the conglomeration of values that they viewed as most essential to themselves. In many respects, it is the Cowellian conception of Ives that persists in concerts halls today, and the composer is still celebrated for his individualistic gumption, transcendentalist spiritualism, and the technical innovations that these traits made possible. That said, however, as a canonical composer, Ives enjoys many constituencies, and in some of them, existing on the fringes of mainstream classical music culture, his image never stopped evolving.

4

The Prison of Culture

Ives, American Studies,
and Intellectual History,
1965–1985

On the evening of Sunday October 20, 1974, the 100th birthday of Charles E. Ives, a concert took place in honor of the composer at his alma mater, Yale University. As the members of the audience filed into Woolsey Hall, they were met by the sight of two enormous banners strung from the proscenium arch, framing the central bank of pipes of the fabled Newberry Memorial organ and draped such that their ends hung just a few feet above where the performers would stand or sit. The twin ionic colonnades running parallel along the length of the hall's side balconies, its richly decorated barrel-vaulted ceiling, and the fussy gilded filigree worked through much of the room—none of this could compete with the banners, declaring with boldfaced sans serif belligerence, "IVES" on the left side of the stage and "100th" on the right. For many of the attendees of that evening's performance, the juxtaposition of the banners' stark design with Woolsey Hall's Beaux Arts architecture (the word "genteel" comes readily to mind) would have been an apt metaphor for their sense of Ives's spirited response to the conservatism he had encountered as a student at Yale (Figure 4.1). Aphorisms drawn from Ives's writings littered the program booklet audience members consulted over the course of the evening, a sampling of his well-known verbal incendiary. "The ears have to be on their own"; "The word 'beauty' is as easy to use as the word degenerate"; "That music must be heard is not essential—what it sounds like may not be what it is."[1]

But music would be heard—and it too reinforced the prevailing consensus about Ives. The repertoire implicitly invited comparison, for it juxtaposed the First Symphony, an early work composed under the tutelage of Horatio Parker, with *The Unanswered Question*, *Second Orchestral Set*, and "West London," which displayed celebrated Ivesian hallmarks: quotations, antiphonal collisions,

Figure 4.1 Yale's Woolsey Hall decked out for the Ives Centennial Festival-Conference, 1974. Courtesy Music Division, The New York Public Library for the Performing Arts, Astor, Lenox, and Tilden Foundations.

and harmonic unorthodoxies. At the end of the concert, the exhausted Yale student ensembles that had scrappily but enthusiastically negotiated this challenging repertoire quit the stage. The lights dimmed, and through the darkened hall drifted the sounds of "The Alcotts" from the "Concord" Sonata, as recorded by Ives himself in 1943. Serving as a musical benediction, the composer's idiosyncratic pianism stood in sharp timbral contrast to the preceding orchestral works. Here, offered in a composite of visual imagery, written word, and music, was the powerful but conventional vision of Ives: the archetypal American individualist, a fulfillment of the Emersonian mandate of abandoning the "courtly muses of Europe" and a testament to the freedoms—artistic and otherwise—of the United States.

It was a vision widely celebrated throughout the country in that centenary year. The birthday concert at Yale was the culminating, though not concluding, event of the five-day Charles Ives Centennial Festival-Conference, extending from October 17 to 21 and held under the joint auspices of Brooklyn College and Yale University. Earlier in October, the New York Philharmonic had presented its own Ives festival, comprised of a series of programs that paired works by Ives with those of other composers: Berg, Ravel, Bartók, Ruggles, Hindemith, Stravinsky, Rudhyar—arch-modernists to a man.[2] Further down the coast, the Governor of Florida designated the Miami-based Charles Ives Centennial Festival an official state event and linked it to the coming U.S. Bicentennial.[3] Organized by music critic F. Warren O'Reilly, the festival featured performances of nearly three quarters of Ives's oeuvre by local and national ensembles and soloists, scattered across the 1975–76 season. In the Midwest, at the University of Minnesota, a lively Ives Festival also transpired, the third in four years. On the Fourth of July, at the State fairgrounds of Danbury, Connecticut, Ives's hometown, Leonard Bernstein and Michael Tilson Thomas led the combined forces of the American Symphony Orchestra and several local ensembles through a program of the composer's music.[4] It was the grandest of homecomings.

While the centenary celebrations served as the capstone for the decades-long process that secured Ives a place in America's musical institutions, they also marked the moment at which fractures began to appear in the effigy of the composer that had stood essentially unaltered in the imaginations of his advocates since the fifties. The signs were visible even amid the Charles Ives Centennial Festival-Conference. A reporter for the magazine *Musical America* remarked that the conference sessions "drew up a clear battle line between older friends and colleagues of Ives, who had known and worked with him, and the bright young academicians who bore in on their subject with scholarly scalpel, lens to eye, and a big bag of accessory tools each from his own field of expertise."[5] The emphasis on the academic milieu of the younger participants was astute. Ives's earliest influential devotees—Henry Cowell, Nicolas Slonimsky, Peter Yates, Aaron Copland—were only occasionally affiliated with universities and colleges. Some among the next generation of Ives partisans, reaching their majority in the forties and fifties, did pursue careers dominated by academic appointments: John Kirkpatrick, before becoming the curator of the Ives collection at Yale University, had served as piano professor at several different institutions; Lou Harrison taught composition at various West Coast colleges; and Gilbert Chase interleaved stints in the foreign service with university appointments. None of these men, though, entered academia along the path that would become requisite for aspirants to the professoriate with the emergence of the big American research universities after the Second World War. They had not passed through graduate school, with its regimen of classes and exams culminating in a thesis project, and if they possessed a doctorate, it was honorary. Almost all the new voices that joined the discourse about Ives in the seventies had what has now become the indispensable lettered pedigree, from BA (or BM) to PhD. Equally important is the fact that the new cohort of Ivesians consisted largely of musicologists and historians, whereas previously, discussion about Ives had been the province of composers and performers. It would be surprising if a transition such as this, at once generational, professional, and institutional, failed to provoke tensions.

This chapter and the next will examine the contributions "bright young academicians" made to discourse about Ives, with particular attention to the methodological frameworks they brought to bear on the subject matter—their "scholarly scalpels." Each chapter covers the same twenty-year period, centered on the centenary and bounded roughly by Stokowski's premiere of the Fourth Symphony in 1965 and the publication of J. Peter Burkholder's *Charles Ives: The Ideas behind the Music* in 1985. This chapter focuses on historians, while the next is devoted to musicologists, an arrangement that reflects the chronological impact these two groups of scholars had on Ives's reception.

Particularly vulnerable to the scrutiny of historians was the long-standing trope of Ives the autonomous man, whose creative life was unimpeded by the cultural constraints that hobbled other Americans. The historian's wont is to create causal linkages, and whether those connections happen to be social, political, or intellectual, the net effect is to bind the subject matter to a specific context. Not the American constitution for its intrinsic virtues, but as a contribution to a trans-Atlantic, Enlightenment-era debate about the nature of good government; not Abraham Lincoln the venerable president, but the Whig turned Republican, whose ideas about race were transformed over the course of his career; not the Hoover Dam as architectural marvel, but as the product of complex political negotiations over infrastructure projects during the twenties and thirties. Thus, when historians examined Ives, instead of focusing on things that set him apart, they looked for correspondences between the composer and his contemporaries. This characteristic practice had its most dramatic and influential impact on Ives's reception through Frank Rossiter's *Charles Ives and His America* (1975). Rossiter, a Princeton-trained historian, fettered Ives with the challenges faced by Gilded Age men of his social class: he possessed their prejudices against professional artists, was forced to accommodate himself to the business culture in which they were expected to pursue careers, and shared their anxieties about the changes wrought by modernity. The composer had not been free at all—indeed, very much the opposite. He was, as Rossiter put it, "a virtual prisoner of his culture."[6] Most historians were not willing to go quite as far as Rossiter, but the principal legacy of their engagement with Ives was to give the composer roots in the loam of American culture, to make him part of a past that extended well beyond the bounds of provincial, postbellum Danbury and even transcendentalist Concord.

Setting the Scene: From the Fourth Symphony Premiere to the Centenary Celebrations

The long journey Ives made from obscurity to concert-hall mainstay was more or less complete with the premiere of the Fourth Symphony in April 1965. The performance, given by Leopold Stokowski and his American Symphony Orchestra, was greeted by unprecedented ballyhoo. The press avidly chronicled the complexities involved, from the painstaking editorial work of compiling a usable score, to the deployment of two assistant conductors to aid Stokowski in negotiating the symphony's antiphonal mash-ups. Once the noise of the premiere died away, what remained was the constant, steady hum of institutional machinery: regular performances of the major works, a growing catalogue of recordings, and a steady stream of reviews and commentaries—all signs that Ives had come to occupy an important place in the American classical-music canon. That place was secured by the symbols that had collected around his person, their potency deriving from resonances with widely held convictions about American identity.

Leonard Bernstein tapped this rich semiotic vein with the title of one of his Young People's Concerts: "Charles Ives: American Pioneer." Aired on Public Television in 1967, it featured Bernstein expatiating on the Yankee gumption of Ives, who braved the rugged musical wilderness and tackled problems that Europeans like Schoenberg and Stravinsky would not confront for several years afterward.[7] Critic and composer Eric Salzman pared back Bernstein's title even further for a 1968 article published in the magazine *Commentary*: "Charles Ives: American." It was not Ives's innovations that mattered most, Salzman opined, but rather that he "was the first important composer whose work stands essentially outside the received Western tradition—so far outside of it that—unlike Schoenberg or Stravinsky, for example—he did not have to overthrow and then labor mightily to rebuild." As such, Ives was free to incorporate whatever elements of the Western tradition he saw fit, an option that was closed to modernists, for whom tradition was an anathema and "making it new" a prerogative. Moreover, those elements coexisted with musics of wildly divergent pedigrees, resulting in a stylistic mélange full of complexities and contradictions. This Salzman relished—and for more than the aesthetic frisson it elicited. The complexity of Ives's scores, he explained, was "just the natural result of many different kinds of music, the conjunction of individual freedoms and free activities."[8] Ives was not only the quintessential American, his music was an embodiment of democratic American culture.

Or, that at least was how the editors of *Commentary* likely interpreted Salzman's article when they received it as a submission. During the fifties, *Commentary* had been one of the main forums in which prominent American intellectuals engaged in a discussion about individual autonomy vis-à-vis the tensions of the Cold War. Ives's music, with its bustling stylistic jumble, was a ready homology for the freedoms of democracy, and as shown in the previous chapter, it had been deployed in that capacity many times over. Salzman had something more modest in mind. Like a number of other university-trained composers of his generation (his pedigree was Princetonian), he had arrived at the conclusion that the ever more rarified refinements of serial technique, the main preoccupation of composers in academia, represented a musical cul-de-sac. Ives offered a way out—freedom—an alternative to serialism, and a historical precedent for the experiments with aleatory, quotation, and "pop art" that were beginning to flourish at the time.[9] Thus the autonomous Ives depicted by Salzman was at once salvation for the ossified musical practices of academe and the sound emanating from the "city on the hill" for Cold War propagandists.

The convergence of Cold War politics and Ives's reception dates back to the midfifties, and specifically to Henry and Sidney Cowell's *Charles Ives and His Music*. Until 1974, this book remained the sole monograph dedicated to the composer; it is thus not surprising to discover that it continued to exert a strong influence in the late sixties and seventies. Salzman explicitly credited the Cowells in the text of his article, and there are many other instances in which their presence is detectable, whether with a clear citation or not. Take, for example, a 1967 article titled "Charles Ives—Lonely American Giant," which appeared in *Gramophone*, a magazine targeted at classical-music record collectors. Here the fusion of Ives with the transcendentalist writers, which the Cowells catalyzed, was on display: "There was a high proportion of rough-hewn New England granite in his skeleton, as well as a conscious identification with the philosophical and literary heritage of Emerson and Thoreau and the New England philosophy of transcendentalism."[10] Now after years of neglect, the author pronounced with satisfaction, Ives was enjoying the public attention he deserved.

John McClure, who wrote the article, was in a position to make authoritative claims about Ives's popularity, for he was a business executive at Columbia Records. More Ives recordings were issued with the imprimatur of Columbia's Masterworks subdivision, which McClure oversaw, than that of any other label.[11]

By 1968, the company could boast an illustrious catalogue that included John Kirkpatrick's two recordings of the "Concord" Sonata (1948, 1968), Leonard Bernstein's recording of the Second Symphony, Stokowski's recordings of the Fourth Symphony, and a newly released box set containing all the symphonic works.[12] And boast it did: a Columbia advertisement that appeared in the Schwann catalogue, then the definitive reference source for the recording industry, featured an array of covers for the company's Ives offerings and the caption "A natural resource. The genius of Charles Ives" (Figure 4.2). This was McClure's article distilled down to an aphorism. The message to Schwann's readership was that Columbia had mined the New England granite, alchemically transformed it into vinyl, and now packaged it for the patriotic American consumer. Directing this enterprise from the loftiest heights of the company executive was McClure's boss, Goddard Lieberson, president of CBS/Records Group and an Ives aficionado since the thirties. Ives had another prominently placed music-industry champion in the person of Oliver Daniel, a producer and executive at Broadcast Music Inc. and a confidante of Leopold Stokowski. McClure, Lieberson, and Daniel were friends for Ives in high places, and though none of them contributed anything new to the nexus of ideas about the composer, their support was crucial to the Ives boom that lasted from the midsixties through the centenary year.

The most significant impetus to public discourse about the composer during the seventies was the desire to celebrate his 100th birthday. Ives well knew that festivals and other commemorative events loom large in our memories, like cognitive magnets that capture and organize vivid impressions along the field lines of shared experience. One need only think of his "Holidays" Symphony or the Fourth of July scenario of "Putnam's Camp," the second movement of *Three Places in New England*, both works in which the listener tumbles through sonic landscapes that surge in and out of definition. The urge is strong to memorialize through celebration, and, in the seventies, the classical-music world had much cause to do so: December 1970 was the bicentenary of the birth of Beethoven, whose position in the canonical pantheon was rivaled only by Bach and Mozart; June 1971 witnessed the 450th anniversary of the death of Josquin des Prez, a recent entrée to the pantheon and upon whom the highest accolades were now bestowed.[13] Lavish celebrations marked both occasions. An important precedent was set by the five-day Josquin International Festival-Conference, which was hosted by the Julliard School in New York and directed by Edward Lowinsky, one of the most prominent musicologists of the time. It featured a mixture of performances, workshops, and scholarly papers, the latter organized into sessions that addressed biographical matters, source studies, editing problems, and a number of other issues. The enormous success of the event was crowned by the publication of its proceedings in 1976. Among the attendees was musicologist H. Wiley

Figure 4.2. Advertisement for Ives recordings on the Columbia label, appearing in the *Schwann* catalogue, June 1967. Courtesy Sony Music Entertainment.

Hitchcock, who would use the Josquin Festival-Conference as a model for the Ives Centennial Festival-Conference, which took place three years later, in 1974.

Hitchcock had earned his spurs in the musicological world for scholarship on seventeenth-century French and Italian music, beginning with his 1954 dissertation, "The Latin Oratorios of Marc-Antoine Charpentier." But he had also interleaved occasional articles and reviews on American topics with his more substantial output of Baroque scholarship. Shortly after securing a professorship at Hunter College in 1961, Hitchcock was approached by Prentice Hall publishers about the prospects of overseeing a series of music-history textbooks. He agreed, planning to dedicate one of the volumes to the subject of American music. Faced with a dearth of musicologists equipped for the task of writing such a book, he decided to do it himself. I will have occasion to explore Hitchcock's *Music in the United States: A Historical Introduction* (1969) in the next chapter; for the moment, suffice it to say that the book proved enormously significant for American music historiography and marked a turning point in Hitchcock's career. Thereafter, his reputation as an Americanist tended to overshadow his Baroque scholarship. Notably, he founded the Institute for Studies in American Music (ISAM) at Brooklyn College, where he was appointed a professor in 1971 (after his death in 2007, the institute was renamed the H. Wiley Hitchcock Institute for Studies in American Music in his honor).[14] As the director of ISAM, Hitchcock set in motion the events that would lead to the Ives Centennial Festival-Conference.[15] He felt that the institute should do something to commemorate the centenary of Ives birth and, accordingly, convened an ad hoc committee early in 1973 to discuss the matter.

One of the members of this group was Vivian Perlis, who had met Hitchcock in the early fifties, when she was a graduate student at the University of Michigan.[16] Perlis credits her graduate years for awakening a cognizance of American music as a historical concept, the result of her interactions with the faculty and other students at the university who were interested in the musical past of the United States. During this period, she also encountered the music of Ives for the first time (on recordings) and felt an immediate affinity for it. That connection would not, however, lead directly to scholarly engagement with Ives: instead she traversed a circuitous and serendipitous route before becoming one of the most important Ives scholars of the seventies.[17]

Perlis left the University of Michigan with a master's degree in 1952 and subsequently devoted herself to motherhood, occasionally taking work as a harpist and pianist and teaching music-history courses. In 1967, to supplement her income, she took a position as a reference librarian at Yale University, where the Ives manuscripts were housed. She recollects becoming entranced by the curious unruliness of the manuscripts, the expressive scrawl across the well-worn pages. Her interest piqued, Perlis began to explore the collection, and, since Kirkpatrick had not yet assumed his position at Yale, she fell into the role of its de facto curator. When Julian Myrick, Ives's erstwhile business partner, contacted the library in 1968, explaining that he had materials that might be valuable to the collection, Perlis was the natural choice to make the trip to New York and assess the items.[18] It was this initial contact with Myrick that prompted Perlis's realization that there were still people alive who had known Ives and whose memories ought to be preserved for posterity—that and a nudge from Hitchcock, who had encouraged historians to use recording technology for just this sort of purpose in a 1968 article.[19] Thus began the Ives Project, which would involve the collection of interviews with fifty-eight people, the preparation of transcriptions, and, ultimately, the publication of Perlis's *Charles Ives Remembered* in 1974, which contained edited versions of the interviews. By early 1973, the final publication details for the book were being coordinated so that its release would occur in the centenary year.

The ISAM exploratory committee evolved into the Ives Society, which, led by Hitchcock and Perlis as president and vice president, respectively, served as the organizing body for the Festival-Conference.[20] The Ives community showed up in force, and many attendees sported a badge made especially for the occasion, declaring "Ives Thrives." Indeed he did, for this was a vibrant festival, marked by a level of excitement that one might aptly characterize as Ivesian. The concerts were often filled to capacity, and the well-attended conference sessions were notable for an animation and engagement rarely attendant upon such proceedings. But it was also fractious—and again, the adjective "Ivesian" is apropos. Although Hitchcock and Perlis had purposefully organized the festival so that it furnished exposure to different perspectives of the composer, they had anticipated neither the diversity of opinions nor the stridency with which some participants chose to express their convictions. Lawrence Wallach, a recent graduate of the musicology program at Columbia, likened the paper panels to the New England town-hall meetings, about which Ives had waxed so effusively. Reporting for *Current Musicology*, the graduate-student run journal of his alma mater, Wallach observed that conference presenters frequently met with opposing opinions from the audience:

> Polarities were the order of the day, all of which were articulated, debated, and left unresolved. They included views of Ives as 1) the theoretical and impractical philosopher-musician, vs. the canny, practical craftsman who knew just what he wanted; 2) the representative of his time, vs. the isolated and bewildered reactionary; 3) the spiritual giant, vs. the tortured neurotic; 4) the composer of self-contained, abstract, and universally available music, vs. the referential and regional tone-poet whose full significance can only be realized in an historical context; 5) the tonal and polytonal composer, vs. the serialist and grouper of pitch-classes; 6) the historical freak whose music is without precedent, vs. the heir to one hundred and fifty years of American musical traditions.[21]

The first view Wallach enumerated—"philosopher-musician"—bears closest resemblance to Ives as portrayed by the Cowells, and there are traces of their influence in some of the others. But there are also a number of perspectives listed here that I have yet to introduce—"bewildered reactionary," "tortured neurotic"—perspectives that were just beginning to make an impact on discourse about the composer.

A panel entitled "Ives and American Culture" proved to be one of the most contentious sessions. Two of the panelists, Frank R. Rossiter and Robert M. Crunden, were historians, and the papers they read presented competing revisionist portraits of the composer. Both scholars situated Ives amid the turmoil of the late nineteenth century, when the United States was transformed by unregulated capitalism, populist agitation, and reform activism; they disagreed, however, about the success with which the composer negotiated the challenges of his time. Gilbert Chase, who chaired the panel, drew attention to the pedigree of Rossiter and Crunden, observing that this was "the first time to the best of my knowledge that cultural historians have been given a major role in interpreting the life and work of a composer in the context of a predominantly musical conference."[22] Beyond invoking their disciplinary background, Chase did not offer an explanation for the impetus behind the revisionist approach characteristic of the historian interlopers. Nor did Rossiter and Crunden, apart from suggesting that that the broader historical perspective that they brought to bear on the subject of Ives served as a much-needed corrective. They were silent about the motivations for employing the specific tools they drew from their methodological arsenal. What went unacknowledged was the fact that historians were facing an upheaval within their discipline—an upheaval linked to the emergence of the New Left in the United States.

Imagining America: The Assumptions of Intellectual History and American Studies

Before describing the contributions historians made to Ives scholarship, it is first necessary to lay some groundwork by examining the structure and assumptions of their field and its connection to American Studies. Academic disciplines have a tendency to divide into fiefdoms, presided over by subdisciplinary specialists who negotiate boundaries with their neighbors even as they tend their own fields. Historians use a host of qualifiers to identify their domains. Consider, for example, a labor historian specializing in late-nineteenth-century England: one qualifier demarks geographic locale, another specifies time period, and still another identifies the kinds of issues that preoccupy the historian in question. It is the last of these that concerns me here, for this category of qualifier, perhaps because it is far less concrete than either place or time, has provoked some of the most hotly contested historiographical confrontations. The sixties and seventies witnessed a protracted skirmish between the practitioners of intellectual history and social history. It spilled over and redefined the amorphous terrain of cultural history, which was sometimes overlapping and sometimes contiguous with the two other subdisciplines. Among the many consequences was an imprecision of nomenclature, as the case of Frank Rossiter illustrates. He self-identified as an intellectual historian but was introduced at the Festival-Conference as a "cultural historian." To unravel the impact of this upheaval on Ives's reception, it is necessary to take a closer look at the profile of intellectual history in American academe, as well as that of its closely related kin, American Studies.

As a bona fide subdiscipline, intellectual history was a relative newcomer to the field, although its subject matter (ideas and the people who originate and develop them) had always been of concern to historians. Vernon L. Parrington's *Main Currents in American Thought*, the three volumes of which were published between 1927 and 1930, was the first attempt at a synopsis of the history of ideas in the United States. As such, it marked a departure from the norm of narratives structured around political events then found in most history monographs, surveys, and textbooks. In his trademark stately voice, which still makes his prose a pleasure to read, Parrington announced his purpose: "I have undertaken to give some account of the genesis and development in American letters of certain germinal ideas that have come to be reckoned traditionally American—how they came into being and how they were opposed, and what influence they have exerted in determining the form and scope of our characteristic ideals and institutions."[23] This grand endeavor depended on two major assumptions about American culture, first, that it was distinct from European culture (despite historical linkages) and, second, that it was coherent in nature. There was an "American mind," and the habits of thought characteristic of that mind, its handling of conflict and resolution, could be discerned by examining the work of the foremost American intellectuals, from John Cotton to F. Scott Fitzgerald. These assumptions constitute what historian Gene Wise dubs the "Parrington Paradigm," and he distills it even further to a single postulate: "America is revealed most profoundly in its 'high' culture."[24]

Parrington's work remained a lonely outlier until the forties, when it was joined by Ralph Gabriel's *The Course of American Democratic Thought* (1940) and Merle Curti's *Growth of American Thought* (1943). Though the appearance of these three books was significant for the discipline, intellectual historians in the United States tend to identify as their locus classicus Perry Miller's *The New England Mind*, comprised of two volumes subtitled *The Seventeenth Century* (1939) and *From Colony to Province* (1953). Prior to the appearance of the first volume, the rubric *intellectual history* was not in wide usage—among either English-language scholars or their colleagues on the European continent. Miller set the precedent for embracing the term, explicitly placing his study under its ambit in his foreword. In

The New England Mind, he at once narrowed and extended Parrington's assumption about intellectuals being the bedrock of the culture in which they lived. He reduced the scope from nation to section, but treated the ideas of Puritan divines holistically, ranging well beyond the political theories that were Parrington's main concern. As historian Felix Gilbert observes of Miller, he "demonstrated that a change in one area of thought involves a realignment of thought and action in all other spheres. The assumption on which Miller's 'intellectual history' is based and which distinguishes his treatment from previous ones is that of the interconnected character of man's concept of life."[25]

The ascendancy of intellectual history was closely entwined with the emergence of American Studies in the forties and fifties. Intellectual historians were an important constituency within the confederacy of scholars allied under the American Studies banner, which, from the moment it was raised, was celebrated as interdisciplinary. In practice, though, American Studies remained comfortably situated at the interstices between history and literature. The texts that became canonical for the field were mostly the work of scholars with backgrounds in history or English departments—F. O. Matthiessen's *American Renaissance* (1941), Henry Nash Smith's *Virgin Land: The American West as Symbol and Myth* (1950), and David M. Potter's *The People of Plenty* (1954), to name three of them. This bias was also reflected in the contents of *American Quarterly*, first published in 1949 and the organ of the American Studies Association after the organization was chartered in 1951. The visual arts, music, and dance made only occasional appearances in early issues of the journal, which gave pride of place to literature, philosophy, and politics.

The assumption about the cultural centrality of intellectuals that undergirded the work of Parrington and Miller was transferred to the first generation of American Studies scholars, whether their pedigree was literary or historical. Exemplary in this regard was Henry Nash Smith, who held a master's from the English department at Harvard and the first PhD from the same institution's "History of American Civilization" program, founded in 1937. The subtitle of Smith's book *Virgin Land: The American West as Symbol and Myth* supplied the appellation "myth and symbol" that came to designate the practices of the literary scholars who first identified themselves with American Studies.[26]

A myth or symbol, as Smith explained, is an "intellectual construction that fuses concept and emotion into an image." In American culture, one such symbol was "the West," which had occupied a prominent place in the American mind from the colonial period to the late nineteenth century, when Frederic Jackson Turner postulated his famous thesis about the role of the frontier in American history. In *Virgin Land*, Smith set out to explore this myth, following Parrington's precedent by using source material associated with "high" culture, the writings of Thomas

Jefferson, Thomas Hart Benton, and James Fenimore Cooper, most notably. But he also devoted a considerable amount of space to dime novels, exploring the mythology of Western heroes like Deadwood Dick and Buffalo Bill. Smith was self-conscious about dipping into such "lowbrow" fare but argued that dime novels were useful because they tend "to become an objectified mass dream, like the moving pictures, the soap operas, or the comic books that are the present-day equivalents."[27] Thus, the myth of "the West" percolated down from the highbrow to the lowbrow sphere, a unitary phenomenon in the American mind.

There was a similar consensus about the coherence of American culture among some of the historians who were Smith's colleagues and contemporaries. Here too, Parrington loomed large, for again the assumption was that intellectuals provided the most cogent expressions of the American mind. But whereas Parrington had traced the developmental trajectory of that mind through points of conflict, these historians argued that it had assumed a fixed and coherent form early in the colonial period. In his influential book *The Genius of American Politics* (1953), Daniel J. Boorstin advanced the thesis that Americans shared a sense of "givenness," a "belief that that values in America are in some way or other automatically defined: *given* by certain facts of geography or history peculiar to us." This shared belief ran as a consistent thread through the history of the United States. It even persisted beneath the surface turbulence of such a momentous event as the American Revolution. Boorstin argued that the Revolution had not been undertaken with a view to imposing a new method of organizing society but rather to restore certain rights granted by the British Constitution and common law. When read in context, the Declaration of Independence "appears a document of imperial legal relations rather than a piece of high-flown political philosophy." Compared to the French Revolution, its impetus was conservative—a desire to restore the status quo ante. The recourse of the founding fathers to existing legal principle was an extension of a general pragmatic attitude, born of the unique challenges that Americans confronted in their natural environment. The Puritans had arrived in the New World with a preformed (European) social dogma, but within two or three generations, it had been revised to meet the exigencies of the "howling wilderness." "The Nazis and Communists," Boorstin observed, "started with blueprints for society and turned to technology as the only means to attain their ends. For our political thought it has been a happy fact that the opposite was true. Nature had to be mastered before society could even survive." Direct confrontation with the land in all its vastness was a solvent to the political theorizing of European revolutionaries. Clearly, Boorstin's work was influenced by the politics of the Cold War, traces of which are also evident in the scholarship of a number of other prominent historians who shared his convictions about the homogeneity of the American past.[28]

A critical 1959 article, entitled "The Cult of the 'American Consensus': Homogenizing our History" and published in *Commentary* magazine, birthed the term *consensus history* that has become ineluctably linked to this cohort. Historian John Higham, author of the article, was disturbed by the essentializing tendency in the work of Boorstin, Richard Hofstadter, David Potter, and Louis Hartz. Higham acknowledged that the efforts of this group had not been coordinated, but they nonetheless converged on a conservative national identity for Americans, marked by its indifference to the utopian ideologies of the far right and left. For these historians, there was, Higham explained, "a unifying framework of ideas and values [that] had created a distinctive American people [and] explained the durability of their society and institutions." Higham complained that the proponents of "American Consensus" had papered over the very real fractures of the past and the multiplicity of the peoples inhabiting the United States. "The conservative frame of reference," he argued, "creates a paralyzing incapacity to deal with the elements of spontaneity, effervescence, and violence in American history."[29] This criticism would grow in time, but for the moment, the assumptions about the unitary nature of the American mind were in ascendancy, the Parrington paradigm governing the "consensus historians" and the "myth and symbol" school alike. With the disciplinary framework laid bare, it is now possible to evaluate the influences of American Studies and intellectual history on Ives's reception, each of which will be taken up in turn.

Ives and American Studies

After Harvard established its "History of American Civilization" doctoral program, American Studies proliferated at universities throughout the country. By 1970, according to the annual survey conducted on behalf of the American Studies Association, there were 168 such programs in the United States.[30] The name Charles Ives, however, had only recently begun to register among the members of the growing American Studies community. And, in keeping with the literary predilections of the discipline, it was Ives's prose that first attracted attention. A 1963 review of Howard Boatwright's edition of *Essays Before a Sonata* marked Ives's debut in the pages of *American Quarterly*.[31] Still, he remained a nominal presence in that journal until the publication of Audrey Davidson's article "Transcendental Unity in the Works of Charles Ives" in 1970.[32]

Davidson was a graduate student at the University of Minnesota, where, unusual for the time, some of the music courses interfaced with the American Studies program on campus. The connection was fostered by Johannes Riedel, a musicologist who displayed (also unusual for the time) a catholicity of scholarly interests, from the music of the Weimar Republic to folk-music traditions of South

America. Riedel offered a sequence of American Music courses that commandeered the framework characteristic of American Studies. Two of his students attempted a distillation of that framework in a brief overview of the university's American music offerings:

> One of the basic concepts stressed in [American Studies] . . . is the interrelationship of all parts of American culture. It is assumed that artistic expression, like religious, political, and social institutions, should be studied for cultural meaning. Art forms incorporate materials and ideas from all the other institutions of a culture, often demonstrating the great preoccupations and cultural values of an age. A student in *American Studies* approaches the arts within a cultural framework, and uses the knowledge he gains about them to confirm, alter, or expand his previous conceptions of that culture.[33]

Once again, the familiar premise: American culture comprises a single entity and changes in one of its parts are necessarily reflected in the others.

The principal way in which Riedel and his students fulfilled the American Studies prerogative of linking Ives to other facets of American culture was to reinforce his connection with transcendentalism. In the *Charles Ives Primer* that Riedel coauthored with his composer colleague Robert Oudal, transcendentalist aesthetics took precedence. Oudal and Riedel supplied a précis of Concordian thought, demonstrating that its central goal was "to show the basic one-ness of the subjective man with objective nature." Ives, they asserted, was so committed to this view that it "permeates all phases of his outlook on life." As corroboration, they cited Ives's essay "The Majority" and quoted from Henry and Sidney Cowell's *Charles Ives and His Music*, which was responsible for securing the primacy of the transcendentalist Ives trope in the first place.[34] Approaching the subject from a somewhat different angle, Audrey Davidson, in her *American Quarterly* article, invoked transcendentalist aesthetics to explain Ives's usage of the word *unity*. It was a mistake, she insisted, to understand that term as meaning structural completeness and coherence, an error made by two of Ives's more prominent critics, Copland and Carter. What was required instead, was a redefinition of the term, more consistent with the intuitive, nature-inspired vision of unity found in transcendentalist thought.[35]

But while certifying Ives's transcendentalist credentials was the main occupation of the Minnesotan scholars who employed the American Studies methodology, some of them did venture comparisons between Ives and other major American figures. Colleen C. Davidson, another alumnus of Riedel's classes, devoted a lengthy two-part article to establishing connections between the career of Ives and the novelist Winston Churchill. Both men, she argued, were infused with the progressive spirit of their era; in their works, "we have a dramatization of the Progressive attempts to define what was right (natural) and what was wrong (unnatural) in the American experience with the intention of formulating some all-encompassing solution that would bring Americans back to the happy purity of the early Republic."[36] Incidentally, the definition of progressivism Davidson employed was derived from Richard Hofstadter's *Age of Reform*, one of the canonical American Studies texts and the work of a scholar I identified earlier with "consensus history." Other Riedel pupils compared Ives with William Faulkner and Henry Adams.[37] The possibilities multiplied, made legitimate by a methodology that postulated the coherence of American culture, even as its adherents might celebrate the lack of coherence (at least in traditional musical terms) of Ives's music.

This trait is also evident in American Studies scholarship devoted to Ives that issued from the University of Texas at Austin, another institution that proved hospitable to the composer.[38] In the early seventies, two doctoral students at the university produced dissertations devoted to Ives. Historian Robert M. Crunden, an American Studies faculty member, served on both of their supervisory committees and would himself author several books in which the composer would figure prominently. Rosalie Sandra Perry's dissertation, "Charles Ives and American Culture" (1971), was completed under the joint auspices of the American Studies and music departments, and Crunden was her principal advisor. By comparison, Charles Ward's dissertation, "Charles Ives: The Relationship between Aesthetic Theories and Compositional Processes" (1974), was more strictly a musicological affair, and for this reason I will postpone its consideration to the next chapter. (Ward did his graduate work in the music department, and Crunden played only a subsidiary role in the writing of his thesis as out-of-department committee member.)

A lightly revised version of Perry's dissertation was published in 1974, part of the crop of midseventies Ives monographs that joined the Cowells' book, which, for nearly two decades, had sat singly on library shelves. The substance of Perry's book hinged on an assertion: "Ives was alert, intelligent, and well-read, the kind of man who was very much the product of intellectual trends and impulses in American civilization." Her objective was to show parallels between the ideas Ives propounded in his various writings (and, insofar as they are possible to glean, his music) to constellations of contemporaneous ideas that were circulating among American intellectuals: the legacy of transcendentalism, the notion of the stream of consciousness, the implications of realism (artistic and otherwise), and pragmatism. The connections were woven, where possible, around references to authors that Ives himself made, but frequently Perry forayed into writings for which there was no evidence of the composer's direct acquaintance. That Ives was "intelligent" and "well-read" was license enough for her to make such connections. To partake of the discourse of American intellectuals, she assumed, was to be wholly caught up by the "intellectual trends and impulses in American civilization," whether one was directly aware of them all or not. Thus, even though Ives never referenced Margaret Fuller, William James, and Charles Sanders Peirce (to name only a handful of the luminaries who make cameo appearances in the dissertation), Perry assumed that their ideas were in the air, as it were, and thus readily accessible to a man of Ives's intellect. The issue of agency—how Ives might have been exposed to various "intellectual trends and impulses"—she passed over rapidly.[39] Perry's work testifies to the vitality of the Parrington paradigm: the notion of a coherent American mind, a unity despite its many currents, legitimizing the assumption that all educated Americans partook of the ideas that coursed through its synapses.

Traces of Parrington are also detectable in the work of Perry's erstwhile advisor, Robert M. Crunden, whose debut as an interlocutor in discourse about Ives took place in 1972. That year witnessed the publication of his third book, *From Self to Society, 1919–1941*, and a highly critical review of Frank Rossiter's dissertation. Both reveal Crunden to have had an omnivorous cross-disciplinary appetite and a predilection for a methodology that relied on men and women "representative of a general position" to chart the course of larger ideas in American intellectual history. In the book, potted biographies of intellectuals and artists coupled with brief synopses of their ideas served to support a thesis about a shift in emphasis from the individual to the community in the interwar period. Although *From Self to Society* was typical of American Studies for harnessing figures as diverse as John Dewey, Margaret Mead, and Ernest Hemingway to its purposes, it was unusual in incorporating composers in the train. Crunden explicitly drew attention to the neglect musicians had suffered at the hands of past historians: "Despite the publication of a number of useful memoirs, and the wide popularity of some of their work, American musicians have never received their due in the cultural history of modern America." To begin correcting this imbalance, he included a chapter that juxtaposed George Antheil and Edgard Varèse with Alfred Stieglitz, John Marin, and Eugene O'Neill. And, in the briefest of references, he adumbrated his strategy for incorporating Ives into a broader narrative about turn-of-the-century American culture. In the twenties, he observed, the music of Ives remained "unpublished and unheard in a confused and dusty pile in the same room where it had been written." It was one of the neglected "legacies of the progressive era" awaiting later discovery.[40] The implication was that Ives was as much a "representative man" of the progressive period as Antheil and Varèse were emblematic of the twenties. Crunden's subsequent activities within the world of Ives scholarship were largely governed by the project of refiguring Ives as a progressive.

The paper Crunden read at the Centennial Festival-Conference as part of the "Ives and American Culture" panel provided the blueprint. He began by attacking Ives literature for the way it made the composer an isolated figure, or, as he put it colorfully, "some kind of freak." The problem was the obverse of the one he had identified in *From Self to Society*: the failure of writers about music to look beyond the bounds of American musical culture. It was not Ives's musical contemporaries who provided the best point of comparison but men and women who had "creative careers" in other fields: educational psychology, politics, and business administration. These were the progressives, and they were linked by a shared set of biographical and social traits. Progressivism, Crunden explained, was an outgrowth of Protestantism, its participants largely a product of New England and their reformist agenda reflecting the deep-seated religious values characteristic of that part of the country. Typically, progressive reforms treated society as an aggregate of individuals and thus tended, as Crunden put it, "to see social problems as personal problems writ large." It was idealistic in the sense that it was "always measuring reality against some abstract standard," but the reform mechanisms devised by its adherents were typically pragmatic in nature. To certify Ives's membership in this group, Crunden cited various passages from *Essays Before a Sonata* and *Memos*. He pointed to Ives's commitment to actuarial "laws of averages," direct democracy, and the limitations on personal property. All of these commitments suggested that Ives was the kindred spirit of Woodrow Wilson, Theodore Roosevelt, and Jane Addams.[41]

The word *progressive* was not wholly alien to Ives's reception; however, past commentators had tended to use it in its more general sense, referring to the stylistic innovations of Ives's music rather than putative connections with social and political movements. The two notable exceptions were Colleen Davidson, one of the University of Minnesota Ivesians, and Perry, Crunden's pupil. What linked these three scholars, even though Crunden seems to have been unaware of Davidson's work (her 1968 article is absent from his citations), is a shared theoretical framework. They approached Ives from the American Studies perspective, which made it possible to jump confidently from the composer to his prominent contemporaries in the literary, political, or psychological worlds. The concept of a unitary American culture was the abstract basis for such leaps, and their practical execution depended on terms like progressivism, pragmatism, and realism. These isms did the work of binding together the convictions of people engaged in vastly different fields of endeavor, no matter how dim their awareness of one another might be. Even transcendentalism, a hoary trope of Ives criticism, underwent a transformation at the hands of American Studies scholars. It remained a set of philosophical principles to which Ives subscribed, but now there was an additional emphasis on the link among people who shared those principles, beyond the foundational group of Concordians. Literary scholar Raymond Ge-selbracht, for example, wrote about a second outburst of transcendentalism at the end of the nineteenth century, manifest in the music of Ives, the architecture of Frank Lloyd Wright, and the choreography of Isadora Duncan.[42] Again, the names proliferate.

Ever since the publication of Henry and Sidney Cowell's *Charles Ives and His Music*, commentators had been in the habit of stressing Ives's autonomy. The standard image was of a composer who soared gloriously free of the concerns and constraints of society. The work of American Studies scholars—the Minnesotans, the Texans, and a handful of others scattered across the country—began to alter that image, fixing tethers to Ives, pulling him to lower altitudes where he might mingle with a company of his most august contemporaries. What persisted in the work of these scholars was the celebratory tone that had always been a hall-mark of Ives partisans. It was something that came naturally to American Studies scholars, for their field was born of the populist nationalism of the thirties and bolstered by wartime patriotism. The celebration reached an apogee with the work of the "consensus historians" in the fifties, who wrote sober paeans to the American spirit for its apparent immunity to the utopian dreams that had violently derailed European history. Perry and Crunden were working a generation later, and although they might write of the late nineteenth century that it was marked by the "decaying sentimentality of a borrowed Victorianism," as Perry did, they celebrated the energies of reform and renewal represented by the progressive movement. Theirs was not an unnuanced affirmation of American culture, but when it came to the American arts and letters, hortatory habits died hard. It is no wonder then that Crunden proved to be one of strongest critics of Frank R. Rossiter, who had a much darker vision of American culture.

Ives and Intellectual History

Rossiter received his AB in 1959 from Harvard University, where, as a history major, he was afforded the opportunity of taking classes with the paterfamilias of intellectual history, Perry Miller. He went on to pursue a masters in education at the University of Pennsylvania in the early sixties, but, after graduating, decided instead to embark on an academic career, entering the PhD program in history at Princeton University in the fall of 1965. Around this time, Rossiter became acquainted with the music of Ives, taking part, as he put it, in "the great upsurge of interest" in the composer.[43] The fusion of his musical and historical interests first occurred in a paper about Ives that he wrote for a seminar led by Civil War historian James McPherson.[44] The paper, in turn, led to a dissertation entitled "Charles Ives and American Culture: The Process of Development, 1874–1921," which he completed in 1970 under the supervision of Martin Duberman, with McPherson serving on the advisory committee. By the fall of 1974, when Rossiter participated in the Ives Centennial Festival-Conference, he had been an assistant professor at the University of Michigan, Ann Arbor for four years and was in the midst of his tenure review.

Even before delivering his paper at the conference session, Rossiter was aware that his research could have an unsettling effect on Ives partisans. Nearing the end of his dissertation in 1970, he had shown completed portions of the document to John Kirkpatrick, who had aided him in negotiating the complexities of the Ives collection at Yale University. Kirkpatrick was nonplussed by what he read and raised his concerns with Rossiter on multiple occasions. The reaction alarmed Rossiter, especially since Kirkpatrick had agreed to submit an evaluation of the thesis to the Princeton History department. In a letter to his advisor, Rossiter worriedly reported, "Kirkpatrick has been at me again. It seems I am debunking Ives and making statements that show no sense of standards, etc. He thinks I am well-meaning but misguided. Heaven knows what he'll write in the evaluation that he's going to send you. I haven't shown him the Conclusion yet."[45] Rossiter's trepidation about the response his conclusions might meet was warranted, for he projected a negative reflection of the view of Ives that Kirkpatrick had long touted. As it turns out though, Kirkpatrick was the consummate professional and, apart from criticizing the "existentialist" tone of the dissertation, his evaluation lauded Rossiter.[46] This did not mean that his misgivings about Rossiter's work were put to rest. Indeed, they surfaced again at the Festival-Conference, where Rossiter presented a paper that synthesized the argument of his dissertation. When voiced, Kirkpatrick's grievances resonated with the reactions of others in attendance. He accused the historian of being a "thoroughly convinced materialist" and of having omitted "the most central fact of Ives's life—that is, its being centered in a spiritual faith."[47]

Indeed, Rossiter had downplayed transcendentalism, to which Kirkpatrick was undoubtedly referring, and instead focused on the psychological impact of American attitudes toward music on Ives. The portrait he offered was without precedent in Ives's reception—much of the reason for the shock it provoked. But the ideas that shaped the portrait, imbuing it with unique textures and shadings, have a lineage that can be traced back to the work of his advisor, Martin Duberman, and beyond, to Richard Hofstadter.

I have fleetingly introduced Hofstadter as a practitioner of consensus history, following the precedent set by John Higham, who first coined the term. But, as a number of scholars have observed, it is not an easy fit for Hofstadter.[48] Like his supposed consensus confreres, he did tend to treat the conflicts of American history as having played out within a fixed frame of shared ideological assumptions.

In fact, the preface to his *The American Political Tradition* (1948) provided the earliest itemization of those assumptions and thus marked the advent of consensus historiography.[49] But unlike Boorstin, Hartz, and other historians who projected ideological homogeneity deep into the American past, Hofstadter was reluctant to celebrate consensus as an unmitigated good. Historian Alan Brinkley writes of Hofstadter that he "recognize[d] that the narrow range of acceptable opinion in American politics, and the centrality within that range of the acquisitive values of competitive capitalism, exacted a significant price—both from the nation's public discourse and from the private lives of its people."[50] Assessing the effects of the toll is the main item of business in Hofstadter's influential *The Age of Reform: From Bryan to F. D. R* (1955), which, not incidentally, was a perennial favorite of Rossiter's, alongside Perry's *The New England Mind* (both were featured regularly in his course reading assignments).

The novelty of *The Age of Reform* lay in its invocation of psychology as a historical explicans. Hofstadter had read widely in the behavioral sciences and sought to apply what he had learned to the populist and progressive movements of the late nineteenth and early twentieth centuries. The populists, he argued, were motivated by their psychological investment in the agrarian myth, the notion that "[t]he American tradition of democracy was formed on the farm and in small villages, and its central ideas were founded in rural sentiments and on rural metaphors." The myth had literary origins, born of the minds of English and American intellectuals, the architects of an imaginary pastoral populated by independent yeoman, whose lives were unmarred by pecuniary demands. But if the myth had little basis in reality (most farmers worked within the system of commercial agriculture and had done so since the middle of the nineteenth century), it could still galvanize a movement of aggrieved late-nineteenth-century rural Americans who discovered that their livelihoods were enchained to the vacillations of the stock market. The progressive movement was also rooted in a psychology of loss arising from the economic transformations of the period. Here though, it was not livelihoods that were threatened, but status. Men who occupied positions that had long been respected—Hofstadter's list included "the old gentry, the merchants of long standing, the small manufacturers, the established professional men, the civic leaders of an earlier era"—discovered that they no longer held the reins of power. "Conditions varied from profession to profession," Hofstadter explained, "but all groups with claims to learning and skill shared a common sense of humiliation and common grievances against the plutocracy." In short, the psychological effect of seeing long-held certitudes unravel was the stimulus for two of the most important turn-of-the-century social movements.[51] Over the subsequent years, the arguments that Hofstadter advanced in *The Age of Reform* proved unable to withstand scrutiny. The book remained influential for its methodology, however, and, in Hofstadter's wake, other American historians turned to the behavioral sciences for theories that would help them explain historical phenomena.[52]

Among them was Martin Duberman, who was just embarking on his career in the early sixties and had gained a reputation for trenchant scholarship on the abolitionist movement. As Duberman observed in a 1962 essay, older historians had tended to portray the abolitionists as impractical visionaries, fanatics whose zealotry reflected the deficiencies of their character rather than a genuine commitment to the freedom of African American slaves. But the research he conducted for his biographies of Charles Francis Adams and James Russell Lowell, one man a sympathizer with the abolitionists and the other a full-fledged participant in the movement, revealed personalities of a very different sort. Historians, Duberman was forced to conclude, had been quick to generalize about group behavior based on paltry evidence and without regard for the range of temperaments represented in the movement. As he put it, "We know far too little about why men do anything—let alone why they do something as specific as joining a reform movement—to assert as confidently as historians have, the motives of whole groups of men." To rectify this shortcoming, Duberman did not suggest that historians abandon the analysis of groups, though he did stipulate that legitimate efforts of this sort would require proficiency with "the techniques of sociology and other related disciplines." Instead, he encouraged a greater attentiveness to individual personalities and suggested that ego psychology might provide the necessary methodological rigor.[53] In Duberman's own work, the formal absorption of ego psychology remained notional, and, by the early seventies, his interest had dissolved, in no small part due to the abysmal failure of psychotherapy to help him come to grips with his own homosexuality.[54] Nonetheless, it left a residue, a preoccupation with the interplay between the psychology of individuals and the social demands imposed on them by the movements in which they participate and the institutions to which they belong.

The same preoccupation is also evident in Duberman's pupil Frank Rossiter. His dissertation unfolds as a psychodrama, and its main theme is the tragic consequence of an artist internalizing the conservative values of his social milieu. This was Ives's tragedy, so Rossiter declared, presenting an argument that upended the conventional view of the composer: "Far from being an 'autonomous' man, Ives was a prisoner of his culture; his attachment to certain American values and institutions was so complete and so literal as to narrow and stifle his career as a creative artist." To substantiate this bold claim, Rossiter set about reevaluating the composer's biography, focusing especially on the decision to pursue a career in business rather than music. Ives's explanation (that American musical culture was conservative, Eurocentric, and provincial, and thus inhospitable to an artist with an experimental bent) did not pass muster with Rossiter. Instead, he argued that a music career had never been a live option. In the nineteenth century, he explained, social mores made music largely the enthusiasm of women, catered to by a handful of professional men who were either European or, if American, the recipients of European training. Thus, despite the fact that George Ives had been much vaunted by his son and his son's enthusiasts, this lone member of the Ives clan to pursue a semiprofessional music career was, in the eyes of his contemporaries, a failure: fathers and sons were expected to show their mettle in the business world, not in the feminized (and thus suspect) sphere of music. Rossiter argued, "Ives accepted the connotations of sociosexual effeminacy that American males attached to all cultivated-tradition music and thus allowed an emotional barrier to form between himself and such music."[55] Here, Rossiter owed a debt to H. Wiley Hitchcock, who had descried the gendered quality of nineteenth-century American musical culture without exploring its implications for Ives's career.[56]

Beyond transforming the decision to pursue music as an avocation into an inevitability, Rossiter also called into question the protomodernist interpretation of Ives's music. This interpretation was central to what Rossiter would dub in the revised, published version of his dissertation, the "Ives Legend" (the constituent tropes are listed in my introduction).[57] Modernists had been the composer's first champions, and it was the innovations in the music that initially attracted and held their attention. Rossiter, however, was more interested in the expressive goals of the music than its techniques (what Ives would call the substance rather than manner), and in these he found a decidedly conservative bent. Ives's output did not take the musical vernacular of his hometown as the launching point for a defiant leap into the musical future. Instead, for all its oddities, it was music saturated with the sepia hues of nostalgia. The imagined musical Danbury that serves as its gravitational center was not the Danbury of Charles Ives's childhood—a city that was experiencing the kind of industrialization and ethnic diversification characteristic of many urban centers in late-nineteenth-century America:

> The music is not concerned with the life of a rapidly growing small city, with its business and professional men, mill workers, immigrants, manufacturing, and railroads. Instead, it presents elements that were already outmoded or fast disappearing when Ives was growing up—farmers, camp meetings, barn dances. It was not so much his own boyhood that Ives was telling about, but rather that of his father before the Civil War—when Danbury had still been rural, Emerson had lectured at the Lyceum, farmers had come to town meetings to speak their minds, and men had been sturdy and independent.

Ives, in other words, was trying to relive the past of his father, and in doing so (though Rossiter did not spell it out explicitly), sought to validate a life that others had deemed a failure.[58]

The most shocking passage of Rossiter's dissertation appears in the conclusion he had so agonized about showing to John Kirkpatrick. Here he took the full measure of Ives's America by comparing it with the Soviet Union under Stalin. Cold War ideologues on either side of the Iron Curtain had reveled in just such comparisons, and, on many occasions, Ives had been commandeered as an icon of American freedom. But Rossiter turned the argument on its head. He rehearsed the familiar events surrounding Shostakovich's censure by Soviet officialdom in the thirties and the so-called Zhdanovschina of the late forties. But instead of indicting Soviet heavy-handedness and totalitarian censorship, he used these events as a mirror to reflect the constraints imposed on artists in the United States. Structurally speaking, Rossiter argued, there were similarities between American society at the turn of the century and the Soviet Union at midcentury. Both were in the throes of massive economic change and to cope, they brought pressures to bear on their "most gifted members," forcing them "to bend their efforts to the common purpose and not to go wandering away in private and irrelevant ventures." Past claims about musical independence and personal autonomy notwithstanding, Ives was just as much in thrall to the mores of Gilded Age America as the composers of the Soviet Union were captive to Communist Party dictates.[59]

Rossiter went further. He drew analogies between the dogma of Soviet realism and gendered American discourse about music, both of which involved vigilant policing of the arts for signs of "decadence." And, stepping into terrain that might well have been treacherous a decade and a half earlier, he argued that the means by which American society controlled its citizenry were far more insidious than those deployed by the Soviet Union. While the pressure to conform was externally imposed for Shostakovich, Prokofiev, and the other composers who were victims of Zhdanov's crackdown, Ives was subject to internal pressures:

> Ives imposed on his music and on his life as an artist an extramusical ideology that reflected the dominant values of American society at the turn of the century. And this ideology was similar in many respects to the official ideology that was imposed later upon Soviet composers; both were products of societies tightly organized to resist decadence. That Ives voluntarily imposed such an ideology upon himself is evidence of the greater effectiveness of the American system of "indoctrination."

Thus was the prophet of American musical independence laid low, victim of the very society that anticommunist intellectuals had championed as a bastion against tyranny and totalitarianism.[60]

In the paper he delivered at the Centennial Festival-Conference, Rossiter did not include his comparison between the constraints of gendered discourse about the arts in the United States and the Zhdanovschina in the Soviet Union. The provocation was enough, even without it. A perturbed Aaron Copland launched the contentious question-and-answer session: "What amazes me is how this cranky man you have depicted, so full of kinks and peculiarities, could have created this *music*! . . . It's the most unusual and most individual creation, coming out of such a background and environment, and that mystery I don't think is going to be solved very soon." Gilbert Chase, who had staked his claim on Ives as the culmination of a Whiggish narrative of American music history, added resoundingly, "Long live the mystery!"[61] And then came Kirkpatrick's accusation that Rossiter was a "thoroughly convinced materialist."

The response to the book version of the dissertation, simply titled *Charles Ives and His America* and published in 1975, was more varied, some critics extolling it, others expressing reservations. Rossiter had ameliorated the polemical tone by substituting the label "An Interpretation" for "Conclusion," retreating into the ambivalent language of the subjective. Still, *Charles Ives and His America* stood out dramatically from anything else that had been written about Ives, a portrait suffused by a dark palette of colors. A few readers even detected an agenda that went beyond situating Ives in his cultural context. Historian John W. Barker observed, "In presenting his picture of Ives, Rossiter really wishes us to go beyond it and confront serious questions and judgments on our whole society. It was that society from which Ives learned to be ashamed of art as 'effete, unmanly, and undemocratic.'"[62]

Barker was close to the mark. A small sheaf of letters dating from the midseventies confirms that Rossiter was indeed tilting at more than the orthodoxies of Ives's reception. His transformation of the composer into a victim—a transformation largely responsible for unfavorable responses to his work—was not simply the gratification of a "boyish glee at throwing shockers," as Kirkpatrick diagnosed it.[63] Something far more serious and personal was at stake. The subject of Ives furnished Rossiter with an opportunity to explore the psychological repercussions of a predicament that bore a close resemblance to what he confronted daily, along with millions of other Americans: how to live as a gay man in a society that placed his desires beyond the pale of decency. Like the Ives he imagined, gay men of Rossiter's generation were forced to suppress their true identities, condemned either to the closet or to marginalization, discrimination, and (something Ives never faced) criminalization.

The letters in question were addressed to Rossiter's erstwhile advisor, Martin Duberman. The pair had not been in regular contact after Rossiter graduated from Princeton, but a book review Duberman wrote for the *New York Times* early in 1974 served as the impetus for renewed correspondence. The subject of the review was the "social autobiography" of American socialist Michael Harrington, *Fragments of a Century*. Duberman was deeply critical of Harrington's decision to address only those aspects of his life that he deemed manifestations of larger social trends, passing over more personal matters—his relationship with his wife, his nervous breakdown. "To suggest that the public and private realms are dichotomous," Duberman declared, "is to block our understanding of those intra/interpersonal elements that are a critical dimension of every political enterprise."[64] Although it may not have occurred to him to do so, Duberman could well have supported this contention by pointing to his own book *Black Mountain: An Exploration in Community* (1972). In this study of the short-lived midcentury college, Duberman revealed his own homosexuality and demonstrated acuity for ferreting out the sexual politics of the institution, particularly its homophobic double standards.[65] Here, the personal and presumably private (by Harrington's criteria) informed the professional and public analysis of a seasoned historian. Duberman's subsequent dual career as active member and chronicler of the gay rights movement was a testimony to the erroneousness of dichotomizing the private and public spheres.

The week after the review was published, Rossiter wrote to Duberman, expressing his appreciation for it and then taking the opportunity to unburden himself:

> I have been following with great interest your public statements on homosexuality. I myself have been coming out more and more over the last seven years—but, unfortunately, not to the extent that you have. The recent convention in New York and the Gay Academic Union [Duberman was a founding member] seem to me worthwhile efforts. . . . Gay discussion groups (rather than social groups or action groups) still seem most attractive to me; in fact, I was very active in one of the earlier discussion groups here at Yale in 1968–69. (I understand even Princeton has some sort of gay movement now!) When I go back to Michigan this summer [Rossiter was at Yale, on a National Endowment for the Humanities grant, finishing his book] I hope that some sort of group for faculty members and graduate students in Ann Arbor can be worked out.[66]

The seven years during which Rossiter had been wrestling with the issue of revealing his homosexuality coincided with the period in which he was at work on Ives. Indeed, his participation in the Yale discussion group was made possible by his move to New Haven in order to conduct research in the Ives collection. Although I am unaware of any extant records of the discussions that transpired among the participants in the group, it does not seem venturesome to suggest that they included the Stonewall Riots of June 28, 1969, which became one of the most important events in the history of the Gay Rights movement.

Even considering the emphasis on gender discourse in Rossiter's dissertation, the fact that he was simultaneously pondering Ives and his own situation does not necessarily mean a direct connection. For many graduate students, psychological vicissitudes of one kind or another are attendant upon the dissertation-writing process, but there is no reason to assume they leave a clear imprint on the content of the final document, and even less so on the book that follows. In Rossiter's case, however, there is corroborating evidence.

For the year and half following the confessional letter, Rossiter and Duberman were in fairly regular correspondence. This was a period that was pivotal for Rossiter's career: it witnessed the failure of his tenure case at the University of Michigan, despite the publication of *Charles Ives and His America*, and his subsequent move to Dallas, where he received a tenure appointment at the University of Texas. Although the letters mostly concern practical matters, there are moments in which Rossiter demonstrates a particular interest in the ways in which Duberman was foregrounding issues of sexuality in his research and teaching. For example, in a letter dated October 12, 1974 (and thus written a week before the Ives Centennial Festival-Conference), Rossiter expressed his fascination about a course on "Sexuality in American History" Duberman was currently teaching, and, in an enthusiastic postscript, suggested that Duberman investigate whether homosexuality had any bearing on the activities of abolitionists by virtue of the shared affinity of victims of prejudice.[67] In another letter, Rossiter speculated about his own future research: "It seems to me that a social and cultural history of the American composer from about 1910 to 1950—which I should like very much to do some day, but most of the nonprinted sources are probably still inaccessible—would have to give serious attention to the homosexual component of the story."[68] Sadly, this project was never realized, but it is prescient of the issues that musicologists would begin to explore in the nineties and antedates Nadine Hubb's *The Queer Composition of America's Sound: Gay Modernists, American Music, and National Identity* (2004) by nearly thirty years.

The same letter contains the most compelling evidence that Rossiter sometimes conflated his own America with that of Charles Ives. Duberman had suggested that Rossiter take legal action against the University of Michigan if he suspected that his homosexuality had played a role in the negative tenure decision. Rossiter responded, "I don't know how many of my colleagues in the Department of History here know or suspect that I'm gay; but since I'm a 'nice' and 'well-behaved' homosexual (I don't 'flaunt it,' etc.), I doubt that even the senior people would have been too disturbed by the knowledge." The choice of words encased in scare quotes is telling. "Nice" and "well-behaved" were the very adjectives Ives invoked in his many diatribes against the concert music culture of his own day; they signaled the feminized conformity that was an anathema to the composer. Whereas for Ives, they were the shackles one bore as a professional musician, for Rossiter, they were the constraints of the closet. And, just as Ives, in Rossiter's view, fell victim to the gender pathologies of American culture, Rossiter felt victimhood was the most likely prospect for gay men. Pondering his future involvement with the gay rights movement, he wrote, "I don't know whether I'll be able to become involved in homosexual groups or not after I make this change in jobs. In general, I feel strongly that the liberated and 'organized' homosexual will never attain a sense of his true identity until he launches an all-out attack upon the family as an institution and until he realizes that (logically) the principal goal of his movement must be to rescue young homosexuals from the disastrous fate of being raised by heterosexual parents." Here is the same combination of stridency and pessimism that is characteristic of *Charles Ives and His America*.[69]

Rossiter, like his Ives, was indeed a victim of American prejudices. In the late eighties, he contracted AIDS, which had spread unchecked through the gay community as most Americans and their political representatives averted their collective gaze. Rather than suffer the ravages of the disease, Rossiter committed suicide in 1989. His death is rendered that much more tragic in light of the fact that he had just agreed to serve as faculty advisor for a gay students organization, the most public affirmation of his identity he ever made.[70]

By this time, Rossiter's scholarly activities had long since dwindled, a result of the heavy teaching load he carried at the University of Texas at Dallas. It would be more difficult to make a case for victimhood here: it is not clear that Rossiter found his teaching-oriented position any less fulfilling than the one he might have enjoyed had he secured tenure at the University of Michigan, where research was the priority. But if there is a culprit, it is American academic culture and, more specifically, disciplinary vicissitudes. Rossiter, having concluded that his homosexuality had not factored into the tenure decision, explained to Duberman, " I think that the general movement away from traditional intellectual history and toward more social history, in the general field of American history today, had a lot more to do with it. . . . [E]litist or not, I still find the history of ideas and the creative arts in America worth doing."[71] Ives too was to be a victim of the shift that so dramatically impacted Rossiter's career.

Rethinking America "From the Bottom Up"

Writing from the vantage of the late seventies, intellectual historian John Higham wistfully reminisced about the cachet his subdiscipline once enjoyed: "The most exciting, as well as the most controversial, single achievement of intellectual historians in the 1950s was a fresh vision of the meaning of America—a vision that comprehended the whole of American history and thus illuminated the present also. According to this approach, a unifying framework of ideas and values had created a distinctive American people. It explained the durability of their society and institutions."[72] In other words, the innovations of intellectual history, first manifest in the work of Vernon L. Parrington and Perry Miller, had laid the groundwork for the integrative investigations of American culture characteristic of "consensus history" and the American Studies movement. There is more than a little irony here—and possibly some regret—for Higham had authored the 1959 *Commentary* article in which the term *consensus history* was coined, its practitioners identified, and their work admonished for effacing the multifaceted nature of the peoples inhabiting the United States. In the interim, Higham's criticisms had gained traction, motivating a younger cohort of historians to revolt against "consensus history" and, confirming the law of unintended consequences, question the very validity of intellectual history. By the seventies, Higham's subdiscipline was under siege. Its profile was dwindling at national conferences and in academic journals, few graduate students were pursuing topics that fell within its traditional ambit, and, in some instances, as Rossiter's failed tenure case at the University of Michigan illustrates, livelihoods were threatened.

The most vocal detractors of the intellectual historian's enterprise were the devotees of what came to be called "New History."[73] Just as Higham applied the rubric "consensus history" retrospectively, after its hallmarks had manifest in the practice of historians during the fifties, "New History" did not enter common parlance until well after its practitioners had established their voice in academe. But unlike the consensus cohort, scholars who identified with the term had long thought of themselves as active agents in an important disciplinary upheaval. Indeed, in the late sixties, terms like *new social history*, *new negro history*, or *New Left history* served as precursors to, and would subsequently be subsumed by, *New History*.[74] All of these terms reflect the affinities of a group of historians heavily invested in the political activism of the late sixties and seventies—their defining feature. Barton J. Bernstein, introducing a collection of essays that featured some of the prominent members of this group, described the genesis of their scholarly convictions as integrally linked to recent events:

> During the early sixties the conservative consensus began to break down. For many, the rediscovery of poverty and racism, the commitment to civil rights for Negroes, the criticism of intervention in Cuba and Vietnam, shattered many of the assumptions of the fifties and compelled intellectuals to re-examine the American past. From historians, and particularly from younger historians, there began to emerge a vigorous criticism of the historical consensus.[75]

Bernstein and his like-minded colleagues regarded the practice of writing history as a political act. Thus, for them, the conservative continuity that the consensus historians touted in the fifties was a reflection of early Cold War suspicions of ideology and radicalism. If the discipline was retooled to focus on poverty, racism, and civil rights, it could be harnessed to a progressive agenda. In their work, practitioners of the "New History" set about restoring conflict to the American past, calling into question the legacies of American liberalism and focusing on the peoples who had been marginalized in past narratives—women, migrants, workers, and minorities. The title of the first essay in Barton's collection, "The American Revolution Seen from the Bottom Up," by Jesse Lemisch, nicely encapsulates the sense of changed perspective characteristic of this cohort and invokes a phrase—"from the bottom up"—that became one of its slogans.

Some of the advocates of history "from the bottom up" found a ready model in the French *Annales* school, which employed the quantitative methodologies of the social sciences to make inferences about the lives of ordinary people. The *Annalistes* dismissed military and political events, the traditional subject matter of historians, as epiphenomena. Instead, they sought to uncover long-lived *mentalités*, collective beliefs shared by specific demographic groups of people. They turned from the evidentiary staples of the discipline—correspondence of major political figures, diplomatic documents, treatises of the intelligentsia—to sources that supplied broader kinds of information: census returns, city directories, and geographical surveys. In the United States, the methods of the *Annalistes* were adopted with a fervor that was also fueled by the tantalizing potential of computers for enabling complex statistical analysis. Thus a dominant strain of "New History" manifested itself as social history with a quantitative bent.[76]

As historiographer Ellen Fitzpatrick demonstrates in *History's Memory: Writing America's Past, 1880–1980*, the conviction that the newfound emphasis on social history marked an abrupt departure from the past was somewhat ill-founded. Studies of race, gender, and class, for example, were produced throughout the century of scholarly endeavor that Fitzgerald documents. Moreover, upon closer inspection, even the historians most closely identified with "consensus" exhibit a broader range than the characterization suggests (one need only think of Hofstadter). The modern "New History" paradigm, Fitzgerald writes, "stripped away many complexities that had come to define a rich historiographical tradition built up over a century of professional American historical writing."[77] But if the claims of "New History" are a myth, imposing a disjuncture where continuity would be more appropriate, its practitioners were marked by self-consciousness, the sense that they were part of a movement. Barton, Lemisch, and their like-minded colleagues envisioned themselves as being engaged in a collective endeavor, stemming from a shared desire to blaze new paths in the old terrain of the American past, provoked by the experience of the present.

Those targeted by "New History" polemics also felt that the battle lines had been clearly demarked. Laurence Veysey, an intellectual historian whose specialization was the history of American universities, drew a series of stark contrasts to dramatize the situation in 1979:

> In substantive terms, social and intellectual history have lately offered versions of American history that are ever more distant. . . . Social history portrays a deeply segmented society, split by race, sex, and social class. Intellectual history either suggests a single culture or dwells on subworlds within the Protestant and Jewish elites. Social history dwells upon blacks, immigrants, women, the poor, New Yorkers, Pennsylvanians, Marylanders. Intellectual history emphasizes ministers, lawyers, radicals, writers, professors, New Englanders, a few whites from the deep South, and . . . the more articulate politicians. For social historians the central institution of the past century is the factory; for intellectual historians, the university. Social history, finally, studies census returns and city directories, sources that offer representative evidence about populations. Intellectual history unashamedly studies some of the most unrepresentative evidence conceivable.[78]

Veysey presented this inventory of subdisciplinary differences as part of a paper he delivered at a conference convened to explore "New Directions in American Intellectual History." The introduction to the published proceedings of the conference occasioned the retrospective musings of John Higham that I quoted at the outset of this section. As one of the principal organizers, Higham could underscore the ebb in fortunes of intellectual history by recounting the difficulties he had encountered securing financial support for the event.

But if the situation was dire, the tone of the conference participants was mostly optimistic, and accommodation rather than entrenchment was the order of the day. Taking to heart the criticisms issuing from social historians, many of the contributors acknowledged that ideas inhabit particular spheres of society and should not be projected onto the whole. David Hollinger, for example, argued that communities of discourse were the main subject matter for intellectual history.[79] Approaching the problem from a different angle, Veysey pointed out that one of the most pressing challenges facing intellectual historians was determining how the mentalities of aggregate groups of people (the main concern of social historians) could impinge upon or respond to the intellectual pursuits of some members within those groups. He offered an illustration:

> We think of the absurdity of trying to understand Charles Ives in the context of the insurance business, but then we recall his relationship to the Fourth of July. We are led to review the intricacies of selectivity in the encounter of such men with the world, the degree of compartmentalization that some persons, perhaps especially intellectuals, experience for long periods in their lives. The degree of

autonomy in one's intellectual life—both from the nonintellectual and from other intellectuals—would seem to be one of the variable conditions of existence.[80]

Ives, like all people, belonged to a number of social groups; however, the values implicit to some of those groups would not necessarily be relevant for a historian intent on shedding light on the composer's creative activities. It was inconceivable to Veysey that the values of the New York business community could have any proximate relation to the music. A clearer case could be made for the relevance of Ives's roots in New England, where the celebration of national holidays was imbued with a particular kind of patriotism. But the relevance of even this connection had to be weighed against the individuality of Ives, the extent to which his compositional decisions were a representation of his own volition and not some aspect of a group *mentalité*.

While Veysey's comments provide a representative sampling of the kind of ruminations rippling through the community of intellectual historians in the seventies, they also reveal something of the scope of Ives's reputation. Veysey, as a matter of course, assumed that an audience of historians would be familiar with the biography of Charles Ives, know something about his music, and would consider the composer a figure proper to the inquiries of their discipline. Indeed an intellectual historian—Frank Rossiter—had already written a biography of Ives that in 1976 had been a runner-up for the National Book Award in the "history and biography" category. Curiously, Veysey seems not to have been aware of Rossiter's book, for if he had been, he would not have thought the linkage between Ives's music and business so absurd. He also would have discovered a biography that showed some evidence of absorbing the grievances of social historians against the traditional practices of intellectual history.

Rossiter, by nature, seems not to have been inclined to engage in historiographical debates. Historian Gerald L. Soliday, a friend and former colleague of Rossiter's at the University of Texas at Dallas recalls that theoretical issues rarely came up in their conversations. Soliday himself was influenced by the *Annales* school, its methodologies informing his work on the social history of early modern Germany.[81] Rossiter probably had some exposure to the varieties of social history that were just beginning to percolate through the field during his graduate student years, even though Princeton was a bastion of academic conservatism. James McPherson, who served on his dissertation committee, was doing history "from the bottom up," having published two books about the experience of African Americans during the Civil War and contributing to Barton Bernstein's edited volume of essays by "New History" practitioners.[82] The scholarly output of Martin Duberman, Rossiter's adviser, fit comfortably under the intellectual-history rubric; however, many of the essays he wrote for more public forums—*Partisan Review*, the *New York Times*, and the *Village Voice*—reveal a respectful engagement with the ideas of the New Left. Possibly, concerns characteristic of social history arose naturally from Rossiter's decision to focus on Ives's psychology. Whatever the case, they are present in both his dissertation and book.

In comparison to other contemporary accounts of Ives's life, Rossiter's stands out for its extensive passages devoted to limning the social environs the composer inhabited. For example, in the first chapter, "The Danbury Experience," he supplied a rich description of nineteenth-century Danbury, Ives's hometown: major demographic trends, labor relations within its main industry (manufacturing hats), and the constellation of values that governed the elite strata of Danbury society of which the Ives family was a member. Rossiter gathered much of this information from a local history of the town augmented by data from the United States Census Office—the kind of information privileged by the Annalistes. Similarly, when discussing Ives's years at Yale, Rossiter lavished attention on the social hierarchy of the various Yale fraternities and discussed at length the place sports, music, and scholarship occupied in the minds of the young men who attended the university. All of this information about social context served to bolster Rossiter's central thesis: Ives, the icon of American cultural freedom valorized in the fifties and sixties, bore little resemblance to the historical Ives, who had been hemmed in by the mores of his social milieu.[83]

Admittedly, the evidence for the impact of "New History" on Rossiter's scholarship is thin; a more solid case can be made for Robert Crunden. Unlike Rossiter, Crunden was a historian who spoke freely about his intellectual commitments and left a sizable body of scholarship that substantiates them. He described himself as a conservative, a term that for him not only signaled certain political allegiances but also reflected, as he explained, assumptions "about which areas of life are generally rewarding for the intelligent person to concentrate upon."[84] In his work, this meant a steadfast commitment to intellectual history, beginning with his dissertation on the novelist and progressive reformer Brand Whitlock. Crunden sought explicitly to meet the challenges of "New History," not by abandoning his own commitment to studying the intelligentsia, but by trying to finesse his methodologies.

Reviewers had savaged Crunden's *From Self to Society* (1972), objecting to his "representative man" approach in which a parade of American notables from the early twentieth century was mustered to illustrate a "general position."[85] Rather than jettison the method, Crunden tried to make it more rigorous. His 1982 book, *Ministers of Reform: The Progressives' Achievement in American Civilization, 1889–1920*, included a methodological note that manages to sound defensive even while it adopts the clinical language of the statistician. Crunden explained that he had selected "one hundred figures who seemed to form a group that was coherent in its values. The group included many minor individuals but also every major figure whom, to my knowledge, scholars had ever called 'progressive,' whatever they may have meant by the term."[86] The approach here is more than reminiscent of the demographic preoccupations of social historians, as they attempted to discern in statistical averages the basic experiences—economic, political, social—of a particular group of people. It differs, of course, in making intellectuals the focus rather than "ordinary people."

Ives was one of the "representative men" in *Ministers of Reform*, and he shared first billing with Frank Lloyd Wright in a chapter entitled "Innovative Nostalgia in Music and Architecture." That chapter grew out of the paper that Crunden presented at the Ives centennial conference, and it retained the purpose of demonstrating that the composer participated in the progressive "climate of opinion." Crunden defined progressivism in much the same way as he had at the conference, although this time he emphasized the paradoxical nature of some of its commitments: preserving the moral framework of Protestantism, progressives had shed its dogmatic particulars; idealistic in their agendas, they were pragmatic in devising reforms that would aid the realization of their goals; confronted with twentieth-century mass culture, they retained the nineteenth-century view of society as an aggregate of individuals. In the arts, progressivism manifested as what Crunden called "innovative nostalgia." He explained, "Progressive artists were neither derivative nor original in any pure sense of those terms. They looked backward for emotional support and secure ideas even as they bravely experimented with federal regulation, instrumentalism, and polyrhythms."[87] According to this view, then, Ives shared the Januslike qualities of his contemporaries, at once looking longingly backward and eagerly forward.

There was more than just methodology at stake for Crunden. The larger goal of *Ministers of Reform* was to buttress the notion of progressivism, which had been the source of debate ever since the publication of Hofstadter's *Age of Reform*—a debate made all the more contentious by the ascendancy of "New History." During the sixties, historians were preoccupied with delineating the causes and commitments of the "progressive movement." There were clear fault lines dividing the presumptive membership—divisions that were evident in the way various constituencies had responded to progressive legislation on matters as varied as the Federal Reserve, the treatment of workers, and women's suffrage. Historians also found themselves divided about the presence of a nativist streak in the movement, the muddle of regional attitudes toward prohibition, and several other key issues. Documenting the resulting disputes, historian Peter Filene despaired of a resolution in a 1970 article facetiously titled "An Obituary for the 'Progressive Movement.'"[88] The term, he concluded, no longer had the strength to support historical argument; it collapsed under the weight of contradictions. Nonetheless, during the seventies, some historians continued to defend the coherence of progressivism, among them Robert Crunden, who, along with two colleagues, published a small book designed to rebut Filene's assertions.[89] At the same time, social historians, building their narratives "from the bottom up," passed by the political leadership of the progressives and focused on the rank and file, a trend that accelerated in the eighties. There were studies of coal miners, ironworkers, glass manufacturers, and cigar makers; regional case studies, examining the experiences of the working classes; monographs devoted to various immigrant groups; and a flood of scholarship investigating the plight of African Americans and women.[90] The progressive period was refracted through the prisms of race, ethnicity, class, and gender, yielding a multiplicity of views, and thus tending to support Filene's argument. In 1982 historian Daniel T. Rodgers discerned an emergent "pluralistic reading of progressive politics . . . in which the fundamental fact of the era is not reform in any traditional sense of the term, but the explosion of scores of aggressive, politically active pressure groups into the space left by the recession of traditional political loyalties." One might be able to discern clusters of ideas that figured in the discourse of progressives, whether self-identified or recognized in hindsight as such by historians, but the fabric would tear if one tried to stretch these ideas over a "static ideological frame."[91] Rodgers's pluralistic vision of progressivism has tended to remain the historiographical norm, with only a few recent exceptions.

When the criterion for membership in the progressive movement became connections formed through active coalitions, Ives was inevitably left out. Though he was passionate about his politics and imbibed some political literature, his sociopolitical activism was minimal.[92] Ives made a cottage on his West Redding property available to the Fresh Air fund, which sought to expose the urban poor to the salutary effects of country living; he was involved in the liberty bond drive during the First World War; and he engaged in some naïve, cantankerous pamphleteering—that was the whole of it. Unlike his wife, Harmony, Ives did not have the experience of working in a settlement house, where he might have had the opportunity to meet with people who inhabited the Jane Addams wing of the progressive movement.[93] With convictions about the unity of American culture on the wane among historians, there was little motivation for connecting Ives to progressivism on the basis of a few ideational resonances found in his prose writings. Despite Crunden's best efforts, Ives dropped from view, not only as a progressive, but also as a participant in the various facets of turn-of-the-century culture. In surveys of the progressive period published after *Ministers of Reform*, one looks in vain for the name "Charles Ives." Even two recent books that revive the integrative approach characteristic of pre-1970 scholarship, Michael McGerr's

A Fierce Discontent: The Rise and Fall of the Progressive Movement in America (2003) and Jackson Lears's *Rebirth of a Nation: The Making of Modern America, 1870–1920* (2009), make no mention of the composer, though they enfold the likes of Theodore Dreiser and Frank Lloyd Wright within otherwise generous sweeps.

To the Margins Once More

The impact of the New Left was felt all along the interdisciplinary front of American Studies and not limited to the ranks of historians. Its effects were first manifest in the midsixties, taking the form of scholarly assessments of the protest movements, which in turn led to political agitation for change within the institutions that supported American Studies. In 1969, several younger scholars, dubbing themselves "The Radical Caucus," organized an informal conference that ran simultaneously with the official national meeting of the American Studies Association (ASA) in Toledo. The ASA council, not wanting a schism, provided the members of the Radical Caucus with an opportunity to air their grievances and was confronted with a series of demands: a greater role for graduate students in the affairs of ASA, fellowships for minority scholars, and a resolution demanding the cessation of hostilities in Vietnam. The council met only the first of these, creating two new seats, one designated for a graduate student and the other for a member of the Radical Caucus. The decision to provide an automatic seat on the council for a disgruntled splinter group provoked controversy, which was further exacerbated by the successful vote for a funding subsidy to go to the Radical Caucus organ, *Connections*. Daniel Boorstin was one of several scholars who resigned from the ASA to signal their disapproval. Organizational changes and accommodations were also accompanied by a broadening of the purview of offerings at ASA conferences, the articles in its journal *American Quarterly*, and, more generally, in the work of its membership, wherever it happened to be published. Among American Studies scholars, belief in the singularity of American experience was becoming superseded by the conviction that plurality was the defining feature of the peoples inhabiting the United States. Surveying the field, historian Allen F. Davis identified the 1973 convention of the ASA, which was held in San Francisco, as a turning point. It was there that "cultural history, the study of material culture and social history—with its emphasis on gender, ethnicity, race and class—became dominant in the association and displaced the emphasis on American exceptionalism and an American consensus."[94]

It may seem puzzling that Davis would pronounce 1973 the year of cultural history's ascendancy; after all, the avowed purpose of scholars who had assumed the American Studies mantle had always been the study of American culture. The term *cultural history* requires some unpacking, all the more so, since I have smuggled it by without comment, embedded in several quotations that have appeared in this chapter. Unlike *intellectual history*, which Perry Miller made common to scholarly parlance in the middle of the twentieth century, "cultural history" has deep etymological roots that are traceable at least as far back as the nineteenth-century German cognate *Kulturgeschichte*. And indeed, from Jacob Burkhardt to V. L. Parrington to Richard Hofstadter, any number of historians might have justifiably claimed the term as a description of their activities. But there are nuances to Davis's usage of "cultural history" that are particular to the seventies, when an increasing number of scholars rallied to its banner (its popularity persists to this day).

A helpful place to start is with the tentative definitions Laurence Veysey offered in his essay about the predicament of intellectual history. While conceding the difficulty of drawing disciplinary distinctions, Veysey proposed a threefold scheme of historical practices: social history, which exposes "social realities"; intellectual history, which examines "formal systems of thought"; and, in an intermediary position, cultural history, which concerns itself with "collective mentalities."[95] Most historians pursued some combination of these categories, whatever descriptor they applied to their scholarship: historians like Perry Miller and Daniel Boorstin had assumed that the ideas they culled from the writings of the intelligentsia were the articulation of convictions held by the wider populace; historians of the *Annales* school gathered data about the social realities of ordinary people with the end in mind of uncovering *mentalités*. In other words, cultural history exerted a magnetic pull toward the center—a pull that was strengthened in the seventies by the influence of anthropology, and more specifically the work of Clifford Geertz, whose *The Interpretations of Culture* (1973) became one of the most frequently cited works of the period.

The essays contained in Geertz's book were intended to demonstrate a refinement of the concept of "culture." Man, Geertz declared, " is an animal suspended in webs of significance he himself has spun, I take culture to be those webs, and the analysis of it to be therefore not an experimental science in search of law but an interpretive one in search of meaning."[96] Shared symbols serve as the matrix within which discourse transpires in any culture, and the anthropologist's objective is to discern and decode those symbols, as manifest in the ways in which people entertain themselves (Geertz's essay on Balinese cock fighting is his most famous), exchange goods, fight, court, practice religious rituals, and even consume food. The symbols of a culture also saturate its written texts, but—and this was the crux of the matter for American Studies, in which close readings of American literature were treated as the barometer of American culture—the act of producing those texts was also enmeshed in the symbolic order, as was their interpretation by readers past and present. Thus, as one of the speakers pointed out at the 1973

ASA conference, *Moby Dick* had only "peripheral significance" for understanding the culture of mid-nineteenth-century Americans since it had largely fallen flat with contemporary audiences.[97] The veneration of Melville's book as part of the American literary canon spoke more to present-day symbolic orders, to the humanist convictions of literary scholars and their conventions of analysis.

The term *cultural history*, as it was commonly invoked from the seventies onward, implied a cognizance of the ideas emanating from the work of Geertz and other anthropologists. Its practice was distinguished by a careful delineation of the social groups that comprised a culture and fine-grained analysis of the symbols encoded in source materials appropriate to those groups. Paradoxically though it might at first seem, even as cultural history underscored the problems of "using imaginative literature as historical evidence," it prepared the way for a rapprochement between the practitioners of "New History" and embattled intellectual historians.[98] One of the purposes of Geertz's *Interpretations of Culture* was to encourage ethnographers to see their cultural analysis as a matter of "sorting out the structures of signification," an enterprise "more like that of the literary critic" than "that of the cipher clerk."[99] The objective was "thick description" (a designation that has become associated with Geertz, though he himself borrowed it from British philosopher Gilbert Ryle), which aimed at decoding the semiotic codes of cultural practices in a fashion analogous to the close readings of literary scholars. Intellectual historians were particularly well positioned to capitalize on the ascendancy of Geertzian ideas, for, like their colleagues in English departments, they were practiced in the art of parsing texts for symbolic nuances, but they did not have the same investment in the aesthetic value of canonical works. Once they learned to think of intellectuals as constituting a community of discourse, to attend to the issues of agency and constituency in making broader generalizations about the influence of ideas on American culture, and to apply their training to texts emanating from spheres outside their traditional purview, they found themselves thriving. By the end of the nineties, intellectual historian Thomas Bender could declare of his field that though "in the 1970s [it] feared being swept aside by social history [it] now finds itself insinuated into nearly every corner of the discipline, mostly under the aegis of the protean concept of culture."[100]

Ives did not fare well amid the changes that beset American Studies, in part because his few advocates, Crunden most notably, were reluctant to abandon older methodologies. Another was Betty E. Chmaj, who had been a member of the ASA Radical Caucus and whose efforts had been instrumental for putting the status of women on the docket for a reformed American Studies. But her radical politics did not translate to the realm of scholarship, where she displayed a decidedly conservative bent. Indeed, a 1979 article titled "Sonata for American Studies:

Perspectives on Charles Ives" finds Chmaj grumbling in the footnotes about "the culturologists in our field" intimidating others into "banishing high literature from the American Studies classroom." Her interpretation of Ives unfolds in a familiar fashion: the composer's aesthetic principles are extracted with the goal of establishing connections with other major American artists. Thus Ives's proclivity for open-ended works exemplified the "idea of the unfinished" that played out in the work of nineteenth-century romantics like Melville, and, more generally, his theories engaged the same issues as "Robert Henri and James Jackson Jarves on painting, William Dean Howells and Henry James on literature, certainly Louis Sullivan and Frank Lloyd Wright on architecture."[101] The framework that made the assemblage of such a pantheon possible also supported the work of Peter Conn, another American Studies scholar who attempted a postcentenary assessment of Ives. Conn avoided the panegyric tone to which some of his colleagues were prone, Chmaj among them, preferring instead a more critical stance. Nonetheless, in *The Divided Mind: Ideology and Imagination in America, 1898–1917* (1983), he managed to thread together the motley assortment of artists in his book, ranging from Charles Ives to the muckraker David Graham Philips, by relying on the idea of a shared American culture, albeit one riven by contradictions. What he detected in the work of all the Americans he surveyed was a "profound internal dialectic, a conflict between tradition and innovation, between control and independence, between order and liberation."[102] In the chapter devoted to Ives, one encounters the innovative nostalgic of Robert Crunden's imagination, constricted by the gendered constraints Frank Rossiter had detected.

The Parrington paradigm, regnant in American Studies until the seventies, made it fairly easy to incorporate and normalize Ives, but, in principle, there was no reason why he could not have been absorbed into the new cultural-history regimen. Occasionally—very occasionally—he has been. Lawrence W. Levine cited Ives's experiences at Yale as evidence for the sacralization of particular musical repertories in his *Highbrow/Lowbrow: The Emergence of Cultural Hierarchy in America* (1988), an exemplary product of cultural history as I have here described it. Less successful was MacDonald Smith Moore's *Yankee Blues: Musical Culture and American Identity* (1985), which tried to identify Ives with a specifically New England aesthetic tradition, distinctive and repugnant for its racist bigotries.[103] But the books of Moore and Levine are rare exceptions.

Already, by the late seventies, Ives's prospects in American Studies seem to have dimmed. "Ives," Chmaj observed, "is seldom taught in basic American Studies courses . . . Stephen Foster, Woody Guthrie, and Bob Dylan appear to earn more attention in American Studies than Ives, who ought to be as much a part of our curriculum as Whitman. Or Winslow Homer, say, or Frank Lloyd Wright."[104] The single article devoted to Ives in the ASA journal *American Quarterly* (authored by Chmaj's friend Audrey Davidson), never found a companion piece, though reviews of books about the composer issuing from elsewhere in academe have occasionally appeared in the journal. What looked to be an incipient interdisciplinary engagement with Ives in his centenary year has turned out, in retrospect, to be an aberration.

5

Musicology Makes Its Mark

Ives and the History of Style, 1965–1985

Two Californian stalwart supporters of Charles Ives were among the celebrants who descended on New York in October 1974 for the Charles Ives Centennial Festival-Conference. Peter Yates had been one of Ives's earliest devotees, a mystical modernist enraptured by the transcendentalist overtones of the later works in the output of the composer. Well before the name Ives became familiar in American musical circles, Yates had promoted the composer's music in Los Angeles, organizing performances as part of his legendary Evenings on the Roof concert series. Lou Harrison made his acquaintance with Ives's music slightly later, but was no less devoted. He had conducted the premiere of the Third Symphony in 1946, an event that was the catalyst for the awarding of the Pulitzer Prize to the work in 1947. Now, nearly thirty years later, Yates and Harrison seated themselves together at one of the conference sessions only to discover that the tenor of the discourse was moving in a disconcerting direction. Yates wrote about the experience: "At the Ives Festival-Conference in New York a couple of musicologists were picking at Ives' character; I was heating up to vocalize. Lou Harrison, beside me, laid a hand on my arm: 'Peter, we've done our work. Now let them do theirs.'"[1]

Yates's recollections ring true, both for what they reveal about the characters of the men involved (Yates was notoriously excitable, Harrison sublimely pacific) and the perceptive recognition that a generational shift was under way. Yates erred, however, in identifying the change with musicologists, because the profession was poorly represented at the Festival-Conference. Most of the individuals named "principal participants" in the printed program would have opted for a different label: composer, performer, music theorist, or maybe even archivist.[2] Likely, Yates was using "musicologist" as a blanket designation for any scholar who studied music. Possibly he was reacting to the papers delivered by intellectual historians Frank Rossiter and Robert M. Crunden, whose session "Ives and American Culture" was especially divisive.

As of 1974, few musicologists had turned their attention to Ives. In fact, the centenary year passed almost without mention of the composer in the *Journal of the American Musicological Society*, organ of the discipline's largest professional association in the United States. The only places in which the name "Charles Ives" appeared were the annual lists of "publications received" and doctoral dissertations.[3] This was symptomatic of the general state of affairs: while established musicologists displayed nominal interest in the composer, younger scholars were beginning to make him the subject of their inquiries. Indeed, for musicological commentary on the Ives centenary events in New York and elsewhere, one has to look to graduate-student journals: *Current Musicology*, which presented several lively reports, and *Student Musicologists at Minnesota*.[4] Elsewhere in the musical scholarly world, occasional articles about Ives could be found in *Musical Quarterly* and *Perspectives of New Music*, neither of which catered specifically to musicologists (the former had a general readership and the latter a constituency of composers and theorists). The first sign of an incipient, widespread engagement with Ives on the part of musicologists came in 1975, when Vivian Perlis's *Charles Ives Remembered: An Oral History* was awarded the top annual prize for a monograph by the American Musicological Society. Even so, a feature article on the composer would not appear in the society journal for another fourteen years.

Although Yates discerned their presence too early, musicologists did reshape discourse about Ives once they entered the conversation. Like the intellectual historians and American Studies scholars I discussed in chapter 4, they came equipped with a set of disciplinary practices and perceptions, habits of thought that conditioned the way in which they portrayed Ives. Their influence also paralleled the historians', for they contributed to the erosion of Cold War commonplaces that cast the composer as a rugged individualist, an American visionary who stood both outside and ahead of classical-music history. Beginning in the late sixties, and culminating with the work of J. Peter Burkholder in the early eighties, musicologists gradually developed a portrait of Ives deeply rooted in European music history. Moreover, Burkholder discovered that Ives's commitment to transcendentalism, much vaunted since the fifties, was not so deep nor did it extend quite so far back as had previously been assumed. In short, the impact of musicology on Ives's reception was just as dramatic as that of American intellectual history.

But these two disciplines could not have been more dissimilar. In the midsixties, intellectual historians were preoccupied with distilling the essence of a particular culture (often that of the United States) by looking for foundational ideas in the work of the intelligentsia. Musicologists sought to uncover and organize the musical manuscripts of the distant past (usually the Medieval or Renaissance eras), the end goal being an account of the various styles at the disposal of a composer in any given period. Obviously, the disparate nature of the materials handled by intellectual historians and musicologists was a determining factor. More significant, though, were the different circumstances under which each discipline acquired membership in American universities. As an outgrowth of history, intellectual history was part of a tradition of scholarly enterprise that had deep roots in the United States. By contrast, musicology was grafted on to departments of music, which, since their beginnings in the late nineteenth century, had been dedicated to providing a practical education to aspiring musicians. The scholarly tradition to which musicologists had recourse was European, and, more specifically, German—for that is where the earliest American scholars in the field took their training. What is striking about the musicological scholarship devoted to Ives, from the sixties to the eighties, is how closely it hewed to this tradition. The most conservative of means, deployed to examine the most peculiar of composers, contributed to the most startling reassessment of Ives's significance.

Defining Musicology: Theory and Practice

The foundational document of modern musicology is Guido Adler's "Scope, Method and Goal of Musicology," published as the lead article in the inaugural issue of the *Vierteljahrsschrift für Musikwissenschaft* in 1884. The "single purpose" of the *Vierteljahrsschrift*, declared its editors in the preface to the issue, was "to serve science," and it was Adler's job to demonstrate that the study of music could be pursued through empirical observation and inductive reasoning.[5] The contents of Adler's article would not have been entirely new to the small Central European readership of the fledgling journal. Indeed, the central thrust had been anticipated in published statements about musical scholarship issued by Friedrich Chrysander and Philipp Spitta, the two men with whom Adler shared the editorship of the *Vierteljahrsschrift*.[6] But in its comprehensiveness, Adler's attempt to define the nascent field of *Musikwissenschaft* stood head and shoulders above anything that had preceded it. Adler offered a view of the field calculated to appeal to an academic community that was skeptical about the prospects of making music subject to scholarly endeavor. It was a bid for legitimacy at a time when Central European universities were undergoing a transformation: the natural sciences were in their ascendancy, while the idealist strain of philosophy, long cherished by German speakers as their special province, was in decline. Evidently it worked—at least as far as Adler's career was concerned:

the following year he gained entry to the halls of academe, winning an appointment at Prague University, and then, in 1889, a position at the University of Vienna, something he had long coveted. Because it was prescriptive and because it was designed as a prospectus for the professoriate, it would be wrong to take Adler's article as an accurate description of musicological activities in the late nineteenth century.[7] For my purposes, it is best seen as a repository of ideas that have engaged musicologists throughout the history of their discipline and that they have affirmed, elaborated, discarded, and even disavowed according to the dictates of their own particular needs.

Under the rubric "musicology," Adler bundled together a wide assortment of pursuits, from the paleographic work of dating manuscripts to the ethnographic study of folk-music practices, from the organization of musical principles for pedagogical purposes to experiments in acoustics (this last conveniently contained within the ambit of the sciences already). Musicology, for Adler, then, meant any kind of rigorous study in which music was the main focus. But though his vision of musicology was broad in scope, Adler imposed a strict order and hierarchy on its many constituent endeavors. He divided the discipline into two sections: first, the historical section, which "organizes itself according to epochs ... or according to peoples, territories, regions, cities, and schools of art"; and second, the systematic section, which establishes the "highest laws in the individual branches of tonal art." According to Adler, the "individual branches" of the systematic section were music theory, aesthetics, pedagogy, and what would now be called ethnomusicology (though the term was not introduced until 1950). Of these four, Adler was most tentative about discussing aesthetics, the subject of the "musically beautiful" having been prone to the sort of metaphysical speculation that he sought to purge in favor of more "scientific" discourse. Though the systematic section might seem most consistent with the objective of distilling general laws, the highest goal of a science, Adler was more committed to the idiographic prospects of the historical section. His theoretical writings about musicology, beginning with the 1884 article, coupled with the example of his own published research provide a clear picture of enterprises falling under the historical section, while the systematic section remains ill-defined. In fact, Adler was explicit about his priorities, declaring that the systematic section rested on the historical section. Except to emphasize the breadth of "systematic musicology"—it encompassed research in fields as varied as acoustics, psychology, and ethnography—I will follow Adler in not lingering over it.[8]

For Adler, the main focus of historical musicology was the musical work, not composers' biographies, musical institutions, performers, or audiences, although these could be studied as an ancillary to the main enterprise. First on the itinerary of the musicologist was the task of establishing the provenance of the work under consideration and determining the kind of repertory to which it belonged. Classification would proceed according to *Gattung*, which can be translated as "species" or "genre," either of which is indicative of the biological metaphors that saturate this article and make it a typical product of late-nineteenth-century Central European intellectual culture.[9] Once a critical number of works had been "defined paleographically," the musicologist could set about the task of tracing the evolution of "laws of music" for different periods, "how, proceeding from the simplest thesis, the artistic norms latent in the tonal products become more and more complicated." This, Adler declared, "takes the highest precedence; this is the actual focal point of all music-historical work."[10]

Adler's article offered only vague outlines for the methodology of classifying works according to species or genre, a lacuna he sought to redress in his *Methode der Musikgeschichte* (1919). Here, he replaced *Gattung* by the notion of "style," his earlier formulation "laws of music" became "style laws" or "style norms," and, accordingly, he dubbed the methodology "style criticism." As he envisioned it, style criticism involved a synthetic process that combined an analysis of form, itself a product of assessing individual musical parameters (rhythm, harmony, melody, etc.), with an analysis of content. Adler remained nebulous about content, suggesting only that it involved more than the eighteenth-century notion of *Affekte*—the generalized mood of a particular piece or some portion thereof. The methodology would facilitate connection between music and its cultural context by means of a threefold division of style, defined with respect to time, place, and author. In each of these divisions, the musicologist was to identify specific periods, tracing the growth and decline of particular style types. Here, for example, is his description of the time division: "We arrange the several style-varieties in periods and study their mutual relationship and opposition, their individuality, their rise and fall. We survey the complexity of the occurrences within a period and seek to isolate the basic style with all its attendant phenomena. We follow the style-varieties in their chronological development."[11] Again, the underpinning metaphor is biological evolutionary processes.

In principle, one could proceed from "style criticism" to the realm of systematic musicology, possibly even to aesthetic evaluation. But in practice, style criticism remained Adler's primary focus; as he pointed out, the task of putting the musicological house in order according to the precepts of his methodology was enormous.[12] There were thousands of musical manuscripts in European libraries, and the scientific rigor to which Adler aspired demanded that as many of them as possible be analyzed in the process of distilling styles. The primacy of this endeavor also pushed aside other kinds of enterprises that had fallen under the ambit of historical musicology as Adler had first defined it (albeit accorded secondary status): biography, institutional histories, and performance practice.

Thus, Adler, as disciplinary patriarch, bequeathed to his successors a methodology that fixated on the musical text to the exclusion of other matters. Moreover, he fostered a habit of thinking linearly in causal and often teleological strings, with the prevailing metaphor of style as organism. This particular facet of Adler's legacy had major ramifications for the reception of Ives, who had been rendered sui generis by many of his early Cold War–era devotees.

Reinforcing Adler's emphasis on the musical text was a commitment on the part of many German intellectuals to an idealism that made instrumental music the crowning glory of the arts. That commitment, which has its own complex history, gave rise to one of the most heated and protracted musical debates of the latter half of the nineteenth century—a debate that embroiled most of the major composers of the period, from Richard Wagner to Johannes Brahms, from Anton Bruckner to Gustav Mahler. The main point of contention concerned the kinds of meanings instrumental music could convey, and more specifically, whether program music amounted to a cheapening of the medium. Did the existence of a program, which might take the form of a prose narrative, a poem, or an image, damage the integrity of music by harnessing it to a limited, lesser medium? A resounding "yes" came from Eduard Hanslick, who was Adler's predecessor at the University of Vienna. In an influential treatise, he identified the beautiful in music with its formal construction, not with the emotions it elicited in the listener or any programmatic content.[13] This was a mature form of what musicologist Carl Dahlhaus described as the "idea of absolute music."[14] Hanslick's formalism not only had a long German pedigree but also, like that of Adler, was motivated by the desire to imbue discourse about music with scientific rigor. Its long-standing legacy for musical scholarship was a bias against hermeneutics and the neglect of music that made a prerogative of invoking things "extra-musical." Herein lies part of the explanation for why musicologists ignored Ives for so long. His music, even when it does not have an explicit program, frequently gestures outside itself through the plethora of musical borrowings.

In the United States, musicology took much longer to become a part of university culture than in Central Europe. Although Adler bears the distinction of holding the first chair in musicology at the University of Vienna, he had been preceded at the same institution by Hanslick, who served under a different title: first associate and then full professor of history and aesthetics of music from 1861–1895. Philip Spitta began his appointment as professor of music history at the University of Berlin in 1873. (Chrysander, the final member of the editorial triumvirate that oversaw the *Vierteljahrsschrift*, remained an independent scholar.) By contrast, the first chair of musicology in the United States was established at Cornell University in 1930. Its occupant, Otto Kinkeldey, had received his doctorate in Germany and, prior to World War I, served as a professor of music history at Breslau University. But Kinkeldey's appointment did not mark the beginning of American musicology. As in Europe, before a professorship became a viable option, those who pursued music scholarship did so independently or under the auspices of other institutions.[15] Early American musicology was as expansive an endeavor as Adler had theorized. Its practitioners tackled all manner of music, from Amerindian songs to Beethoven symphonies, and the orientation of their scholarship ranged across the "historical" and "systematic" subdivisions.[16]

Musicology did not flourish in American academe until after the Second World War, when it benefited from the massive expansion of the university, itself a consequence of the influx of veterans funded by the GI Bill and Cold War anxieties about American intellectual preeminence. Departments of music had been present in American universities since the late nineteenth century; the one at Yale, Ives's alma mater, was founded in 1890.[17] Such departments, though, were geared toward musicians who sought technical training in the Western European art-music tradition. There was a scholarly component in the mandatory music history and theory courses, but scholarship was ancillary to the goal of producing competent classical-music performers and composers. Typically, the instructors were faculty members whose specialization lay elsewhere—composing, in the case of Horatio Parker, who taught music history at Yale. Hiring scholars to teach these courses relieved Parker and his ilk of an onerous burden; it was a practical solution made possible by the expanded financial resources of postsecondary institutions during the forties and fifties. It also meant that the scholarly inclinations of musicologists hired to fill the new posts typically ran to subjects concerning classical-music history, excluding those whose interests lay elsewhere.[18] Thus, although American scholars continued to pay lip service to the broad definition of musicology, as set out by Adler, the benefits of institutionalization accrued mostly to those who carried out their work in the historical subdivision.[19] Under these circumstances, Adlerian style criticism flourished, along with the paleographic enterprises that were its necessary precursor. Just how central the concept of style was to musicologists is revealed by a definitive (and oft-quoted) pronouncement in the preface to Donald J. Grout's *A History of Western Music* (1960), a textbook that would serve generations of music students: "The history of music is primarily the history of musical style."[20]

American scholars whose interests did not lie in the history of classical music did find opportunities in the postwar university, fostering alliances with or winning appointments in anthropology departments, and to a lesser extent, folklore departments.[21] But they were increasingly marginalized in the conferences and publications of the major professional musicological organization, the American Musicological Society (AMS). Dissatisfaction with this state of affairs was partly responsible for the founding of the Society for Ethnomusicology in 1955.[22] Music scholarship would be further sundered in the seventies, when music theorists, who occupied themselves with formal analysis of works in the classical canon without necessarily attending to issues of stylistic evolution, formed their own society.[23] The configuration that emerged from this process of division and specialization still obtains in most music departments today: a trio of cohabiting disciplines, each with its own distinctive objectives, identified by the rubrics music theory, ethnomusicology, and musicology. In the seventies, the latter was usually understood to refer to the historical study of the Western European art-music tradition. (Since then, musicologists have been venturing further afield, into the realms of jazz, film, and popular-music scholarship).

The first dissertations on Ives began to appear in the late sixties and early seventies, some twenty years after the establishment of PhD programs in musicology across the country. The delay stemmed in part from the fact that Ives was still a new phenomenon, his canonical status only recently secured through the championship of Henry Cowell, Leonard Bernstein, Leopold Stokowski, and other high-profile musicians. A more significant hindrance, however, was the biases inherent in contemporary musicological practice.

Consider the case of Clayton W. Henderson, who received his graduate training in musicology at Washington University in the midsixties. Henderson's scholarly apprenticeship began with a slate of courses heavily weighted toward Medieval and Renaissance topics. It culminated with a dissertation project in which he set out to transcribe and study the contents of a book of lute tablature issued by the sixteenth-century Italian publisher Ottaviano Petrucci.[24] Echoed implicitly in this regimen were the priorities Claude Palisca expressed in a landmark 1963 survey of the musicological discipline as practiced in the United States: "At the present stage in the development of musicology, the most urgent task remains to make available through modern editions the vast quantity of music and primary literary sources of the period before 1800 that still exist only in manuscript and early printed editions."[25] Unlike Adler's foundational article, this was not a prescription. Palisca's survey revealed that the period attracting the most attention of scholars at any stage of their career was the Renaissance, followed by the Medieval and Baroque eras. The classical and romantic periods occupied only a handful of musicologists, and the twentieth century more or less fell outside of the disciplinary domain.

Henderson conducted the preliminary work on his dissertation under the supervision of Paul A. Pisk, one of several prominent Central European émigré scholars who then dominated the discipline, reinforcing the Germanic legacy in American musicological practice.[26] Pisk's credentials were impeccable. He had completed his musicological training under the guidance of Guido Adler at the University of Vienna in 1916, specializing in sixteenth-century German music.

By the time he arrived at Washington University, he had produced several critical editions, penned a clutch of articles, and was joint author of a textbook with a title that revealed its Adlerian patrimony, *A History of Music and Musical Style* (1963).[27] What set Pisk apart from other musicologists was the dual nature of his career, for he was also a composer who enjoyed the cachet of having been a member of Arnold Schoenberg's Viennese circle. He was, as a result, one of the few musicologists whose scholarship addressed twentieth-century topics.

Roughly eighteen months into his project, Henderson ran into a problem. He discovered that another scholar was on the cusp of publishing material pertaining to the Petrucci book and decided it would be best to relinquish his claim on the subject. Starting from scratch, he embarked on a new dissertation project that was at once unorthodox in its subject matter, conventional in its objectives, and virtually free of competing scholarly claims.[28]

Henderson was drawn to Ives amid the upsurge of interest in the sixties presided over by Leonard Bernstein and Leopold Stokowski. He was intrigued by the jostling quotations of Ives's music, and he found that he recognized some of this borrowed material from his own musical past as a New England chorister and church organist. Encouraged by the handful of Americanists he knew among his musicological acquaintances, he decided to make the quotations of Ives the subject of his thesis.

When Henderson proposed the topic to Pisk, a long silence ensued. And then came the remonstrations. Ives was a dilettante composer, Pisk objected, an amateur who lacked musical refinement, and, besides, Ives quoted popular music—hardly the sort of thing worthy of a musicologist's time. Henderson refused to be dissuaded, and, to his credit, Pisk relented, thereafter supporting his advisee's work. Nonetheless, Pisk never gave up his misgivings about Ives, or, for that matter, his general prejudice against American music, the latter reflecting a eurocentricity that was then typical of musicology.[29] Parenthetically, it bears mentioning that not all émigré scholars were as dismissive of Ives as Pisk was. Columbia's Paul Henry Lang and Yale's Leo Schrade, authors of the earliest musicological assessments of Ives, were mostly positive.[30]

When Henderson graduated in 1969, he was only the second PhD student to have written a dissertation about Ives.[31] Although he was blazing a trail in terrain where few musicologists had ventured, the equipment with which he worked was standard issue. The title of his thesis is the first clue that Adlerian precepts inform the project: "Quotation as a Style Element in the Music of Charles Ives." Consistent with the taxonomical predilections of his grand-teacher, Henderson devoted nearly a third of the dissertation to appendixes in which he listed all known borrowed sources, supplied transcriptions, and cross-referenced them to the Ives works in which they appeared.[32] Much of the main text was given over to classifying borrowings according to the frequency with which they appeared in individual works. But Henderson also attempted to distill some general principles for Ives's techniques of making alterations to borrowed material. His urge, again, was to approach the task in a taxonomical fashion, and, accordingly, he identified several subsets of practices in Ives's approach to the individual elements of melody, rhythm, and harmony. "Fragments used as generating points for immediate sequence," "shifting of original pulse or accents," and "interval mixtures," are only three of the many subheadings he used to label the techniques, but they give enough of the flavor of his approach.[33] This was nothing less than style criticism, the central pillar of Adlerian musicological practice: the identification of the idiosyncratic ways in which a particular composer handles musical parameters. One thing Henderson steadfastly ignored was the issue of meaning, the expressive purposes behind Ives's borrowings. And here too he was consistent with the precedent of his German forebears.

The traits of musicology Henderson encountered at Washington University—the antiquarian focus, neglect of American music, persistence of style criticism, and avoidance of hermeneutics—also shaped the experiences of other Ives scholars who received their training in the late sixties and seventies. In the early 1970s, when Harvard graduate student Geoffrey Block went to consult with faculty advisors about the possibility of making Ives his thesis topic, the director of graduate studies asked patronizingly, "You don't want to do him do you?" Block ended up writing a dissertation about the genesis of two Beethoven piano concerti instead and did not venture any scholarship devoted to Ives until the eighties.[34] At Berkeley in the midsixties, Judith Tick, like Henderson, experienced a regimen of courses heavily weighted toward documentary studies and early music. After completing her masters in 1967, she took a brief hiatus from graduate school. When she decided to return, now determined to study American music, it was obvious that Berkeley was a poor fit for her interests and she decided to apply elsewhere. Tick was accepted to the PhD program at the City University of New York, where H. Wiley Hitchcock had just established the Institute for Studies in American Music for the purpose of fostering scholarship in a field long neglected.[35] Though Tick wrote her application essay on Ives and published a revised version of it while she was still a graduate student, she too would postpone more extensive engagement with the composer until later in her career.[36] Possibly, Tick might have changed her mind about Berkeley if she had remained there. Larry Starr, who entered the program the year she left, recalls that Richard Felciano, a newly appointed member of the composition faculty, incorporated the music of Ives into his classes. For a time, Starr contemplated doing a dissertation on Ives with Felciano but, for reasons he can no longer recall, opted instead to work on Bartók's *Mikrokosmos* under the supervision of Andrew Imbrie, another

Berkeley composer.[37] Starr's case reveals that, by the seventies, a determined musicology graduate student could pick a twentieth-century subject, but that guidance would have to come from outside the field, typically through the good graces of a composer-scholar.

For this cohort of musicological initiates, style loomed large among the constellation of ideas and concepts they absorbed as graduate students. J. Peter Burkholder described the legacy of Guido Adler as being in "the very air I was breathing," particularly during his time at Earlham College as an undergraduate in the midseventies, before he moved on to the University of Chicago for his PhD.[38] Larry Starr, remembers "style" being used as a term of differentiation, never applied to individual works, but serving instead in a generic sense to demark "whole periods, groups of composers, and individual composers."[39] Unlike Burkholder, Starr did not invoke Adler, though the ongoing influence of the German musicological patriarch is manifest in the threefold classification scheme to which he refers. A college textbook authored by Berkeley faculty member Richard Crocker, titled *A History of Musical Style* (1966), is testament to the centrality of style in the pedagogical framework of that university at the time. When I asked Geoffrey Block about his graduate work at Harvard University in the early seventies, he was quick to respond that style had not figured much at all. But then, upon further reflection, retracted. In fact it seemed to be quite pervasive, from courses that explicitly dealt with matters of style (Block mentioned seminars on the Renaissance period and the *galant* style) to the cultivation of an analytical methodology that sought out the stylistic idiosyncrasies in any given piece.[40] It would seem that style analysis was such a familiar and unremarkable part of the mental furniture of musicologists that it could escape notice, even in a moment of retrospection.

By the early seventies, musicologists were beginning to express misgivings about style analysis, and gradually it would ebb from the forefront of musicological concerns.[41] Even so, in 1977, musicologist Howard Mayer Brown could still complain that questions "dealing with style, genre and compositional technique . . . seem to pre-occupy musicologists almost to the exclusion of everything else."[42] The context for Brown's complaint was an article in which he examined the musical practices depicted in Boccaccio's *Decameron* in order to see what they might reveal about the social place of music during the fourteenth century. Style played a major role in his argument, a comparison of extant trecento monophonic secular and religious song being critical to his conclusions, but it was a means, not an end. Brown's work is indicative of an expansion of the kinds of problems that preoccupied musicologists in the seventies. Accordingly, archival work, to which there was a renewed dedication at the time, turned outward, from matters pertaining to "music itself" to the structure of musical institutions, the nature of patronage systems, and developments in printing technology. While style moved to a subsidiary position within the broader field of musicology, it retained its central place for musicologists who took on the polystylistic Ives.

Defining Ives Paleographically

But before Ives could be made the subject of style history, his manuscripts, which were in disarray at the time of his death, had to be put in order and usable editions needed to be prepared and published. As it turns out, these two paleographic enterprises were not at first undertaken by musicologists. The earliest people to struggle with Ives's manuscripts were the copyists hired by the composer to ready his music for printing. They faced a tangle of variants and emendations, a scrawl that sometimes drifted into illegibility, and a habit of revising that made it difficult to fix any given work in final form. Ives identifies some of these copyists by name in both his correspondence and the copious marginalia of the manuscripts themselves. Vivian Perlis even managed to track down one of them for her Ives oral history project, George F. Roberts, whom Ives employed regularly during the thirties and forties.[43] Other copyists are identifiable only by the distinctive traits of their writing.

Ives scholars know little about George Price, who was admonished on the manuscript of *The Fourth of July*, "Please don't try to make things nice! All the wrong notes are *right*. Just copy as I have—I want it that way."[44] Whoever Price might have been, this oft-quoted marginalia reveals that Ives did not initially extend to his copyists the same kind of interpretive leeway that he afforded those who performed his music. As his eyesight worsened and his health declined, however, he became increasingly reliant on the judgment of others. Ives was more comfortable relinquishing control in the last two decades of his life, when the music was in the hands of dedicated devotees like Henry Cowell and Lou Harrison. Frequently, Ives would instruct his trusted editors to "do whatever seems best," an injunction that suggests he regarded them as creative collaborators.[45]

When Ives died, Henry Cowell and John Kirkpatrick undertook the business of sorting through Ives's papers jointly, with Harmony Ives serving as a go-between. Henry's involvement, as usual, meant that Sidney too was drawn into the process, and the Cowells also recruited an archivist from the New York Public Library named Joseph Braunstein. Tensions ensued since there were different ideas about what to do with the material: for Cowell, the goal was to get it all in print as soon as possible; Kirkpatrick recommended proceeding more deliberately, organizing the variants of any given work so as to show something of the creative evolutionary process; Cowell pushed the Library of Congress as the repository for Ives's manuscripts; Kirkpatrick was more inclined to see them at Yale.[46] Characteristically, however, Cowell's involvement petered out after several months, and, by the summer of 1955, Kirkpatrick had more or less complete control over the project. For the next five years, he worked at cataloguing Ives's manuscripts whenever his performance schedule and commitments as a faculty member at Cornell permitted. Kirkpatrick's papers, housed at Yale University alongside those of Ives, contain ample evidence of the labor he expended on the wordily titled *Temporary Mimeographed Catalogue of the Music Manuscripts and Related Materials of Charles Edward Ives 1874–1954* (1960).[47] In addition to the many letters Kirkpatrick exchanged as he attempted to locate and identify all extant Ives manuscripts and correspondence, Kirkpatrick's papers also include the lengthy questionnaires that he prepared for Ives's friends, family, and associates (business and musical), inquiring after any bit of information that would help establish dates for the manuscripts.

Although the *Temporary Mimeographed Catalogue* was intended to be precisely that—temporary—and Kirkpatrick hoped to produce a more refined version, it was not replaced for nearly forty years. Vivian Perlis's register of Ives's literary writings provided a supplement in 1983, but it was James B. Sinclair's *A Descriptive Catalogue of the Music of Charles Ives* (1999) that finally superseded Kirkpatrick's work. Even so, Sinclair grants the *Temporary Mimeographed Catalogue* continued importance, "mainly for its identification of paper types and as a guide to the manuscripts kept . . . in the Yale Music Library's rare book room."[48] As musicologist Drew Massey aptly remarks, Kirkpatrick's catalogue was the "Rosetta stone for an entire generation of Ives scholarship."[49]

After having imposed order on Ives's manuscript, Kirkpatrick's next major paleographical enterprise was to prepare an edition of Ives's unpublished writings, including the autobiographical "Memos" from the thirties, which had furnished the Cowells with much of the information for their book about the composer. Kirkpatrick proceeded in the same assiduous fashion as he had with the catalogue, a task facilitated by his appointment as professor of piano and curator of the Ives collection at Yale University in 1968. And again, even the most cursory examination of the Kirkpatrick papers cannot but turn up some material from the extensive paper trail that the project created. The end result was published in 1972 as *Memos*, though its appendixes, containing Ives's other previously unpublished prose writings, occupy more page space than the eponymous autobiography. When the Ives Society set out in 1973 to create a complete critical edition of the composer's music, Kirkpatrick was the obvious choice to fill the role of executive editor.

It bears repeating that Kirkpatrick had not received professional musicological training—in fact, he had never completed the undergraduate degree he began at Princeton University. Massey points out that one stimulus to Kirkpatrick's editing was his perception that it would legitimize his presence in academia.[50] Kirkpatrick was certainly not wrong in viewing editing as one of the main activities of musical scholarship at the time. But it is difficult to gauge the extent to which he was aware of the methodologies musicologists employed in the construction of critical editions, despite a few tantalizing hints in his correspondence. Potentially revealing is a letter he wrote to Howard Boatwright in the summer of 1961, when Boatwright was in the final stages of the work on his edition of *Essays Before a Sonata*. Kirkpatrick reported that he had started the task of editing Ives's *Psalms* at the behest of music publisher Mercury and that, "just like renaissance stuff . . . the text-underlay is one of the biggest headaches." In musicological circles, much ink had indeed been spilled over the issue of text underlay; Kirkpatrick may well have become acquainted with the problem by reading the critical commentary for the editions of works he selected for performance in his capacity as a choir director (a role he assumed in some of the academic positions he had occupied). In the same letter, he mentioned Beethoven scholar Dagmar Weise, who "has helped me a lot in various musicological directions."[51] Weise served as the editor for two critical editions of Beethoven sketchbooks issued by the Beethoven-Haus in Bonn. The extant correspondence between Kirkpatrick and Weise is extensive, but, apart from an exchange about the Beethoven manuscript holdings in the Yale library, it is mostly of a personal nature and does not shed any light on the "musicological directions" to which Kirkpatrick was referring.[52]

The same year in which the Ives Society embarked on its project of creating an Ives critical edition, Kirkpatrick and Elliott Carter exchanged "open letters" about the nature of Ives's musical legacy. Though these letters were intended for publication, they did not appear in print until 2007, when Massey published them as appendixes to an article about the Ives Society critical editions.[53] Kirkpatrick, who instigated the exchange, sought to address the issue of Ives's primacy with respect to the use of dissonance outside the realm of accepted tonal practice. Carter had famously raised this issue in his review of the 1939 New York premiere of the "Concord" Sonata, suggesting that Ives had revised the piece so many times (something Carter had himself witnessed) that it would be difficult to determine whether the composer really had been the first to use such sonorities. Drawing on his extensive work dating the manuscripts, Kirkpatrick adduced early examples—free of revisions—that seemed to provide incontrovertible evidence of Ives's precedence over his European modernist contemporaries. Carter, by this time, had adopted a rather different view of Ives, choosing to see him less as a modernist pioneer, taming virgin musical ground, and more as a participant in a larger history of dissonance, alongside Scriabin and Strauss. What is significant in this exchange, as Massey points out, is Kirkpatrick's ongoing commitment to the Ives-as-innovator trope, for it would inform his activities as executive editor of the critical edition: "Kirkpatrick's conviction that Ives's original ideas were already sufficiently dissonant led to editions in which presenting Ives's initial intention became the goal. In other words, Kirkpatrick and other Ives Society members inscribed Ives's priority as an innovator into their editions through editorial intervention."[54]

Kirkpatrick affirmed his preferences at the 1974 Ives Centennial Festival-Conference as a member of a panel discussion devoted specifically to the problems of editing Ives. The chair asked him directly, "How do you feel about the idea that the last version is the best?" Kirkpatrick responded, "I do often find that Ives's first idea was best. Painters often say that a sketch, even a pencil sketch toward a painting, is apt to have a freshness that somehow the painting never preserves."[55] Kirkpatrick subsequently codified this perspective in the editorial guidelines that were distributed to editors who worked on Ives Society critical editions: "One should hold a skeptical but open view of [Ives's] later revisions, which were often touches of genius illuminating the original concept, but too frequently were unnecessary added dissonances or elaborated details sidetracking the original directness."[56] Kirkpatrick's prescription was at odds with the principle that generally guided editors who worked on critical editions for other composers, namely to assemble a score that captured "final authorial intent"—the *Fassung lezter Hand*, to use the German phrase.

It is not surprising, then, that the first few volumes of the Ives critical edition were greeted with puzzlement and, on occasion, outright rejection. Massey provides an extensive sampling of critical reaction to the editions, but for my purposes, it will suffice to quote two of them. First, the devastating assessment of German musicologist and Ives specialist Wolfgang Rathert, excerpted from his 1989 review article that surveyed all the critical editions released by the Ives Society thus far: "Do these editions hold their own judged by common editorial criteria or by the specific demands of the works? On the contrary, there are no uniform editorial principles, the musicological underpinnings are obviously inadequate, and there is a resulting carelessness in the handling of the music."[57] More nuanced and more forgiving was American musicologist Charles Hamm's review of *Forty Earlier Songs*, edited by Kirkpatrick himself. Hamm observed, "Kirkpatrick's approach to these songs is sometimes more in the spirit of creative collaboration than of critical, musicological editing." After listing a number of questionable editorial interventions, he concluded, "musicologists who are not performers have much to learn from Kirkpatrick's insistently musical approach to editing."[58] Neither of these quotations is focused specifically on the issue of privileging original versions, but they both reveal that the Ives Society editions fell short of musicological expectation—and the key word here is musicological. Hamm's comments are particularly perceptive because he drew a distinction between performing editions and critical editions, situating Kirkpatrick's work somewhere in between. And what was true for Kirkpatrick, executive editor of the series, carried over to the other editors he oversaw.

In an influential review of the 1939 premiere of the "Concord" Sonata, critic Lawrence Gilman had applied the sobriquet "Unobtrusive Minister of Genius" to John Kirkpatrick.[59] Massey has adopted it as the title for his thesis about Kirkpatrick's editorial activities, and it is equally apt as a description of Kirkpatrick's role in Ives's reception. *Minister* couples nicely with Kirkpatrick's official title at Yale: *curator*. Both words are evocative of the ecclesiastical world, *curate* being a close cognate of *curator*. They name roles within an official church hierarchy—upholders, protectors, and promoters of doctrine, not its creators (the business of prophets, who generally stand outside such hierarchies). The doctrine Kirkpatrick defended, and that guided his actions for the tenure of his executive editorship of the Ives Society critical editions, was the view of Ives as transcendentalist innovator. Though arguably its most ardent promoter, Kirkpatrick was not the originator of this view. It was the creation of the first generation of Ives devotees in the twenties and thirties, filmed over by a metaphysical patina courtesy primarily of the writing of Henry and Sidney Cowell. Ultimately, Kirkpatrick would prove to be flexible in his ministerial role, for when a new cohort of scholarly Ivesians, most of them bona fide musicologists, set about examining the legacy of the composer from the standpoint of their own dogma, he accepted their discoveries—if sometimes grudgingly.

Square Pegs and Round Holes:
The Music of Ives and Style Criticism I

For most musicologists working in the late sixties and early seventies, twentieth-century music seemed a daunting prospect. Some held the conviction that the music of the recent past—even going back as far as the turn of the century—lacked the requisite historical distance for forming objective assessments. Another deterrent, perhaps more formidable, was the unsuitability of this music to the application of standard methodologies.[60] The modernist mandate, which demanded near perpetual innovation from its adherents, had beset most composers working in the classical-music tradition during the twentieth century. As a result, the contemporary musical landscape was littered with a startling and unprecedented array of styles, and common-practice musical language stood in eclipse (though reports of its demise were greatly exaggerated). In such a landscape, categorizing the flora and fauna was a difficult task: it was possible to discern some coherent genera and even, with a bit of squinting, the dim outlines of stylistic evolution, but closer scrutiny tended to yield confusion. Musicologists who braved the music of the twentieth century were forced to find a compromise between their subject matter and the kinds of linear narratives they were accustomed to constructing. Fitting Ives into such narratives was especially difficult, as a survey of three of the earliest efforts attests—the work of William W. Austin, H. Wiley Hitchcock, and Robert Morgan.

Austin, a colleague of Kirkpatrick's at Cornell University, was one of the first American musicologists to hazard a history of twentieth-century music and the first to incorporate Charles Ives within such a narrative.[61] His *Music in the 20th Century* (1966) was the final volume in a seminal music-history series issued by W. W. Norton publishers. Austin solved the problem of contemporary music by making the styles of seven composers—Debussy, Schoenberg, Stravinsky, Bartók, Prokofiev, Hindemith, and Webern—landmarks relative to which he mapped out the rest of the stylistic terrain.[62] Throughout the book, his modus operandi was to introduce a biographical sketch of each composer, proceed to discussing the traits of the composer's style, and then conclude with some tentative critical assessments. Within this tripartite structure, it was style that received the greatest attention. "It should be needless to warn," Austin noted near the beginning of the book, "that our passing attention to biographies remains quite subordinate to our constant attention to the music itself." His comments about the prospects of linking style to matters of historical context broader than biography are also revealing: "Patterns of social and economic change can be found to parallel the patterns of stylistic change. Economic changes surely condition the stylistic changes, and perhaps, in some sense, determine them. But the facts are so many, so varied, and so incompletely known that a conscientious historian must propose any pattern as a tentative hypothesis. Any pattern of parallel patterns is a mere speculation, not an explanation." This brief reference to Marxist theory (the term appears in the index pointing to this very page, but not in the text) is unusual for a music history published in English at this time, but the convictions about the proper limitations of musicology are wholly typical. And it is a measure of Austin's success within the field and according to those limitations that the American Musicological Society bestowed upon his book the first Kinkeldey Award, an annual prize for the most distinguished book of the year.[63]

The principal criterion for Austin's assessment of any composer was the extent to which his or her music displayed an integrated, controlled style. On those grounds, Ives failed. Austin declared deficient the composer's "command of musical materials" and likened the jumbled nature of Ives's prose writings to his "heap[ed] up motifs and chords." Elaborating further, Austin explained, "[Ives's] own melodies [as opposed to those he quoted] are not memorable. His own rhythms are often sluggish or jerky. His chords are mostly opaque blocks of six or more notes tightly spaced and doubled in octaves." The pedigree of Austin's criticisms runs back to the writings of Elliott Carter, prominently cited in his bibliography. And, like Carter, Austin was not wholly dismissive of Ives's music. The composer, he conceded, had never been interested in "finding a style or a perfect form" anyway, since his transcendentalist commitments, spelled out in *Essays*, privileged substance over manner. Ultimately it was "his boldness of imagined 'substance' that compels admiration, and in some of his music a sympathetic listener finds unique delights, along with moral challenge." Thus transcendentalism covered a host of Ives's musical sins. Austin acknowledged that, by the sixties, the composer had become "a legendary figure, inspiring and consoling many young Americans," but he exerted little musical influence. As far as the history of style in the twentieth century was concerned, Ives stood in a cul-de-sac.[64]

Austin was to play a minimal role in shaping Ives's reception (in his 1983 dissertation, J. Peter Burkholder would make a point of rebutting the vision of Ives supplied in *Music in the 20th Century*).[65] But his work is illustrative of the preoccupations of musicologists and the difficulties they faced in absorbing Ives into their disciplinary framework. Lines of development or continuity, antecedents and consequences, causal strings—all of these centered on style: this is what musicologists sought.

In 1969, three years after the publication of Austin's book, H. Wiley Hitchcock tried his hand at the historical survey genre. His book, *Music in the United States: A Historical Introduction*, is imbued with the fervent convictions of an avowed American exceptionalist—convictions he inherited from earlier studies of American culture. As explained in chapter 4, scholars associated with the American Studies movement in its early post–World War II phase had worked under the assumption that the American people possessed a singular essence. Seminal figures like Henry Nash Smith and David M. Potter maintained that the United States stood apart from Europe, that it had its own myth and symbols, and that identifying them would require a uniquely collaborative effort across many disciplines. Although music was of peripheral concern to the first cohort of American Studies scholars, their convictions were shared by the handful of people concurrently devoting themselves to the study of American music. Gilbert Chase, in particular, argued strenuously that the United States had a unique music history, the chronicling of which demanded a resourceful scholar, willing to pursue "every pertinent discipline, through all the sciences of man."[66] Such a wide-ranging endeavor was not easily contained by the bounds of musicological practice in the sixties and early seventies. Hitchcock drew attention to this problem in a 1968 article, observing that while Americans had been delinquent in preserving the musical past of this country, the ends toward which musicologists often strove—*Denkmäler*, *Gesamtausgaben*, *Monumenta*—were not well-suited to the particular nature of American music history. Note the usage of German and

Latin terminology, a (perhaps unconscious) means of underscoring the foreignness of the musicological enterprise. The problem, as Hitchcock diagnosed it, was that the best of American music emerged from folk and popular traditions, which lent themselves less readily to the production of scholarly editions. Much of what made this music special could not be captured on the printed page as it had more to do with performance practice.[67]

Hitchcock was especially indebted to Chase, whose resounding affirmation of American folk music he absorbed and projected into the pages of *Music in the United States*. Although much less polemical than Chase, Hitchcock made his allegiances clear. His favor lay with American music that was part of the "vernacular tradition," a rubric he coined to identify music "understood and appreciated simply for its utilitarian or entertainment value." It had its counterpart in the "cultivated tradition," defined as "a body of music that America had to cultivate consciously, music faintly exotic, to be approached with some effort, and to be appreciated for its edification, its moral, spiritual or aesthetic values." In effect, the "cultivated tradition" was a synonym for Western European classical music. Hitchcock's terms have since become part of the standard lexicon of musicologists who specialize in American music, an indication of the role he played in shaping the field. Irrespective of the tradition with which he was dealing, though, his main objective was to chart the history of its musical styles. While he offered the following passage as an explanation for the selection of post–World War I composers represented in *Music in the United States*, it is exemplary of his general criteria: "I have emphasized the principal stylistic trends and the predominant musical attitudes. Many fine composers have thereby gone unmentioned; they have had to make way, with my apologies, for the few who seem to me to have been the ones in whose work the major themes of twentieth-century American music have been expressed most clearly, boldly, and influentially."[68]

Foremost among those composers Hitchcock deemed influential was Charles Ives, whom he accorded a full chapter, just as Chase had done in *America's Music*. Ives was the only composer to receive such extensive treatment and, by way of justification, Hitchcock asserted, "[Ives's] thought and his music stand as continuing, fertile challenge to American musical evolution."[69] Chase had made Ives the culminating figure for his narrative, and accordingly, he placed him at the very end of the book, disrupting its chronology. By contrast, in Hitchcock's book, the Ives chapter served as the central structural pillar. Ives stood at the apex of a narrative arc that began with the eclectic character of American musical culture during the colonial period and early republic, separated into the vernacular and cultivated traditions during the nineteenth century, achieved a synthesis with Ives, and then devolved into heterogeneity once more in the twentieth century.

But it was a peculiar kind of synthesis that Ives achieved, because it involved the juxtaposition of vernacular and cultivated musics, not their integration. Here, Hitchcock faced the challenge of the unitary concept of style then dominant in musicological practice—a concept whose criteria had proved devastating for Ives when William Austin applied them. Rather than surmounting the obstacle, Hitchcock went around it by invoking transcendentalism. Yes, it was true that Ives's music displayed a "tumultuous congregation of materials" and an "apparent lack of continuity." Yes, it was also true that the composer's "planar, heterophonic polyphony [is] occasionally so dense that the ear simply cannot distinguish the separate strands."[70] But transcendentalism saw unity in diversity. For Hitchcock, the music worked in much the same way as Emerson's writing, as described by Ives in *Essays*: "His [Emerson's] underlying plan of work seems based on the large unity of a series of particular aspects of a subject rather than on the continuity of its expression. As thoughts surge to his mind, he fills the heavens with them, crowds them in, if necessary, but seldom arranges them along the ground first."[71] Thus, transcendentalism explained the disparate musics that populated Ives's sonic landscapes, the episodic nature of his works, and his predilection for quotation—that and the musical open-mindedness Ives inherited from his father.[72] In short, Hitchcock reached much the same conclusions as Austin, but without denigrating Ives's musical craftsmanship en route. The Cowellian trope of transcendentalist-inspired individualism once again served as the glue that made Ives and his music coherent, despite its sounding surface.

While the issue of style remained paramount for Hitchcock and Austin, this was not the case for Robert Morgan, who took up the question of Ives and his place in music history in an influential pair of articles published in the midseventies. Morgan's career embodies the shift of discourse about Ives within the musical world from the domain of composers to that of musicologists. He was a composer by training, having received his PhD in composition from Princeton University in 1969. Over the course of the seventies, Morgan gradually shifted his efforts to scholarship and eventually abandoned composition completely. He does not recollect when he first encountered Ives, but in the course of his graduate-student years, he developed a strong affinity for the composer—and this despite the fact there was little love lost for Ives among the composition faculty at Princeton. The composers there tended toward arch-modernism and placed a premium on rigorous structural coherence. Some of them required that all notes be accounted for by musicotheoretical principles, notably Milton Babbitt, who was then the most vocal Princetonian.[73] If a high level of systematic organization was the criterion, Ives's music, particularly those pieces that were a patchwork of musical quotations, seemed dubious. But for Morgan, searching for an independent compositional voice, Ives's eccentricities were an inspiration, whether because of their close affiliation with, or refusal to follow, logical postulates. Thus, when he began to write about Ives, he stressed the possible avenues of development opened up by the composer's innovations. In effect, he gave a new lease on life to the modernist apologias that had been offered up on Ives's behalf in the late twenties. Morgan, in responding to a paper given by the Yale theorist Allen Forte, even went so far as to question the imposition of systematic order on the music of Ives.[74]

Provocatively titled "Rewriting Music History: Second Thoughts on Ives and Varèse," the first of Morgan's Ives articles sought an explanation for recent trends in composition that seemed to defy the historiographical consensus about the twentieth century (such as it was). Several European scholars had taken on the subject of contemporary music, and their accounts, which tended to be more linear than that of Austin, provided a tentative evolutionary trajectory.[75] According to this narrative, the century began with a period of experiment, prompted by the collapse of nineteenth-century tonality, from which emerged the new orthodoxies of Stravinskian neoclasscism and Schoenbergian serialism. After the Second World War, avant-garde composers extrapolated from Schoenberg's methods of handling pitch, applying serial techniques to other parameters of music—rhythm, dynamics, texture. Thus "total serialism" became the reigning paradigm, with Stravinsky's "conversion" serving as final validation. For Morgan, this narrative was undoubtedly reinforced by his experience at Princeton, where serialism was widely cultivated. That kind of pedigree meant that the experience of witnessing the widespread abandonment of serial techniques, as began to happen in the midsixties, must have been especially jarring—and exciting, given Morgan's urge toward compositional independence. A gleeful sense of crisis is palpable in his writing:

> Yet today we seem to be at an historical impasse. The music of the past decade or so has brought about developments which, however confusing and contradictory in most regards, have in common the characteristic of seeming to run directly counter to this prevailing philosophy of twentieth century music. And since this philosophy is still generally held by most of our historians (at least there is very little evidence to the contrary), it is scarcely surprising that recent music remains so totally incomprehensible to them.[76]

This impasse, Morgan argued, necessitated a replacement of the prevailing historical narrative by something that could account for the variety of contemporary music.

His solution was to propose a reevaluation of the priority of composers within the canon. "It may well have been Ives and Varèse," Morgan suggested, "who

represented the true center of twentieth-century music history." These two composers responded to the crisis of tonality not by negating it, as Schoenberg and
his total serialist progeny had done, but by embracing the fact that they were no
longer constrained by a unitary system. Eclecticism could be the rule, and the
"problem of unity" within a particular piece could be solved, not "by a consistent
adherence to one compositional approach or even one musical style, but by a
consistent attitude toward the use of different approaches and styles."[77] In Morgan's second article, he advanced much the same solution, with Mahler replac-
ing Varèse as Ives's European partner in innovation.[78] What Morgan had done
was to renovate the hoary trope about Ives being ahead of his time by adopting
a different temporal perspective. Ives had made use of serial-like practices, but
his rhythmic devices and the "staggering complexity" of his textures made him
the proper forebear of composers like Stockhausen, Xenakis, Ligeti, and Pen-
derecki. In addition, Ives's expostulations about the world of "classical music"
were akin to Satie and Cage's efforts to deflate the pretensions of the traditional
concert hall. Finally, Ives's use of quotation represented a solution to the "crisis
of tonality" that found "radically new contexts for the old material." Morgan
observed, "it is no coincidence that this solution has reappeared . . . in the past
few years, when the aura of crisis has reasserted itself due to the questions raised
by total serialism."[79]

In addition to solving the historiographical problem presented by recent music, Morgan's articles also sought an alternative to Ives apologias that stressed the
composer's American-ness. By placing Ives at the center of twentieth-century
music history, relating his music to radical European developments, Morgan
invoked compositional concerns as explicans. This was a different approach
from past Ivesians, who had invoked the unique qualities of American musical culture to explain the peculiarities of Ives's music. It is no coincidence that
Morgan's first article about Ives is the rare post-Cowellian treatment of the
composer that does not invoke transcendentalism, a philosophy long treasured
for its autochthonous roots.

Although Morgan presents a history centered on technical innovation, there
is common ground shared by his work and the kind of style histories produced
by scholars trained as musicologists. He shares with his musicological confreres
a set of four assumptions about the business of conducting musical scholarship.
First, the "music itself" is the subject matter proper, with social or political concerns playing a peripheral role. Second, where the "music itself" is concerned,
the transference of ideas does not require direct association between composers.
Morgan acknowledged that Ives's creative life played out in isolation from the
larger American musical world, much less the European avant-garde. And yet
Morgan could place Ives at the center of twentieth-century music history because

of resemblances between his music and those of recent composers—even if, again, those composers did not cite Ives as a direct influence. Third, although Morgan understood the construction of history to be a malleable process working in service of the present, he, like most musicologists, aimed to construct a unitary narrative. Thus Ives, despite his isolation, became an actor in a larger drama, the "crisis of tonality" driving the plot forward for all composers at the beginning of the twentieth century. Morgan explained that once tonality was lost as a system, "it was as lost to Ives and Varèse as it was to anyone else."[80] Finally, the personalities paramount to musical scholarship are composers, not the musicians who perform their music, audiences who attend concerts where it is performed, or the critics and scholars who write about it.

In greater or lesser degree, these four assumptions also underpin the work of Austin and Hitchcock. Austin, in his later writing about Ives, reached the conclusion that multiple narratives could accommodate the composer. But each one of the narratives he outlined was essentially linear in and of itself, and Ives could be placed either in the mainstream of development or a side tributary.[81] Hitchcock, for his part, offered a style history featuring vernacular and cultivated musics side by side. But this was a broadening of the scope of disciplinary endeavor, not a fundamental rupture in its methodologies. What Austin, Hitchcock, and Morgan also shared, and what sets them apart from writers who had previously addressed the subject of Ives, was a desire to give the composer a musical past—one not confined only to his experiences of Danbury music making. Their efforts showed that the discourse of musical scholarship, and specifically musicology, was flexible enough to encompass a composer who had often been portrayed as the fully formed product of America's virgin musical soils.

Making Square Pegs Round:
The Music of Ives and Style Criticism II

One of the most imposing monuments of post–World War II musicology is the *Neue Bach-Ausgabe*, an edition of J. S. Bach's complete works consisting of over a hundred volumes, the first issued in 1954 and the last in 2007, each of which is accompanied by a separately published critical report. Coordinated by the Johann Sebastian Bach Institute in Göttingen and the Bach-Archiv in Leipzig, the massive endeavor of producing this edition involved scholars on either side of the Atlantic. It is a triumph of international collaboration, a demonstration of the most rigorous methods of source criticism, and a celebration of the sort of paleographical enterprises that were, for nearly a hundred years after the inception of *musikwissenschaft*, the sine qua non of musicological practice. But with triumph came trauma.[82] As musicologists sifted through Bach's manuscripts in the fifties and sixties, they discovered that the chronology proposed by the nineteenth-century German musicologist Phillipp Spitta had serious errors. A patriarch of the field, Spitta was venerated for having adapted the paleographic methodologies used by scholars in literary fields—methodologies upon which musicologists still relied. Especially notable was his use of watermarks for establishing a chronology of Bach's output. With the refined paleographic techniques available to scholars in the fifties—techniques that were nonetheless wholly in keeping with Spitta's positivistic framework—it became apparent that there were problems with the dating of the chorale cantatas. The evidence suggested that Bach had not spent his last years in Leipzig devoutly ruminating over the musical possibilities of the Lutheran chorale and producing the cantatas that Spitta regarded as the crowning achievement of the composer's career. Much to the consternation of the scholars at work on the new edition, Spitta, who had seemed a model empiricist, had fallen prey to German nationalist ideology, which cast Bach as the Great Lutheran Cantor. Could the present endeavor be similarly compromised? Musicologists would not make peace with that possibility until the eighties.[83]

Something similar to the "great trauma" occurred within the realm of Ives research. A radical reenvisioning of Ives resulted from the wholly conventional enterprises of seeking out structural and stylistic unities within individual pieces, trying to chart a stylistic evolution across Ives's oeuvre, and, building on the preliminary work of Austin, Hitchcock, and Morgan, positioning Ives with respect to the broader style history of the classical tradition. Taking the analogy further, John Kirkpatrick stood roughly in relation to the first generation of musicologists who studied Ives as Spitta did to the scholars who worked on the *Neue Bach-Ausgabe*. Like Spitta, Kirkpatrick was known for his meticulous dating and cataloguing work. And, like Spitta's view of Bach, Kirkpatrick's conception of Ives was reinforced by one of the prevailing ideologies of his time. In fact, in the late fifties (the period in which he was hard at work on the Ives catalogue), Kirkpatrick's vehement anticommunism led him to promote the music of the all-American transcendentalist Ives as an antidote to the red menace.[84]

Beginning in the late sixties, several musicologists, most of them younger, set about scrutinizing the nature of Ives's practice of leavening his work with borrowed music—marches, parlor songs, hymns, and the like. They were not all in agreement, but the consensus drifted toward the idea that Ives's borrowings could be accounted for on musical grounds, a function of structural and stylistic concerns explainable without invoking transcendentalism. This line of thought culminated with the work of J. Peter Burkholder, whose 1983 dissertation (and the two books that grew out of it) showed that Ives's commitment to transcendentalism came much later in his creative life, and that the composer's borrowing practices had clear roots in the European classical-music tradition. In short, Ives was not quite the vaunted Emersonian maverick celebrated since the publication of Henry and Sidney Cowell's *Charles Ives and His Music* in 1955.

The roots of the discussion about borrowing are traceable back to the Cowells' seminal study. They proffered the following explanation:

> Ives . . . uses musical reminiscence as a kind of stream-of-consciousness device that brings up old tunes with their burden of nostalgic emotion. These snatches of hymns, minstrel songs, college songs, fiddle tunes, and so on, sewn through the fabric of his music, are never left as quotations only; certain fragments soon develop a life of their own, and some aspect of their musical structure is always made the basis of the piece's subsequent behavior, so that ultimately the music stands independent of any literary or other extra-musical connection.[85]

Little was offered in the way of substantiating evidence. Although the Cowells presented a readily testable hypothesis, it was neglected for over a decade, most writers choosing to focus instead on the programmatic possibilities presented by the snatches of borrowed music. Part of the responsibility lies with the Cowells' larger argument about Ives as a transcendentalist, which proved to be enormously resonant. In effect, it made the entirety of the composer's output programmatic, a realization in sound of the philosophies of Emerson and Thoreau. In addition, Ives's own pronouncements about the value of "substance" over "manner" seem to have deterred his proponents from exploring the manner of his music (though critics from Elliott Carter to William W. Austin maintained that his weaknesses lay in precisely this department).

The first musicologist-authored paper about Ives's borrowings was published in 1967, the work of Sydney Robinson Charles, who was otherwise a Renaissance specialist.[86] She set out to show that the borrowed material in the Second Symphony of Ives was not simply "a memoir of Ives' musical experience" in Danbury, as Leonard Bernstein had described it in the liner notes for his 1958 Columbia recording of the work.[87] Instead, it was possible to demonstrate that much of the borrowed material was integrated into the structure of the music and could be considered apart from its denotative function. Charles separated the borrowings in the symphony into three different categories, illustrating each with multiple examples: those that had no structural importance, those that were structurally essential within the context of a single movement, and those that had significance across multiple movements. To strengthen her argument, she also pointed out that in instances in which Ives had combined borrowed melodies to create a new one, the main criterion was musical resemblance, not the subject matter of the texts associated with the original tunes. The crux of the matter was this: "A close examination of the score from the beginning to end shows that Ives, in fact, has spared no effort to unify the Symphony by recurring thematic links drawn from borrowed and unborrowed material alike. The intricate, yet cohesive structure which results demonstrated eloquently that Ives, in selecting and working out his borrowed material was intensely concerned with its musical qualities." This was nothing less than a complete refutation of the line of argument Austin had advanced in *Music in the 20th Century*. Charles insisted that Ives's music did display precisely that structural, and, one might infer, stylistic coherence that had been his major criterion for assessing the music of other composers. Ives was a competent craftsman, whose music displayed "qualities which distinguish good music of all periods: well chosen material organized in a suitable structural frame, the whole bearing the stamp of a composer of originality and genius." Here was an affirmation of Ives resting on the most conservative of criteria.[88]

So too was Clayton Henderson's 1969 dissertation, "Quotation as a Style Element in the Music of Charles Ives," which I have already had occasion to sample. Henderson sorted through Ives's oeuvre, identifying borrowings and distilling systematic principles. He did not move much beyond this basic itemization, however, but he did detect stylistic evolution across the composer's oeuvre: "[I]f these composition[s] are arranged according to their original date of creation, there is evidence of increasing sophistication."[89] Summarizing his findings in a 1974 article, Henderson declared that Ives possessed "[a] definite concept of structure, with borrowed music serving as a point of reference."[90] What this meant was that the composer's output had "musical merit" that would allow it to survive the passing of the borrowings as living symbols, when their sources ceased to be a matter of common knowledge.

Henderson's dissertation was the most substantial piece of scholarship produced in the wake of Charles's efforts, but a number of other scholars also weighed in on the issue of Ives's borrowings in the late sixties and seventies. In 1968, Dennis Marshall advanced much the same argument as Charles and Henderson, using Ives's First Piano Sonata as his main example and describing the way in which the various hymn tunes borrowed therein were deployed. "It now seems clear," Marshall concluded, "that Ives has chosen his borrowed material very carefully, and the term 'quotation' seems hardly adequate to describe the fundamental importance of these hymn tunes as formal models and as unifying factors in the sonata."[91] Marshall was the first to problematize the term "quotation," and it was ultimately superseded by the looser concept of "borrowing" advocated by J. Peter Burkholder. The material in Marshall's article was intended to be part of his dissertation, which was to have yet another telling title: "Charles Ives and the Synthesis of Diverse Elements." Unfortunately, his untimely death left the project incomplete.

Gordon Cyr, a composer rather than musicologist, turned his attention to the many borrowings in the Fourth Symphony in 1971. Cyr took to task past commentators who had suggested that this appropriated material was of extra-musical significance. Such an evaluation made little sense, he maintained, since the subject matter of the borrowed hymns and popular songs sprawled across such a wide range of topics. Instead, what the borrowings shared was a similar melodic profile, "a *tendency* toward that form of the pentatonic scale equivalent to the diatonic collection minus the fourth and seventh degrees."[92] In Cyr's view, Ives had created a music that was integrated by the intervallic structure of its constituent melodies—borrowed or newly invented.

Not all the interlocutors involved in the discussion were willing to focus ex-clusively on "musical matters." Colin Sterne, for example, offered a program-matic reading of the Second Symphony that depended on the borrowings, while Christopher Ballantine argued more broadly that the experience of Ives's music was greatly impoverished by ignoring the web of associations evoked by the borrowings.[93] The same point was made more pugnaciously by Charles Wilson Ward in his 1974 dissertation, "Charles Ives: The Relationship between Aesthetic Theories and Compositional Processes." Ward launched an attack on the prevail-ing concept of style. It was deleteriously limiting, he opined, to believe that "the single criterion for truth . . . can be found in an objective analysis for the way a composer manipulates his musical materials." Style analysis applied to the music of Ives would yield meager results, for this was a music that referred outside itself, the product of a philosophy that had its roots in the aesthetics of transcenden-talism. Thus, while denying the validity of conventional musicological practice, Ward affirmed an entirely conventional view of Ives that made *Essays* the Rosetta stone for all of the composer's output. Despite his strident denunciation of style analysis, even Ward agreed that the borrowed music in Ives's pieces was present, at least in part, "as object for musical manipulation."[94]

Regardless, then, of where scholars stood on the question of the programmatic significance of the borrowings, there was a general agreement that they figured in Ives's music not merely as surface adornments, a kind of semantic icing on the cake, but as integral parts of the larger structure. H. Wiley Hitchcock put it succinctly toward the beginning of his 1977 monograph, simply titled *Ives*:

> Ives's "quotations" have nothing to do with nationalism, folklorism, or mere lo-
> cal colour. Like those of Joyce, Pound, or Picasso, they were as natural to him as
> pure invention: the pre-existent melodies that so often figure in his compositions
> were simply part of his auditory experience, just as susceptible to reworking into
> an artistic present as the storehouse in memory of a novelist or poet, or the vi-
> sual experience (whether of nature or prior art) of a painter. Of course the tunes
> that Ives borrowed had associations for him, but his use of them usually goes far
> beyond mere associative value. Borrowed melodies are sometimes the very basis

of the musical fabric, and they are treated variously, from the baldest verbatim quotations of single tunes or collage-like assemblages of them to the most subtle cloudy allusions, reminiscences, and half-rememberings.

Ives, Hitchcock affirmed, was a capable craftsman who worked borrowed material into his musical language in a careful manner, yielding works that were coherent and compelling.[95]

To render Ives truly susceptible to the analytical tropes of musicological discourse would require, however, that those tropes be reconfigured so that they might bind together all the loose ends of his sprawling music. Larry Starr, who had cut his teeth on the music of Bartók, the subject of his PhD dissertation, managed just such a reconfiguration in three articles published in the late seventies and early eighties that subsequently became the core of his 1992 monograph *A Union of Diversities: Style in the Music of Charles Ives*.[96] Unlike the other musicologists discussed so far, Starr was not focused exclusively on Ives's borrowings; instead, he was concerned with a broader category of phenomena that included the deployment of preexisting music as a subset: the rapid-fire style changes that were the most salient feature of many of Ives's best-known works. Compelling though such changes might be for many listeners, they confounded the analytical discourse of musical scholarship, which placed a premium on unity. Starr illustrated the problem at the beginning of his first article about Ives, published in 1977, by surveying the changes in the brief twenty-measure song "Ann Street." By his count, there were nine stylistically coherent sections in this piece, which meant that style was changing more or less every two measures. And so the quandary: "The essential problem confronting the analyst here, as in so many Ives pieces, is that of understanding whether overall unity and coherence lie behind all the surface changes—whether, in fact, unity and coherence appear to be compositional desiderata at all for Ives and, if so, in what way. And if unity and coherence do not seem to be significantly present, what, if anything, may be found in their place?"[97]

Starr did not answer the last of these questions, for he devised an ingenious way of demonstrating that unity did indeed lie beneath the surface changes. Style in Ives's hands, he suggested, was a musical parameter just as susceptible to manipulation as timbre, harmony, melody or rhythm. It too could be used a means of creating a coherent, unified narrative across the length of a work. From this standpoint, "Ann Street" could be described as an arch-shape, with the first stylistic section treated as an introduction. Beginning with the second section, the piece traces a trajectory through several styles to arrive, roughly at the song's midpoint, at one distantly removed from the second, and then roughly retraces the path to return to the point of stylistic departure at the end of the song.[98]

In *A Union of Diversities*, Starr expanded the analytical approach he developed for "Ann Street" and applied it to a representative sampling of Ives's songs. He argued that the informed listener could understand Ives's music without a particular knowledge of the context in which it was composed, without recourse to literalistic programs (whether Ives supplied one or not), and without familiarity with the motley of musical Americana that paraded across the surface of so much of the composer's output. With respect to the last of these, Starr was especially insistent:

> In terms of the artistic form and meaning of his music, Ives's quotations, however they may have functioned for him personally, need not be viewed as evocations of specific kinds of occasions, time periods, or landscapes. They may be heard as quotations of *styles*. Their function is a formal one. They create meaning and stimulate emotion, not through dependence on personal association, but through their interaction with the other stylistic elements in a particular work, and through the formal and affective associations their styles create in the context of the surrounding music.[99]

Thus Starr threw in his lot with the scholarly faction comprised of Charles, Henderson, Cyr, and (by the time *A Union of Diversities* was published) J. Peter Burkholder, who all contended that the borrowings could be explored as purely musical phenomena. Starr, however, was concerned with the meanings that could be gleaned from Ives's music, and, as a result, his analyses were not limited to the kinds of formalistic investigation characteristic of some of the other members of this group. Ives, he showed, used style in a number of different ways to convey meaning. Particularly common was the juxtaposition of styles to evoke a physical or mental journey. But there were also a number of other techniques: styles could be layered, either to create a composite style or to create a texture of independent strata; they could be subjected to a process of simplification; and, in a few rare instances, they could be made more complex. The crux of the matter was that style had both structural and semantic functions, working in intricate counterpoint to the texts of Ives's songs.

The manipulation of style also provided Starr with a means of charting Ives's musical evolution in a 1983 article, a first step toward the periodization of the composer's oeuvre—and another step toward making Ives fit conventional musicological narratives. Starr observed that prior to 1902, when Ives abandoned music as a profession, the composer produced pieces that were stylistically consistent throughout. Some of the works displayed a "conservative manner," essentially music that adhered to the conventions of late-nineteenth-century tonality. Others employed a "radical manner," Ives's early Psalm settings for example, each of which "is distinctive in degree and kind of departure from traditional late-nineteenth-century thinking. Each presents an individual stylistic 'area,' explored with reasonable and sometimes extraordinary consistency."[100] What did not happen in these early works though, was a mixing of the two manners. Stylistic diversity within the context of a single piece was something that Ives began to explore only after he had resigned from his post at the Central Presbyterian Church in New York. Here, Starr argued, was the basis for separating Ives's music into early and mature periods. Thus Ives, despite his musical peculiarities—or, in fact, because of them—could be made subject to the kinds of evolutionary narrative that musicologists applied to the output of more conventional composers. Working concurrently with Starr, J. Peter Burkholder, who would become the dominant figure in Ives scholarship from the eighties onward, developed an even more comprehensive account of the composer's style history.

Dispelling the Transcendentalist Myth

Burkholder's serious engagement with the music of Ives began with a mandatory course on twentieth-century musical analysis, which he undertook as a composition graduate student at the University of Chicago in 1976. Ever since he had first encountered Ives's music as a college sophomore, he had been attracted to its unusual features and evocative qualities. There were interesting harmonies and a mixture of tonality and atonality, in service of music that seemed to map out three-dimensional space and represent the multiple layers of lived experience. Now an aspiring composer himself, Burkholder settled upon an analysis of the final movement of Ives's Third Symphony for his seminar paper. He produced a moment-by-moment analysis, parsing each vertical sonority into the tonic, dominant, and subdominant key areas. When he showed it to Robert Morgan, newly appointed to the University of Chicago faculty in 1978, Morgan found it tedious. Though inauspicious, this exchange marked the beginning of Morgan's role as mentor to Burkholder, who, by this time, had abandoned his goal of becoming a composer and set his sights on musical scholarship instead. In the fall of 1979, Burkholder prepared a dissertation proposal that signaled his intention to focus on Ives. Morgan would serve as advisor.[101]

Initially, Burkholder wanted to write a dissertation that was solely analytical, examining the ways in which Ives deployed and amplified nineteenth-century techniques in his mature music. There was even a direct precedent in the 1972 dissertation of David Eiseman, which demonstrated Ives's rootedness in the European symphonic tradition.[102] But, as anyone who has completed a dissertation in the humanities will attest, what one sets out to write rarely resembles the final product. Roughly one-third of Burkholder's dissertation is indeed devoted to showing how, as he put it, "each major aspect of Ives's musical method developed by a process of exaggeration from starting points in common 19th-century procedures and assumptions."[103] This section, however, proved to have far less importance for the field of Ives studies than the other two-thirds of the dissertation. That two-thirds began humbly as Burkholder set out to write a fifteen-page introductory chapter intended to summarize conventional wisdom about the unifying aspects of Ives's career, namely his commitment to transcendentalism and use of borrowed music. The idea was to dispense with the two issues that had dominated Ives scholarship, clearing the ground for the main business of analysis. As Burkholder read Ives's writings, perused the published literature, examined the writings of Ives's mentors, worked in the Yale Ives archive, and made inquiries with Ives's friends and family, he found himself reaching very different conclusions. Consequently, Burkholder was compelled to change his plans and devote space—considerable space—to the very issues he had thought to pass over rapidly. In its final form, the dissertation consists of three parts bearing separate titles: "Ives's Artistic Aims and their Development" (which is mostly concerned with transcendentalism), "Ives's Use of Existing Music," and "Techniques: Traditional Roots and Contemporary Parallels."[104]

It bears repeating that Burkholder, like the other musicologists who studied Ives during the seventies, carried out his research well within the bounds of conventional musicological practice. Establishing continuities of style and technique between Ives's music and the broader nineteenth-century repertory was precisely the sort of thing musicologists had been doing since the founding of the discipline. In fact, Burkholder started from the most conservative of disciplinary premises. In the acknowledgements section of his dissertation, he credited his undergraduate professors at Earlham College with teaching him "to look at the music first and to read what has been said about it later, after approaching the music on its own terms."[105] The conviction that music could be encountered in an unmediated fashion, unencumbered by the ideas of others, had lingered at the center of musicological discourse, albeit sometimes uncomfortably, for nearly a century. When Adler spoke of uncovering the "laws of Art" in 1885; when Oscar Sonneck advocated the study of "*Das ding an sich*" in 1929; and when Jan LaRue claimed that his style-analysis methodology provided a means of "understanding music based directly on the notes themselves" in 1970; each scholar was giving voice to this belief.[106] The musicological imperative to focus on the "notes themselves" is most obviously borne out in the second and third parts of Burkholder's dissertation. But it was also a spur to the first, an attempt, as Burkholder explained, "to clear away the underbrush that had grown up around Ives's music and obscured 'the music itself' through a transcendentalist fog."[107]

Part I turns the essentialist spirit of musicologists on the prose writings of Ives—the texts in themselves, as it were. The main subject of Burkholder's scrutiny was *Essays Before a Sonata*, which had long been the locus classicus for Ivesian aesthetics. Ever since the Cowells' study of Ives in the fifties, the assumption had been that the composer's advocacy of the transcendentalists in *Essays* meant that he shared their philosophical outlook completely. Burkholder's approach was to set aside, for the moment, the subject matter of the book (the Concord cohort) and focus instead on what the text revealed about the writer's habits of thought. Reading *Essays* from this vantage revealed three characteristics: first, Ives displayed a pattern of approaching issues in a dualistic fashion (substance and manner being the most famous pairing); second, he repeatedly expressed his belief in the "innate goodness of humankind"; and, third, he tended to privilege intuition and experience over external authority.[108]

Having distilled the essence of Ives's thought, as represented by *Essays*, Burkholder compared it with the ideas of the transcendentalist writers themselves. There proved to be some similarities but also some significant differences. To begin with, Ives's habit of dualistic thinking displayed a moralistic character that was alien to Emerson, who wrote about polarities contained within a larger unity. Citing specific examples, Burkholder pointed to the value-laden distinctions Ives drew between "artistic strength" and "moral weakness" or "the majority" and "the minority." To Burkholder, such dichotomies owed more to the ongoing influence of Puritan thinking than to anything Emerson had ever written. Even in those passages of *Essays* that seemed closest kindred to transcendentalist thought, Ives deployed his own terms, which suggested that the composer had arrived at the same conclusions independently. Moreover, *Essays* displayed a circumscribed conception of transcendentalism, limited primarily to Emerson and Thoreau, and, even within their writings, a rather selective reading. "[Ives's] Thoreau," Burkholder observed, "is the author of *Walden*, the contemplative listener, rather than the social rebel of *Civil Disobedience*." Finally, Burkholder noted that music had not occupied a prominent place in the thinking of most transcendentalists, with the notable exception of John Sullivan Dwight, whose musical conservatism stood at some remove from Ivesian aesthetics.[109]

Moving from texts to matters biographical, Burkholder found more reasons to contest the view that the transcendentalists occupied a central place in Ives's life, from cradle to grave. The first target of his scrutiny was the composer's childhood. Burkholder wrote Sidney Cowell, inquiring whether her research had turned up any evidence to support the vision of a transcendentalist-infused home life; examined the list of books in the Ives family library; and consulted with Bigelow Ives, the composer's nephew. Cowell was unable to recollect what sources justified the claim that she and Henry had made about Emerson and Thoreau being foundational for Ives. The family library, while attesting to a strong interest in religious matters and social justice (especially abolition), yielded relatively little in the way of transcendentalist writings. It did contain Theodore Parker's *A Discourse on Matters Pertaining to Religion* (1842), but Parker did not serve as a major point of reference in Ives's prose. Nor could Burkholder find the copies of Emerson and Thoreau that Sarah Ives, the composer's grandmother, was supposed to have cherished. Bigelow recollected that as a boy, he knew Emerson and Thoreau only as "books on the shelf." Coming up empty-handed, Burkholder concluded, "there is no evidence to support the assumptions that enthusiasm for Emerson continued unabated in the Ives family from the 1850s until Charles Ives left home to enter college nearly half a century later, that Ives was himself directly affected by it, that the importance of transcendentalist ideas for Ives remained constant from his youth to his old age, or the even more sweeping assumption that the essential elements of Ives's aesthetic philosophy originated in Emerson and Thoreau."[110] When Burkholder turned his attention to sources pertaining to Ives's college life, he also found them lacking evidence for an ongoing affinity with the transcendentalists. What was needed, therefore, was a wholesale biographical revaluation that attended closely to the development of Ives's philosophical and aesthetical commitments. This Burkholder supplied, refiguring in the process, the role of three people in Ives's life: George Ives, Horatio Parker, and Harmony Ives.

As in most accounts of the composer's biography, Burkholder's made George Ives a central figure: he was the source of Charlie's experimental enthusiasms and open-mindedness, a musical idealism that was not specifically transcendentalist in nature. But Burkholder's Ives was not a figure fully formed at childhood's end—neither the vaunted musical transcendentalist of Cowellian imagination nor the prisoner of sociosexual mores who Frank Rossiter described in his influential 1975 biography. Burkholder perceived a dichotomous way of thinking in the musical activities of George, implanted in his son but then superseded in the younger man's mature music. George, the evidence suggested, drew a distinction between his musical experiments on the one hand—polytonal superimpositions, microtonal sonorities, unusual scales—and music for performance on the other. The experiments were intended for private edification, not public entertainment.[111] By contrast, in Ives's later works, they stood cheek by jowl with music of a more conservative nature.

Unlike many past biographers, Burkholder did not portray Horatio Parker as a pedant who exerted little influence on Ives's musical development. Instead, Parker imparted to Ives another kind of musical idealism, which, though again not transcendentalist, shared the German provenance of ideas that animated the Concord cohort. It emphasized the moral dimension of art, demanding of the artist that he or she strive toward the highest ends. Music conceived in this fashion had a moral purpose and not a utilitarian one; it was an expression of the will of the composer, which was not to be swayed by matters of public taste. The word Parker used to describe this dimension was "substance," one-half of Ives's favorite binary. The other, "manner," Burkholder traced back to an essay on Debussy written by Ives's friend John Griggs.[112]

Most significant of all was Harmony Ives. Here, Burkholder turned even more abruptly away from biographical precedent, for past writers, if they dealt with Harmony at all, consigned her to the role of ideal helpmate, the epitome of nineteenth-century domesticity. In Burkholder's narrative, she became the catalyst for Ives's mature style and the impetus for his transcendentalist enthusiasms. Her family had its own idealism rooted in the literary tradition of New England churchmen—a tradition to which Emerson himself belonged. In extant correspondence between Charles and Harmony from the period of their engagement (late 1907 to June 1908), Harmony extolled the virtues of reading and spurred her future husband to literary pursuits. Burkholder argued that it was her urgings that would eventually lead Ives to his deep engagement with Emerson and Thoreau. The evidence, he conceded, was circumstantial,

> but it is very strong: there is a shift of topic in Ives's chosen texts towards spiritual, Transcendentalist, and later progressive political ideals, coinciding with the composition of the "Concord" Sonata, the beginning in the 1910s of Ives's application of Transcendentalist thinking to his concerns in the insurance business and the larger political issues, and his marriage to Harmony. This combination of circumstances suggests strongly that, whatever Ives's earlier contact with Emerson's writings, he returned to them in earnest around the time of his engagement to Harmony, and their influence grew to affect every aspect of his life.

Equally influential was Harmony's conception of the experience of art, also revealed in letters to Ives from the period of their courtship. Burkholder identified two salient traits: "first, she focuses on 'putting into expression' not merely emotions but specific moments or events, moments which are individual, indeed unique and irreplaceable; second she recognizes that writing words or music about 'one's happiest moments' is normally done after the moment is over, through the memory." Ives, already prone to nostalgia by the acutely felt absence of his father, adopted these traits. Harmony thus stimulated a retrospective introspection in her husband, prompting him to sift through the past for salient experiences that could be put into musical expression.[113]

When Burkholder published the first part of his dissertation as *Charles Ives: The Ideas behind the Music* in 1985, invariably, it was his demolition of the transcendentalist myth that commanded first attention from reviewers.[114] In removing Emerson and Thoreau from the center of Ives's intellectual life, he had deprived the composer's devotees of an explanation for the jostling musical multitudes that inhabited his works. But invocations of transcendentalism had struck Burkholder as having something of an air of desperation anyway:

> Explaining Ives's uses of borrowed music as being "probably due to a transcendentalist's faith in the validity of traditional or popular expressions to voice his own thoughts," as John Kirkpatrick has suggested, is really no explanation at all; this only confuses the issue by excusing Ives's extraordinary reliance on borrowed music as a symptom of a mystical orientation, thereby confounding two separate strands of Ives's development with one another.[115]

Having untangled one strand, Burkholder turned to the other in the second part of his dissertation.

There was, by this time, ample precedent to such an endeavor. Sidney Robinson Charles, Clayton Henderson, and Larry Starr were just three of the scholars who had offered affirmative assessments of Ives that attempted to subjugate his stylistic heterogeneity (in which the borrowings played a major role) to standard disciplinary narratives. Burkholder's accomplishment was to provide a cogent account of Ives's borrowing practices that was more strongly in compliance with the patterns of musicological discourse than any of his predecessors. That account, as Burkholder explained, demonstrated that the borrowings could be "understood in purely musical terms."[116] In other words, it obviated transcendentalist apologias that made recourse to the notion of an underpinning spiritual unity.

The impetus for Burkholder's approach to Ives's borrowings was a seminar on the Renaissance Mass of the late fifteenth and early sixteenth centuries, which he took as part of his graduate coursework at the University of Chicago. Howard Mayer Brown, who led the seminar, had devoted considerable work to imitation in the secular genre of the French Chanson. Burkholder produced a seminar paper that used Brown's work as a foundation for examining borrowed material in the masses of the fifteenth-century composer Johannes Martini. (Shortly after completing his dissertation, Burkholder reworked the paper and published it in the *Journal of the American Musicological Society*—strong testament to his facility in the world of Renaissance scholarship, which supplied the bread and butter of so many musicologists. The article won the 1986 Alfred Einstein Prize, awarded annually by the AMS to an outstanding article by a young scholar. As further evidence of contemporary musicological priorities, it is worth noting that it beat out another article published by Burkholder that year, "Quotation and Emulation: Charles Ives's Use of His Models.")[117] With the perspective he had gained through his exploration of the borrowing techniques of fifteenth- and sixteenth-century composers, Burkholder perused the literature on Ives borrowings, including Clayton Henderson's dissertation, then the most extensive study of the subject.

The first item of business was typology. Burkholder believed that past scholars had erred in describing the borrowed music in Ives as "quotation." This suggested that the music was preserved intact when transported into Ives's works, which was rarely the case. Instead, he argued, there were several different musical techniques involved, each of which deserved itemization. Apart from simple settings and variations, Burkholder identified five techniques: modeling, in which the structure and possibly some of the melodic material was adopted from a preexisting piece; paraphrasing, in which a melody was altered to form a new one, usually with similar structural characteristics; cumulative setting, in which the borrowed tune or tunes do not present themselves in their entirety until the end of the piece; quoting, understood in the strictest sense; and quodlibet, in which two or more melodies were combined vertically or horizontally, "often as a joke or technical tour de force." Burkholder stressed that these techniques were frequently found in combination, especially in Ives's "mature works," where one encounters "*collage*, a swirl of quoted tunes added, quodlibet-style, to a musical structure based on modeling, paraphrase, or cumulative form, and *patchwork*, where quodlibet and modeling meet." Four of the techniques had antecedents in the music of the Renaissance—modeling, paraphrasing, quoting, and quodlibet—but "cumulative setting" was Burkholder's invention, made necessary by Ives's borrowing habits.[118]

Burkholder was not, by any means, the first to observe the composer's practice of unveiling borrowed music in its whole form at the end of a piece. As is often the case with Ives scholarship, there is precedent in the perceptive observations of the Cowells' *Charles Ives and His Music*.[119] Lou Harrison, describing the violin sonatas, named the technique "reconstruction," a designation subsequently taken over by Charles Ward in his dissertation; and there were others too who made a note of the practice.[120] Burkholder was different, though, in stressing that this technique, however named, had been prefigured in the music of earlier composers. It resembled the form of Bach's chorale preludes and was much like a sonata form with the exposition missing. Indeed this was Burkholder's central point:

> All of these techniques are richly anticipated in the music of earlier composers in the traditions of both European art music and American vernacular music, from the parody and paraphrase masses of the Renaissance to the programmatic quodlibet in Heinrich Biber's Battle Sonata, from the use by nineteenth-century composers of earlier classical music as models for their own to settings of familiar tunes in styles as diverse as the chorale preludes of J. S. Bach and the medley marches of John Philip Sousa.[121]

What was remarkable about Ives was not that he borrowed music but the catholicity of his sources and the "extremes to which he took the emulative procedures which he had inherited."[122]

Once he had established his typology and categorized Ives's works accordingly, Burkholder discovered that not all of the borrowing techniques were used in equal measure across the length of the composer's career. There was, instead, a "logical evolution" that could be correlated with the aesthetic developments documented in the first part of his dissertation. Cumulative settings, for example, first began to surface in Ives's output around 1902, coinciding with his decision to abandon professional music making, and they became his preferred form in the years of musical maturity (1907–1920), a period that began with his marriage.[123]

The end result of Burkholder's efforts was a much more dynamic view of Ives that, at the same time, rendered him more conventional with respect to the European art-music tradition. Just like Beethoven or Bach, his output could be periodized—though Burkholder did forgo the traditional early-middle-late partitioning in favor of a sevenfold division. Those periods were demarked by major changes in Ives's biography, reflected in his shifting aesthetic concerns, and manifest in the music through the changing blend of borrowing techniques. To put it differently, Ives underwent compositional development like any other composer, a process that could be carefully documented by the attentive scholar and that displayed a degree of unity—in the looser sense of a set of shared general characteristics that evolved logically over time. Even more significantly, Ives's compositional development not only resembled that of European composers but was rooted in the same tradition, absorbing borrowing techniques that had a lengthy pedigree within that tradition.

Burkholder devoted roughly two hundred pages to the part of his dissertation about the borrowing practices of Ives, and, as with the first part concerning Ives's aesthetics, it would become the basis of a stand-alone volume. In this case, however, the material was substantially revised and expanded, the product of twelve years of additional work. From the roughly forty pieces discussed in the dissertation, he increased the purview to some two hundred, providing comprehensive coverage of Ives's oeuvre. He also incorporated new findings about the dates of Ives's compositions, supplied extensive discussion of sketch materials for several pieces, and ventured into the realm of hermeneutics. But the most significant change was the implementation of a more nuanced borrowing typology that consisted of fourteen categories.[124] Published in 1995, the resulting monograph, *All Made of Tunes: Charles Ives and the Uses of Musical Borrowing*, weighs in at over 550 pages. It brings us a long way from the inauspicious beginnings of musicologists' engagement with Ives in the midsixties as represented by William Austin's *Music in the 20th Century*, but perhaps not quite as far as might at first seem. Certainly it is true that where Austin had perceived disorder and poor craftsmanship, Burkholder saw order and consummate craftsmanship; while Austin placed Ives in the backwaters, apart from the rushing current of musical development, Burkholder situated him in the mainstream; where Austin heard a musical farrago that made sense only as sonic realization of transcendentalist principles, Burkholder heard music that could be explained "on its own terms," apart from any programmatic allusions. And yet, for all these differences between Austin, circa 1966, and Burkholder, circa 1995, they did not dispute the criteria for and objective of assessing the music of Ives. Both men worked within the framework of musicological discourse as established in the 1960s—a framework that made style a priority and unity its essential condition.

Burkholder affirmed his continuing commitment to the traditional pursuits of musicology in a talk delivered in 1989, amid disciplinary upheavals that were to broaden considerably the ambit of musical scholarship (the details will have to wait until the next chapter). "My interest in why composers make the choices they do," he explained, "leads to a study of musical style, the traditional core of historical musicology, for composers make choices within, among and sometimes in defiance of the prevailing style or styles." Burkholder's talk was one of three contributions to a panel on the relationship between musicology and music theory, which was experiencing more strain than usual as a new cohort of musicologists marginalized their theorist colleagues by seeking interdisciplinary alliances elsewhere. Burkholder mounted a careful defense of the value of both fields as traditionally conceived and contended that they were inextricably linked. The analogy he drew to explain this relationship is striking for its historical resonances: music theory was to musicology as biological taxonomy was to evolution, he suggested. "Though they have separate histories, today these are not two fields, but one. Taxonomy is the classification of living things according to how closely related they are. Evolution is the retracing of the family tree of all life. Evolution is the historical basis for taxonomy, and taxonomy provides evidence for evolution."[125]

The natural sciences had served as an aspiration for the founders of musicology, who strove, in the latter half of the nineteenth century, to make the study of music sciencelike. In his talk, Burkholder invoked the natural sciences as a point of reference, a simile, and not as the paragon of scholarly virtue. Nonetheless, by resorting to this simile, Burkholder's comments reveal that over a century after Adler published his "The Scope, Method, and Aim of Musicology," the language of evolutionary biology still came readily to hand for a prominent musicologist.[126] And it bears mentioning that Burkholder's study of Ives's borrowing unfolded in an analogous fashion to the dual vision he articulated here: the task of taxonomy, the classification of borrowing techniques led to the arrangement of those techniques in a chronological sequence. Burkholder was not repudiating what has since become known as "New Musicology." Rather, he was making a case for the continuing validity of older disciplinary practices—practices that had proven to be effective for generating new insights about Ives, from dispelling the transcendentalist myth to revealing the composer's connections with the European art-music tradition.

6

Ives at Century's Turn

"Is an icon becoming a has-been?"[1] This was the question *New York Times* critic Donal Henahan posed in April 1987, after Leonard Bernstein decided to cancel a scheduled performance of Ives's Fourth Symphony. Indeed there was evidence that a certain amount of ennui had set in with respect to Ives. A few weeks earlier, in a *Times* survey of high-profile musicians, several participants had nominated him "most over-rated composer."[2] On the other side of the country, Los Angeles critic Herbert Glass observed that there had been a "general decline in Ives's stock since the overexposure attending the 1974 centenary," and, he added, it was a shame that the "lovely, listenable" works had been consigned to oblivion "along with the more off-putting creations of Ol' Charlie, sometime musical bogeyman and ear-stretcher."[3] Glass's quip at Ol' Charlie's expense was mild in comparison to the accusation musicologist Maynard Solomon leveled against the composer that fall. Ives, Solomon pronounced, had engaged in a "systematic pattern of falsification" to safeguard his claims at the patent-house of musical modernism. During the twenties, he had methodologically upped the dissonance in his compositions, crafted lists that backdated his works, and added marginalia in the manuscripts that would corroborate the false dates.[4] For Ives scholars, Solomon's indictment was especially irksome because of the forum in which it was lodged: the preeminent publication of musical scholarship, the *Journal of the American Musicological Society*. Never before had the journal's editors deigned to publish a feature article about Ives, and now in 1987, some twenty years after Ives had become par for musicological discourse, he made his debut as one of the greatest musical perjurers of all time.

Though Solomon's criticisms were devastating, they served as the catalyst for an explosion of scholarly activity centered on Ives in the nineties. Rebutting

Solomon became a vital industry that attracted a host of musicologists, long-time Ives stalwarts and neophytes alike. Their approaches varied, some working within the traditional framework of musicological methodologies, others venturing tactics associated with what came to be known as "New Musicology." The old tools of paleographic and stylistic analysis were deployed alongside new techniques that prioritized social context and stressed the contingency of musical meaning. Ultimately, Solomon's accusations would be rebuffed, but to this day, his article remains unsurpassed as the most influential scholarly essay ever written about Ives.

As Ives scholarship boomed in the nineties, his sagging reputation in the concert hall also lifted, though for different reasons. The main factor was the broad acceptance of a new version of an old myth. Ives was no longer simply the icon of American individualism and lone pioneer of musical modernism, but the patriarch of a lineage of composers linked by their penchant for experiment: the American Mavericks. The etiology of this myth and the vicissitudes of Ives scholarship at the turn of the twentieth century are the subjects of this final chapter.

Ives on the Couch

When, in 1987, Solomon broached the question of chronology in Ives's oeuvre, he did so from a vantage that was unusual in the field of musicology. The evidence he mustered to support his assertion about Ives's duplicity was paleographical and comfortably within the bounds of disciplinary discourse. It was harnessed, however, to a psychoanalytical theory about the motivations behind the campaign of misinformation Solomon imputed to Ives. Psychobiography had been a preoccupation of Solomon's ever since he entered the musicological world in the seventies with a controversial biography of Beethoven. As far as the output of musical scholars was concerned, that book and the subsequent Ives article sat on a sparsely populated shelf. But there was ample precedent in other academic disciplines.

Beginning in the fifties, a subset of professional historians had availed themselves of the explanatory potential of psychoanalysis.[5] On the whole, their preference was not for orthodox Freudianism but for so-called "ego psychology," which focused on the member of the psychoanalytic tripartite that mediated between the unconscious animal drives of the Id and the dictates of society issuing from the Superego. Ego psychology appealed because it stressed conditioning factors arising from social (and thus historical) context, mitigating the biological reductionism of Freud. One of its most influential practitioners, Erik Erikson, provided a model in his *Young Man Luther: A Study in Psychoanalysis and History* (1957). The book hinged on the concept of "identity crisis," Erikson's famous neologism for the pivotal and fraught moment he believed everyone confronted in late adolescence. But if universal, it had specific historical manifestations and solutions. Erikson attributed Luther's crisis to the tension he experienced between his father's expectation that he pursue a career as a lawyer and his own sense of spiritual calling. It was resolved by a rethinking of theological doctrine, the consequences of which rumbled through European history in the form of the Reformation.[6] In the two decades following the publication of Erikson's book, psychobiography flourished, its subjects as varied as Goethe, Thaddeus Stevens, Woodrow Wilson, Adolph Hitler, and Richard Nixon. Alongside this biographical literature, studies of mass movements rooted in psychological theorizing also thrived.[7]

Seen against this backdrop, the publication of Maynard Solomon's *Beethoven* (1977) was a continuation of a vibrant, if somewhat controversial, tradition. In fact, conservative would be an apt characterization of the book, because Solomon hewed closely to orthodox Freudian doctrine and evinced little influence of the social concerns of ego psychology. He argued that some of the long-known peculiarities of Beethoven—his uncertainty about his birth date, his pretense at being a member of the nobility, his predilection for unavailable women—pointed toward a classic Freudian neurosis, the "family romance."[8] Ten years later, Solomon turned his attention to Ives, and, just as he had done with Beethoven, mingled careful documentary study with psychoanalytical theorizing. The end result was his inflammatory 1987 article "Charles Ives: Some Questions of Veracity."

Again, Solomon opted for Freudian orthodoxy, depicting Ives as a victim of an Oedipus complex, the desire of the son to replace his father and the attendant feelings of guilt. On some fronts, Charlie was successful at trumping George his father: Charlie became a prosperous businessman and succeeded as a composer; George had been a mere performer. But on other fronts, he could not compete: as Mollie's husband, George had a stronger claim on her than Charlie did as son, and Charlie could never get around the fact that he was the offspring of George. Thus, Solomon concluded, "Unable to surpass his father in his most fundamental roles and perhaps hoping to avoid reprisals for imagined transgressions, we may surmise that Ives was impelled to make his father his permanent collaborator, idealizing their relationship, purifying his own motives, and professing a filial piety of immaculate quality."[9] To vouchsafe the status of his father, Charlie turned to the issue of priority, ascribing to George the invention of a host of modernist devices, from polytonality to quarter-tone expansions of the diatonic pitch set. To sustain the claim that the usage of these devices in his own compositions stemmed from George, Charlie had to disavow the influence of any contemporary composers— from Debussy to Stravinsky—on his music. This, Solomon explained, was the motivation for the massive project of revising and backdating manuscripts.

On the whole, musicologists shied clear of the psychoanalytical content of Solomon's article, preferring to focus on paleographical evaluation of the evidence for or against the "systematic pattern of falsification." The only scholar to address the Freudian thesis at the heart of the article was Stuart Feder, who, unlike Solomon, was a professional psychoanalyst. In his book *Charles Ives, 'My Father's Song': A Psychoanalytic Biography* (1992), Feder agreed that the oedipal complex had played a part in Ives's psychological development, as was the case with all human beings. But, Feder averred, Solomon had imposed the complex onto the facts of Ives's life in a procrustean way, neglecting factors arising from the broader social context in which the father-son relationship played out. Moreover, to focus exclusively on the oedipal moment was to deny the significance of other stages of psychological development, the postadolescent period, for example, which, as Feder argued, had been crucial for both George and Charlie.[10] As young men, both experienced an identity crisis shaped in part by ideals deeply embedded in Danbury culture that made music and masculinity incommensurate.

For George, the crisis came while he was serving as an army bandmaster during the Civil War. Feder uncovered documents revealing that amid the pivotal Siege of Petersburg, George requested that he be removed from his position, demoted to private, and presumably deployed right into the fray. Making the point emphatically, he destroyed his cornet and failed to show up for regular duty. This incident, which earned George a court martial, Feder interpreted as symptom of a failure to negotiate the passage from boyhood to manhood. While the pomp attendant upon band performances made George temporarily and ritually a leader of men, his musical endowment could never substitute for the bloody heroism of a frontline infantryman or, beyond the Civil War, the business acumen that allowed his elder brothers to prosper. The values of Danbury precluded this, and Danbury he could not escape. Feder wrote, "Events in the years following the war reveal that George continued to be unprepared to leave home literally; events of later life suggest that he was never fully able to do so psychologically."[11]

Charlie left home physically, but as with his father, not psychologically. Here oedipal factors did come into play. As a baby, Charlie was confronted with the noisy disruptions—musical certainly, sexual probably—of his bandmaster father. George was thus responsible for making Charlie aware of the world beyond his mother, who, for her part, was a silent presence and left little trace in her son's autobiographical writings. Feder asserted that the music Charlie heard in those early years, the hymns and marches of his father's repertoire, became ineluctably bound to his mental representation of George. Thus, throughout Charlie's life, his musical imagination would keep him connected to George, and through George, to Danbury and its environs. George died the first year Charlie was away from home, precisely that moment at which he was beginning to assert his own identity and succeed where his father had not, becoming an independent man. And so Charlie's crisis. The correspondence between father and son during the final months of George's life shows tensions, the consequence of a son's impatient desire to move forward and a father's urge toward cautious restraint. Feder hypothesized that the death of George "represented the fulfillment of his [Charlie's] most despised wishes and initiated a state of mourning which is necessarily complex. For his most beloved opponent had been rendered so completely helpless as to make the struggle meaningless. Worse was the enduring self-suspicion of mortal responsibility. Thus was loss burdened with guilt." Charlie spent much of the subsequent two decades engaged in a protracted mourning process. Its vicissitudes played out in his musical imagination, where George continued to live, and where Charlie could engage in what Feder described as an "intrapsychic" collaboration with his father.[12]

On the surface, there are resemblances between the analyses Solomon and Feder proffered, both of them homing in on Ives's complex relationship with his father and activating issues of gender and sexuality in the process. But they part ways because of their different interpretations of psychoanalysis, Solomon being an amateur Freud enthusiast and Feder a professional, whose Freudianism was inflected by Eriksonian ego psychology. In the larger scope of things, this difference matters little. By the early nineties, psychobiography had been on the wane for some time, its fortunes ebbing as psychoanalysis in its various flavors lost credibility in academe.[13] As far as the reception of Ives is concerned, no one has followed Solomon and Feder further down the path of psychological speculation, and with both men absent from the world of Ives scholarship (Solomon has moved on to other subjects and Feder passed away in 2005), this seems to be the state of things for the foreseeable future. In any case, from the moment Solomon published his Ives article in 1987, it was his paleographical analysis rather than the Freudian interpretation it supported that claimed musicologists' attention.

The Great Paper Chase

Solomon called into question the dates for Ives's compositions listed in John Kirkpatrick's *Temporary Mimeographed Catalogue*. In compiling it, Kirkpatrick relied primarily on evidence that originated with the composer himself: information contained in diaries and letters; various lists of dates that Ives compiled, beginning in the late twenties; and marginalia in the manuscripts, particularly addresses that could be identified with specific periods of Ives's life.[14] Solomon argued that the contradictory nature of much of this evidence was so serious that it could not serve as the basis of a valid chronology. Without attempting an exhaustive dismantling of the catalogue, he adduced a few examples to illustrate the problems.

Among them was the second movement of the *First Orchestral Set*, entitled "Putnam's Camp," a perennial favorite of Ivesians past and present. In the middle section of the piece, Ives superimposes two different marches at different tempi, mimicking his father's most famous musical experiment—and the only one for which there is external corroboration.[15] The marginalia for the autograph of "Putnam's Camp" includes the following bit of political commentary: "Wanted in these you-beknighted states! . . .—more independence—more gumption!—Less Parties and Politics. Election Day 1908—[William Howard] Taft" (Figure 6.1). Scrawled in block capitals, it is clearly in a later hand than the music. Moreover, the date 1908 conflicts with another Ives supplied elsewhere in the manuscripts for this piece: "Whitman's House, Hartsdale N.Y., Oct. 1912." Solomon was skeptical that the piece was composed on either of these dates, noting pointedly, "There is no independent evidence that this work was composed prior to the première of *Le Sacre du printemps* on 29 May 1913, or, indeed, completed much before its own first public performance on 10 January 1931." This example, and many like it, suggested to Solomon that Ives had backdated his scores, making it appear that he had slipped into the musical patent office before modernist notables like Igor Stravinsky.[16]

The pages of the *Journal of the American Musicological Society*, where Solomon's article was published, had long been the site of paleographic autopsies. Over the years, readers of the journal had seen many manuscripts subject to the kind of critical scrutiny Solomon directed toward the Ives material. But whereas contesting the provenance of a Medieval or Renaissance manuscript had few repercussions in the larger musical world, throwing into question the chronology of Ives's music was big news—big enough to garner the front page of the Sunday Arts and Leisure section in the *New York Times*. "Did Ives Fiddle with the Truth?" blared the headline at the top of a summa of Solomon's findings. Critic Donal Henahan soberly announced,

> Because recent research has largely dissipated the aura of integrity and rugged independence that surrounded the name of Ives and inevitably rubbed off on his music, it is going to be impossible for many of us ever again to hear an Ives piece in quite the same way as before. The New Englander who fired our imaginations as the Last Transcendentalist, the artistic descendant of Emerson and Thoreau, appears now to have something in common with a shady accountant.[17]

It was a blow to the national musical psyche to have Ives exposed as a fraud.

The immediate wake of Henahan's article stirred up irate letters from *Times* readers.[18] But the scholarly response to the issues Solomon raised was slower in coming. In the fall of 1988, a meeting of the Greater New York chapter of the American Musicological Society brought Solomon face to face with several

Figure 6.1. Manuscript for *Putnam's Camp*, mm. 107–108. Courtesy Yale University Irving S. Gilmore Music Library.

prominent Ives scholars: H. Wiley Hitchcock, J. Peter Burkholder, theorist Philip Lambert, and editors Paul C. Echols and Jim Sinclair, who were at the helm of the Ives Society's critical editions project. The feature event was a panel discussion entitled "Charles Ives: Trying to Answer Some Questions of Veracity." Burkholder contributed a prepared statement, welcoming Solomon's contribution to Ives scholarship as an "important corrective." He agreed that it was quite likely that Ives had fallen victim to the modernist propaganda issued on his behalf, and, as a result, engaged in some legerdemain when dating his compositions.[19] For Burkholder, whose own work had divested Ives of the transcendentalist legacy, the stakes were very different than for someone like Henahan, who retained the popular image of Ives that had been in circulation since the fifties.

Apart from Burkholder's statement, the contributions of the panelists did not make it to print. But an exchange between Lambert and Solomon published in the *Journal of the American Musicological Society* opens another window on the early stages of the scholarly discussion prompted by Solomon's article. Lambert, whose research mostly centered on Ives's experimental works, acknowledged that the composer was inconsistent about his dates. However, the evidence was open to multiple interpretations, and one need not arrive at Solomon's conclusion that Ives was an inveterate liar. One could, for example, take a copybook containing harmony and counterpoint exercises in the hand of both George and Charles Ives as evidence substantiating the son's recollections of early musical experiments shared with his father.[20]

With respect to the copybook, Solomon retorted, there was no way to show decisively that all of Ives's additions were made during his father's lifetime. In fact, some of the writing in Ives's hand, particularly the marginalia, looked like it had been added some thirty years later. This was just another instance in which the "Ives mythology" unduly swayed scholarly interpretation. The best approach was to jettison all of Ives's dates. We need, Solomon asserted, "to rely upon the traditional methods of historical musicology—documentary and paper studies, handwriting comparisons, and a detailed analytic reconstruction of the compositional process of each work."[21] To a large extent, the dating controversy would proceed to a resolution according to these very terms, an exemplary display of conventional disciplinary practice.

One of the first scholars to take up the challenge was Carol K. Baron, who filed a PhD thesis about Ives's *Three Page Sonata* in 1987, the same year Solomon published his inflammatory article. To address the dating problem and vindicate Ives, Baron adopted a classic paleographic dual strategy. First she constructed an argument based on "internal evidence," information gleaned from the characteristics of the music alone. The goal was to demonstrate that some of Ives's revisions actually made the music less dissonant, thereby deflecting the accusation that the composer had reworked his scores to bolster his claims as a modernist pioneer. Although Baron's analysis met with skepticism, she did set a precedent, and a number of other scholars have since essayed arguments along the same lines.[22] The second part of her strategy was to muster "external evidence," hard material facts about the provenance of the manuscripts. Here she turned to handwriting analysis, identifying three manuscripts from different periods of Ives's life that could be dated precisely because they were for pieces that had verifiable first performance dates. For each of these manuscripts, Baron tabulated handwriting characteristics—the general size of the characters, the direction and length of note stems, the shape of noteheads, clefs, and accidentals, and so on. The handwriting in other manuscripts could then be compared against the tables to determine a rough date. Though this method was imprecise, Baron felt it provided sufficient evidence to conclude that "Putnam's Camp" dated from early enough to vouchsafe the composer's claim as innovator.[23]

A more complete exoneration came at the hands of Gayle Sherwood, another scholar just beginning her career in the late eighties. Sherwood had first encountered Ives in an undergraduate course that was part of the music-history survey sequence at McMaster University, where she completed her bachelor's degree. She remembers a shock of recognition: many of the hymn tunes Ives borrowed inhabited the sonic landscape of her own childhood and brought back memories of the small church in Brantford, Ontario, that her father, a minister, had led when she was a girl. Even while she experienced the music as nostalgic, Sherwood marveled at the audaciousness of including simple hymn tunes like "In the Sweet By and By" and "What a Friend We Have in Jesus" in a genre as august as the symphony. "When I heard Ives," she recollects, "it just lit up for me." Over the course of her undergraduate career, Sherwood's interest in Ives deepened, and when she took an intensive research and bibliography course in her third year, she submitted as a final project an annotated bibliography on the composer. That project laid the groundwork for the Ives research and information guide she would later publish with Routledge—a guide that has become indispensable to Ives scholars (along with Geoffrey Block's *Charles Ives: A Bio-Bibliography*) and is now in its second edition. When, in 1989, she was offered a graduate fellowship at Yale, where the Ives manuscripts were housed, her mind was made up: she would do a dissertation about Ives.[24]

The musicology curriculum Sherwood encountered at Yale was conservative and substantially unchanged from what an aspiring scholar in the discipline would have encountered in the sixties and early seventies. The emphasis was on pre-1700 music, and the skill set the musicology faculty sought to inculcate was mostly centered on primary-source studies: establishing provenance, identifying style traits, and, should manuscripts present the opportunity, sketch studies geared toward documenting compositional processes. These were the tools that Solomon had suggested would resolve the dating controversy and, as Sherwood acquired them, she remembers being surprised that no Yale musicology graduate students had ever brought them to bear on the Ives manuscripts housed literally a block away. Fortunately for Sherwood, a newly arrived member of the theory faculty was extraordinarily well-suited for supervising a dissertation on Ives: Robert Morgan, who had overseen Burkholder's dissertation at the University of Chicago.[25]

The period during which Sherwood completed her PhD was one of tremendous upheaval in musicology, when traditional preoccupations and practices came under fire from multiple quarters. But Sherwood's dissertation, "The Choral Works of Charles Ives: Chronology, Style, Reception," which she filed in 1996, is free of the vexations that otherwise beset the field. The product of Yale's conservative milieu in which the status quo ante was preserved, the dissertation rests firmly on the twin pillars of conventional musicological practice: paleography and style criticism. To be sure, Sherwood ventures a discussion of reception, a concern of more recent vintage within the world of musicological scholarship. But, by and large, the dissertation is an affirmation of the blueprint drawn up some hundred years earlier by the discipline's patriarch, Guido Adler. Indeed, traditionalist factions in the larger disciplinary debate could have made recourse to it for evidence of the continuing effectiveness of orthodox methodologies.

As her first task, Sherwood devised a method for dating Ives's manuscripts modeled on the paper analyses that figured in classic musicological studies of the output of Bach, Mozart, Beethoven, and other composers. The paper types found in Ives's manuscripts had already been indexed by John Kirkpatrick in his *Temporary Mimeographed Catalogue*. Using this information, Sherwood determined the dates during which each of the companies that produced the paper was active, thereby establishing a terminus post quem for any page. Companies tend to change some of the characteristics of their paper from time to time, watermarks or other insignias being the most readily detectable alterations, but records of when such changes are made are hard to come by. To overcome this problem, Sherwood sought out dated manuscripts from the collections of other composers who were active in the New York and New Haven areas between 1881 and 1941 and who used the same paper types as Ives. As a result, for any given paper type, she determined a rough span of time in which it was used by Ives's contemporaries. Further refinement was possible for the paper types used by the professional copyists Ives occasionally employed. Dated correspondence between Ives and the copyist could help pin down a more precise period of usage. Sherwood created a cross-correlation mechanism by expanding Baron's handwriting study to include some additional manuscripts that could be definitively dated. This provided her with a finer-grained understanding of the way in which Ives's handwriting changed over the course of his life. Together, Sherwood's tables of paper types and their period of usages and her refined handwriting typology constituted the most accurate means of dating Ives's manuscripts yet devised.[26]

Even before Sherwood filed the dissertation, her work was filtering through the Ives community, disseminated through conference talks and an article she published in a high-profile journal. Anticipation was high for here, at last, was the means to issue a definitive ruling on the charges Solomon had leveled against Ives. Had he engaged in a systematic pattern of falsification, backdating his works so that all European modernist influences were obscured? Yes, she conceded, "Ives musical development was more gradual and more strongly influenced by other composers than he was willing to admit." But—and here, the sound of relieved sighs is almost audible—"the early results of this objective chronology verify Ives's reputation as an innovator and experimenter at the turn of the century and thus help to confirm his unique role in the development of North American music."[27] The composer was vindicated, though the tarnish of the Solomon controversy would take some time to remove.

In the classic model of musicological practice that Sherwood absorbed at Yale, paleography served as a precursor to style criticism, and that is indeed the place it occupied in her dissertation. To keep the scope manageable, she chose to focus on Ives's choral output, projecting its changing style traits onto the kind of narrative arc that musicologists had traced through the oeuvres of many composers—an arc that relied upon biological metaphor for coherence. The archetypal model, which can be traced back to Guido Adler and the first generation of university-based musicologists, located in the earliest pieces of a composer the seed of future genius. In turn come works in which the budding composer wrestles with stylistic influences, then the full flowering of artistic maturity, and, finally, the retrospection of a "late period." Sherwood departed from this model in only two respects. First, following Peter Burkholder's precedent, she bifurcated Ives's mature period (post-1907), considering experimental research works separately from those she describes as being "written in the concert music tradition." Second, she forewent the term "late period," though the defining retrospective characteristic is present in her description of some of the last works. Sherwood writes, for example, that Ives's setting of Psalm 90, his final sacred choral work, "combines original approaches with a stylistic catalogue of previous techniques to make a unified and integrated whole."[28]

The effect of Sherwood's revised chronology had its greatest impact on the portion of the evolutionary style narrative concerned with Ives's efforts to sort through his various musical influences. Preeminent among those influences, were, of course, George Ives and Horatio Parker, but Sherwood also detected some additional ones. The new dates she had generated for the choral music Ives composed prior to 1902, when he abandoned music professionally, suggested that his output was conditioned by the church positions he occupied. Ives had become adept at working with the medium of the so-called quartet choir, preferred by two prominent American church musicians, Harry Rowe Shelley and Dudley Buck. Comprised of four professional soloists backed by an amateur choir, the quartet choir was a configuration ideal for the limited resources of churches. Generally speaking, Shelley, Buck, and their many imitators (Ives among them), played the quartet off of the larger choir, infusing the parts sung by the former with a chromaticism that was close kindred to the barbershop style associated with glee clubs. The quartet-choir had its detractors, reformers who wanted to rid church music of the sickly hymns and harmonies they associated with it, and Horatio Parker was one of the most vociferous. Thus, as a pupil of Parker's at Yale, Ives was confronted with a direct challenge to the kind of music he performed and composed as a professional musician. Sherwood demonstrated that this confrontation played out in Ives's musical output, most notably in his cantata *The Celestial Country*, which was long assumed to be a straightforward homage to Parker's *Hora Novisimma*. The cantata, she explained, was Ives's attempt to integrate the quartet-choir and the reformed style of his Yale Professor, creating a "true hybrid" that anticipates the stylistic plurality that would become one of the most celebrated hallmarks of Ives's musical maturity.[29]

The net effect of Sherwood's dissertation was to stabilize scholarly discourse about Ives, mitigating the dating controversy and adding more clarity to his process of stylistic development. In other words, Sherwood sharpened without substantially altering the image of Ives that musicologists had been reconstructing since the late sixties. As with her predecessors, she relied upon the conventional tools of her discipline—indeed, her dissertation is a masterly demonstration of classic musicological methods. Rhetorically speaking, this is part of the point. Ives, for all his unconventionality, could be investigated in the same manner as any other composer: his oeuvre bore the earmarks of consummate craftsmanship, displayed the sort of progressive growth natural to any major artist, and could sensibly be integrated into the larger history of classical music. In other words, Ives merited his place in the canon and ought to enjoy all the attendant privileges that canonicity bestowed.

By the time Sherwood filed her dissertation in 1995, however, conventional musicological tools and the questions they were designed to address had been the subject of a protracted and heated debate within the discipline. Paleography and style analysis seemed wholly inadequate to probe the relationships between music and its sociopolitical contexts, the kind of inquiry that a mostly younger cohort of musicologists felt the field had neglected to its detriment. Gender, sexuality, race, and class—these were the issues that animated so-called "New Musicology."

Ives and Recent Musical Scholarship

Before going any further, the term "New Musicology" requires some clarification. Sometimes it is used in a broad sense to describe the hegemony under which most musicologists now operate, where a premium is placed on studying music in its cultural context. But the sense in which I invoke it is more limited, referring to a contingent of scholars who commanded the spotlight in the late eighties and early nineties, agitating for disciplinary reform. Without being exhaustive, a list of prominent members includes Susan McClary, Rose Subotnik, Ruth Solie, and Lawrence Kramer, all of whom produced books and articles that ventured far afield from the concerns that had previously dominated music scholarship.[30] Their work was certainly a catalyst for "New Musicology" in the first and broader sense. But sometimes, as the case of Ives scholarship illustrates, their impact was more indirect, exerting a quickening effect that stimulated discussion of issues that were already part of the discourse, rather than working a full-scale transformation.

The main targets of New Musicological opprobrium were the modes of criticism that were de rigueur in the field. Still dominant was Adlerian style criticism, which was concerned solely with the organization of the constitutive elements of music—melody, harmony, rhythm, timbre—and avoided speculation about meaning. This was intentional, for Adler and the other nineteenth-century musicological patriarchs sought to create a rigorous "scientific" discourse that, distinct from more popular forms of criticism, offered impressionistic interpretations. At the same time, Adler's emphasis on matters of formal construction was reinforced by an aesthetic tradition that privileged "absolute music." According to this tradition, the instrumental works that stand at the pinnacle of the classical music canon do not possess meanings that can be indexed to the physical or emotional world. Instead they exist on their own separate plane. To freight a symphony with a dramatic narrative or to associate it with the flux of emotions is to laden it with unnecessary baggage, for its true value lies in its formal construction.

For New Musicologists, the privileging of form to the exclusion of all else impoverished musical experience. They argued that since music is the product of social context, its connections to that context—its meanings—should be a prerogative of the discipline. Lawrence Kramer, assuming a hortatory mode that is typical of New Musicology pronouncements, encouraged his colleagues to engage in "modes of hermeneutic and historical writing that . . . position musical experience within the densely compacted, concretely situated worlds of those who compose, perform, and listen."[31] To do this, New Musicologists looked outside the field, adopting theoretical frameworks that thrived elsewhere in the humanities: neo-Marxian critical theory, various flavors of structuralism and post-structuralism, feminist and queer theory. So armed, they set about the business of hermeneutics, generating readings of musical works that prioritized issues of identity, with gender and sexuality topping the list of concerns.

A salient example is an essay about Ives that appears in Kramer's 1995 book *Classical Music and Postmodern Knowledge*. Kramer meshes a premise about art and its immanent link to society advanced by critical theorist Theodor Adorno with a theory about the nature of "democratic social space" developed by literary critic Philip Fisher. Turned loose on Ives, this theoretical apparatus reveals a music that is fraught with the contradictions of early-twentieth-century American culture, juxtaposing progressive innovation with reactionary misogyny and racism. Here Kramer reveals a hallmark of New Musicological practice: the burden of proof lies on the interpretive virtuosity of the scholar rather than documentary evidence. Kramer does not seek to prove that anyone ever heard Ives's music this way before, whether the composer himself or his auditors, but that it can (and, he insists, should) be heard this way.[32] Thus Kramer, like the other New Musicologists, garbs himself in the critic's mantle, not the historian's.[33] It is perhaps not surprising then, to find that New Musicologists were also critical of the paleographical work that had consumed so much of musicologists' energy in the past, what Joseph Kerman, one champion of interpretive criticism, famously characterized as "positivist musicology."[34]

Since New Musicologists set out to interrogate the basic assumptions of the discipline, the most obvious targets were the scholarly edifices that supported major canonical composers. Even at the height of his prominence in the midseventies, Ives had never rivaled a Bach or Beethoven for public or scholarly attention. Comparatively speaking, only a small band of the spectrum of musicological enterprise was ever dedicated to Ives, and the energies it contained were mostly directed toward the project of fitting the composer into conventional narratives. Kramer's Ives essay was a rare New Musicological exploration of the composer, and it proved not to exert much influence on subsequent discussion. But New Musicology would have an indirect impact on Ives scholarship by fomenting change in the broader discipline. It stimulated an engagement with social context that was already present in the field—despite what New Musicology polemics sometimes suggested.

Combing musicological monographs and articles from the late seventies and early eighties, one encounters numerous examples of scholars looking beyond the "music itself," before the advent of New Musicology. There were Renaissance specialists who examined the sociopolitical complexities of patronage systems and musical institutions at the courts of the Italian peninsula.[35] Opera scholars had begun to explore the ways in which issues of nationalism impinged on their various repertoires.[36] And, on the fringes of the discipline, a group of Americanists banded together as the Sonneck Society (now renamed the Society for American Music) in 1975, part of their purpose being to study music as a social phenomenon on this continent. Richard Crawford, a charter member, recollects that the society was founded "in a climate where curiosity about music centered on its role in history, not its artistic excellence."[37] New Musicology would help legitimize and draw attention to these various enterprises, even if the scholars involved in them did not necessarily adopt the New Musicological method of preference: hermeneutics fueled by high-octane theory.

The work of Judith Tick, one of the members of the Sonneck Society, is a case in point. Tick was exploring issues of gender over a decade before the "New Musicology" cohort appeared on the scene, the impetus coming from her own political commitments. While a graduate student at Berkeley, from 1964–1967, she became involved with the women's liberation movement. Like many second-wave feminists, Tick was reacting to the ingrained sexism of academia, from the condescending treatment some faculty members meted out to female students, to the narrow range of professional opportunities for women within the university. At first, her social concerns did not impinge much upon the substance of her scholarly work. In 1970, when Tick decided to continue her graduate studies at the City University of New York, she submitted a paper rooted in style analysis that examined Ives's use of ragtime. She showed that many of the composer's most adventurous rhythmic explorations took ragtime as a point of departure, testament to his awareness of turn-of-the-century popular music and evidence against the then-prevalent image of the composer working in splendid musical isolation.[38] H. Wiley Hitchcock, with whom Tick hoped to study at CUNY, liked the paper so much he recommended that she submit it to the *Journal of the*

American Musicological Society. But Tick hesitated, intimidated by the patriarchal mien of contemporary academe, and, in the end, she did not follow through. As she eloquently explains, "When you are on the margins, you often don't see your way to the center clearly." The article would not be published until 1974, and then in the less prestigious (though vibrant) *Current Musicology*, a journal run by graduate students at Columbia University.[39]

Tick remained interested in Ives as a graduate student, but by the time she was in a position to select a dissertation topic, she had acquired a sense of urgency about one of the central projects of the nascent women studies movement: "rewriting women back into history."[40] She produced a paper about professional women musicians in late-nineteenth-century America for a seminar taught by Gilbert Chase, who visited CUNY in 1973. At Chase's urging, Tick published an expanded version of the paper in *Annaurio*, a journal unusual for its catholicity of subjects and thus one of the few forums hospitable to this rare example of musical scholarship engaged with social history.[41] After completing the article, Tick decided that she would make the history of American women composers in the nineteenth century her dissertation topic. At the time, she observes in retrospect, "I did not fully appreciate the implications of *not* studying a 'great man.'"[42]

Although the subject of her *Annaurio* article and dissertation would seem to have little bearing on Ives, it was motivated by Tick's response to recent scholarship dedicated to the composer. She had read Frank Rossiter's dissertation and was aghast at the way he made women culpable for Ives's alienation from American musical culture. This, she felt, granted women far more agency than they actually had, for the sphere they inhabited was just as much a prison as the psychological chains with which Rossiter bound Ives.[43] Tick set out to examine the sphere of women's confinement, arguing that social values determined its practical and aesthetical dimensions: the sanctioned contexts in which women could create music, whether as performers or composers, and the styles with which they were associated. The emergence of women as composers in the late nineteenth century, she argued, prompted a "sexual aesthetics" that reinforced gender prejudices and was built on long-standing distinctions between "feminine" and "masculine" music. The former was sentimental, lyrical, and emotive, best realized in the "smaller forms" of parlor song and short piano pieces; the latter was virile, powerful, and intellectual, its qualities revealed in the "higher" forms of the symphony, string quartet, and the like. Tucked in at the end of the article, Tick pointed out that Ives's gendered rhetoric was of a piece with this pervasive sexual aesthetics: "Ives's opinions were aberrant only in the violent lengths to which they were carried. His vocabulary was very much a part of his time."[44]

For over a decade after the publication of her *Annaurio* article, Tick pursued the study of women composers with only a few companions.[45] She could take some solace in the activism of her female composer colleagues, who had formed organizations like the League of Women Composers in order to create greater opportunities for women in the world of contemporary music.[46] Paradoxically, the burgeoning women's studies movement proved inhospitable to the sort of work Tick was doing. One of the foundational figures in the field, Gerda Lerner, wrote scathingly of histories that focused on "notable women," a rubric that inevitably applied to the composers that Tick studied. Such history, Lerner proclaimed, "does not tell us much about those activities in which most women engaged, nor does it tell us about the significance to society as a whole of women's activities. The history of notable women is the history of exceptional even deviant women, and does not describe the experience and the history of the mass of women."[47] Thus Tick's lonely position within the field of musicology was compounded by the studied indifference of the historians who might have been her closest scholarly kin. Possibly, she might have found interested interlocutors among the practitioners of feminist criticism in the arena of literary studies. Tick's inclinations however, ran more toward social history than criticism. Her work was concerned with what documentary evidence had to reveal about the situation of women musicians in the nineteenth century, not with interpretations of the way feminine identity was constructed in specific pieces of music.

By the end of the eighties, the study of women no longer persisted on the fringes of the discipline, New Musicology having galvanized interest in the intersection between music and gender. Tick now had more allies, among them Ruth Solie, editor of the landmark multiauthored volume of essays *Musicology and Difference: Gender and Sexuality in Music Scholarship* (1993). As Solie acknowledges, it was Tick who originally conceived of assembling the collection, but other commitments (a biography of composer Ruth Crawford Seeger) prevented her from taking on the task of editing. However, Tick did supply a contribution, an essay entitled "Charles Ives and Gender Ideology," that marks her return to the world of Ives scholarship after a nearly twenty-year hiatus. This return was not an abrupt departure from her recent work, for she had initially intended her essay to use Ives's aesthetics as a foil to those of Crawford Seeger. In comparison to the other offerings in the volume, Tick's is characteristically free of references to literary and critical theory. She moves quickly to documentary evidence that supplies a much-needed context for understanding the gendered nature of Ives's language. Again, it is social history that is her focus, and she devotes herself to unpacking the composer's prose writings rather than offering a theory-driven reading of a specific piece.

The scholars who had been most active in addressing Ives's gendered language—Frank Rossiter, Stuart Feder, and Maynard Solomon—had all opted for a psychological approach, interpreting Ives's vituperations about the emasculation of art as symptoms of a deeper pathology. For Tick, such explanations were insufficient because they failed to take the larger social context into account. Gendered language, as she had been arguing for years, was pervasive in nineteenth-century American culture, and Ives was exceptional only in the vehemence of some of his pronouncements. Addressing Solomon and Feder specifically, she writes, "[A] psychoanalytic perspective masks the power of society to transmit gendered views of culture, rife with prejudice and viable precisely because issues other than sexuality are engaged through tropes of masculinity and femininity." Ives was deploying a "grammar of prejudice" to attack those who occupied positions of power in the musical world, not to defend his or his father's masculinity. When he raged about "sissies," "lilypads," and "ladies," Ives was articulating the frustration of an American composer who felt the oppressive weight of the European classical-music tradition. These were the tropes that came ready to hand, and they were not necessarily the symptom of a virulent reactionary misogyny.[48]

This is a very different conclusion from the one Kramer reached, even though the politics of gender also figure prominently in his arguments. That difference is a function of methodology, for while Kramer is quick to soar to hermeneutical heights lofted by critical theory, Tick hovers closer to documentary evidence.

Generally speaking, in the last decade and a half, Ives scholars have taken Tick's lead rather than Kramer's. They have not neglected the business of interpreting Ives's works, but the preference has been to hem in modest hermeneutical readings with primary source material that bolsters plausibility. For Denise Von Glahn, an exploration of the turn-of-the-century preservation movement, specifically its modes of memorializing war heroes, serves as a backdrop to parsing the first movement of *Three Places in New England*.[49] David Metzer examines how Victorian constructions of childhood tinge the nostalgic patina and subject matter of Ives's music.[50] And both Michael Broyles and Judith Tick have examined the intricacies of contemporary political discourse and its ramifications for Ives's music and prose.[51] These examples skim the surface of an extensive literature, but they are characteristic in furnishing few encounters with the French or German intellectuals whose literary, critical, and social theories swept into the field with the advent of New Musicology. This is not to say that Ives scholarship proceeds without theory, for whether or not scholars choose to make their presuppositions explicit, they are necessarily present. Rather, the premises with which Ives scholars tend to operate bear more resemblance to those employed by historians than literary critics—premises about cause and effect, the role of documentary evidence, and the relationship between the scholar and his or her materials.

There are notable exceptions. Charles Hiroshi Garrett, in his book *Struggling to Define a Nation* (2008), follows Kramer in invoking Adorno and pursuing a mode of "immanent critique" to explore the social implications of Ives's use of ragtime.[52] Significantly, Garrett's book is a revision of the dissertation he completed at the University of California, Los Angeles, a bastion of New Musicology. Michel Foucault's notion of "discourse" figures prominently in Thomas Clarke Owen's 1999 dissertation, "Charles Ives and His American Context: Images of 'Americanness' in the Arts."[53] Owens is the third and final musicologist to have completed a PhD thesis about Ives under Robert Morgan's supervision—Peter Burkholder and Gayle Sherwood preceded him—and his work reveals that in the final years of the twentieth century, New Musicology had even established a foothold at conservative Yale University. On the whole though, the impact of New Musicology on Ives scholarship has been less direct. It has not spelled the end of older disciplinary concerns like establishing stylistic continuities between the music of Ives and the European classical tradition.[54] But it has served to open up space around and draw attention to issues of cultural context, formerly the demesne of the handful of historians and American Studies scholars who had ventured into the Ives arena in the late sixties and seventies.

The possibilities of the enlarged space in which musicologists could now operate are illustrated by the postdissertation work of Gayle Sherwood. Her output, culminating with the only musicologist-authored biography of the composer, *Charles Ives Reconsidered* (2008), traces a trajectory away from paleographical and style-critical concerns that commanded her attention as a graduate student and toward a broader engagement with American culture.

The first point along the trajectory is a 1999 article that reiterates one of the major arguments of her dissertation, namely that Ives's *Celestial Country* is a stylistic mélange that mingled the influence of Horatio Parker with elements of the popular quartet-choir repertoire that the Yale professor detested. The article departs from the dissertation by overlaying a new interpretive framework borrowed from the work of cultural historian Lawrence Levine. Sherwood suggests that *Celestial Country* inhabited the increasingly untenable middleground between classical and popular music, a division Levine traced to the late nineteenth century in his seminal book *Highbrow/Lowbrow: The Emergence of Cultural Hierarchy in America* (1988). "Quite literally," Sherwood writes, "Ives was caught between the populist style [the quartet-choir tradition] . . . with which he had grown up and elitist views of Parker that were gaining support throughout educated American society."[55] The style-critical tools of the musicological trade are much in evidence in Sherwood's article, but the perspective is reoriented, directed outward, from scores to changing cultural mores.

Just two years later, Sherwood was exploring terrain well outside the traditional domain of musicology. Her second postdissertation Ives article was published in the *Journal of the American Musicological Society*, where still, in 2001, Ives's name was an infrequent presence.[56] Titled "Charles Ives and 'Our National Malady,'"

Sherwood's article sifts through the documentary evidence pertaining to Ives's health breakdowns in 1906 and 1918. Though past biographers had suggested these were a consequence of heart problems, family correspondence and medical records spoke of "nervous collapse," which pointed to one of the most common diagnoses of the period: neurasthenia. According to George M. Beard, the physician who coined and popularized the term in the 1880s, the disease was a by-product of modernity and its main sufferers were upper-middle-class businessmen who were required to process unprecedented amounts of information. Heredity too was a factor, those most susceptible being from the educated and refined classes. And Americans seem to have been afflicted earlier and in far greater numbers than any other people in the Western World. Perverse though it may seem, this was a point of pride for Beard and his followers because they took it as an indication that the United States was on the vanguard of modern development. In fact, as Sherwood discovered, the diagnosis "neurasthenia" was a mark of status, medical acknowledgment that a man occupied an illustrious stratum of American society. That same stratum was responsible for the sacralization of art, the distinction between highbrow and lowbrow tastes that was, as Levine argued, cultivated by members of an embattled Anglo-American elite faced with the immigrant horde. Sherwood explained the connection: "[T]he alliance between American high culture and European musical traditions on the one hand, and the American upper class and neurasthenia on the other, reveals a kind of cultural crossroads." And it was there that she situated Ives. Seen from this perspective, the music the composer began to write in 1907, after taking the "rest cure" and beginning his courtship of Harmony Twichell (both prescribed treatments for neurasthenia), is cast in a reactionary light:

> By conjoining the vernacular music that he learned as a child and mostly associated with his father with the Euro-American forms that he learned at Yale—a bastion of white male privilege—Ives preserved and "elevated" this music. The fusion of these genres in Ives's mature works embodied a musical reaction against the threatened eradication of his world—that of the educated Anglo-Saxon white male—that acts as a compositional analogue to his physiological reaction in the form of neurasthenia.

This is a far cry from the kind of argument Sherwood had advanced in her dissertation.[57]

In 2008, now working under her married name Magee, she uses the greater space afforded by a book to flesh out the arguments of her postdissertation articles. But in *Charles Ives Reconsidered*, Magee also ventures into territory that she had not previously covered—again, the driving impulse being to situate Ives more completely in his culture. For example, in her account of Ives's mature period, which she identifies with the twelve years bookended by his 1906 and 1918 break-downs, Magee emphasizes the various attempts the composer made to introduce his music to others. Though yielding little result, whether Walter Damrosch's reading of the First Symphony or the infamous contretemps with violinist Franz Milcke, those incidents point not to a composer determinedly aloof from the musical culture of his time but one seeking to break back into it. Ives "continuously presented his works to musicians that he hoped would be sympathetic," but it was not until the twenties that he would find the "right product, the right sales pitch, and receptive customers in the form of a modernist community of composers and performers." Once Ives joined that community, he was a willing collaborator in the process of revising his life to make it conform more closely to the modernist and nationalist precepts of Henry Cowell's circle. This last assertion was not new, of course, other scholars—Peter Burkholder and Maynard Solomon—made it in the past. All told, though, Magee's account of Ives's career presented a composer far more bound up with the idiosyncrasies of American culture than anyone had previously offered.[58]

The musical commentary Magee supplies also departs from the traditional mode of style analysis, and markedly so in the case of her readings of the works Ives produced in and around the First World War. At the time, she observes, Americans were preoccupied with the issue of immigration and the loyalty of hyphenated Americans. These same kinds of concerns were manifest in Ives's music, because concurrently "Ives was fleshing out several major compositions that expressed his own, unhyphenated identity in conjunction with a new emphasis on musical militarism." Magee is even more specific when she tackles individual works, the richness of her comments about the "Concord" Sonata bringing her close to the hermeneutic realm of New Musicology. She suggests that by "[a]nchoring the work in a place known simultaneously for brass-knuckles warfare against a foreign entity [it was where the Revolutionary War had begun], and the advocacy of nonviolent resistance (voiced in Thoreau's *Civil Disobedience* of 1849), . . . [Ives] may have been offering a complicated reflection of his own time." In addition, he was perhaps making an assertion about the vitality of American amateur music making. Honing in on the most obvious borrowings featured in the piece, the opening motive from Beethoven's Fifth Symphony, Magee explains:

> Throughout the sonata, Ives enshrines the work in a pianistic reduction similar to the arrangements of Beethoven's symphonies that he played as a teen. In so doing, Ives reclaims the nineteenth-century American amateur performance context of this work from the forces of the early twentieth-century concert establishment that insisted on "authentic" readings of the work by trained, professional symphony orchestras.

Magee is always careful to lace her readings with conditional auxiliary verbs. But even with this cautionary measure in place, she has traveled far from the safe precincts of traditional musicology.[59]

The end result fulfills the promise of the book title: Magee does indeed present an Ives reconsidered. There are resemblances to the psychologically damaged Ives of Stuart Feder's imagination, bereft after the early death of his father. But for Magee, Ives's ailment has broader cultural connotations, extending well beyond the immediate family relationships that preoccupy psychoanalysts. There are resemblances to the well-trained classical musician of Peter Burkholder's imagination, but Magee's Ives has more nuanced musical commitments that are inextricably bound up with social milieu. There are also resemblances to the victim of American cultural mores of Frank Rossiter's imagination, but Magee's Ives has more agency and responds to his changing circumstances with the shrewdness of a businessman (though not without misfires). There are much fewer resemblances to the isolated, autonomous Ives that the Cowells so successfully projected in the fifties, though Magee does rehabilitate the composer's reputation as an innovator.

As a codicil to this section, it is worth bringing in one further text for comparison, Jan Swafford's 1996 Ives biography. Swafford's work also provides a convenient way to begin mitigating the effects of the diachronic organization of this book, a task that will preoccupy me for most of the remaining pages. Thus far, I have presented the reception of Ives as if it has been dominated by a successive series of images (more or less mapped out in reverse order in the preceding paragraph). But, as these various Iveses have appeared, they have tended not to supplant the ones that preceded them. Instead they have coexisted, often sustained by the different, sometimes overlapping spheres that comprise American musical culture. Swafford's book exists in one of the overlaps, for it is the product of a composer-critic nominally involved in musical academe and intent on engaging a general audience.

In the preface to *Charles Ives: A Life with Music*, Swafford declares, "This biography follows no schools or theories. . . . Rather than theories I have facts and materials, and I tried to draw no conclusions until the facts and materials demanded them." But elsewhere in the preface, one learns that Swafford's book is animated by several convictions—which is another way of saying that it is underpinned by "theory" (pace Swafford). First and foremost is the belief that the lives of artists tend to unfold in a more predictable fashion than most, a function of the compulsion to realize an inner creative impulse. "Even more than an artist's life," Swafford goes on to add, "the lifework has a roughly predicable shape, coalescing toward an approach, a voice, a maturity—call it a style. Often that style moves toward some sort of zenith and consummation, sometimes followed by decline." Here is the residue of older musicological narratives that conflate style development with the growth of biological organisms, metaphor collapsing into identity.[60] A second conviction Swafford expresses in his preface concerns the relationship between the composer and cultural context, which would seem, at first sight, to nudge him closer to the issues Magee addresses in her biography. Swafford asserts, "We cannot adequately understand [Ives] without reference to the spirit of his age: Progressive, Pragmatist, and Realist." The appeal to zeitgeist, however, is more evocative of the precepts of American Studies scholars operating around 1970—Sandra Rosalie Perry and Robert M. Crunden, for example—than those preferred by musicologists in the nineties. Indeed, the sources that Swafford relies upon to characterize American culture generally, and progressivism, pragmatism, and realism specifically, almost all date from before the advent of "New History," which left the American past a tangled skein of narratives.[61]

But while Swafford relies upon dated musicological and historical frameworks to support his biography, he demonstrates a comprehensive knowledge of both the Ives manuscripts and Ives scholarship, from Cowell to Magee. His tendency is to mitigate the extreme qualities in the images of Ives created by his predecessors. Thus, for example, he is willing to accept Rossiter's contention that the feminization of American musical culture left an indelible mark on Ives, but not to imbue the composer with the pathos of victimhood. Similarly, he acknowledges that Ives suffered from depression, but refrains, unlike Solomon and Feder, from plumbing the depths using psychoanalytical theory. If there is one thing Swafford is intent upon, it is safeguarding Ives's image as innovator, something he returns to time and again. In sum, the book is a conservative one. It is unmatched by any of the Ives biographies in its level of detail, but the portrait it offers is a mingling of the more moderate elements drawn from the work of others. This Ives stands in the middle ground between academia, where disciplinary vicissitudes had made over the image of the composer several times, and the broader, more public arena of classical-music devotees, where much older conceptions of the composer continued to thrive—though with an important modification.

The Maverick Tradition

As the culmination of the millennial concert season, the San Francisco Symphony, led by its music director, Michael Tilson Thomas, presented a ten-concert festival that featured the work of twenty-two composers, collectively identified as "American Mavericks." To commemorate the festival, the orchestra issued a lavish volume sized for the coffee table and printed on durable glossy stock. Interleaved with and sometimes printed on pages swathed in bold colors are vignettes, biographical blurbs, and brief essays about the maverick composers. Pride of place in the volume belongs to Charles Ives. Chronology was certainly a factor, Ives being the earliest composer included on the festival programs. But the authors, a bevy of critics and commentators who supply annotations for the San Francisco Symphony, offer other justifications:

> [Ives] found his way to polytonality, atonality, polyrhythms, and other devices that, like Leonardo's bicycle and contact lenses and ball bearings, all had to be reinvented by others. He even anticipated ideas dear to some composers in the 1960s: that any sound is potential music, that a stylistically neat and consistent articulation of musical materials is not a necessary part of the musical experience, and that a work need not be "fixed," but might be work-in-progress as long as its creator lived.[62]

Quite simply, Ives had foreseen the whole of twentieth-century musical development.

Prima facie, this is nothing more than the recitation of dogma, the belief in Ives's primacy first espoused by modernists in the twenties and then sedimented into doctrine through endless repetition in the fifties and sixties. Its presence in a book targeted at a general audience would seem to be an indication of the static nature of public discourse about Ives, as against its dynamic scholarly counterpart. On closer inspection, however, the narrative in which the book places Ives departs from the one espoused in the heyday of Bernsteinian and Stokowskian advocacy. For the Ives that appears here is not only the great anticipator but also the paterfamilias of a specifically American tradition of musical experimentalists. This is a narrative that traces a lineage from Ives, through Henry Cowell, John Cage, the minimalists, and ultimately to John Adams. It is a narrative that bifurcates the history of American classical music, valorizing those composers who have foregone the patronage of the university (particularly in the form of tenure appointments) and the styles of modernism that have flourished there. It is, in short, an antiestablishment narrative, though as the San Francisco Symphony's "Maverick Festival" demonstrates, it has, ironically, found support from some of the most established musical institutions in the classical-music world. How that happened is the last story I have to tell. And, as with many things Ives, it requires me to return again to Henry Cowell.

In the late twenties, Cowell initially promoted Ives as a part of a group of American composers. Known occasionally then, and more frequently now, as the "ultra-moderns" (hyphen optional), the group was eclectic stylistically and aesthetically, encompassing the occult-inclined Dane Rudhyar and the mercurial Carl Ruggles. Of course, Cowell regarded Ives as a composer-ethnographer, an American Bartók whose music was rooted in the exuberant practices of amateur, small-town musicians. As different as the ultramoderns were, Cowell found a way of linking them in a 1933 essay entitled "Trends in American Music." He cast Rudhyar, Ruggles, Ives, and the rest as experimentalists, who either by dint of training or choice, stood at some remove from European musical traditions. They were, Cowell implied, genuinely American composers, unlike the contingent of New York–based cosmopolitans following "either modern French or 'neoclassical tendencies'"—men like Aaron Copland and Virgil Thomson, who just so happened to dominate the influential League of Composers.[63] Ultramodernism, as musicologist Carol Oja observes, "stood for an assertion of regional validity, a reaction against the perceived hegemony of East Coast institutions."[64]

Ives, as it turned out, found his way to the broader public singly as an "autonomous man" and not in the company of the ultramoderns. But Cowell's convictions about divisions in the contemporary music scene persisted in the writings of two of his pupils, Lou Harrison and John Cage.[65] For example, in a 1945 review of a concert featuring the music of Cage, Harrison sketched a lineage shaded by familiar nationalist undertones: "The three works on this program, it seems to me, definitely establish Cage as the newest member of the great American independents, along with Ives, Ruggles, Cowell, and Varèse."[66] Cage reciprocated the compliment in an influential 1959 article entitled "History of Experimental Music in the United States." Harrison figures as a member of the youngest generation of experimentalists alongside Christian Wolff, Earle Brown, and Morton Feldman, three composers who were then closely associated with Cage. Their ancestry is traced back to Ives and Varèse, while Stravinsky and Schoenberg, modernism's usual patriarchs, are deemed irrelevant to the history of experimental music. Here nationalist convictions occupy the foreground. "America," Cage pronounced, "has an intellectual climate suitable for radical experimentation. We are, as Gertrude Stein said, the oldest country of the twentieth century." It is the most American of tendencies "to easily break with tradition, to move easily into the air . . . [to exhibit a] capacity for the unforeseen, . . . for experimentation." That said, however—and here Cage closely echoed Cowell—experimentalists have been the outsiders, neglected by the most influential new music organizations in the United States, including the League of Composers. Thus, familiar protagonists, complemented by recruits from a younger generation, are made to face off against equally familiar antagonists.[67]

Peculiar though it might seem, Cage's article was first published in German translation. It appeared in the 1959 issue of the *Darmstädter Beiträge* and was not available in English until 1961, when Wesleyan University Press included it in a collection of Cage's essays. This delay is symptomatic of the lack of institutional support that Cowell and Cage complained about, and, at the same time, points to a complicated process of transnational exchange. Though the formative ideas about American experimentalists originated with Cowell and his confederates, they fused into a coherent and persistent narrative in the context of post–World War II central Europe.

In the years immediately following the war, competition among the four occupying powers in Germany had given rise to a vibrant cultural infrastructure comprised of public radio stations, New Music festivals, performance ensembles, and well-stocked libraries.[68] This infrastructure remained intact with the advent of political independence and the creation of the Federal Republic of Germany in 1949. The bountiful commissions, performance opportunities, and speaking engagements available in West Germany made it possible for American composers to earn a respectable living from their métier, something few of them had experienced in the United States. Musicologist Amy Beal, who has chronicled the history of postwar American-German musical relations, memorably explains that for American composers, West Germany was "a place to ply their wares with dignity."[69] Moreover, as Beal also shows, it proved to be a place particularly receptive to views of American musical culture of Cowellian pedigree, the result of a fortuitous resonance with long-held stereotypes about the United States.

Cage's music was first played on West German radio in 1952, debuting on an influential late-night New Music program broadcast out of Cologne. Composer Herbert Eimert, who produced and hosted the program, offered some commentary to establish context for his listeners. Audiences in the United States, he explained, were poorly informed about music; however, this ignorance freed them from the "holy eternal criteria of value" that held tyrannical sway over the German musical establishment.[70] As a result, Americans were more open to experimentation, and a figure like Cage could emerge unfettered by the weight of tradition. This caricature of American culture was standard fare, the sort of thing German commentators had glibly dispensed for decades. But it happened to harmonize with Cowellian ideas about the autochthonous nature of experimentation in the United States—ideas that Cage recycled in his *Darmstädter Beiträge* article six years later.

The emergent West German narrative about Cage crystallized in a lecture Wolfgang Edward Rebner delivered in 1960 at the famed *International Fereinkürse für Neue Musik* in Darmstadt. Rebner, a German composer who had spent considerable time in the United States, titled his lecture "American Experimental Music" and supplied his audience with a more coherent version of the lineage Cage had sketched. Beal describes Rebner's lecture as "crucial to the development of a German narrative about American modern music, a narrative stretching from Ives to Cowell to Varèse to Cage" and "the first clear articulation of a historical position that linked these four composers through an established musical tradition."[71] Over the subsequent decades, the fertile climate of West Germany nourished the historiography Cage and Rebner propounded. It was cultivated by Germans and visiting Americans; strengthened by repetition in concert-hall commentary, lectures, program notes, and radio programs; and grew to absorb subsequent generations of experimentalists.

Perhaps the most important sustaining factor was the vigor of German musical discourse, the long tradition of polemics about aesthetic theory and the future of music that extended back to the beginning of the nineteenth century. In the fifties and sixties, a node of this discourse was the debate about the systematization of music as represented by the "total serial" works of composers like Pierre Boulez and Karlheinz Stockhausen. From Rebner's lecture onward, the experimentalists served as the antithesis to this tendency, "the sensual foil," as Beal puts it, because they emphasized the nature of sound rather than its rigorous organization. When, in the late sixties, musical debates were conflated with a larger, more heated conflict about the nature of society, the experimental lineage, which now extended from Ives to the minimalists, was freighted with New Left symbolism. The protests and strikes that beset Europe with particular ferocity during the *annus horribilus* 1968 were fueled by the conviction that traditional institutions and conventional authority had failed. Though the anger of young revolutionaries was also directed at the United States and its Cold War policies, in the musical world, the antiestablishment narrative burnished the reputation of American experimentalists. It helped that Cage and some of his confreres had embraced the American New Left.[72]

By and large, the revolutionary tincture that seeped into European discourse about the experimentalists had little impact on the American reception of the experimentalist patriarch Charles Ives. But there was one notable instance in which it did impinge, and with predictably divisive results. Among the offerings of the 1974 Ives Centennial Festival-Conference held in New York was a round-table session called "International Views." Several participants chose to invoke the vexed politics of the moment, including Dutch composer Louis Andriessen. "The growing importance of Ives's music in Holland," he maintained, "had directly to do with the democratic movement there, with its development after the revolution in Paris in 1968 and the democratic movement at the universities and conservatories. Not until this very lively period in Europe—I would say a revolutionary period—did we recognize the revolutionary aspects of Charles Ives's music."[73] Even more emphatic was the contribution of Hans G. Helms, a West German filmmaker and writer. Helms recast Ives as a social revolutionary who understood "the necessity for enhancing musical and ideological communication with his audience" and, as a result, created music freed of the hegemonic aesthetic sensibilities of the petty bourgeois.[74] Ideologically speaking, Helms suggested, Ives most closely resembled communist composer Hans Eisler. This was a comparison he repeated in a scathing review of the Ives Festival-Conference published a year later. Helms accused the organizers of having behaved in a manner typical of "musical officialdom," ignoring the underlying "socio-economic and political or ideological motivations" that informed Ives's activities. The composer's work was not best understood as a celebration of American culture, as the conference organizers would have it, but a revolt against it. Ives's political writings were, Helms tendentiously asserted, "a premonition of a development which reached its climax with the Watergate affair."[75]

Helms's invective prompted a response from Richard Taruskin, a musicology graduate student at Columbia University who had also attended the Festival-Conference. In a letter to the editor of the journal that had published Helms's critique, Taruskin explained that he did not object to Helms's obvious Marxist perspective but to the display of ignorance about American intellectual history. Ives was not a "crypto-Eisler," a musical advocate of socialism, but rather a "dreamy Utopian," as the nineteenth-century transcendentalists had been. Moreover, Taruskin contended, Helms had engaged in a highly selective reading of Ives's political writings, cherry-picking those quotations that supported his own ideological agenda. The certitude with which Helms made his pronouncements on American culture bespoke Old World snobbery—something Taruskin detected among several panelists in the "International Views" session. Nor was he alone, for he recollected that one of the spectators "exhorted the smug Europeans around the table to 'know our history as well as we are made to learn yours,' and drew a round of spontaneous and tension-relieving applause."[76] Indeed, as Taruskin supposed, Old World stereotypes about American culture had informed Helms's views of Ives. What Helms supplied was the New Left variant of the narrative about the experimentalists that had coalesced in West Germany some twenty years earlier, German clichés about American culture having been a decisive factor.

If, however, the specific European political connotations of the experimentalist narrative failed to resonate in the United States, the process of repatriation had begun. Partly this was a consequence of English-language books about the experimentalists written by European authors—notably Michael Nyman's *Experimental Music: Cage and Beyond* (1974) and Walter Zimmermann's *Desert Plants* (1976).[77] Another crucial factor was the activity of American experimentalists themselves, who, despite limited opportunities, made efforts to perform and disseminate their music on this side of the Atlantic, conditioned by the reception they received in Europe.

During the sixties, three members of Cage's New York milieu—James Tenney, Malcolm Goldstein, and Philip Corner—founded a contemporary music ensemble and bestowed upon it the name "Tone Roads," borrowing Ives's title for a collection of three of his more venturesome scores. The tribute implied by the name was reflected in the programming, which featured performances of many Ives works. For example, a 1965 program included Ives's Second String Quartet, *The Anti-Abolitionist Riots*, and *Some South-Paw Pitching*. Rounding out the program were works by a familiar complement of composers: Cage's Aria for Voice with Concert for Strings and *Fontana Mix*, Cowell's Quartet Pedantic, and Carl Ruggles's *Evocations*.[78] As Peter Garland, a former pupil of Tenney, has observed, the repertoire of this ensemble "connected the 'maverick' influence of John Cage to the more 'classic' American tradition of Varèse and Ives." Garland is wrong in asserting that Tone Roads created "the idea of a continuous, radical American tradition," for in actual fact the idea had already taken root overseas.[79] But the activities of Tenney and his collaborators helped lay the groundwork that would allow it to flourish at home.

So did the books of a trio of American authors, who, during the fifties and sixties, ventured rare assessments of contemporary music. Gilbert Chase, in his landmark *America's Music: From the Pilgrims to the Present* (1955), devoted a chapter entitled "The Experimentalists" to composers from Cowell to Cage. Notably absent was Ives, whom Chase placed in splendid isolation at the end of the book, reflecting the contemporaneous view of the composer as an autonomous man. In contrast, both Peter Yates and Eric Salzman, who published separate surveys of twentieth-century music in 1967, identified Ives as a foundational figure for the experimentalists.[80] Of these three authors, only Yates deployed the rubric "American Experimental tradition," affixing it at the head of a two-part chapter.[81]

Broader circulation of the concept of an experimental tradition did not occur until the late seventies and eighties, when a process of organization and institutionalization lodged it more firmly in public modes of musical discourse. The watershed was a 1979 festival called New Music, New York, which took place at The Kitchen, a SoHo performance space that had long been hospitable to avant-garde art. In the course of a tightly programmed nine days, the festival featured a veritable "who's who" of New York experimentalists, including Philip Glass, Steve Reich, Meredith Monk, Pauline Oliveros, and dozens of others. Tom Johnson, reporting for the *Village Voice*, described it as a coming-out celebration for music that had existed "on the fringes of official culture."[82] *New York Times* critic John Rockwell struggled to describe the eclectic assemblage: "They come mostly from the realm of 'classical' avant-gardism, what might very loosely be called the post-Cageian school of American music. But there are also people from the loft jazz scene, the underground, 'no wave' New York rock scene, sound-related performance art and more." Taking a slightly different tact, Rockwell observed that as inclusive as the festival seemed to be, it excluded "what might be called 'uptown' or 'midtown' contemporary classical music," by which he meant the music of composers associated with Columbia University, the Julliard School of Music, and those who had been lucky enough to receive performances in the hallowed precincts of Lincoln Center or Carnegie Hall. Here Rockwell fell back on a dichotomy—uptown versus downtown—that commentators of the New York art scene had invoked going back at least to the sixties, and which he himself had used frequently in his popular music criticism.[83] The uptowners enjoyed the benefits of mainstream credibility and institutional support, while the downtowners were forced back on their own resources, making a go of it by themselves or forging local alliances. Rockwell made no secret about where his sympathies lay: "A case can be made that much of the finest American music has been composed by rugged individualists, cut off by geographical or psychological isolation from the mainstream of American culture."[84] The name "Charles Ives" does not appear here, but it lingers in the offing.

The success of New Music, New York—the concerts regularly filled to capacity—served as the impetus for an annual event with the generalized name New Music America. What had been a local (New York) celebration of downtown experimentalists became a peripatetic, annual festival held in different cities across the country throughout the eighties.[85] The downtown/uptown binary also stuck, in large part due to Rockwell's repeated recourse to it in his own writing, both for and apart from the *New York Times*. It figured prominently in his *All American Music: Composition in the Late Twentieth Century* (1983), the first book to attempt an accessible overview of the eclectic contemporary music scene in the United States. He did not employ the binary in his article on "Experimental Music" for the *New Grove Dictionary of American Music* (1986), but it was there by implication in his discussion of the vibrant New York nexus of performance art, rock, jazz, and experimental music that coalesced in the sixties and seventies. The article is significant for consolidating the experimental-tradition narrative in the premiere reference source for American music, thereby granting it an unprecedented degree of historiographical legitimacy. "Experimental music in the USA," Rockwell explained, "reaches back at least as far as Charles E. Ives. . . . Ives, like many American inventors and tinkerers, musical and otherwise, who preceded him, struck out on his own. His works were largely ignored while he was active as a composer . . . but after they gained an audience in the 1920s the experimental tradition found a wider resonance."[86] Thus began a familiar trajectory, its terminus now extended beyond the minimalists so as to include all the artists involved in the downtown scene and other experimentalist outposts across the country.

Further scholarly sanction for the experimentalist narrative came from the work of English musicologist David Nicholls, whose 1990 book *American Experimental Music, 1890–1940* offered a thorough-going analysis of the output of three generations of experimentalists.[87] The following year, in what would become a widely used textbook on twentieth-century music, Robert Morgan declared that Ives had the "voice of an authentic American maverick" and that he was "the initiator of an 'alternative' stream in twentieth-century American music, dedicated to the pursuit of highly personal compositional approaches largely unencumbered by European precedents." The title of the section dedicated to this alternative stream? "The Experimental Tradition in American Music."[88]

In 1994, the New York Philharmonic, under the baton of its music director, Kurt Masur, offered a concert dubbed "The American Eccentrics," which juxtaposed Ives with Ruggles, Henry Brant, and Wallingford Riegger.[89] The rubric "eccentric" was perhaps not the most flattering of choices from the array of synonyms that identified this tradition over the years—experimentalist, innovator, pioneer, maverick. However, the concert did signal the moment at which Cowell's ultramoderns and their progeny entered mainstream concert culture as a coherent group, rather than appearing singly as they had done in the past. The dalliance of the New York Philharmonic with the eccentrics was soon eclipsed by a more dedicated and protracted engagement on the part of Michael Tilson Thomas and the San Francisco Symphony. It persists to this day—and in the Bay Area, the term of preference is "maverick."

From early on in his career, Thomas cultivated an interest in the music of the mavericks. A lifelong engagement with Ives began in the late fifties, when Thomas heard the composer's music for the first time as a young teenager. By 21, already launched on his meteoric climb to conducting celebrity, he had led a performance of *Three Places in New England* by the Los Angeles–based Debut Orchestra at a time when Ives was rarely heard in Southern California.[90] The same year, 1966, Thomas gave a piano recital entitled "Pioneers of Music . . . Past and Present," which featured the works of Cowell and Cage alongside more traditional fare: Bach, Mozart, Liszt, and Ravel.[91] He was still in his twenties when, as associate conductor of the Boston Symphony Orchestra, he made his first Ives recording, pairing *Three Places in New England* with Carl Ruggles's *Sun-treader*.[92] Again, at the helm of the Boston Symphony, he created a stir at Carnegie Hall in 1973 by presenting a program that featured Steve Reich's *Four Organs*.[93] Thus, by the time he was thirty, Thomas had a performance repertoire that included representation of all generations of experimentalists, from Ives to the minimalists. There is no evidence, however, that he conceived of them as part of a unified tradition. Indeed, with respect to Ives, his views were actually drifting in the other direction.

During the eighties, Thomas partnered with the Charles Ives Society to make the first recordings of the major orchestral works using the society-sanctioned critical editions. In the liner notes for the earliest of these recordings, which featured the Second Symphony, Thomas explained that he had first been attracted to Ives's "dissonant later works" and that "it took me a while to realize the Romantic spirit that pervaded them, and I proceeded back to the source of this spirit in his earlier tonal works."[94] Whether or not this perspective was a direct consequence of his interaction with Ives scholars, it certainly resonates with the project of rooting Ives in the nineteenth century that dominated contemporary American musicological endeavor. It also has the effect of directing attention away from Ives's would-be legatees, the future-oriented ultramoderns and the subsequent generations of experimentalists.

The album art quite literally overlaid a retrospective patina on Ives, reinforcing his connection to the past (Figure 6.2). It featured a montage of black and white photographs, superimposed on a sepia background and slightly colorized to create an autochrome effect. The foreground is dominated by a grainy 1913 image of Ives standing in New York's Battery Park, cropped around his silhouette and pasted on top of a photograph of the Danbury Fair Grounds, effectively relocating him from an urban to rural setting. In italics, above the composer's name, appears an imprimatur that vouches for the authenticity of the LP: "First Recording of the Critical Edition." This design, which was retained for the other recordings in the series, broadcasts the documentary aspirations of the project (despite the sleight-of-hand of moving Ives the New York businessman to the hometown where he would never live again). A quick glance at the collection of album covers pictured in the 1967 Columbia Ives advertisement reproduced in chapter 4 reveals something of the distance at which Thomas's recordings stand from other items in the Ives discography. Certainly some of the images link Ives to the past, but they tend to opt either for dreamy nostalgia or patriotic American symbols—stars and stripes—without the trappings of historical authenticity (the abstract design of William Masselos's recording of the Piano Sonata points decidedly forward).

In the nineties, with the Critical Edition recordings behind him, Thomas's perspective shifted, reflecting the extent to which the notion of an American experimentalist tradition, with Ives as its founder, had become pervasive in discourse about contemporary classical music. Since taking the helm as music director of the San Francisco Symphony in 1995, he has regularly offered concerts featuring the music of "American mavericks." The earliest of these took place in June 1996, a pair of concerts that made a considerable splash, in part because the guest artists included the living members of the Grateful Dead.[95] Repeated success with this repertoire prompted Thomas to organize a festival entirely devoted to the American mavericks as the culmination of the 1999–2000 season. And, as I write, the plans have been laid for a more modest four-program series to figure as part of the San Francisco Symphony's centenary season, 2011–2012.

Over the years, Thomas and the San Francisco Symphony have had their share of critics, most of the objections having to do with the indiscriminate way in which the rubric maverick is dispensed. Richard Taruskin, who wrote a largely

Figure 6.2. Cover of Columbia recording of Ives's Second Symphony, 1982.
Courtesy Sony Music Entertainment.

positive review of the 2000 festival in the *New York Times*, could not help but observe that the inclusion of Milton Babbitt, "the very icon of tenured palefacery," was at odds with what the mavericks were supposed to represent. Taruskin also reported that online classical-music forums were flooded with bids and nominations for Maverick membership; every composer wanted to be a part of "the in-group of outsiders, the icons of iconoclasm."[96] Few traces of this discussion survive, the transience of information on the internet being what it is, but on the American Mavericks website, launched in 2003 under the joint sponsorship of the San Francisco Symphony and National Public Radio, the criteria for inclusion are even looser. Notably Elliott Carter is represented by an interview, despite the fact that Thomas deemed him too "Eurocentric" and "brainy" to figure on the 2000 program. Visitors to the website will observe that "American Mavericks" is now a registered trademark—an irony too delicious not to point out.[97]

From a cynical standpoint, this eager readiness to confer the maverick mantle smacks of commercial opportunism. From another perspective, it points to the trait of omnivorousness that is unique to the discourse (or discourses) that yielded and supported the concept of the American experimental tradition. This concept has always been flexible, absorbing successive generations of American composers, proliferating in ways that are impossible for the other terms deployed by scholars, critics, and composers to categorize contemporary music. The musical historiography of the twentieth and twenty-first centuries is littered with terms of this latter sort—impressionism, expressionism, serialism, neoclassicism, minimalism, neoromanticism, postminimalism—each identified with a discrete group of works or composers. But "maverick tradition" is endlessly versatile, unencumbered by specific style criteria, and immune, apparently, to being absorbed by mainstream classical-music institutions that might otherwise spell its logical demise. It is rooted in the myth of the outsider, a perennial favorite of American culture in most all of its constituencies, regardless of the proximity of those constituencies to whatever one might choose to define as "inside."

Among the current scions of the maverick tradition is a composer whose access to public and high-profile classical-music forums has been unmatched in recent American music history, save perhaps by Leonard Bernstein. John Adams, the composer in question, is uniquely in a position to shape the reception of his music, and he has done so by tracing his musical lineage back to Ives, explicitly and implicitly. Sometimes, assuming the role of conductor, he has surrounded his own works with those of other mavericks. In 1999, for example, serving as guest conductor for the Chicago Symphony Orchestra, Adams offered programs that featured two of his pieces, Ives's *Three Places in New England*, and compositions by Lou Harrison, Philip Glass, and Aaron Copland (Copland is the odd man out here).[98] But it is his scores that provide the strongest evidence of his commitment to the idea of the maverick tradition and his own sense of place within that tradition.

Two of Adams's recent orchestral works, *On the Transmigration of Souls* (2002) and *My Father Knew Charles Ives* (2003), pay homage to the maverick patriarch. The New York Philharmonic commissioned the earlier work to commemorate the victims of the terrorist attacks on September 11, 2001. In a 2004 interview, Adams recollected that he struggled to find the right tone, not wanting to lapse into the "Coplandesque brand of sentiment." His solution was the "elevated philosophical mode" that Ives assumed in pieces like *The Unanswered Question* and the Fourth Symphony. Portions of the former appear in *On the Transmigration of Souls*, "a ghost in the background . . . [that] every once in a while . . . peeks through [the] screen of activity."[99]

Far and away the strongest testament to Adams's sense of connection to the maverick patriarch is *My Father Knew Charles Ives*, which was commissioned by the San Francisco Symphony. It is a work of musical rather than factual auto-biography, for Adams's father did not know Ives. Instead, the piece grew out of Adams's sense that as a child, he had shared with his father a relationship that had parallels to the one enjoyed by George and Charles Ives. Adams's father was part of a New England milieu of amateur music makers, redolent of postbellum Danbury and its lively vernacular musical traditions. Like Ives, Adams gained entrée to the musical world through his father, who served both as his first music teacher and companion in his earliest ensemble experiences. For attendees of the premiere performance of *My Father Knew Charles Ives*, the San Francisco Symphony program annotator offered an evocative scenario: Adams senior and junior playing alongside "local worthies such as the town jeweler, garage mechanic, and English Teacher, . . . [in] such organizations as the band of the town's mental hospital and the Nevers Second Regimental Band." Here was the beloved community of Ives's imagination preserved in aspic and reanimated in the middle of the twentieth century. The sounds too of Ives's musical world swirl nostalgi-cally through *My Father Knew Charles Ives*, which, as Adams has joked, might alternately be titled *Three Places in New England, Only a Little Further North* (his hometown Worcester, Massachusetts, lies some one hundred miles to the Northeast of Danbury, Connecticut).[100]

Shortly after the premiere of *My Father Knew Charles Ives*, critic Joshua Kos-man asserted in the *San Francisco Chronicle* that the work made explicit some-thing that had long been implicit. "What Adams is attempting is to define the terms of an indigenous American musical tradition. And the assertion is twofold: the tradition begins with Ives, and is encapsulated today by Adams's music."[101] This is true as far as it goes, but it neglects the fact that others have been complicit in promoting the experimentalists as the authentic American lineage of compos-ers. And certainly, among them, Michael Tilson Thomas has been one of the most influential. Thomas has cultivated the relationship between the San Francisco Symphony and Adams, who is based in the Bay Area. Together, with the support of California critics, program annotators, and the scholars who have sometimes been involved in San Francisco Symphony projects, Adams and Thomas have formed a virtuous circle that reinforces the idea of the "maverick tradition" and venerates Charles Ives as founding father.[102]

Thus the peripatetic trope of the American experimentalist has returned from whence it originated, though now it finds its seat not in the Bohemian enclaves of the Bay Area that Henry Cowell frequented, but in one of the most important institutions of the modern-day classical-music world. Conceived by Cowell, who regarded himself as the perennial outsider, it had been forged abroad amid the vibrant contemporary music world of postwar Germany, was burnished at home by the eclectic downtown scene of New York, and acquired its final sheen as it entered the lore of the concert hall in San Francisco.

And Now?

The fiftieth anniversary of Ives's death occurred in 2004, and like the centenary of the composer's birth three decades earlier, served as the motivation for festivals celebrating Ives across the United States. Although the anniversary did not occasion anything on the scale of the Ives Centennial Festival-Conference, with its international profile and near-complete roster of then-prominent Ivesians, there were multiple opportunities to hear Ives. New York proved especially vibrant, the season's offerings including a six-concert festival held under the auspices of the Julliard School of Music and a three-week extravaganza titled "Charles Ives— An American Original in Context" sponsored by the New York Philharmonic.

In anticipation of the latter event, the *New York Times* made space for its classical-music critics to list their favorite Ives recordings and supply some commentary. A panoply of Iveses paraded by. Anthony Tomassini depicted the composer in his oldest guise, as modernist innovator, noting that blurry chords in one of his songs "seem to anticipate the atmospheric harmonies of Gyorgy Ligeti." Further down the page, Allan Kozinn and Anne Midgette stressed Ives's connection to the late-nineteenth-century romantics, a view that dates back to the seventies, when musicologists set about connecting the composer to the European Classical tradition. Sandwiched between Kozinn's and Midgette's contributions, Jeremy Eichler's presented the fiercely individualistic Ives, by-product of the concerns about autonomy that animated the early Cold War period.[103] A week into the festival, *Times* readers were furnished with yet another perspective, this one courtesy of musicologist Richard Taruskin. Invoking the gender issues that animated more recent Ives scholarship, Taruskin observed that *Essays* "shows Ives to have been . . . no modernist at all but a nostalgist, with all that the word implies in cultural and social conservatism."[104]

Here, in the space of one week's worth of concentrated commentary on Ives, are most of the portraits from the full span of the composer's eighty-year reception history. The only major image missing is the conception of Ives as an American music ethnographer. But one need not range far in the anniversary-year criticism published in the *Times* to discover that it too remained in circulation. Several months earlier, in a review of a concert that was part of the Julliard festival, Eichler had noted, "One of Ives's outstanding qualities was his brash confidence in the vitality of American music at a time when the country still lingered deep in Europe's shadow."[105]

The Iveses refracted through the pages of the *New York Times* in 2004 were also dispersed in other mass-market newspapers and magazines—sometimes singly, sometimes in multiples. Certain images figured more prominently than others, particularly the view of Ives as the patriarch of the maverick tradition—a view that essentially updated the earliest conception of Ives as a modernist. What did not happen, in contrast to the 1974 centenary celebration, was the unveiling of new, controversial interpretations of the composer. The discourse was multifarious, but it was also static. And it remains so today, insofar as occasional appearances of Ives in mass-market publications can be said to constitute a discourse.

Such appearances are increasingly rare, a reflection of a much broader decline in coverage of classical music. Traditional newspapers have seen their subscriber base dwindle as they struggle to compete with new media, and when executives make cuts to compensate, arts critics are obvious targets since they can be removed without affecting the resources and personnel committed to "hard news." Across the country, full-time classical-music critics have been replaced by stringers, and in some cases, newspapers and magazines have stopped covering classical music completely.[106] Under these circumstances, it is not surprising that Gayle Sherwood Magee's *Charles Ives Reconsidered* (2008) passed mostly without notice in major newspapers and magazines. Only *The Nation* saw fit to publish a review, a marked contrast to the considerable attention that Jan Swafford's *Charles Ives: A Life with Music* attracted just twelve years earlier.[107]

If discourse about Ives in the public square is greatly diminished, there is one place where Ives continues to thrive: American colleges and universities. Evidence of this vitality comes in many forms, the most obvious being the number of Ives festivals that have taken place under the aegis of academic institutions. The 1974 Ives Centennial Festival-Conference, of course, was jointly sponsored by the City University of New York and Yale University. But there are many more recent examples, including the 1996 Bard College music festival, "Charles Ives and His World," which yielded a book of essays and documentary sources (amply cited in this book), and the Wesleyan-sponsored Ives Vocal Marathon, a four-year series of concerts that covered all of Ives's vocal repertoire, capped by a four-day event in 2009 that melded concerts and scholarly panels. Outside of such celebratory occasions, the music of Ives is a fairly regular presence in the repertoire of collegiate choirs and chamber ensembles. Perhaps more significant though is the increased space devoted to Ives in recent editions of *A History of Western Music*, the standard music-history textbook used in American universities. Beginning with the seventh edition, Ives scholar J. Peter Burkholder has been the custodian of this venerable textbook, ensuring that for the foreseeable future, virtually every American undergraduate who studies music will encounter Ives at least once in the course of his or her education.[108]

As for Ives scholarship, which has largely been supported by the patronage of the university, it remains a growth industry. Since 2000, there has been a steady supply of new books and articles about the composer, though not quite matching the prolific nineties. Even the *Journal of the American Musicological Society*, which was inhospitable to Ives for many years, has been a reliable source for new Ives scholarship.

Given the multitudinous nature of public discourse about Ives (to the extent it persists), it is not surprising that that the output of Ives scholars is also variegated. One major strand is constituted of work concerned with placing Ives in his social context, a stimulus for which, as I have suggested in this chapter, was the advent of New Musicology. Alongside and sometimes entangled with this strand, is another that is rooted in traditional musical analysis. Among the more notable contributions are Philip Lambert's extensive investigations of Ives's experimental music and Geoffrey Block's analysis of the "Concord" Sonata.[109] As theorist John McGinness has aptly pointed out, this scholarship continues the project initiated during the seventies and most influentially sustained by Burkholder's work.[110] The goal is to show that there are systematic regularities in Ives's music, that his compositions are not the result of haphazard intuition but the product of a refined musical craftsmanship, and that, consequently, he belongs to the European art-music tradition. In addition to these two central strands of modern Ives scholarship, a number of others coexist, including studies of documentary sources and reception.

And so work on Ives proceeds apace. But even as it does, the sanctum of academe stands in jeopardy. The financial crisis of 2008 and the subsequent economic unraveling placed many colleges and universities under duress. Cuts and furloughs have become the order of the day as administrators are forced to manage with fewer resources, and in this climate, questions about the value of a humanities education have begun to resound. It is too soon to say what this portends for American music departments, but their fate will determine that of Ives. Irony of ironies: today, the reputation of a composer who, in old age, raged about the narrow-mindedness of "Doctors of Music," hinges on the ongoing commitment of an embattled professoriate.

Postscript

"So What Do You Think about Ives?"

It was a Sunday morning, the last session of a sleepy meeting of the Pacific-Southwest chapter of the American Musicological Society, and perilously close to lunchtime. A handful of stalwarts were scattered sparsely around the lecture hall as I stepped to the podium to read my paper. Many of the attendees of the two-day meeting had already slipped out in order to make their journey home, cognizant of the unpredictability of California traffic. After mine, there was one more paper to go, and the meeting's supply of goodwill and enthusiasm was near exhausted. At most, I thought to myself, I'll get a few polite questions, and possibly nothing at all, because the topic of the paper—an early version of the material in chapter four about the impact of intellectual history and American Studies on Ives's reception—would be unfamiliar ground. As it turns out, I did get a few questions and they *were* all polite. But one of them, coming from an attendee near the back of the hall, sent me reeling. "So what do *you* think about Ives?" he asked pointedly.

I was stunned and momentarily tongue-tied. My paper examined the factors contributing to the way in which a constituency of scholars had portrayed the composer in the 1970s. Now, some forty years later, what possible bearing could my view of Ives have on the subject? I used the standard stalling tactic of repeating the question, and then mumbled something incoherent about sharing the perspective advanced in recent Ives scholarship, particularly Gayle Sherwood Magee's book, *Charles Ives Reconsidered*. The moment passed and I limped on to another polite inquiry.

I have since come to realize that the question was not as irrelevant as it first seemed to me. My paper had an implicit premise (one that is paramount also to the present book), namely that the convictions we hold about historical figures are always a function of our own ideologies. Or, to put it differently, no matter who is writing about Ives—whether an ardent devotee, a skeptical critic, or a scholar—the image projected is never an exact replica of the historical Ives. The difference is a function of the habits of thought of the writer, which, in turn, are conditioned by such factors as political commitments, aesthetic beliefs, social milieu, and, notably in the case of scholars, disciplinary frameworks. With the ascendancy of postmodernism in the humanities, this has become something of a historiographical truism, and a raft of theory, from Foucault to Gadamer, has been generated in support of it. What I forgot on that Sunday morning was that the truism applied to me as much at it did the Ivesians I was speaking about. I was being pressed on just this point, and the question, expressed in an alternative form, might have been phrased something like this: "If the view of Ives advanced by scholars in the 1970s was a construction, the byproduct of debates then raging in American universities, what factors shape your view of Ives now?"

In the months after the chapter meeting, while conducting research for the remaining portions of this book, I interviewed a number of Ives scholars and found myself asking them variants of this very question. What did Ives mean to them and could they identify the factors that contributed to their understanding of the composer? As I tried to piece together a coherent, overarching narrative from the answers they gamely and graciously supplied, I kept turning the question back on myself. It seemed to me that I was obligated at least to hazard an answer, especially after having exposed the scaffolding that supported the Ives research of so many of my colleagues. At the risk of appearing self-indulgent then, I offer in closing some thoughts about what Ives has meant to me, or, to be more precise, why I decided to write a book about his reception.

· · ·

I'm not quite sure when I first heard Ives's music. I suspect it was through the good graces of the Canadian Broadcasting Company, which, in the eighties, still programmed mostly classical music. But I do remember the first time Ives left a strong impression on me. It was during my first term as an undergraduate student in music composition at the University of British Columbia, when the campus orchestra, of which I was a part, offered an all-American program. We performed two Ives works, *The Unanswered Question* and *Central Park in the Dark*, and I found the former so haunting that I rushed to the nearest record store to find a recording. The CD I purchased also included *Three Places in New England* and the Third Symphony, both of which were revelatory in their own way. The atmospheric final movement of *Three Places in New England* captivated me, and, to this day, it has remained one of my favorite Ives works. The Third Symphony was full of borrowed music familiar from my own childhood, for I had grown up regularly attending a church where "What a Friend We Have in Jesus" and "O for A Thousand Tongues to Sing" were staples. I cannot say though that this was the beginning of a dedicated engagement with Ives and that a straight line runs from that early college experience to the current book. In truth, the book had motivations that had little to do with an abiding passion for Ives's music.

By the middle of my sophomore year, I had become disillusioned with the composerly guild into which I was being initiated. Most of its members, whether students or faculty, remained obsessed with modernist innovation and disparaged composers who wrote music that was retrospective enough in its stylistic language to hold out an immediate appeal to a member of the average public. It seemed to me that the compositional world had become a modern-day tower of Babel—a tower that was mostly shunned by the capable, budding performers who were my fellow students and whose musicality I respected enormously. I became a musicologist because I wondered why this state of affairs had arisen. I went to Berkeley to pursue graduate studies because a member of its music faculty, Richard Taruskin, had supplied some compelling answers.

Musicologists will undoubtedly detect Richard's influence on this book, and he even makes several cameos in the final chapter, first as a graduate student and then in his current guise as the field's most prominent public intellectual. His acclaim rests in no small part on his ability to penetrate modernist cant and to demonstrate that it often disguises critical sociopolitical factors that influence composers' music and, just as important, what they say about it. When I began graduate school, several of Richard's pupils were at work on dissertations pertaining to the Cold War, and it was initially my intention to join them. The intersection between music and politics during that period seemed particularly fraught, and among its yields were PhD composition programs in North American universities that fostered prickly brands of modernism.

In my third year, I ventured outside the department of music to take a course on American intellectual history from 1929 to 1963, which seemed an ideal way to broaden my knowledge of the period. I was grievously unprepared to step into such a course, not even knowing quite what the rubric "intellectual history" meant, and when I glanced over the syllabus, found myself confronted with a list of names—from Reinhold Neibuhr to Henry Luce—that were mostly unfamiliar to me. David Hollinger, who taught the course, and the other enrolled graduate students (all of them from the history department), were courteous and welcoming, managing the feat of integrating my awkward, halting contributions into the larger discussions. The breadth of knowledge on display was both terrifying and exhilarating, and I was awed by the way my fellow students moved deftly from one realm of thought to another—literature, theology, political history, philosophy, psychology, film, art. They seemed to know something about everything—

everything that is, except music. As an aspiring composer in college, I had felt alienated from the broader musical world; now a new sense of isolation began to nag at me as I became aware of how little classical music registered in the minds of other scholars of my generation.

Around the same time I took the intellectual history course, I also conducted preliminary work to familiarize myself with American musical culture during the fifties and sixties. That work led me to believe that classical music had once enjoyed a large constituency among educated Americans, and that a generation or two ago, I might have discovered historians who were classical-music aficionados. My dissertation, I decided, would explore the values projected onto classical music during the Cold War period, focusing specifically on orchestral repertoire. I hoped that maybe I could convince intellectual historians that even if they did not particularly care for classical music now, it was important enough in the past to merit further attention. I wrote a lengthy prospectus titled "The Orchestra in the Cold War" and set to work on a chapter addressing shifts within the canonical repertoire that might reveal something about contemporary American cultural values. As I was well aware, the most dramatic development of my time period was the surge of interest in the music of Gustav Mahler and Charles Ives, and so I chose to make the reception of these two composers the centerpiece of the chapter. In some sense, I never stopped working on it.

In the end, my dissertation was titled "Converging Paths to the Canon: Charles Ives, Gustav Mahler, and American Culture," and it chronicled the reception of the titular composers from the beginning of the century up to 1965, when Stokowski premiered Ives's Fourth Symphony. But the dissertation was more than a plea for relevance on the grounds that Mahler and Ives had once mattered a great deal to Americans. It was also an attempt to demonstrate that ideas about composers could be treated in the same way that intellectual historians treated ideas about anything. And moreover, that the ideas about these two particular composers happened to grow out of some of the most important episodes in twentieth-century American intellectual history, from the Greenwich Village revolt of the teens to the ideological battles of the Cold War.

This book is an extension of the Ives portion of the dissertation project and, indeed, supersedes it by bringing the story of the composer's reception more or less to the present. The prerogatives have not changed. Once again, my goal has been to show that both the narratives and methodologies employed by intellectual historians can illuminate, and be illuminated by, the reception history of a major composer.

While working on this book, my concerns about the marginalization of the music we musicologists have traditionally studied have only increased. My encounters with colleagues in other departments have replicated many times over the experience I had as a graduate student in David Hollinger's intellectual history course. I am no longer surprised to encounter historians of the United States who have never heard of Ives (and, after writing chapter four, I understand the reasons).

Perhaps I can put it most succinctly by returning to Stanley Fish's concept of "interpretive communities," which I glossed in the introduction to this book. My motivations for writing about Ives's reception came about from a sense that the scholarly community of musicologists to which I have been inducted, and to which my work is presumably directed, stands in jeopardy. Not that we'll disappear tomorrow any more than Ives will, or, for that matter, classical music. But I do think we are confronted with a dwindling constituency and that we are likely fated to become (if we are not there already) antiquarians in the narrowest sense of the word. Of course, New Musicology was largely about broadening the purview of the discourse, of expanding the musicological interpretive community by raising issues of gender, race, sexuality, and class. I would never have been attracted to the field if those issues had not been on the table, and they have certainly made acceptable the sort of interdisciplinary venture that yielded this book. That interdisciplinarity, however, has seemed rather one-sided, a matter of musicologists exploring other fields with few outside scholars making excursions into our domain. It is my hope that this book will find its way into the hands of Americanists who are not musicologists, and that it will serve as an invitation to take a closer look at what we study by making a compelling case for why it matters.

Notes

Introduction

1. L. Bernstein, "Thursday Evening Preview Scripts," 4.

2. Rossiter, *Charles Ives and His America*, 249.

3. Jauss, "Literary History as a Challenge to Literary Theory," 5.

4. Dahlhaus, "Problems in Reception History."

5. For two wide-ranging essays about reception and its attendant issues, replete with useful bibliographies, see Everist, "Reception Theories, Canonic Discourse, and Musical Value"; Samson, "Reception."

6. Fish, "Is There a Text in This Class?"; Hollinger, "Ethnic Diversity, Cosmopolitanism, and the Emergence of the American Liberal Intelligentsia."

7. Fish, "Is There a Text in This Class?" 306.

Chapter 1. Conservative Transcendentalist or Modernist Firebrand?

1. Not everyone received both *Essays* and "Concord." Clifton Joseph Furness got the sonata first; *Essays* came only after he sent an appreciative letter to the composer. See Swafford, *Charles Ives*, 322.

2. For a detailed examination of neurasthenia and its implications for Ives's breakdowns, see Sherwood, "Charles Ives and 'Our National Malady,'" 555–584.

3. Swafford, *Charles Ives*, 284–285.

4. For Ives's efforts to stimulate interest in his music prior to publishing *Essays* and "Concord," see Magee, "A New Sweet World," in *Charles Ives Reconsidered*, 90–116.

5. Ives, *Memos*, 70.

6. Owens, commentary in Ives, *Selected Correspondence of Charles Ives*, 56.

7. For a discussion of the musical decisions Ives made in preparing *Concord*, see Block, *Charles Ives: Concord Sonata*, 27–30. Magee suggests that Ives tempered the nationalist ele-

ments of the work to accord with the mood of postwar America. Magee, *Charles Ives Reconsidered*, 146–147.

8. Gross, "The Celestial Village," 251–281. Of course, Concord also enjoyed fame as the site of the earliest conflict in the American Revolutionary War.

9. The evidence is carefully assessed in Burkholder, *Charles Ives*, esp. 20–32.

10. Kleinfield, "The Structure of Emerson's Death," 175–199.

11. Teichgraeber III, "'More Than Luther of these Modern Days,'" 48–74.

12. Baym, "Early Histories of American Literature," 459–488.

13. Beers, *Initial Studies*, 95, 99, 94, 123.

14. Incidentally, Pancoast uses the term *manner* and Trent *substance* in exactly the same way Ives does. See note 16.

15. Ives, "Author's Preface," in *Essays*, xxv.

16. Ives uses the terms *substance* and *manner* extensively in *Essays*, but gives the most succinct definition in his "Epilogue": "Substance has something to do with character. Manner has nothing to do with it. The substance of a tune comes from somewhere near the soul, and the manner comes from—God knows where" (*Essays*, 77). J. Peter Burkholder has shown that this terminology was not original to Ives, and that he borrowed it from an article about Debussy written by a friend, John Cornelius Griggs. See Burkholder, *Charles Ives*, 68–72. But other turn-of-the-century writers used *substance* and *manner* as Ives did.

17. Ives, *Essays*, 11, 16, 17, 18.

18. Phelps to Ives, July 4, 1920, in Ives, *Selected Correspondence*, 71.

19. Ives, *Essays*, 22.

20. Carlyle to Emerson, November 3, 1844, in Emerson, *The Correspondence of Thomas Carlyle and Ralph Waldo Emerson*, 81.

21. Beers, *Initial Studies in American Letters*, 106.

22. Ives, *Essays*, 22.

23. Gougeon, "Abolition and the Biographers," 1–23.

24. Ives, *Essays*, 27.

25. Ibid., 31.

26. Mitchell, *Individualism and its Discontents*, 5.

27. Ibid., 198, note 9.

28. Ives, *Essays*, 35.

29. "Ives Scholastic Record (1894–98)," in Ives, *Memos*, 182.

30. Ives, *Essays*, 36.

31. Ibid., 67–69.

32. Something of the flavor of Ives's marketing ideas is conveyed in his parable "Broadway," in *Memos*, 229–235.

33. Baym, "Early Histories of American Literature," 459.

34. Twichell to Charles Ives, in Rossiter, *Charles Ives and His America*, 173.

35. Arnold, "Culture and Anarchy," 409–410. For the impact of Arnold on American culture, see Rubin, *The Making of Middlebrow Culture*, 14–15.

36. Ruland, *The Rediscovery of American Literature*, 13–23.

37. Babbitt, *Rousseau and Romanticism*, 129–139.

38. Babbitt, *Democracy and Leadership*, 240.

39. Rubin, *The Making of Middlebrow Culture*, 45–48.

40. Ibid., 3.

41. Emerson, "Spiritual Laws," 133.

42. Babbitt, *The Masters of Modern French Criticism*, 353, 357.

43. For a summary of their views, see Mitchell, *Individualism and Its Discontents*, 38–46 and Ruland, *The Rediscovery of American Literature*, 33–56, 57–96.

44. Ives, *Essays*, 26.

45. Ibid., 35.

46. In *Essays*, Ives projects his beliefs onto Emerson, claiming that the philosopher "realizes the value of '*the many*,'—that the law of averages has a divine source. He recognizes the various life values *in reality*—not by reason of their closeness or remoteness, but because he sympathizes with men who live them, and the *majority* do" (33–34).

47. Ibid., 35.

48. V. W. Brooks, *America's Coming-of-Age*, 3, 4, 7.

49. Brooks is probably referring to Emerson's "Thoughts on Modern Literature."

50. V. W. Brooks, *America's Coming-of-Age*, 41, 40.

51. Frank, *Our America*, 72. For a more extensive account of Frank's attitude toward Emerson, see Mitchell, *Individualism and its Discontents*, 52–54.

52. Santayana, "The Genteel Tradition in American Philosophy."

53. Blake, *Beloved Community*, 124.

54. V. W. Brooks, *America's Coming-of-Age*, 85, 87.

55. Bourne, "Trans-National America," 181. Incidentally, Bourne departed from Brooks and Frank in expressing admiration for Emerson, but Bourne's views about the literary past were far less developed because he mostly wrote about social issues. See Blake, *Beloved Community*, 117.

56. Although the attacks that Brooks and his colleagues leveled from their Bohemian enclave were the most vocal and direct assault on nineteenth-century values, popular culture had already begun to shift. Studying self-help literature of the time, Warren I. Susman has noted the ascendancy of the term *personality* at first coexisting with *character* and then eclipsing it. In contrast to inward-directed *character*, *personality* was outer-directed and intent on establishing identity with respect to others. Susman notes that the train of adjectives associated with personality—fascinating, stunning, attractive, magnetic—consisted of words that "would seldom if ever be used to modify the word *character*" (Susman, "'Personality' and Twentieth-Century Culture," 277).

57. Broyles, "Charles Ives and the American Democratic Tradition."

58. Swafford, *Charles Ives*, 381.

59. Michael Broyles has suggested that Ives was aware of *The Masses*, which became the venue for other voices issuing from Greenwich Village. See Broyles, "Charles Ives and the American Democratic Tradition," 144–146.

60. Phelps to Ives, July 4, 1920, in Ives, *Selected Correspondence*, 71.

61. Goldstein to Ives, March 10, 1921, in Ives, *Selected Correspondence*, 58.

62. Ives, undated sketch for reply to Goldstein, in Ives, *Selected Correspondence*, 59. This may have been written much later, for the mode of expression is more consistent with the persona Ives would later adopt, when he had a vested interest in proving his musical independence.

63. Swafford, *Charles Ives*, 318.

64. Cadman to Ives, March 9, 1921, in Ives, *Selected Correspondence*, 57–58.

65. Stringham, "Ives Puzzles with His Cubistic Sonata and 'Essays'"; A. Kramer, "A Pseudo-Literary Sonata!!!" 36; Bellamann, "Reviews: 'Concord, Mass., 1840 1860,'" 169. All three reviews are reproduced in *Charles Ives and His World*, ed. Burkholder, 280–286, 278–279.

66. Townsend, *Sherwood Anderson*, 187.

67. Busoni, *Sketch of a New Esthetic of Music*, 10–11.

68. Ibid., 34.

69. Bellamann, "Notes on the New Aesthetic of Poetry and Music," 260, 261, 264, 262. Incidentally, Bellamann acknowledged Busoni but shied away from admitting the extent to which he was indebted to the composer. He claimed that the notion of "pure idea" and its inherent potential are "not the exclusive property of a Benedetto Croce or a Ferruccio Busoni. It is the sum total of a tendency perceived in isolated and unrelated works" (261).

70. Bayne, "A Critical Study of Henry Bellamann's Life and Work," 40.

71. Lowell, "Preface," in *Some Imagist Poets*, vii.

72. Bellamann, "Reviews: 'Concord, Mass., 1840–1860,'" 167, 166, 169.

73. Katherine Bellamann quoted in Bayne, "A Critical Study of Henry Bellamann's Life and Work," 51. For an extensive discussion of Ives's gendered rhetoric, see Tick, "Charles Ives and Gender Ideology."

74. Swafford, *Charles Ives*, 321.

75. Wiecki, "Two Musical Idealists—Charles E. Ives and E. Robert Schmitz."

76. Ives, "Some 'Quarter-Tone' Impressions," in *Essays*, 110.

77. See, for example, Downes, "Franco-American Musical Society."

78. Monique Schmitz Leduc, interview by Perlis, *Charles Ives Remembered*, 125.

79. Magee, *Charles Ives Reconsidered*, 152.

80. Bellamann, "The Music of Charles Ives," 16.

81. Bellamann, "Charles Ives," 46, 47, 48.

82. Swafford, *Charles Ives*, 323–324.

83. Clifton J. Furness cited in Swafford, *Charles Ives*, 322.

84. Whitmer, "New Music," 5–6.

85. Ives, "Postface to *114 Songs*," in *Essays*, 130.

86. Magee, *Charles Ives Reconsidered*, 147.

87. Swafford, *Charles Ives*, 323, 335; Owens, discussing the publication of *50 Songs*, in Ives, *Selected Correspondence*, 63.

88. For a sampling, see Ives, *Selected Correspondence*, 60–70.

89. Ibid., 151. Among these works are the unfinished *Universe Symphony* and the songs "On the Antipodes," "Yellow Leaves," and "Peaks," the latter two being settings of poems by Henry Bellamann.

90. Ives, "Music and its Future," 197, 192.

91. John Kirkpatrick, who edited the published edition of *Memos*, describes it as "an autobiographical scrapbook of reminiscence." Kirkpatrick, preface to Ives, *Memos*, 16.

92. Ibid, 26.

93. Magee, *Charles Ives Reconsidered*, 164.

94. Ives, *Memos*, 27, 133. These are just three of the many epithets Ives hurls. Several commentators have ascribed the tone of *Memos* to the composer's degenerating physical and mental health. See, for example, Feder, *Charles Ives*, 309, 313; Swafford, *Charles Ives*, 387–392.

95. Ives, *Memos*, 28.

96. Magee, *Charles Ives Reconsidered*, 151, 156–162.

97. Ives, *Memos*, 36.

98. J. Peter Burkholder, who has also addressed the shift of Ives's self-depiction from *Essays* to *Memos*, describes Ives objective in writing the latter as "disinherit[ing] himself from European music" ("Charles Ives and His Fathers," 10).

99. Ives, *Memos*, 42–43, 132.

100. Ibid., 49.

101. Yellin, review of *The Celestial Country*.

Chapter 2. Songs of Our Fathers

1. H. Cowell quoted in Weisgall, "Music of Henry Cowell," 498.

2. In *Charles Ives and His Music*, Henry Cowell claimed to have "heard Ives's name for the first time" in the early twenties, when "obvious and vulgar jokes" circulated about Ives following the publication of *Essays Before a Sonata*, the "Concord" Sonata, and *114 Songs* (Cowell and Cowell, *Charles Ives and His Music*, 90–91). His writings make no mention of Ives until 1925.

3. Hicks, *Henry Cowell, Bohemian*, 122.

4. Two earlier articles by Cowell mention Ives, but only as brief examples of recent stylistic developments. See H. Cowell, "America Takes a Front Rank in Year's Modernist Output" and "Our Inadequate Notation."

5. H, Cowell, "American Composers IX," 24.

6. H. Cowell, "Three Native Composers," 185.

7. H. Cowell, "American Composers IX," 26–27.

8. Ibid., 29.

9. Ibid., 27, 28.

10. H. Cowell, "Moravian Music," 25, 26, 29.

11. H. Cowell, "The Value of Eclecticism," 265.

12. For a discussion of the different approaches anthropologists adopted in transcribing Amerindian music, see Ellingson, "Transcription."

13. See, for example, Densmore, *Northern Ute Music.*

14. H. Cowell, "Our Inadequate Notation," 30.

15. Pescatello, *Charles Seeger*, 72–73, 61–62. For a discussion of Seeger's engagement with anthropology, see Baranovitch, "Anthropology and Musicology."

16. H. Cowell, "Our Inadequate Notation," 33.

17. Paul, "From American Ethnographer to Cold War Icon," 410–411.

18. Bluestein, *The Voice of the Folk*, 93.

19. Rosenfeld, *An Hour with American Music*, 31.

20. Lomax, "Some Types of American Folk-Song," 1.

21. Kodish, *Good Friends and Bad Enemies*, 36–37.

22. McGill, *Folk Songs of the Kentucky Mountains*, v.

23. Taruskin, "Nationalism."

24. Dvořák, quoted in Creelman, "Real Value of Negro Melodies," 28. For a more extensive discussion, see Beckerman, *New Worlds of Dvořák.*

25. MacDowell cited in Gilman, *Edward MacDowell*, 83–85.

26. Ives, *Essays*, 78, 79–80.

27. Bellamann, "Reviews: 'Concord, Mass., 1840–1860' (A Piano Sonata by Charles E. Ives)," 166.

28. Ibid., 168.

29. Bellamann, "Program Notes."

30. The Second Violin Sonata was premiered as part of a recital devoted to modern violin sonatas performed by Jerome Goldstein (violin) and Rex Tilson (piano). Tryon's review of the performance, which focused on the Ives sonata, appeared as part of a summary of the week's musical events (Tryon, "'Freischütz' at the Metropolitan").

31. Tryon, "Folk Song and Hymn Tunes of America."

32. Tryon, "Of Ives and Others."

33. Oja, "Creating a God," in *Making Music Modern*, 25–44.

34. See Shirley, "Folk Music," in *Modern Music.* The only notable exception to the cosmopolitan trend among the modernists with whom Cowell associated was Ruth Crawford. Carl Sandburg recruited her to supply piano accompaniments for the material he had collected for *The American Songbag.* This was a brief venture for Crawford, and it was not until the thirties that she, like Charles Seeger (whom she married in 1931), became seriously committed to American folk music. Tick, *Ruth Crawford Seeger*, 53–57.

35. S. Johnson, "Henry Cowell, John Varian, and Halcyon," esp. 3–4.

36. H. Cowell, "Hidden Irish Treasure," 31.

37. Ibid., 33.

38. Paul, "From American Ethnographer to Cold War Icon," 417–418.

39. The arrangement is discussed in two letters contained in the Henry Cowell Papers: Cowell to Walton, August 27, 1927, Henry Cowell Papers, folder 500, box 17; Cowell to Walton, undated (Sidney Cowell has penciled in 1927), Henry Cowell, Papers, folder 501, box 17.

40. Henry Cowell to Olive and Harry Cowell, December 20, 1927, Henry Cowell Papers, folder 501, box 17.

41. Bartók, "The Relation of Folksong to the Development of the Art Music of Our Time."

42. Ibid., 324–325.

43. Ibid., 326, 321.

44. For a discussion of the concept of social evolution roughly contemporaneous with Cowell's early explorations of Ives, see Goldenweiser, "Evolution, Social." The terms *diffusion* and *independent invention* are thoroughly discussed in Stocking, "Franz Boas and the Culture Concept in the Historical Perspective."

45. Boas, "Summary of the Work of the Committee in British Columbia," cited in Stocking, "Franz Boas and the Culture Concept," 214.

46. H. Cowell, "American Composers IX," 24.

47. The New School for Social Research was the one place that could be counted upon to furnish interested listeners with samplings of Ives's music on a semiregular basis. Beginning in 1928, at least one piece by Ives was included among its eclectic offerings for six of the next seven years. For more on the New School, see Bick, *The Musical Legacy of the New School for Social Research*.

48. "House paradigm" is my coinage, but I am drawing here on the assertions of Peter M. Rutkoff and William B. Scott, who, in their history of the New School, identify the principles of the institution with the ideas of historian James Harvey Robinson. The major influences behind Robinson's work, and thus the New School, were the instrumentalism of John Dewey and the anthropology of Franz Boas (Rutkoff and Scott, *New School*, 1–18).

49. Rutkoff and Scott note that Johnson "invariably assigned topics addressed to important normative and methodological issues to close friends, such as philosophers Morris Cohen, John Dewey, Horace Kallen, and Sidney Hook" (ibid., 72).

50. For a complete list, see Paul, "From American Ethnographer to Cold War Icon," 400, note 1.

51. Hicks, *Henry Cowell, Bohemian*, 133.

52. Slonimsky, *Perfect Pitch*, 108–120.

53. Anonymous reviewer for *Les Dérnières Nouvelles* quoted in Cowell and Cowell, *Charles Ives and His Music*, 108.

54. Herrmann claims that it was a copy of the *114 Songs* that he and Jerome Moross discovered at the New York public library. Moross, however, recalls that it was the "Concord" Sonata, and that the pair had stumbled onto it at the Half-Price Music Shop. See Herrmann and Moross interviews in Perlis, *Charles Ives Remembered*.

55. Herrmann, "Charles Ives," 99.

56. Berger, "Charles Ives."

57. In addition to Berger, Herrmann, and Moross, the other members were Elie Siegmeister, Henry Brant, Irwin Eilner, Israel Citkowitz, Lehman Engel, and Vivian Fine. Bukoff, "Charles Ives, a History and Bibliography of Criticism."

58. Rosenfeld, "Musical Chronicle," 358.

59. Oja, *Making Music Modern*, 305. For more on Rosenfeld's somewhat contradictory critical stance, see Broyles, *Mavericks and Other Traditions*, 102–105.

60. Rosenfeld, "Charles E. Ives," 262.

61. Rosenfeld, "A Musical Tournament," 121.

62. Rosenfeld, "Charles E. Ives," 263.

63. Rosenfeld, "Ives," 318.

64. Wilson, "Paul Rosenfeld," 15.

65. Hughes, *Oswald Spengler*, 72.

66. Mumford, "Spengler's *The Decline of the West*," 220, 223.

67. Rosenfeld, "The Nazis and 'Die Meistersinger,'" 90, 91.

68. Rosenfeld, "The Advent of American Music," 51.

69. Carter in Perlis, *Charles Ives Remembered*, 142.

70. Between 1936 and 1938, publications on Ives were few and far between and the number of performances dwindled. For the details of Cowell's incarceration, see Hicks, "The Imprisonment of Henry Cowell."

71. V. W. Brooks, "On Creating a Usable Past," 338, 337, 339.

72. Ibid., 340.

73. Hoopes, *Van Wyck Brooks*, 127.

74. V. W. Brooks, "On Creating a Usable Past," 340.

75. Hoopes, *Van Wyck Brooks*, 134–140.

76. Copland and Perlis, *Copland*, 125.

77. Copland, "The Composer in Industrial America," 104.

78. Pollack, *Aaron Copland*, 107.

79. Copland, "The Composer in Industrial America," 99–106. This whole passage is redolent of Young America rhetoric—from comments about the organic relationship between the arts and everyday life in France (as opposed to the United States where no such connection existed) to the disparagement of the genteel composers active in the late nineteenth and early twentieth centuries.

80. Copland and Perlis, *Copland*, Vol. 1, 204.

81. Mumford, *The Golden Day*, 3.

82. Ibid., 20, 52, 58, 73. The trajectory Mumford traces, from organic medieval culture to the machine civilization of the modern age, is reminiscent of *The Decline of the West*. However, Mumford, did not read Spengler's treatise until 1926, *after* he had finished writing *The Golden Day*. D. Miller, *Lewis Mumford*, 300–302.

83. Ibid., 85.

84. Mumford, *The Golden Day*, 278, 97.

85. Ibid., 136.

86. Van Wyck Brooks quoted in D. Miller, *Lewis Mumford*, 252.

87. Hoopes, *Van Wyck Brooks*, 162–163.

88. D. Miller, *Lewis Mumford*, 253.

89. Hoopes, *Van Wyck Brooks*, 176.

90. Capper, "'A Little Beyond,'" 516.

91. Brooks was also influenced by the work of folklorist Constance Rourke, who, like Henry Cowell, used the diffusionist model of culture to validate and explore American folk culture. See Rubin, "Culture."

92. V. W. Brooks, *The Flowering of New England*, 541–542.

93. Cowley, "The Puritan Legacy," 80. Cowley also addresses some of the misgivings that others had had about Brooks's *The Flowering of New England*.

94. Capper, "'A Little Beyond,'" 518–519. I am borrowing the list Capper has assembled of books about the transcendentalists published during the late thirties and early forties.

95. Matthiessen readily acknowledged his debt to Mumford, describing the appearance of *The Golden Day* as "a major event in my experience" (Matthiessen, "Acknowledgments" in *American Renaissance*, xvii).

96. Capper, "'A Little Beyond,'" 521–523.

97. P. Miller, *The Transcendentalists*, 3.

98. Massey, "An 'Unobtrusive Minister of Genius,'" 75–116.

99. Rossiter, *Charles Ives and His America*, 278.

100. Gilman, "Music," 318, 317, 320.

101. See, for example, Downes, "Tardy Recognition."

102. Bukoff's bibliography lists 23 articles for 1939, not quite a match for the 30 published in 1933 (Bukoff, "Charles Ives, a History and Bibliography of Criticism ([1920–1939]," 168–180).

103. Some of the Ives articles mentioning Gilman include Taubman, "Records"; Slonimsky, "Bringing Ives Alive"; Moor, "On Horseback to Heaven"; and "Musical Whitman" (*Newsweek*). On at least one occasion, the renown of the review was helped along by Ives himself, who sent a copy to critic-impresario Peter Yates early on in their correspondence (D. Crawford, *Evenings On and Off the Roof*, 34).

104. "Insurance Man" (*Time*).

105. Fletcher, "A Connecticut Yankee in Music."

106. Herrmann, "Four Symphonies by Charles Ives," 215.

107. Copland, "One Hundred and Fourteen Songs," 61.

108. Carter in Perlis, *Charles Ives Remembered*, 139.

109. Carter, "The Case of Mr. Ives," 175, 174.

110. Berger, "Spotlight on the Moderns"; Thomson, "The Ives Case."

Chapter 3. Winning Hearts and Minds

1. Harrison, "Ruggles, Ives, Varèse," 16–17.

2. Miller and Lieberman, *Lou Harrison*, 13, 16.

3. Ibid., 33.

4. Strauss, "Symphony by Ives in World Premiere"; Downes, "Tardy Recognition."

5. Clifton was on the jury committee from 1943 to 1960; the other members changed from year to year. Fischer, "History and Development of the Pulitzer Prize for Music."

6. Swafford, *Charles Ives*, 422.

7. Rossiter, *Charles Ives and His America*, 296.

8. "Charles E. Ives" (*Life*), 45. Swafford describes the photography session in some detail and reproduces one of Smith's unusable photographs: an amusing, faintly tragic image of Ives, recoiling in terror from the camera and strenuously protesting the whole affair (Swafford, *Charles Ives*, 423–424).

9. Moor, "On Horseback to Heaven," 66, 67.

10. Taubman, "Posterity Catches Up with Charles Ives," 15.

11. Ibid.

12. Moor, "On Horseback to Heaven," 67, 68.

13. Rutkoff and Scott, "The Politics of Disillusionment," in *New School*, 107–127.

14. Fromm, *Escape from Freedom*, 31, 35, 36.

15. "Other-direction" was one of three character types Riesman and his coauthors developed, a typology that they linked to three major stages of societal development. The other two were "tradition-directed" and "inner-directed." Riesman, Denney, and Glazer, *The Lonely Crowd*, 40, 23.

16. Ibid., 278, 314.

17. Ibid., 325.

18. The members of bohemian enclaves, Riesman, Denney, and Glazer explained, "are often zealously tuned in to the signals of a group that finds the meaning of life, quite unproblematically, in an illusion of attacking an allegedly dominant and punishing majority of Babbitts and Kwakiutl chiefs" (ibid., 296).

19. It is possible that Glazer learned about Ives as a result of his work as an assistant editor for *Commentary*. This magazine regularly published the work of music critic Kurt List, an Ives aficionado since the midforties. List was also the editor of his own magazine, *Listen*, which dedicated its November 1946 issue to Ives and featured articles by Elliott Carter and Lou Harrison. Letters preserved in the Henry Cowell papers reveal that List tried to publish some of Ives's music in 1948, but the endeavor came to naught. See Henry Cowell to Charles Ives, October 15 and 19, 1948, Henry Cowell Papers, folder 581, box 19.

20. Saunders, "Marxists at the Waldorf," in *The Cultural Cold War*, 45–56.

21. Manifesto of the Congress for Cultural Freedom, quoted ibid., 82–83.

22. The involvement of the CIA in CCF activities is richly chronicled in Saunders, *The Cultural Cold War*.

23. Hook, "On the Battlefield of Philosophy," 252.

24. The American Committee for Cultural Freedom reactivated an organization founded by John Dewey and Sidney Hook in 1939 to combat totalitarianism in both its communist and fascist incarnations.

25. Nicolas Nabokov, quoted in Caroll, *Music and Ideology in Cold War Europe*, 8.

26. For a thorough discussion of the politics and aesthetics that governed the programming criteria for the Paris Festival, see Carroll, *Music and Ideology in Cold War Europe*, 8–24.

27. Shortly after Soviet apparatchik Andrey Zhdanov issued a 1948 decree condemning "formalism," Slonimsky gave a talk denouncing Soviet cultural policy for the Council for

American-Soviet Friendship. Needless to say, it was his last contact with the organization (Slonimsky, *Perfect Pitch*, 189).

28. Slonimsky, "Sur la musique Américaine," 29.

29. Slonimsky, "Bringing Ives Alive," 49.

30. Slonimsky, "Musical Rebel," 7.

31. Emerson, "The American Scholar," 42.

32. Dayton, "Charles Ives in the USIA," 90–91.

33. Hoffman, "A Great Visionary Musician"; Ioannidis, contribution to roundtable "Ives Viewed from Abroad," in Hitchcock and Perlis, *An Ives Celebration*, 49.

34. Whoever sets out to tell that story will have to begin by perusing the extensive records of the USIA housed at the National Archive in College Park, Maryland.

35. Harmony Ives to Charlotte Ruggles, in Miller and Collins, "The Cowell-Ives Relationship," 474.

36. Henry Cowell to Nicolas Slonimsky, in Slonimsky, *Perfect Pitch*, 152. For Cowell's other inquiries after Ives, see Miller and Collins, "The Cowell-Ives Relationship," 476–478.

37. Miller and Collins, "The Cowell-Ives Relationship," 486, 481–483.

38. Harmony Ives to Charlotte Ruggles, in ibid., 474.

39. Henry Cowell to Harmony Ives, September 15, 1941, Henry Cowell Papers, folder 561, box 19.

40. Harmony and Charles Ives to Henry Cowell, September 18, 1941, Henry Cowell Papers, folder 243, box 9.

41. Harmony Ives to Henry Cowell, October 4, 1945, Henry Cowell Papers, folder 243, box 9.

42. Cowell's correspondents include the likes of John J. Becker, Arthur Berger, and Katherine Bellamann, wife of Henry Bellamann, Ives's earliest champion.

43. S. Cowell, "The Cowells and the Written Word," 86.

44. Oxford University Press, not Prentice Hall, ultimately published *Charles Ives and His Music*. Sidney gives a detailed account of this far-from-smooth transition. Ibid., 86–87.

45. Ibid., 86.

46. Paul, "From American Ethnographer to Cold War Icon," 431–439.

47. Cowell and Cowell, *Charles Ives and His Music*, 144.

48. Ibid., 6, 92, 64.

49. Kerst, "Sidney Robertson and the WPA Northern California Music Project."

50. Cowell and Cowell, *Charles Ives and His Music*, 4, 40, 115.

51. Ibid., 173, 178, 180, 178–179, 74.

52. Ibid., 94, 95.

53. Bell, *The End of Ideology*, 370, 373.

54. Cowell and Cowell, *Charles Ives and His Music*, 94–95.

55. Hollinger, "Ethnic Diversity, Cosmopolitanism, and the Emergence of the American Liberal Intelligentsia," 58.

56. Pells, *The Liberal Mind in a Conservative Age*, 132.

57. Cowell and Cowell, "Charles Ives."

58. Laughlin, "The Function of This Magazine," 5–6.

59. For a good account of the Composer's Collective, see Pescatello, *Charles Seeger*, 109–119,

60. Slonimsky gives an amusing account of his brush with the FBI in *Perfect Pitch*, 107.

61. H. Cowell, "Music Is My Weapon," in *Essential Cowell*, 48.

62. Higgins, editorial comments on "Music Is My Weapon," in *Essential Cowell*, 47. Hicks briefly discusses the circumspect manner in which Cowell carried out his affairs amid the suspicions of the early Cold War period (Hicks, *Henry Cowell, Bohemian*, 148–149).

63. For the German leg of Cowell's tour, see Beal, "The Army, the Airwaves, and the Avant-Garde." In 1956, the FBI launched a routine investigation into Cowell's past activities before he was sent abroad on official business. They turned up nothing incriminating. Hicks, *Henry Cowell, Bohemian*, 148.

64. H. Cowell, "A Composer's World," *Essential Cowell*, 311, 315, 320.

65. Chase notes his admiration for Rourke in his acknowledgments, writing that her work "must always remain a source of inspiration to anyone trying to grasp what is really native and traditional in our culture" (Chase, *America's Music*, xi).

66. Rourke, *The Roots of American Culture and Other Essays*. For more on Rourke's's intellectual pedigree, see Rubin, "Culture."

67. Chase, *America's Music*, 658, xvii.

68. Ibid., xxi.

69. Ibid., 678.

70. Becker, "Charles E. Ives," part 1, 20.

71. Becker, "Charles E. Ives," part 2, 46.

72. Kirkpatrick, "Ives's Transcendental Achievement."

73. Kirkpatrick, "Ives, Transcendentalist in Music."

74. Ibid.

75. Yates, "Charles Ives" (1961), part 2, 4. Yates's other articles about Ives were published in 1944 and 1955 and are listed in "Works Cited." For more on Yates, see D. Crawford, *Evenings On and Off the Roof*.

76. Boatwright, introduction to Ives, *Essays*, xiv, xv.

77. Leonard Bernstein to Aaron Copland, in Burton, *Leonard Bernstein*, 50.

78. L. Bernstein, "The Absorption of Race Elements into American Music," 96, 94. Bernstein completed his bachelor's thesis in 1939.

79. Sabin, "Bernstein Conducts Ives Symphony No. 2"; Kastendieck, "Ives Symphony Is Interesting"; Downes, "Symphony by Ives Is Played in Full."

80. McMahan Jr., Letter to the Music Editor.

81. L. Bernstein, "Thursday Evening Preview Scripts," 4, 6, 10.

82. See, for example, Lang, "Music"; Sargeant, "Musical Events."

83. For a detailed account of the American National Exhibition and its effects, see Hixson, *Parting the Curtain*, 151–213. Bernstein figured prominently in the exhibition. In addition to the performances he gave with the New York Philharmonic, his music served as the soundtrack for a slide montage of American life that ran continuously in the central exhibit building, the

geodesic dome. The main event in a variety show hosted by Ed Sullivan at Gorki Park was also a performance of Bernstein's *Serenade*, which was rendered as a ballet with choreography by Jerome Robbins.

84. Frankel, "Bernstein Work Heard in Moscow."

85. Bernstein's version of the incident appears in "Speech to the National Press Club."

86. Lawrence Gilman to Leopold Stokowski, February 15, 1939, Leopold Stokowski Papers, folder 62.

87. Leopold Stokowski to Lawrence Gilman, February 21, 1939, ibid.

88. The exchange with Gilman disproves Oliver Daniel's claim that he was responsible for prompting Stokowski's interest in Ives. Daniel, *Stokowski*, 577–579.

89. The other major contributors to the endeavor were Kurt Stone, editor in chief of Associated Music Publishers, which owned the rights to the score, and Theodore Seder, the curator of the Fleisher Music Collection in the Free Library of Philadelphia.

90. Leopold Stokowski, program notes for Fourth Symphony premiere quoted in Daniel, *Stokowski*, 798–789.

91. Schonberg, "A Complex Score Is Ives' No. 4." For Schonberg's earlier Ives criticism, see, for example, "Stubborn Yankee."

92. Schonberg, "Music: Stokowski Conducts Ives's Fourth Symphony in World Premiere after 50 Years."

93. Hall, "Charles Ives," 43; Hall, "Premiere and Cultural Turning Point," 58.

94. "The Transcendentalist" (*Newsweek*), 102.

Chapter 4. The Prison of Culture

1. Hitchcock, *Charles Ives Centennial Festival-Conference*, 7, 29, 76, 81.

2. Schonberg, "Music: The Pulse of America Beats in the Music of Ives."

3. Reuben Askew, Governor's Proclamation, reproduced in O'Reilly, *South Florida's Historic Ives Festival*, 3.

4. Tueville, "Festival in Ives Country."

5. Fleming, "Of Ives, Elephants, and Polish Independence," MA-27.

6. Rossiter, *Charles Ives and His America*, 324.

7. L. Bernstein, "Young People's Concerts Scripts."

8. Salzman, "Charles Ives, American," 37, 42.

9. Salzman, email to author.

10. McClure, "Charles Ives," 516.

11. Warren, *Charles E. Ives*.

12. Charles Ives, The "Concord" Sonata, John Kirkpatrick, Columbia MM-749 (1948) and Columbia MS-7192 (1968); Charles Ives, Symphony No. 2, New York Philharmonic, Leonard Bernstein, Columbia KL-5489 (1958); Charles Ives, Symphony No. 4, The American Symphony Orchestra, Leopold Stokowski, Columbia ML-6175 (1965).

13. Higgins, "The Apotheosis of Josquin des Prez and Other Mythologies of Musical Genius," 443–510.

14. Hitchcock, "Changing History."

15. Hitchcock may have also been motivated by F. Warren O'Reilly's plans for a Miami-based festival celebrating the Ives centenary. O'Reilly conceived the idea in 1972 and, by the winter of 1973, assembled an illustrious Festival Committee that included Leonard Bernstein, Leopold Stokowski, Lou Harrison, and John Cage. Some years after the fact and in a fit of high dudgeon, O'Reilly accused the Ives Society of stealing his idea, hastily arranging their own competing event, and engaging in a protracted campaign of sabotage against his efforts. O'Reilly, *South Florida's Historic Ives Festival*, 9.

16. In addition to Perlis, Hitchcock's committee included Gilbert Chase, composer William Bergsma, theorist Benjamin Boretz, musicologist Barry S. Brook, archivists David Hall and Richard Jackson, and graduate student Judith Steinberg.

17. Perlis, interview by author.

18. Ibid.

19. Hitchcock, "A Monumenta Americana?"

20. A previous Ives Society had been founded by John McClure in 1967, who intended the organization to serve as a clearinghouse for all things Ives. John McClure to John Kirkpatrick, June 6, 1967, John Kirkpatrick Papers, folder 74, box 7. After a single meeting, the momentum dissipated and the organization became defunct until Hitchcock reactivated it.

21. Wallach, "The Ives Conference," 33.

22. Chase, introduction to "Ives and American Culture," 3.

23. Parrington, *Main Currents in American Thought*, iii.

24. Wise, "'Paradigm Dramas' in American Studies," 180.

25. Gilbert, "Intellectual History," 143. For another, more recent, overview, see Bender, "Intellectual and Cultural History."

26. For a concise overview, see Bull, commentary on "Can 'American Studies' Develop a Method?"

27. Smith, *Virgin Land*, vii, 91.

28. Boorstin, *The Genius of American Politics*, 32, 9, 84, 65.

29. Higham, "The Cult of the 'American Consensus,'" 94, 100.

30. "American Studies Programs in the United States" (*American Quarterly*).

31. Hansen, review of *Essays*.

32. A. Davidson, "Transcendental Unity in the Works of Charles Ives."

33. Boody and Peterson, "University of Minnesota," 16.

34. Riedel and Oudal, *A Charles Ives Primer*, 3.

35. A. Davidson, "Transcendental Unity."

36. C. Davidson, "Winston Churchill and Charles Ives," 170.

37. Manfred, "Ives and Faulkner"; Larson, "Charles Ives and American Studies."

38. No doubt, the presence of Gilbert Chase on the faculty was an important factor in stimulating interest. He was the founding editor of *Anuario Interamericano de Investigacion Musical*, which was issued jointly under the sponsorship of the Department of Music and the Institute of Latin American Studies. Chase's journal represents a continuation of the vision of the Pan American Association of Composers, which sought to promote the music of all nations in the Americas. Numerous articles on Ives were featured in the journal's pages.

39. Perry, *Charles Ives and the American Mind*, xvi.

40. Crunden, *From Self to Society 1919–1941*, ix, 57, 5.

41. Crunden, "Charles Ives's Place in American Culture," 5, 6.

42. Geselbracht, "Transcendental Renaissance in the Arts."

43. Rossiter, *Charles Ives and His America*, xi.

44. Rossiter, "Charles Ives and American Culture," ii.

45. Frank R. Rossiter to Martin Duberman, June 23, 1970, Martin B. Duberman Papers, folder marked "1970, L–S," box 17.

46. John Kirkpatrick to Martin Duberman, July 20, 1970, John Kirkpatrick Papers, folder 330, box 30.

47. Kirkpatrick, response to "Charles Ives: Good American and Isolated Artist," by Rossiter, in *An Ives Celebration*, 27.

48. See, for example, Pells, *The Liberal Mind in a Conservative Age*, 150–155; Singal, "Beyond Consensus"; Lasch, foreword to *The American Political Tradition*, vii–xxiii.

49. Hofstadter, *The American Political Tradition*, xxxvi–xxxix.

50. Brinkley, "Hofstadter's *The Age of Reform* Reconsidered," 149.

51. Hofstadter, *The Age of Reform*, 7, 137, 149.

52. David M. Potter, another of the consensus historians, also invoked the behavioral sciences in *People of Plenty*, which actually predates Hofstadter's *Age of Reform*. Potter, however, was dealing with the broader issue of national character rather than homing in on phenomena constrained to a particular time period.

53. Duberman, "The Abolitionists and Psychology," 8, 13.

54. Duberman, *Cures*.

55. Rossiter, "Charles Ives and American Culture," 3–4, 58.

56. Hitchcock, *Music in the United States*, 43–53.

57. Rossiter, *Charles Ives and His America*, 248–250.

58. Rossiter, "Charles Ives and American Culture," 154–155.

59. Ibid., 340.

60. Ibid., 340, 345.

61. Copland and Chase, responses to Rossiter, "Charles Ives: Good American and Isolated Artist," 26.

62. Barker, "Who Owns Charles Ives?" 448.

63. John Kirkpatrick to Charles Ward, June 17, 1970, John Kirkpatrick Papers, folder 212, box 18.

64. Duberman, "Those Parts of a Life That Contain the Evidence of History."

65. Duberman, *Black Mountain*, esp. 225–227, 329–333.

66. Frank Rossiter to Martin Duberman, February 1, 1974, Martin Duberman Papers, folder marked "1974 J–R," box 25.

67. Frank Rossiter to Martin Duberman, October 12, 1974, Martin Duberman Papers, folder marked "1974, J–R," box 25.

68. Frank Rossiter to Martin Duberman, May 16, 1975, Martin Duberman Papers, folder marked "1975, M–V," box 28.

69. Ibid.

70. Soliday, interview by author.

71. Frank Rossiter to Martin Duberman, May 16, 1975, Martin Duberman Papers, folder marked "1975, M–V" box 28.

72. Higham, introduction to *New Directions in American Intellectual History*, xi–xii.

73. There are many accounts of the rise of "New History." See, for example, Veysey, "The New Social History in the Context of American Historical Writing"; Bender, "Intellectual and Cultural History."

74. Ellen Fitzpatrick, who has carefully traced historiographical currents in American history, shows that the term "New History" only began to appear frequently in the Seventies. Fitzpatrick, *History's Memory*, 240–242.

75. B. Bernstein, introduction to *Towards a New Past*, ix.

76. For an overview essay with a substantial bibliography, see Kessler-Harris, "Social History."

77. Fitzpatrick, *History's Memory*, 248.

78. Veysey, "Intellectual History and the New Social History," 7.

79. Hollinger, "Historians and the Discourse of Intellectuals."

80. Veysey, "Intellectual History and the New Social History," 9.

81. Soliday, interview by author.

82. McPherson, *The Struggle for Equality* and *The Negro's Civil War*.

83. Rossiter, "Charles Ives and American Culture," 5–89, 90–144.

84. Meikle, Fishkin, and Foley, "In Memoriam."

85. For example, Sklar, review of *From Self to Society*.

86. Crunden, *Ministers of Reform*, 275.

87. Ibid., x.

88. Filene, "An Obituary for the 'Progressive Movement.'"

89. Buenker, Burnham, and Crunden, *Progressivism*.

90. For an extensive sampling, see Diner, "Bibliographical Essay."

91. Rodgers, "In Search of Progressivism," 114, 123.

92. Broyles, "Charles Ives and the American Democratic Tradition"; Tick, "Charles Ives and the Politics of Direct Democracy."

93. Possibly the first movement of Ives's Second Symphony was performed at the New York Settlement School in 1910 or 1911, conducted by Edgar Stowell, a violinist who taught there. But this performance, if it happened at all, arose through personal connections, not progressive commitments. Magee, *Charles Ives Reconsidered*, 104.

94. Davis, "The Politics of American Studies," 368.

95. Veysey, "Intellectual History and the New Social History," 11.

96. Geertz, *The Interpretation of Culture*, 5.

97. Kelly, "Literature and the Historian," 93.

98. Ibid., 91.

99. Geertz, *The Interpretation of Culture*, 9.

100. Bender, "Intellectual and Cultural History," 181.

101. Chmaj, "Sonata for American Studies," 5, 10.

102. Conn, *The Divided Mind*, 1.

103. Among other things, the reviewer for the *American Quarterly* called Moore to task for failing to establish a coherent linkage, aesthetical or otherwise, among his cohort of "Yankee composers." S. Levine, "Euterpe and the Bigots."

104. Chmaj, "Sonata for American Studies," 47.

Chapter 5. Musicology Makes Its Mark

1. Yates, "Charles Ives," 321.

2. Hitchcock, *Charles Ives Centennial Festival-Conference*, 6–7.

3. "Publications Received" (*JAMS*); Adkins and Dickinson, "Supplement (1974) to Doctoral Dissertations in Musicology."

4. *Current Musicology* 18 (1974), 19 (1975), 20 (1975); *Student Musicologists at Minnesota: Centennial Ives Issue Celebrating the USA's 200th Birthday* 6 (1975/76).

5. Friedrich Chrysander, Philip Spitta, and Guido Adler, quoted in Karnes, *Music, Criticism, and the Challenge of History*, 41.

6. Karnes, *Music, Criticism, and the Challenge of History*, 40, 25.

7. Karnes warns against too literal a reading of "Scope, Method, and Goal of Musicology." Adler, Chrysander, and Spitta were not "crusading positivists"; they struggled with and were sometimes ambivalent about the business of fusing *Musik* and *Wissenscahft*. Ibid., 16.

8. Mugglestone, "Guido Adler's 'The Scope, Method, and Aim of Musicology (1885),'" 7, 15.

9. See Mugglestone's commentary on the article, ibid., 3–4.

10. Ibid., 7, 8.

11. Adler, "Style Criticism," 174.

12. Ibid., 176.

13. Hanslick, *On the Musically Beautiful*, 39.

14. Dahlhaus, *The Idea of Absolute Music*.

15. During the twenties, Kinkeldey served as head of the music division at New York Public Library; at the Library of Congress, Oscar Sonneck, who headed the music division from 1902–1917, and his successor Carl Engel (1922–1934), presided over a group of scholar-librarians who did important spadework. Sonneck and Engel, like Kinkeldey, were trained in Germany.

16. For early surveys of American musicology, see Kinkeldey, "American Scholarship in Music since 1876"; Stevenson, "American Musical Scholarship."

17. For an overview, see Kerman, *Contemplating Music*, 11–30.

18. Nettl, "The Institutionalization of Musicology."

19. Claude V. Palisca, for example, offered this definition in a seminal 1963 essay: "The musicologist is concerned with music that exists, whether as an oral or written tradition, and with everything that can shed light on its human context" ("American Scholarship in Western Music," 116).

20. Grout, *A History of Western Music*, xiii.

21. Bohlman, "Ethnomusicology's Challenge," 121–123, 128.

22. Nettl, "The Institutionalization of Musicology," 295–296.

23. Forte, "Comment and Chronicle."

24. Henderson, email to author.

25. Palisca, "American Scholarship in Western Music," 178.

26. See, for example, P. Potter, "From Jewish Exile in Germany to German Scholar in America."

27. Ulrich and Pisk, *A History of Music and Musical Style*.

28. Henderson, email to author.

29. Ibid.

30. Lang, "Hearing Things"; Schrade, "Charles E. Ives."

31. The first was Newman's "The Songs of Charles Ives." There were precedents to the work of Newman and Henderson in the form of senior undergraduate theses and master theses.

32. Refining these appendices has dominated Henderson's subsequent career, and the results of his efforts are published in the two editions of *The Charles Ives Tunebook*.

33. Henderson, "Quotation as a Style Element in the Music of Charles Ives," 136, 143, 157.

34. Block, interview by author.

35. Tick, interview by author.

36. Tick, "Ragtime and the Music of Charles Ives."

37. Starr, interview by author.

38. Burkholder, interview by author.

39. Starr, interview by author.

40. Block, interview by author.

41. See, for example, Leo Treitler's plea that musicologists recognize that style is inextricably linked to the intentionality of the composer and the preconceptions of the listener, thus belying the possibility of its "objective" assessment through a neutral methodology. Treitler, "Methods, Style, Analysis."

42. Brown, "Fantasia on a Theme by Boccaccio," 326.

43. See the George F. Roberts interview in Perlis, *Charles Ives Remembered*, 183–188.

44. Ives, quoted in Sinclair, *A Descriptive Catalogue of the Music of Charles Ives*, 28.

45. Harmony Ives to Lou Harrison, June 28, 1946, in Ives, *Selected Correspondence*, 326.

46. The details of this discussion play out in the correspondence between Kirkpatrick and Harmony in the months after Ives's death, see John Kirkpatrick Papers, folder 204, box 18.

47. Kirkpatrick's plans for creating an Ives catalogue date back to the thirties. See John Kirkpatrick to Charles Ives, July 22, 1936, in Ives, *Selected Correspondence*, 245.

48. Sinclair, *A Descriptive Catalogue of the Music of Charles Ives*, xi.

49. Massey, "An 'Unobtrusive Minister of Genius,'" 63. This section is heavily influenced by Massey's work.

50. Ibid., 52.

51. John Kirkpatrick to Howard Boatwright, July 14, 1961, John Kirkpatrick Papers, folder 36, box 3.

52. The surviving correspondence with Weise begins in 1960, just as Kirkpatrick was completing his catalogue. John Kirkpatrick Papers, folder 55, box 5. The nature of the early exchanges suggests prior acquaintance, but unfortunately there is no record of what Weise and Kirkpatrick discussed before 1960.

53. Kirkpatrick to Carter, May/June 1973, and Carter to Kirkpatrick, June 16, 1973, in Massey, "The Problem of Ives's Revisions, 1973–1987," 631–635, 635–638.

54. Massey, "The Problems of Ives's Revisions," 608.

55. Kirkpatrick and Alan Mandel, in Hitchcock and Perlis, *An Ives Celebration*, 72–73. Mandel served as panel chair. The other members were James Sinclair, Kirkpatrick's protégé, and Lou Harrison.

56. Kirkpatrick and Paul C. Echols, quoted in Massey, "The Problems of Ives's Revisions," 614.

57. Rathert, "The Unanswered Questions of the Ives Edition," 576.

58. Hamm, "Review of *Forty Earlier Songs*," 1125.

59. Gilman, "Music."

60. For a perceptive contemporaneous exploration of the problem, see Treitler, "The Present as History."

61. Gilbert Chase had made Ives the culmination of a history of American music, but unlike Austin, he had not passed through a doctoral program in musicology.

62. Austin, *Music in the 20th Century*.

63. Ibid., 41, 48.

64. Ibid., 59, 57.

65. Burkholder, "The Evolution of Charles Ives's Music," 685–689.

66. The passage in full reads as follows: "Being one of those few who are committed to exploring the musical history of the American peoples, I am impelled to seek, by every possible means, from every pertinent discipline, throughout all the sciences of man, the modes of thought and the methods of work that may enable us to know and understand, and to set forth discursively in writing, all that we can hope to learn of 'man as music-maker and music-user'" (Chase, "A Dialectical Approach to Music History," 5).

67. Hitchcock, "A Monumenta Americana?" As it turns out, in 1988, the American Musicological Society launched a forty-volume series of critical editions entitled *Music of the United States of America (MUSA)*. Hitchcock, ironically, would edit the MUSA edition of Ives songs.

68. Hitchcock, *Music in the United States*, 44, 43, 9, iv.

69. Ibid., x.

70. Ibid., 152, 151.

71. Ives, quoted in ibid., 152.

72. Ibid., 149.

73. For a discussion of the importance of theoretical rigor and systematic organization for Babbitt, see Brody, "'Music for the Masses.'"

74. Morgan, interview by author.

75. Morgan cites H. H. Stuckenschmidt, *Neue Musik* (1951); Karl H. Woerner, *Neue Musik in der Entscheidung* (1956); Juan Carlos Paz, *Introducción a la Música de Neustro Tiempo* (1955); Theodor W. Adorno, *Philosophie der Neuen Musik* (1948); André Hodeir, *Since Debussy* (1961); and Donald Mitchell, *The Language of Modern Music* (1963).

76. Morgan, "Rewriting Music History," 4.

77. Ibid., 5, 6.

78. Morgan, "Ives and Mahler," 72–81.

79. Morgan, "Rewriting Music History," 9.

80. Ibid., 5.

81. Austin, "Ives and Histories."

82. Here, I am indebted to Richard Taruskin, who uses the rubric "great trauma" to characterize the Bach crisis when he introduces it to Berkeley graduate students in his "Introduction to Scholarship" course.

83. For an overview, see Kerman, *Contemplating Music*, 50–55.

84. See chapter 3.

85. Cowell and Cowell, *Charles Ives and His Music*, 147.

86. Charles, "The Use of Borrowed Material in Ives' Second Symphony." Charles completed her PhD in 1959, filing a dissertation that analyzed the musical contents of a fifteenth-century English manuscript—another doctoral project wholly typical of the time. Charles, "The Music of the Pepys Manuscript 1236."

87. L. Bernstein, liner notes for Charles Ives, *Symphony No. 2*.

88. Charles, "The Use of Borrowed Material in Ives' Second Symphony," 108, 111.

89. Henderson, "Quotations as a Style Element in the Music of Charles Ives," 191.

90. Henderson, "Ives' Use of Quotation," 28.

91. Marshall, "Charles Ives's Quotations," 53.

92. Cyr, "Intervallic Structural Elements in Ives's Fourth Symphony," 292.

93. Sterne, "The Quotations in Charles Ives's Second Symphony"; Ballantine, "Charles Ives and the Meaning of Quotation in Music."

94. Ward, "Charles Ives," 6–7, 157.

95. Hitchcock, *Ives*, 10.

96. The articles were Starr, "Style and Substance," "Charles Ives," and "The Early Styles of Charles Ives."

97. Starr, "Style and Substance," 24.

98. Ibid., 29.

99. Starr, *A Union of Diversities*, 16.

100. Starr, "The Early Styles of Charles Ives," 76.

101. Burkholder, interview by author.

102. Eiseman, "Charles Ives and the European Symphonic Tradition."

103. Burkholder, "The Evolution of Charles Ives's Music," 468.

104. Burkholder was actually forced to rethink the structures of his dissertation twice.

First, when he discovered the issue of transcendentalism had not been sufficiently addressed (at which point he conceived of making the dissertation a two-part document) and second, when he found that borrowing, too, needed its own section—thus the final three-part form. Burkholder, email to author.

105. Burkholder, "The Evolution of Charles Ives's Music," x.

106. Sonneck, "The Future of Musicology in America," 320; LaRue, *Guidelines for Style Analysis*, ix.

107. Burkholder, email to author.

108. Because the content of this portion of Burkholder's dissertation appears with little alteration in his subsequent book *Charles Ives*, I have included citations for both sources, separating them with a semicolon as follows: Burkholder, "The Evolution of Charles Ives's Music," 16; *Charles Ives*, 9.

109. Burkholder, "The Evolution of Charles Ives's Music," 54, 55, 57–59; *Charles Ives*, 27, 28, 28–29.

110. Burkholder, "The Evolution of Charles Ives's Music," 75, 44; *Charles Ives*, 38, 22.

111. Burkholder, "The Evolution of Charles Ives's Music," 94–96; *Charles Ives*, 49–50.

112. Burkholder, "The Evolution of Charles Ives's Music," 118–120, 129; *Charles Ives*, 64–65, 70.

113. Burkholder, "The Evolution of Charles Ives's Music," 195–196, 174; *Charles Ives*, 106–107, 96–97.

114. See, for example, Block, review of *Charles Ives*; Swartz, review of *Charles Ives*.

115. Burkholder, "The Evolution of Charles Ives's Music," 6.

116. Ibid., 422.

117. Burkholder, "Johannes Martini and the Imitation Mass of the Late Fifteenth Century" and "Quotation and Emulation."

118. Burkholder, "The Evolution of Charles Ives's Music," 216–218.

119. The Cowells write of Ives, "He feels that music, like other truths, should never be immediately understood; there must always remain some further element yet to be disclosed. A complete musical statement, in all its clarity and simplicity, like any absolute truth, is an ultimate, not a beginning. Ives reserves it, therefore, for the culmination of a work" (Cowell and Cowell, *Charles Ives and His Music*, 142).

120. Harrison, liner notes for Ives, *Sonatas for Violin and Piano*. Ward writes, "In Ives' peculiar treatment of this principle [reconstruction], the opening thematic statements are omitted, so that the form consists of thematic development followed by the *only* statement of the theme as whole" (Ward, "Charles Ives," 89). Burkholder acknowledged the precedence of Cowell, Harrison, Ward, and others.

121. Burkholder, "The Evolution of Charles Ives's Music," 218.

122. Ibid., 219.

123. Ibid., 220. Burkholder describes the discovery himself in "The Uses of Existing Music."

124. The fourteen "procedures for using existing music," as Burkholder describes them,

are modeling, variations, paraphrasing, setting, cantus firmus, medley, quodlibet, stylistic allusion, transcribing, programmatic quotation, cumulative setting, collage, patchwork, and extended paraphrase. Burkholder, *All Made of Tunes*, 3–4.

125. Burkholder, "Music Theory and Musicology," 11, 13. Backing away from one of the central precepts of musicology, Burkholder did argue, "[W]e have misunderstood most music from most eras by thinking in terms of single styles, when in fact stylistic heterogeneity has been a basic tool of musical construction from at least the alternation in medieval liturgical music of solo polyphony with choral chant. . . . The elevation of organic unity to a supreme value, inherited from nineteenth-century aesthetics, has blinded us (and especially those of us who do musical analysis) to the diversity and contrast that people for over a thousand years have apparently found genuinely valuable in their own music" (22).

126. Burkholder mentioned to me that in the mideighties he was doing a translation of Adler's essay, not realizing that a translation already existed. Burkholder, email to author.

Chapter 6. Ives at Century's Turn

1. Henahan, "Is an Icon Becoming a Has-Been?"
2. Page, "Judging Composers."
3. Glass, "Mainstream Americana."
4. Solomon, "Charles Ives," 463.
5. Langer, "The Next Assignment." Psychoanalysts had already tried their hand at analyzing historical figures. See, for example, Freud, "Leonardo da Vinci and a Memory of His Childhood" and "Dostoevsky and Parricide," published in 1910 and 1928, respectively.
6. Erikson, *Young Man Luther*.
7. For an extensive list, see Crunden, "Freud, Erikson, and the Historian," 63–64.
8. Solomon, *Beethoven*.
9. Solomon, "Charles Ives," 446.
10. Feder, *Charles Ives*, 351–357.
11. Ibid., 46.
12. Ibid., 80, 136.
13. For the problems psychoanalysis has confronted since the seventies, see Hale, "Popular Images of Controversy" and "The Crisis of American Psychoanalysis."
14. Kirpatrick, *A Temporary Mimeographed Catalogue*, vii–viii.
15. Philip Sunderland in Perlis, *Charles Ives Remembered*, 16.
16. Solomon, "Charles Ives," 457–458.
17. Henahan, "Did Ives Fiddle With the Truth?"
18. Notably, composer William Bolcolm accused the *Times* of an "anti-Ives campaign" (Bolcolm, "Of Ives, Music and Insurance").
19. Burkholder, "Charles Ives and His Fathers," 10.
20. Lambert, letter to the editor, 204.
21. Solomon, letter to the editor, 212.

22. For criticism of Baron's analysis, see Zaher, letter to the editor. For an example of a similar argument applied to different materials, see Block, "Remembrance of Dissonances Past."

23. Baron, "Dating Charles Ives' Music," 51.

24. [Sherwood] Magee, interview by author.

25. Ibid.

26. Sherwood, "The Choral Works of Charles Ives," 36–68.

27. Sherwood, "Questions and Veracities," 444.

28. Sherwood, "The Choral Works of Charles Ives," 215, 202.

29. Ibid., 148.

30. Among the relevant titles are L. Kramer, *Music as Cultural Practice*; McClary, *Feminine Endings*; Subotnik, *Developing Variations*; Solie, *Musicology and Difference*; Brett, Wood, and Thomas, *Queering the Pitch*.

31. L. Kramer, *Classical Music and Postmodern Knowledge*, 18.

32. Indeed, despite being an avowed postmodernist, Kramer declares, "When [Ives's] musical innovations lead toward [a truly democratic space] he intervenes to arrest it with signs of mastery, signs that confound innovation with belligerent masculinity and America with its antebellum past. Not to hear this in the music would be not to hear it at all" (ibid., 198).

33. Kramer was, in fact, trained as a literary critic, having completed a dissertation entitled "Keats and the Structure of Consciousness" (1972) under the supervision of Harold Bloom at Yale University. He currently holds dual appointments in the English and Music departments at Fordham University.

34. Kerman, *Contemplating Music*, 43–44.

35. A far from exhaustive list would include Fenlon, *Music and Patronage in Sixteenth-Century Mantua*; Newcomb, *The Madrigal at Ferrara*; Prizer, "Isabella d'Este and Lucrezia Borgia as Patrons of Music."

36. For an especially notable example, see Taruskin, "Glinka's Ambiguous Legacy and the Birth Pangs of Russian Opera."

37. R. Crawford, "MUSA's Early Years," 9.

38. Tick, "Ragtime and the Music of Charles Ives."

39. Tick, interview by author.

40. Tick, email to author.

41. Tick, "Women as Professional Musicians in the United States."

42. Tick, email to author.

43. Tick, interview by author.

44. Tick, "Women as Professional Musicians in the United States," 127.

45. Two other important pioneers were Adrienne Fried Block and Nancy Reich.

46. Van de Vate, "The American Woman Composer," MA19.

47. Lerner, "Placing Women in History," 357. Thanks to Judith Tick for this reference.

48. Tick, "Charles Ives and Gender Ideology," 89, 84.

49. Cooney, "A Sense of Place." This article is an outgrowth of her dissertation, "Recon-

ciliations," which in turn forms the basis of a chapter of a book about American music and place (Von Glahn, "From Country to City in the Music of Charles Ives").

50. Metzer, "Childhood and Nostalgia in the Works of Charles Ives."

51. Broyles, "Charles Ives and the American Democratic Tradition"; Tick, "Charles Ives and the Politics of Direct Democracy."

52. Garrett, "Charles Ives's *Four Ragtime Dances.*"

53. Owens, "Charles Ives and His American Context."

54. See, for example, Block and Burkholder, *Charles Ives and the Classical Tradition.*

55. Sherwood, "'Buds the Infant Mind,'" 186.

56. In the fourteen years since Maynard Solomon's article, the flagship musicological journal had only included one other dedicated to Ives—and that in 1999. The author was H. Wiley Hitchcock, and his article laid out the careful archival work that had gone into the critical edition of Ives songs he was then preparing, all classic musicology. Hitchcock, "Ives's 114 [+15] Songs and What He Thought of Them."

57. Sherwood, "Charles Ives and 'Our National Malady,'" 557–560, 577, 576. Sherwood notably takes on Stuart Feder. She writes, "Depression, psychosomatic symptoms, unresolved issues—all perfectly understandable, defensible, and applicable terms in our post-Freudian world. But they would have meant little or even nothing to Ives and his contemporaries. Notwithstanding Feder's excellent study, his diagnosis is anachronistic" (556). For the subsequent exchange between Feder and Sherwood, see Feder, "Heard Maladies Are Sweet"; Sherwood, "Ives and Neurasthenia."

58. Magee, *Charles Ives Reconsidered*, 105, 106, 155.

59. Ibid., 125, 133, 135.

60. Swafford, *Charles Ives*, xii, 88.

61. For a critique of Swafford's treatment of progressivism from a scholar who remained invested in the concept, see Crunden, "Review of *Charles Ives: A Life with Music.*"

62. Key and Rothe, *American Mavericks*, 19.

63. H. Cowell, "Trends in American Music," 5.

64. Oja, *Making Music Modern*, 193.

65. For more on the link between Cowell and his pupils, see L. Miller, "The Art of Noise."

66. Harrison, "The Rich and Varied New York Scene," 183.

67. Cage, "History of Experimental Music in the United States," 73.

68. My principal source here is Beal's *New Music, New Allies.*

69. Beal, "A Place to Ply Their Wares with Dignity."

70. Eimert, Musical Night Program, November 27, 1952, in Beal, *New Music, New Allies*, 57.

71. Beal, *New Music, New Allies*, 63.

72. Ibid., 252, 64, 135–136.

73. Louis Andriessen, quoted in Hitchock and Perlis, *An Ives Celebration*, 49.

74. Helms, "Some Reflections on Charles E. Ives," 59.

75. Helms, "Charles Edward Ives—Ideal American or Social Critic?" 38.

76. Taruskin, letter to the editor, 35, 36.

77. Beal, *New Music, New Allies*, 176.

78. Klein, "20th-Century Music Is Offered in a Concert at the New School."

79. Garland, "The American Experimental Tradition," 12.

80. Yates, *Twentieth Century Music*; Salzman, *Twentieth Century Music.*

81. Yates is also notable for his position within the network of associations that stretched from California to West Germany. He had been part of Cowell's extended contemporary music circle and was also a friend of Wolfgang Rebner, who had been involved in Yates's "Evenings on the Roof" concert series while living in Los Angeles in the late forties and early fifties. Beal, *New Music, New Allies*, 63–64.

82. T. Johnson, "New Music New York New Institution."

83. See, for example, Parmenter, "The World of Music." The earliest Rockwellian example I have found is an article on the minimalists: "Sound of New Music Is Likened to Art."

84. Rockwell, "Underground Music Surfaces for a Nine-Day Festival."

85. I. Brooks, "New Music America History."

86. Rockwell, "Experimental Music," 92.

87. Nicholls, *American Experimental Music, 1890–1940.*

88. Morgan, *Twentieth-Century Music*, 296.

89. Ross, "The Eccentrics Who Declared Independence for America."

90. Riley, "Debut Orchestra Gives Tour of 'New England.'"

91. "Musicale Calendared" (*Los Angeles Times*).

92. Thomas, dir., *Three Places in New England*, by Ives; Thomas, dir., *Sun-treader*, by Ruggles.

93. Schonberg, "Music: A Concert Fuss."

94. Thomas, liner notes for *Symphony No. 2.*

95. Kosman, "American Festival Rocks Davies."

96. Taruskin, "Corralling a Herd of Musical Mavericks."

97. American Public Media, "American Mavericks."

98. Delacoma, "Balancing Conducting, Composition."

99. Adams, "John Adams Discusses *On the Transmigration of Souls*," 198, 197.

100. Steinberg, "My Father Knew Charles Ives (2003)," 207.

101. Kosman, "Voice of America."

102. One of those scholars was Michael Broyles, whose recent book *Mavericks and Other Traditions in American Music* extends the tradition backward in time, to the eighteenth-century psalmodist William Billings.

103. Tomassini, Kozinn, Eichler, Midgette, and Oestreich, "A Radical in a Suit and Tie."

104. Taruskin, "Underneath the Dissonance Beats a Brahmsian Heart."

105. Eichler, "The American Canon's Unabashed Patriot."

106. Wakin, "Newspapers Trimming Classical Critics."

107. Schiff, "Ives's Ears."

108. Grout, Palisca, and Burkholder, *A History of Western Music.*

109. Lambert, *The Music of Charles Ives*; Block, *Charles Ives: Concord Sonata.*

110. McGinness, "Essay."

Works Cited

"American Studies Programs in the United States: A Quantitative Survey." 1970. *American Quarterly* 22, no. 2, pt. 2 (Summer): 418–426.

"Charles E. Ives." 1949. *Life* 27, no. 18 (October 31).

"Insurance Man." 1939. *Time* (January 30): 44–45.

"Musicale Calendared." 1966. *Los Angeles Times* (March 6).

"Musical Whitman." 1954. *Newsweek* 43 (May 31): 78.

"Publications Received." 1974. *Journal of the American Musicological Society* 28, no. 1 (Spring): 131–134.

"The Transcendentalist." 1965. *Newsweek* 65 (May 10): 102.

Adams, John. 2006. John Adams discusses *On the Transmigration of Souls*. Interview by Daniel Colvard. In *The John Adams Reader: Essential Writings on an American Composer*, 196–204. Edited by Thomas May. Pompton Plains, N.J.: Amadeus Press.

Adkins, Cecil, and Alis Dickinson. 1974. "Supplement (1974) to Doctoral Dissertations in Musicology." *Journal of the American Musicological Society* 27, no. 3 (Autumn): 475–514.

Adler, Guido. 1934. "Style Criticism." Translated by Oliver Strunk. *Musical Quarterly* 20, no. 2 (April): 172–176.

American Public Media. "American Mavericks." http://musicmavericks.publicradio.org/. Accessed January 28, 2012.

Arnold, Matthew. 1961. "Culture and Anarchy." In *Poetry and Criticism of Matthew Arnold*, 407–475. Edited by A. Dwight Culler. Boston: Houghton Mifflin Company.

Austin, William W. 1966. *Music in the 20th Century*. New York: W. W. Norton.

Austin, William W. 1971. "Ives and Histories." In *Bericht über den internationalen musikwissenschaftlichen Kongress, Bonn 1970*, 299–301. Kassel: Bärenreiter.

Babbitt, Irving. 1912. *The Masters of Modern French Criticism*. Boston: Houghton Mifflin.

Babbitt, Irving. 1919. *Rousseau and Romanticism*. Boston: Houghton Mifflin.

Babbitt, Irving. 1924. *Democracy and Leadership*. Boston: Houghton Mifflin.

Ballantine, Christopher. 1979. "Charles Ives and the Meaning of Quotation in Music." *Musical Quarterly* 65, no. 2 (April): 167–184.

Baranovitch, Nimrod. 1999. "Anthropology and Musicology: Seeger's Writings from 1933 to 1953." In *Understanding Charles Seeger, Pioneer in American Musicology*, 150–171. Edited by Bell Yung and Helen Rees. Urbana: University of Illinois Press.

Barker, John W. 1976. "Who Owns Charles Ives?" *Reviews in American History* 4, no. 3 (September): 442–450.

Baron, Carol K. 1990. "Dating Charles Ives's Music: Facts and Fictions." *Perspectives of New Music* 28, no. 1 (Winter): 20–56.

Bartók, Béla. 1921. "The Relation of Folksong to the Development of the Art Music of Our Time." *Sackbut* 2, no. 1 (1921): 5–11. Reproduced 1976, in *Béla Bartók Essays*, 320–333. Edited by Benjamin Suchoff. New York: St. Martin's Press.

Baym, Nina. 1989. "Early Histories of American Literature: A Chapter in the Institution of New England." *American Literary History* 1, no. 3 (Autumn): 459–488.

Bayne, Harry McBrayer. 1990. "A Critical Study of Henry Bellamann's Life and Work." PhD diss., University of Mississippi.

Beal, Amy. 2002. "A Place to Ply Their Wares with Dignity: American Composer-Performers in West Germany, 1972." *Musical Quarterly* 86, no. 2 (Summer): 329–348.

Beal, Amy C. 2003. "The Army, the Airwaves, and the Avant-Garde: American Classical Music in Postwar West Germany." *American Music* 21, no. 4 (Winter): 474–513.

Beal, Amy. 2006. *New Music, New Allies: American Experimental Music in West Germany from the Zero Hour to Reunification.* Berkeley: University of California Press.

Becker, John J. 1956. "Charles E. Ives." Parts 1 and 2. *Etude* 74, Part 1 (May-June): 11, 20, 49, 57; 75, Part 2 (July-August): 14, 46.

Beckerman, Michael. 2003. *New Worlds of Dvořák: Searching in America for the Composer's Inner Life.* New York: W. W. Norton.

Beers, Henry A. 1895. *Initial Studies in American Letters.* New York: The Chatauqua Press.

Bell, Daniel. 1960. *The End of Ideology: On the Exhaustion of Political Ideas in the Fifties.* Glencoe, Ill.: The Free Press.

Bellamann, Henry. 1921. "Reviews: 'Concord, Mass., 1840–1860' (A Piano Sonata by Charles E. Ives)." *Double Dealer* 2 (October): 166–169.

Bellamann, Henry. 1923. "Notes on the New Aesthetic of Poetry and Music." *Musical Quarterly* 9, no. 2 (April): 260–270.

Bellamann, Henry. 1927. "The Music of Charles Ives." *Pro Musica Quarterly* (March 27): 16–22.

Bellamann, Henry. 1927. "Program Notes." Pro Musica Concert, January 29. Charles Ives Papers, Mss. 14, folder 2, box 50. Irving S. Gilmore Music Library, Yale University. New Haven.

Bellamann, Henry. 1933. "Charles Ives: The Man and His Music." *Musical Quarterly* 19, no. 1 (January): 45–58.

Bender, Thomas. 1997. "Intellectual and Cultural History." In *The New American History.* 2nd ed., 181–202. Edited by Eric Foner. Philadelphia: Temple University Press.

Berger, Arthur. 1933. "Charles Ives." Typescript for Pan American Concert, June 4. Charles Ives Papers. Mss. 14, folder 2, box 56. Irving S. Gilmore Music Library, Yale University. New Haven.

Berger, Arthur. 1954. "Spotlight on the Moderns: Ives in Retrospective." *Saturday Review* 37, no. 31 (July 31): 62–64.

Bernstein, Barton J. 1968. Introduction to *Towards a New Past: Dissenting Essays in American History*, v–xiii. Edited by Barton J. Bernstein. New York: Pantheon Books.

Bernstein, Leonard. 1958. "Thursday Evening Preview Scripts: Opening of the New York Philharmonic Season of 1958–1959." October 2. Leonard Bernstein Collection, folder 13, box 75. Music Division, Library of Congress, Washington D.C. Available at http://hdl.loc .gov/loc.music/lbtep.0152. Accessed January 27, 2012. © Amberson Holdings LLC. Used by permission of the Leonard Bernstein Office, Inc.

Bernstein, Leonard. 1967. "Young People's Concerts Scripts: Charles Ives: American Pioneer." February 23. Leonard Bernstein Collection, folder 04, box 111. Music Division, Library of Congress, Washington D.C. Available at http://hdl.loc.gov/loc.music/lbypc.0413. Accessed January 27, 2012. © Amberson Holdings LLC. Used by permission of the Leonard Bernstein Office, Inc.

Bernstein, Leonard. 1982. "The Absorption of Race Elements into American Music." In *Findings*, 36–99. New York: Doubleday.

Bernstein, Leonard. 1982. "Speech to the National Press Club." In *Findings*, 160–162. New York: Doubleday.

Bick, Sally. Forthcoming. *The Musical Legacy of the New School for Social Research.*

Blake, Casey Nelson. 1990. *Beloved Community: The Cultural Criticism of Randolph Bourne, Van Wyck Brooks, Waldo Frank, and Lewis Mumford.* Chapel Hill: University of North Carolina Press.

Block, Geoffrey. 1987. Review of *Charles Ives: The Ideas behind the Music* by J. Peter Burkholder. *Journal of Musicology* 5, no. 2 (Spring): 308–311.

Block, Geoffrey. 1988. *Charles Ives: A Bio-Bibliography.* New York: Greenwood Press.

Block, Geoffrey. 1996. *Charles Ives: Concord Sonata.* Cambridge: Cambridge University Press.

Block, Geoffrey. 1997. "Remembrance of Dissonances Past: The Two Published Editions of Ives's *Concord Sonata.*" In *Ives Studies*, 27–50. Edited by Philip Lambert. Cambridge: Cambridge University Press.

Block, Geoffrey. 2010. Interview by author, November 5.

Block, Geoffrey, and J. Peter Burkholder, eds. 1996. *Charles Ives and the Classical Tradition.* Yale: Yale University Press.

Bluestein, Gene. 1972. *The Voice of the Folk.* Boston: University of Massachusetts Press.

Boatwright, Howard. 1962. Introduction to *Essays Before a Sonata, and Other Writings*, by Charles Ives. Edited by Howard Boatwright. New York: W. W. Norton.

Bohlman, Philip. 1992. "Ethnomusicology's Challenge to the Canon; the Canon's Challenge to Ethnomusicology." In *Disciplining Music: Musicology and Its Canons*, 116–136. Edited by Katherine Bergeron and Philip Bohlman. Chicago: Chicago University Press.

Bolcolm, William. 1988. "Of Ives, Music and Insurance." *New York Times* (March 13).

Boody, Charles G., and Margaret Peterson. 1970. "University of Minnesota: American Music Program." *Current Musicology* 10: 16–18.

Boorstin, Daniel J. 1953. *The Genius of American Politics*. Chicago: University of Chicago Press.

Bourne, Randolph. 2001. "Trans-National America." In *The American Intellectual Tradition: A Sourcebook*. 4th ed. Vol. 2, 171–181. Edited by David A. Hollinger and Charles Capper. New York: Oxford University Press.

Brett, Philip, Elizabeth Wood, and Gary C. Thomas, eds. 1994. *Queering the Pitch: The New Gay and Lesbian Musicology*. New York: Routledge.

Brinkley, Alan. 1998. "Hofstadter's *The Age of Reform* Reconsidered." In *Liberalism and Its Discontents*, 132–150. Cambridge: Harvard University Press.

Brody, Martin. 1993. "'Music for the Masses': Milton Babbitt's Cold War Music Theory." *Musical Quarterly* 77, no. 2 (Summer): 161–192.

Brooks, Iris. 1992. "New Music America History: A Caterpillar or a Butterfly?" In *New Music Across America*, 6–11. Edited by Iris Brooks. Valencia: California Institute of the Arts.

Brooks, Van Wyck. [1915] 1958. *America's Coming-of-Age*. Reprint, New York: Doubleday Anchor Books.

Brooks, Van Wyck. 1918. "On Creating a Usable Past." *Dial* 64, no. 7 (April 11): 337–341.

Brooks, Van Wyck. 1936. *The Flowering of New England*. New York: E. P. Dutton and Co.

Brown, Howard Mayer. 1977. "Fantasia on a Theme by Boccaccio." *Early Music* 5, no. 3 (July): 324–339.

Broyles, Michael. 1996. "Charles Ives and the American Democratic Tradition." In *Charles Ives and His World*, 118–160. Edited by J. Peter Burkholder. Princeton: Princeton University Press.

Broyles, Michael. 2009. *Mavericks and Other Traditions in American Music*. New Haven: Yale University Press.

Buenker, John D., John C. Burnham, and Robert M. Crunden. 1977. *Progressivism*. Cambridge: Shenkman Publication Company.

Bukoff, Ronald Nick. 1988. "Charles Ives, a History and Bibliography of Criticism (1920–1939) and Ives's Influence (to 1947) on Bernard Herrmann, Elie Siegmeister, and Robert Palmer." PhD diss., Cornell University.

Bull, Lawrence. 1999. Commentary on "Can 'American Studies' Develop a Method?" by Henry Nash Smith. In *Locating American Studies: The Evolution of a Discipline*, 13–16. Edited by Lucy Maddox. Baltimore: John Hopkins University Press.

Burkholder, J. Peter. 1983. "The Evolution of Charles Ives's Music: Aesthetics, Quotation, Technique." PhD diss., University of Chicago.

Burkholder, J. Peter. 1985. *Charles Ives: The Ideas behind the Music*. New Haven: Yale University Press.

Burkholder, J. Peter. 1985. "Johannes Martini and the Imitation Mass of the Late Fifteenth Century." *Journal of the American Musicological Society* 38, no. 3 (Autumn): 470–523.

Burkholder, J. Peter. 1985. "Quotation and Emulation: Charles Ives's Use of His Models." *Musical Quarterly* 71, no.1: 1–26.

Burkholder, J. Peter. 1988. "Charles Ives and His Fathers: A Response to Maynard Solomon." *ISAM Newsletter* 18, no. 1 (November): 8–11.

Burkholder, J. Peter. 1993. "Music Theory and Musicology." *Journal of Musicology* 11, no. 1 (Winter): 11–23.

Burkholder, J. Peter. 1994. "The Uses of Existing Music: Musical Borrowing as a Field." *Notes* 50 (March): 852–859.

Burkholder, J. Peter. 1995. *All Made of Tunes: Charles Ives and the Uses of Musical Borrowing*. New Haven: Yale University Press.

Burkholder, J. Peter. 2010. Interview by author, November 4.

Burkholder, J. Peter. 2011. Email to author, August 8.

Burkholder, J. Peter, ed. 2002. *Charles Ives and His World*. Princeton: Princeton University Press.

Burton, Humphrey. 1994. *Leonard Bernstein*. New York: Doubleday.

Busoni, Ferrucio. 1911. *Sketch of a New Esthetic of Music*. Translated by Theodore Baker. New York: G. Schirmer.

Cage, John. 1961. "History of Experimental Music in the United States." In *Silence*, 67–75. Middletown, Conn.: Wesleyan University Press.

Capper, Charles. 1998. "'A Little Beyond': The Problem of the Transcendentalist Movement in American History." *Journal of American History* 85, no. 2 (September): 502–539.

Caroll, Mark. 2003. *Music and Ideology in Cold War Europe*. Cambridge: Cambridge University Press.

Carter, Elliott. 1939. "The Case of Mr. Ives." *Modern Music* 16 (March-April): 172–176.

Charles, Sydney Robinson. 1959. "The Music of the Pepys Manuscript 1236." PhD diss., University of California, Berkeley.

Charles, Sydney Robinson. 1967. "The Use of Borrowed Material in Ives' Second Symphony." *Music Review* 28, no. 2 (May): 102–111.

Chase, Gilbert. 1955. *America's Music: From the Pilgrims to the Present*. New York: McGraw-Hill Book Company.

Chase, Gilbert. 1958. "A Dialectical Approach to Music History." *Ethnomusicology* 2, no. 1 (January): 1–9.

Chase, Gilbert. 1977. Introduction to "Ives and American Culture." In *An Ives Celebration*, 3. Edited by H. Wiley Hitchcock and Vivian Perlis. Urbana: University of Illinois Press.

Child, Francis James. 1883–1898. *The English and Scottish Popular Ballads*. 10 vols. Boston: Houghton, Mifflin and Company.

Chmaj, Betty E. 1979. "Sonata for American Studies: Perspectives on Charles Ives." *Prospects*: 1–58.

Conn, Peter. 1983. *The Divided Mind: Ideology and Imagination in America, 1898–1917*. Cambridge: Cambridge University Press.

Cooney, Denise Von Glahn: *see also* Von Glahn, Denise.

Cooney, Denise Von Glahn. 1995. "Reconciliations: Time, Space and American Place in the Music of Charles Ives." PhD diss., University of Washington.

Cooney, Denise Von Glahn. 1996. "A Sense of Place: Charles Ives and 'Putnam's Camp, Redding, Connecticut." *American Music* 14, no. 3 (Fall): 276–312.

Copland, Aaron. 1934. "One Hundred and Fourteen Songs." *Modern Music* 11, no. 2 (January-February): 59–64.

Copland, Aaron. 1952. "The Composer in Industrial America." In *Music and Imagination: The Charles Elliott Norton Lectures, 1951–1952,* 96–111. Cambridge: Harvard University Press.

Copland, Aaron, and Vivian Perlis. 1984. *Copland: 1900 through 1942.* New York: St. Martin's Griffin.

Cowell, Henry. 1925. "America Takes a Front Rank in Year's Modernist Output." *Musical America* 41, no. 23 (March 28): 5, 35.

Cowell, Henry. 1925. "The Value of Eclecticism." *Sackbut* 5, no. 9: 264–265.

Cowell, Henry. 1927. "Moravian Music." *Pro-Musica Quarterly* 5, no. 2 (1927): 25–29.

Cowell, Henry. 1927. "Our Inadequate Notation." *Modern Music* 4 (March-April): 29–33.

Cowell, Henry. 1929. "Hidden Irish Treasure." *Modern Music* 6, no. 4: 31–33.

Cowell, Henry. 1930. "Three Native Composers." *New Freeman* 1, no. 8 (May 3): 184–186.

Cowell, Henry. 1932. "American Composers IX: Charles Ives." *Modern Music* 10, no. 1 (November-December): 24–32.

Cowell, Henry. 1933. "Trends in American Music." In *American Composers on American Music: A Symposium,* 3–13. Stanford: Stanford University Press.

Cowell, Henry. 2001. *Essential Cowell: Selected Writings on Music.* Edited by Dick Higgins. Kingston: McPherson.

Cowell, Henry. Papers. JPB 00-03. Music Division, The New York Public Library for the Performing Arts. New York. Quotations from the Henry Cowell Papers are used with the permission of The Richard and Sylvia Teitelbaum Fund, as successors to Henry and Sidney Cowell.

Cowell, Henry, and Sidney Cowell. 1955. "Charles Ives." *Perspectives, USA* 13 (Autumn): 38–56.

Cowell, Henry, and Sidney Cowell. 1955. *Charles Ives and His Music.* New York: Oxford University Press.

Cowell, Sidney. 1990. "The Cowells and the Written Word." In *A Celebration of American Music: Words and Music in Honor of H. Wiley Hitchcock,* 79–91. Edited by Richard Crawford, R. Allen Lott, and Carol J. Oja. Ann Arbor: University of Michigan Press.

Cowley, Malcolm. 1936. "The Puritan Legacy." *New Republic* 88 (August 26): 80.

Crawford, Dorothy Lamb. 1995. *Evenings On and Off the Roof: Pioneering Concerts in Los Angeles, 1939–1971.* Berkeley: University of California Press.

Crawford, Richard. 2005. "MUSA's Early Years: The Life and Ties of a National Editing Project." *American Music* 23, no. 1 (Spring): 1–38.

Creelman, James. 1893. "Real Value of Negro Melodies." *New York Herald* (May 21): 28.

Crunden, Robert. 1973. "Freud, Erikson, and the Historian: A Bibliographical Survey." *Canadian Review of American Studies* 4, no. 1 (Spring): 48–64.

Crunden, Robert M. 1972. *From Self to Society, 1919–1941*. New Jersey: Prentice Hall.

Crunden, Robert M. 1978. "Charles Ives's Place in American Culture." In *An Ives Celebration*, 4–15. Edited by H. Wiley Hitchcock and Vivian Perlis. Urbana: University of Illinois Press.

Crunden, Robert M. 1982. *Ministers of Reform: The Progressives' Achievement in American Civilization 1889–1920*. New York: Basic Books.

Crunden, Robert M. 1997. Review of *Charles Ives: A Life with Music* by Jan Swafford. *Modernism-Modernity* 4, no. 3 (September): 154–159.

Cyr, Gordon. 1971. "Intervallic Structural Elements in Ives's Fourth Symphony." *Perspectives of New Music* 9/2–10/1 (Spring/Winter): 291–303.

Dahlhaus, Carl. 1983. "Problems in Reception History." In *Foundations of Music History*, 150–165. Translated by J. B. Robinson. Cambridge: Cambridge University Press.

Dahlhaus, Carl. 1989. *The Idea of Absolute Music*. Translated by Roger Lustig. Chicago: University of Chicago Press.

Daniel, Oliver. 1982. *Stokowski: A Counterpoint of View*. New York: Dodd, Mead, and Company.

Davidson, Audrey. 1970. "Transcendental Unity in the Works of Charles Ives." *American Quarterly* 22, no. 1 (Spring): 35–44.

Davidson, Colleen C. 1968. "Winston Churchill and Charles Ives: The Progressive Experience in Literature and Song." *Student Musicologists at Minnesota* 3: 168–194.

Davis, Allen F. 1990. "The Politics of American Studies." *American Quarterly* 42, no. 3 (September): 353–374.

Dayton, Daryl D. 1975–1976. "Charles Ives in the USIA." *Student Musicologists at Minnesota* 6: 87–94.

Delacoma, Wynne. 1999. "Balancing Conducting, Composition." *Chicago Sun-Times* (May 6).

Densmore, Frances. 1922. *Northern Ute Music*. Washington, D.C.: Government Printing Office, 1922.

Diner, Steven J. 1998. "Bibliographical Essay." In *A Very Different Age: Americans of the Progressive Era*, 276–299. New York: Hill and Wang.

Downes, Olin. 1925. "Franco-American Musical Society." *New York Times* (February 15).

Downes, Olin. 1946. "Tardy Recognition." *New York Times* (April 14).

Downes, Olin. 1951. "Symphony by Ives Is Played in Full." *New York Times* (February 23).

Duberman, Martin. 1969. "The Abolitionists and Psychology." In *The Uncompleted Past*, 3–14. New York: Random House.

Duberman, Martin. 1972. *Black Mountain: An Exploration in Community*. New York: E. P. Dutton.

Duberman, Martin. 1974. "Those Parts of a Life That Contain the Evidence of History." *New York Times* (January 27).

Duberman, Martin. 1991. *Cures: A Gay Man's Odyssey*. New York: Dutton.

Duberman, Martin B. Papers. MssCol 848. Manuscripts and Archives Division, The New York Public Library. Astor, Lenox and Tilden Foundations.

Eichler, Jeremy. 2004. "The American Canon's Unabashed Patriot." *New York Times* (January 28).

Eiseman, David. 1972. "Charles Ives and the European Symphonic Tradition: A Historical Reappraisal." PhD diss., University of Illinois, Urbana-Champaign.

Ellingson, Ter. 1992. "Transcription." In *Ethnomusicology: An Introduction*, 122–125. Edited by Helen Meyers. New York: W. W. Norton.

Emerson, Ralph Waldo. 1840. "Thoughts on Modern Literature." *Dial* 1, no. 2 (October): 135–158.

Emerson, Ralph Waldo. 1880. "Spiritual Laws." In *Works of Ralph Waldo Emerson*. Vol. 1, 105–133. Boston: Houghton, Osgood and Company.

Emerson, Ralph Waldo. 1883. *The Correspondence of Thomas Carlyle and Ralph Waldo Emerson, 1834–1872*. 3rd ed. Vol. 2. Boston: James R. Osgood.

Emerson, Ralph Waldo. 1968. "The American Scholar." In *Ralph Waldo Emerson: Essays and Journals*, 31–47. New York: Doubleday.

Erikson, Erik H. 1958. *Young Man Luther: A Study in Psychoanalysis and History*. New York: W. W. Norton.

Everist, Mark. 1999. "Reception Theories, Canonic Discourse, and Musical Value." In *Rethinking Music*, 378–402. Edited by Nick Cook and Mark Everist. Oxford: Oxford University Press.

Feder, Stuart. 1992. *Charles Ives, 'My Father's Song': A Psychoanalytic Biography*. New Haven: Yale University Press.

Feder, Stuart. 2001. "Heard Maladies Are Sweet ('But Those Unheard Are Sweeter'): A Response to Gayle Sherwood." *Journal of the American Musicological Society* 54, no. 3 (Fall): 627–641.

Fenlon, Iain. 1980–1982. *Music and Patronage in Sixteenth-Century Mantua*. 2 vols. Cambridge: Cambridge University Press.

Filene, Peter. 1970. "An Obituary for the 'Progressive Movement.'" *American Quarterly* 22, no. 1 (Spring): 20–34.

Fischer, Heinz-Dietrich. 2001. "History and Development of the Pulitzer Prize for Music." In *Musical Composition Awards 1943–1999: From Aaron Copland and Samuel Barber to Gian-Carlo Menotti and Melinda Wagner*, xvii–xxvi. Edited by Heinz-Dietrich Fischer and Erika J. Fischer. München: K. G. Saur.

Fish, Stanley. 1980. "Is There a Text in This Class?" In *Is There a Text in This Class? The Authority of Interpretive Communities*, 303–321. Cambridge: Harvard University Press.

Fitzpatrick, Ellen. 2002. *History's Memory: Writing America's Past, 1880–1980*. Cambridge: Harvard University Press.

Fleming, Shirley. 1975. "Of Ives, Elephants, and Polish Independence." *High Fidelity/Musical America* 25, no. 2 (February 1975): MA 26–29.

Fletcher, Lucille. ca. 1939. "A Connecticut Yankee in Music." Charles Ives Papers. Mss. 14, folder 5, box 54. Irving S. Gilmore Music Library, Yale University. New Haven.

Forte, Allen. 1979. "Comment and Chronicle." *19th-Century Music* 2, no. 3 (March): 284–285.

Frank, Waldo. 1919. *Our America*. New York: Boni and Liverright.

Frankel, Max. 1959. "Bernstein Work Heard in Moscow." *New York Times* (August 24).

Freud, Sigmund. [1910] 1989. "Leonardo da Vinci and a Memory of His Childhood." In *The Freud Reader*, 443–481. Edited by Peter Gay. Reprint, New York: W. W. Norton.

Freud, Sigmund. [1928] 1997. "Dostoevsky and Parricide." In *Writings on Art and Literature*, 234–255. Reprint, Stanford: Stanford University Press.

Fromm, Erich. 1941. *Escape from Freedom*. New York: Rinehart and Company.

Garland, Peter. 1991. "The American Experimental Tradition: A Personal Perspective." In *In Search of Silvestre Revueltas: Essays 1978–1990*, 5–16. Santa Fe: Soundings Press.

Garrett, Charles Hiroshi. 2008. "Charles Ives's *Four Ragtime Dances* and 'True American Music.'" In *Struggling to Define a Nation: American Music and the Twentieth Century*, 17–47. Berkeley: University of California Press.

Geertz, Clifford. [1973] 2000. *The Interpretation of Culture*. Reprint, New York: Basic Books.

Geselbracht, Raymond H. 1975. "Transcendental Renaissance in the Arts: 1890–1920." *New England Quarterly* 48 (December): 463–486.

Gilbert, Felix. 1972. "Intellectual History: Its Aims and Methods." In *Historical Studies Today*, 141–158. Edited by Felix Gilbert and Stephen R. Graubard. New York: W. W. Norton.

Gilman, Lawrence. 1908. *Edward MacDowell: A Study*. New York: John Lane Company.

Gilman, Lawrence. 1939. "Music: A Masterpiece of American Music Heard for the First Time." *New York Herald Tribune* (January 21). Reproduced 2002, in *Charles Ives and His Music*, 316–321. Edited by J. Burkholder. Princeton: Princeton University Press.

Glass, Herbert. 1987. "Mainstream Americana." *Los Angeles Times* (January 18).

Goldenweiser, Alexander. 1930–1935. "Evolution, Social." In *The Encyclopaedia of the Social Sciences* Vol. 5, 656–662. Edited by Edwin R. A. Seligman. New York: Macmillan.

Gougeon, Len. 2010. "Abolition and the Biographers." In *Virtue's Hero: Emerson, Antislavery, and Reform*, 1–23. Athens: University of Georgia Press.

Gross, Robert A. 1999. "The Celestial Village: Transcendentalism and Tourism in Concord." In *Transient and Permanent: The Transcendentalist Movement and Its Context*, 251–281. Edited by Charles Capper and Conrad Edick Wright. Studies in American History and Culture, No. 5. Boston: Massachusetts Historical Society.

Grout, Donald J. 1960. *A History of Western Music*. New York: W. W. Norton.

Grout, Donald J., Claude V. Palisca, and J. Peter Burkholder. 2005. *A History of Western Music*. 7th ed. New York: W. W. Norton.

Hale, Philip. 1995. "Popular Images of Controversy: Freud's Changing Reputation and the Psychotherapy Jungle" and "The Crisis of American Psychoanalysis." In *The Rise of Crisis of Psychoanalysis in the United States: Freud and the Americans 1917–1985*, 345–359 and 360–379. New York: Oxford University Press.

Hall, David. 1964. "Charles Ives: An American Original." *HiFi/Stereo Review* 13, no. 3 (September): 43–58.

Hall, David. 1965. "Premiere and Cultural Turning Point: Charles Ives' Fourth Symphony." *HiFi/Stereo Review* 15, no. 1 (July): 55–58.

Hamm, Charles. 1995. Review of *Forty Earlier Songs*. *Notes*, 2nd series, 51: 1124–1125.

Hansen, Chadwick. 1963. Review of *Essays Before a Sonata and Other Writings*, by Charles Ives. Edited by Howard Boatwright. *American Quarterly* 25, no. 4 (Winter): 593–594.

Hanslick, Eduard. [1854] 1986. *On the Musically Beautiful: A Contribution towards the Revision of the Aesthetics of Music*. Translated by Geoffrey Payzant. Indianapolis: Hackett.

Harrison, Lou. 1945. "The Rich and Varied New York Scene." *Modern Music* 22, no. 3 (March-April): 181–185.

Harrison, Lou. [1945] 1987. "Ruggles, Ives, Varèse." In *A Lou Harrison Reader*, 16–17. Edited by Peter Garland. Reprint, Santa Fe: Soundings Press.

Helms, Hans G. 1974. "Some Reflections on Charles E. Ives." In *Charles Ives Centennial Festival Conference*, 56–59. Edited by H. Wiley Hitchcock. New York: G. Schirmer, Inc., and Associated Music Publishers.

Helms, Hans G. 1975. "Charles Edward Ives—Ideal American or Social Critic?" *Current Musicology* 19: 37–44.

Henahan, Donal. 1987. "Is an Icon Becoming a Has-Been?" *New York Times* (April 5).

Henahan, Donal. 1988. "Did Ives Fiddle With the Truth?" *New York Times* (February 21).

Henderson, Clayton W. 1969. "Quotation as a Style Element in the Music of Charles Ives." PhD diss., Washington University.

Henderson, Clayton W. 1974. "Ives' Use of Quotation." *Music Educators Journal* 61, no. 2 (October): 24–28.

Henderson, Clayton W. 1990. *The Charles Ives Tunebook*. Warren, Mich.: Harmonie Park Press.

Henderson, Clayton W. 2008. *The Charles Ives Tunebook*. 2nd ed. Bloomington: Indiana University Press.

Henderson, Clayton W. 2010. Email to author, December 9.

Herrmann, Bernard. 1932. "Charles Ives." *Trend* 1, no. 3 (September, October, November): 99–101.

Herrmann, Bernard. 1945. "Four Symphonies by Charles Ives." *Modern Music* 22, no. 4 (May-June): 215–222.

Hicks, Michael. 1991. "The Imprisonment of Henry Cowell." *Journal of the American Musicological Society* 44, no. 1 (Spring): 92–119.

Hicks, Michael. 2002. *Henry Cowell, Bohemian*. Urbana: University of Illinois Press.

Higgins, Paula. 2004. "The Apotheosis of Josquin des Prez and Other Mythologies of Musical Genius." *Journal of the American Musicological Society* 57, no. 3 (Autumn): 443–510.

Higham, John. 1959. "The Cult of the 'American Consensus': Homogenizing Our History." *Commentary* 27 (February): 93–100.

Higham, John. 1979. Introduction to *New Directions in American Intellectual History*, xi–xix. Edited by John Higham and Paul K. Conkin. Baltimore: John Hopkins University Press.

Hitchcock, H. Wiley. 1968. "A Monumenta Americana?" *Notes*, 2nd series, 25, no. 1 (September): 5–11.

Hitchcock, H. Wiley. 1969. *Music in the United States: A Historical Introduction*. New Jersey: Prentice Hall.

Hitchcock, H. Wiley. 1977. *Ives*. London: Oxford University Press.

Hitchcock, H. Wiley. 1999. "Ives's 114 [+15] Songs and What He Thought of Them." *Journal of the American Musicological Society* 52, no.1 (Spring): 97–144.

Hitchock, H. Wiley. 2002. Interview by Frank J. Oteri. "Changing History: At Home with H. Wiley Hitchock." http://newmusicbox.org/44/interview_hitchcock.pdf. Accessed October 6, 2010.

Hitchcock, H. Wiley, ed. 1974. *Charles Ives Centennial Festival-Conference*. New York: G. Schirmer, Inc. . and Associated Music Publishers.

Hitchcock, H. Wiley, and Vivian Perlis. 1977. *An Ives Celebration*. Urbana: University of Illinois Press.

Hixson, Walter L. 1997. *Parting the Curtain: Propaganda, Culture and the Cold War*. New York: St. Martin's Press.

Hoffman, Alfred. 1974. "A Great Visionary Musician." In *Charles Ives Centennial Festival-Conference*, 60. Edited by H. Wiley Hitchcock. New York: G. Schirmer and Associated Music Publishers.

Hofstadter, Richard. [1948] 1989. *The American Political Tradition: And the Men Who Made It*. Reprint, New York: Vintage Books.

Hofstadter, Richard. 1955. *The Age of Reform: From Bryan to F. D. R.* New York: Vintage Books.

Hollinger, David. 1979. "Historians and the Discourse of Intellectuals." In *New Directions in American Intellectual History*, 42–63. Edited by John Higham and Paul K. Conkin. Baltimore: John Hopkins University Press.

Hollinger, David A. 1985. "Ethnic Diversity, Cosmopolitanism, and the Emergence of the American Liberal Intelligentsia." In *In the American Province: Studies in the History and Historiography of Ideas*, 56–73. Baltimore: John Hopkins University Press.

Hook, Sidney. 1949. "On the Battlefield of Philosophy." *Partisan Review* 16 (March): 251–253.

Hoopes, James. 1977. *Van Wyck Brooks: In Search of American Culture*. Amherst: University of Massachusetts Press.

Hughes, H. Stuart. 1952. *Oswald Spengler: A Critical Estimate*. New York: Charles Scribner's Sons.

Ives, Charles. 1920. *Essays Before a Sonata*. New York: Knickerbocker Press. Reprinted 1962, in *Essays Before a Sonata, and Other Writings*. Edited by Howard Boatwright. New York: W. W. Norton.

Ives, Charles. 1933. "Music and Its Future." In *American Composers on American Music*, 191–198. Edited by Henry Cowell. Stanford University: Stanford University Press.

Ives, Charles. 1956. *Sonatas for Violin and Piano*. Rafael Druian. John Simms. Mercury MG-50096 and MG-50097.

Ives, Charles. 1958. *Symphony No. 2*. New York Philharmonic. Leonard Bernstein. Columbia KL-5489.

Ives, Charles. 1972. *Memos*. Edited by John Kirkpatrick. New York: W. W. Norton.

Ives, Charles. 2007. *Selected Correspondence of Charles Ives*. Edited by Thomas Clarke Owens. Berkeley: University of California Press.

Ives, Charles. Papers. Mss. 14. Irving S. Gilmore Music Library, Yale University. New Haven.

Jauss, Hans Robert. 1982. "Literary History as a Challenge to Literary Theory." In *Toward an Aesthetic of Reception*, 3–45. Translated by Timothy Bahti. Minneapolis: University of Minnesota Press.

Johnson, Steven. 1993. "Henry Cowell, John Varian, and Halcyon." *American Music* 11: 1–27.

Johnson, Tom. 1979. "New Music New York New Institution." *Village Voice* (July 2).

Karnes, Kevin. 2008. *Music, Criticism, and the Challenge of History: Shaping Modern Musical Thought in Late Nineteenth-Century Vienna*. Oxford: Oxford University Press.

Kastendieck, Miles. 1951. "Ives Symphony Is Interesting." *New York Journal-American* (February 23).

Kelly, R. Gordon. 1999. "Literature and the Historian." In *Locating American Studies: The Evolution of a Discipline*, 91–113. Edited by Lucy Maddox. Baltimore: John Hopkins University Press.

Kerman, Joseph. 1985. *Contemplating Music: Challenges to Musicology*. Cambridge: Harvard University Press.

Kerst, Catherine Hiebert. 1994. "Sidney Robertson and the WPA Northern California Music Project." *Sonneck Society Bulletin* 20, no. 3 (Fall): 5–9.

Kessler-Harris, Alice. 1997. "Social History." In *The New American History*. 2nd ed., 231–256. Edited by Eric Foner. Philadelphia: Temple University Press.

Key, Susan, and Larry Rothe, eds. 2001. *American Mavericks*. Berkeley: University of California.

Kinkeldey, Otto. 1928. "American Scholarship in Music since 1876." *Music Teachers National Association: Proceedings* 23: 244–256.

Kirkpatrick, John. 1958. "Ives's Transcendental Achievement." Typescript for talk given July 4. John Kirkpatrick Papers. Mss. 56, folder 568, box 61. Irving S. Gilmore Music Library, Yale University. New Haven. Used by permission of Daisy Kirkpatrick.

Kirkpatrick, John. 1960. *A Temporary Mimeographed Catalogue of the Music Manuscripts and Related Materials of Charles Edward Ives* (1874–1954). New Haven: Library of the Yale School of Music.

Kirkpatrick, John. 1961. "Ives, Transcendentalist in Music." Typescript for talk given October 26. John Kirkpatrick Papers. Mss. 56, folder 568, box 61. Irving S. Gilmore Music Library, Yale University. New Haven. Used by permission of Daisy Kirkpatrick.

Kirkpatrick, John. 1977. Response to "Charles Ives: Good American and Isolated Artist," by Frank R. Rossiter." In *An Ives Celebration*, 27. Edited by H. Wiley Hitchcock and Vivian Perlis. Urbana: University of Illinois Press.

Kirkpatrick, John. Papers. Mss. 56. Irving S. Gilmore Music Library, Yale University. New Haven.

Klein, Howard. 1965. "20th-Century Music Is Offered in a Concert at the New School." *New York Times* (June 5).

Kleinfield, H. L. 1968. "The Structure of Emerson's Death." In *Ralph Waldo Emerson: A Profile*, 175–199. Edited by Carl Bode. New York: Hill and Wang.

Kodish, Debora. 1986. *Good Friends and Bad Enemies: Robert Winslow Gordon and the Study of American Folksong*. Chicago: University of Illinois Press.

Kosman, Joshua. 1996. "American Festival Rocks Davies—Ex-Grateful Dead at Symphony Concert." *San Francisco Chronicle* (June 17).

Kosman, Joshua. 2003. "Voice of America: John Adams Speaks for the Nation." *San Francisco Chronicle* (May 18).

Kramer, A. Walter. 1921. "A Pseudo-Literary Sonata!!!" *Musical America* 33, no. 23 (April 2): 36.

Kramer, Lawrence. 1990. *Music as Cultural Practice, 1800–1900*. Berkeley: University of California Press.

Kramer, Lawrence. 1995. *Classical Music and Postmodern Knowledge*. Berkeley: University of California Press.

Lambert, Philip. 1989. Letter to the editor. *Journal of the American Musicological Society* 42, no. 1 (Spring): 204–209.

Lambert, Philip. 1997. *The Music of Charles Ives*. Yale: Yale University Press.

Lang, Paul Henry. 1946. "Hearing Things: Charles Ives." *Saturday Review of Literature* 29, no. 22 (June 1): 43–44.

Lang, Paul Henry. 1958. "Music." *New York Herald Tribune* (October 4).

Langer, William L. 1958. "The Next Assignment." *American Historical Review* 63, no. 2 (January): 321–363.

Larson, Gary O. 1975–1976. "Charles Ives and American Studies." *Student Musicologists at Minnesota* 6: 237–249.

LaRue, Jan. 1970. *Guidelines for Style Analysis*. New York: W. W. Norton Publishers.

Lasch, Christopher. 1989. Foreword to *The American Political Tradition: And the Men Who Made It*, by Richard Hofstadter. New York: Vintage Books.

Laughlin, James. 1952. "The Function of This Magazine." *Perspectives USA* 1 (Fall): 5–6.

Lerner, Gerda. 1976. "Placing Women in History: A 1975 Perspective." In *Liberating Women's History: Theoretical and Critical Essays*, 357–368. Edited by Bernice A. Carroll. Urbana: University of Illinois Press.

Levine, Lawrence W. 1988. *Highbrow/Lowbrow: The Emergence of Cultural Hierarchy in America*. Cambridge: Harvard University Press.

Levine, Stuart. 1986. "Euterpe and the Bigots." *American Quarterly* 38, no. 4 (Autumn): 675–680.

Lomax, John. 1915. "Some Types of American Folk-Song." *Journal of American Folklore* 28, no. 144: 1–17.

Lowell, Amy, ed. 1915. *Some Imagist Poets*. Boston: Houghton and Mifflin.

Magee, Gayle Sherwood: *see also* Sherwood, Gayle.

Magee, Gayle Sherwood. 2008. *Charles Ives Reconsidered*. Urbana: University of Illinois Press.

Magee, Gayle Sherwood. 2010. Interview by author, November 6.

Manfred, Frederick. 1975–1976. "Ives and Faulkner." *Student Musicologists at Minnesota* 6: 1–4.

Marshall, Dennis. 1968. "Charles Ives's Quotations: Manner or Substance?" *Perspectives of New Music* 6, no. 2 (Spring/Summer): 45–56.

Massey, Drew. 2007. "The Problem of Ives's Revisions, 1973–1987." *Journal of American Musicological Society* 60, no. 3 (Fall): 599–645.

Massey, Drew. 2010. "An 'Unobtrusive Minister of Genius': John Kirkpatrick and the Editing of Contemporary American Music." PhD diss., Harvard University.

Matthiessen, F. O. 1941. *American Renaissance: Art and Expression in the Age of Emerson and Whitman.* London: Oxford University Press.

McClary, Susan. 1991. *Feminine Endings: Music, Gender, and Sexuality.* Minneapolis: University of Minnesota Press.

McClure, John. 1967. "Charles Ives—Lonely American Giant." *Gramophone* 44, no. 527 (April): 516–517.

McGill, Josephine. 1917. *Folk Songs of the Kentucky Mountains.* New York: Boosey and Co.

McGinness, John. 2006. "Essay: Has Modernist Criticism Failed Charles Ives?" *Music Theory Spectrum* 28: 99–109.

McMahan Jr., H. E. 1951. Letter to the music editor. *New York Times* (March 11).

McPherson, James. 1964. *The Struggle for Equality: Abolitionists and the Negro in the Civil War and Reconstruction.* Princeton: Princeton University Press.

McPherson, James. 1965. *The Negro's Civil War: How American Negroes Felt and Acted During the Civil War and Reconstruction.* New York: Pantheon Books.

Meikle, Jeffrey L., Shelley Fisher Fishkin, and Neil Foley. 2000–2001. "In Memoriam: Robert Crunden." http://www.utexas.edu/faculty/council/2000–2001/memorials/Crunden/crunden.html. Accessed December 20, 2010.

Metzer, David. 2003. "Childhood and Nostalgia in the Works of Charles Ives." In *Quotation and Cultural Meaning in Twentieth-Century Music*, 15–46. Cambridge: Cambridge University Press.

Miller, Donald L. 1989. *Lewis Mumford: A Life.* New York: Weidenfeld and Nicolson.

Miller, Leta E. 2000. "The Art of Noise: John Cage, Lou Harrison, and the West Coast Percussion Ensemble." In *Perspectives on American Music, 1900–1950*, 215–263. Edited by Michael Saffle. New York: Garland.

Miller, Leta E., and Frederic Lieberman. 1998. *Lou Harrison: Composing a World.* Oxford: Oxford University Press.

Miller, Leta E., and Rob Collins. 2005. "The Cowell-Ives Relationship: A New Look at Cowell's Prison Years." *American Music* 23, no. 4 (Winter 2005): 473–492.

Miller, Perry. 1950. *The Transcendentalists: An Anthology.* Cambridge: Harvard University Press.

Mitchell, Charles E. 1997. *Individualism and Its Discontents: Appropriations of Emerson, 1880–1950.* Amherst: University of Massachusetts Press.

Moor, Paul. 1948. "On Horseback to Heaven: Charles Ives." *Harpers* 197 (September): 65–73.

Moore, MacDonald Smith. 1985. *Yankee Blues: Musical Culture and American Identity.* Bloomington: Indiana University Press.

Morgan, Robert P. 1973. "Rewriting Music History: Second Thoughts on Ives and Varèse." *Musical Newsletter* 3, no. 1 (January): 3–14.

Morgan, Robert P. 1978. "Ives and Mahler: Mutual Responses at the End of an Era." *19th-Century Music* 2, no. 1 (July): 72–81.

Morgan, Robert P. 1991. *Twentieth-Century Music: A History of Musical Style in Modern Europe and America*. New York: Norton.

Morgan, Robert P. 2010. Interview by author, October 21.

Mugglestone, Erica. 1981. "Guido Adler's 'The Scope, Method, and Aim of Musicology' (1885): An English Translation with an Historico-Analytical Commentary." *Yearbook for Traditional Music* 13: 1–21.

Mumford, Lewis. 1924. *Sticks and Stones: A Study of American Architecture and Civilization*. New York: Bone and Liveright.

Mumford, Lewis. 1926. *The Golden Day: A Study in American Literature and Culture*. New York: Boni and Liveright.

Mumford, Lewis. 1939. "Spengler's *The Decline of the West*." In *Books That Changed Our Mind*, 217–235. Edited by Malcolm Cowley and Bernard Smith. New York: The Kelmscott Editions.

Nettl, Bruno. 1999. "The Institutionalization of Musicology: Perspectives of a North American Ethnomusicologist." In *Rethinking Music*, 287–310. Edited by Nicolas Cook and Mark Everist. New York: Oxford University Press.

Newcomb, Anthony. 1980. *The Madrigal at Ferrara: 1579–1597*. Princeton: Princeton University Press.

Newman, Philip Edward. 1967. "The Songs of Charles Ives." PhD diss., University of Iowa.

Nicholls, David. 1990. *American Experimental Music, 1890–1940*. Cambridge: Cambridge University Press.

Oja, Carol. 2000. *Making Music Modern: New York in the 1920s*. Oxford: Oxford University Press.

O'Reilly, F. Warren, ed. 1976. *South Florida's Historic Ives Festival 1974–1976*. Miami: University of Miami.

Owens, Thomas Clark. 1999. "Charles Ives and His American Context: Images of 'Americanness' in the Arts." PhD diss., Yale University.

Page, Tim. 1987. "Judging Composers: High Notes, and Low." *New York Times* (March 22).

Palisca, Claude V. 1963. "American Scholarship in Western Music." In *Musicology*, 89–213. Edited by Frank L. Harrison, Mantle Hood, and Claude V. Palisca. Englewood Cliffs, N.J.: Prentice Hall.

Pancoast, Henry S. 1898. *An Introduction to American Literature*. New York: Henry Holt.

Parmenter, Ross. 1964. "The World of Music: I.S.C.M. Concert 'Under the Lippolds' Will Benefit Its Downtown Series." *New York Times* (February 9).

Parrington, Vernon Louis. 1930. *Main Currents in American Thought: An Interpretation of American Literature from the Beginnings to 1920*. New York: Harcourt, Brace, and Company.

Paul, David C. 2006. "From American Ethnographer to Cold War Icon: Charles Ives through the Eyes of Henry and Sidney Cowell." *Journal of the American Musicological Society* 59, no. 2 (Summer): 399–458.

Pells, Richard H. 1985. *The Liberal Mind in a Conservative Age: American Intellectuals in the 1940s and 1950s.* New York: Harper and Row.

Perlis, Vivian. 1974. *Charles Ives Remembered: An Oral History.* New Haven: Yale University Press.

Perlis, Vivian. 2008. Interview by author, March 19.

Perry, Rosalie Sandra. 1974. *Charles Ives and the American Mind.* Kent: Kent State University Press.

Pescatello, Ann M. 1992. *Charles Seeger: A Life in American Music.* Pittsburgh: University of Pittsburgh Press.

Pollack, Howard. 1999. *Aaron Copland: The Life and Work of an Uncommon Man.* New York: Henry Holt and Co.

Potter, David M. 1954. *People of Plenty: Economic Abundance and the American Character.* Chicago: University of Chicago Press.

Potter, Pamela. 1999. "From Jewish Exile in Germany to German Scholar in America: Alfred Einstein's Emigration." In *Driven into Paradise: The Musical Migration from Nazi Germany to the United States*, 298–321. Edited by Reinhold Brinkmann and Christoph Wolff. Berkeley: University of California Press.

Prizer, William F. 1985. "Isabella d'Este and Lucrezia Borgia as Patrons of Music: The Frottola at Mantua and Ferrara." *Journal of the American Musicological Society* 38, no. 1 (Spring): 1–33.

Rathert, Wolfgang. 1989. "The Unanswered Questions of the Ives Edition." Translated by James Lum. *Musical Quarterly* 73 (1989): 575–584.

Riedel, Johannes, and Robert Oudal. 1969. *A Charles Ives Primer.* Minneapolis: University of Minnesota.

Riesman, David, with Reuel Denney and Nathan Glazer. 1950. *The Lonely Crowd: A Study of the Changing American Character.* New Haven: Yale University Press.

Riley, Robert. 1966. "Debut Orchestra Gives Tour of 'New England.'" *Los Angeles Times* (March 6).

Rockwell, John. 1973. "Sound of New Music Is Likened to Art." *New York Times* (January 3).

Rockwell, John. 1979. "Underground Music Surfaces for a Nine-Day Festival." *New York Times* (June 3).

Rockwell, John. 1983. *All American Music: Composition in the Late Twentieth Century.* New York: Alfred A. Knopf.

Rockwell, John. 1986. "Experimental Music." In *The New Grove Dictionary of American Music*, 91–95. Edited by H. Wiley Hitchcock and Stanley Sadie. London: Macmillan Press.

Rodgers, Daniel T. 1982. "In Search of Progressivism." *Reviews in American History* 10, no. 4 (December): 113–132.

Rosenfeld, Paul. 1927. "Musical Chronicle." *Dial* 82 (April): 358.

Rosenfeld, Paul. 1929. *An Hour with American Music.* Philadelphia: J. B. Lippincott.

Rosenfeld, Paul. 1932. "Charles E. Ives." *New Republic* (July 20): 262–264.

Rosenfeld, Paul. 1932. "A Musical Tournament." *New Republic* (June 15): 119–121.

Rosenfeld, Paul. 1936. "Ives." In *Discoveries of a Music Critic*, 315–324. New York: Harcourt, Brace, and Company.

Rosenfeld, Paul. 1936. "The Nazis and 'Die Meistersinger.'" In *Discoveries of a Music Critic*, 89–99. New York: Harcourt, Brace, and Company.

Rosenfeld, Paul. 1939. "The Advent of American Music." *Kenyon Review* 1, no. 1 (Winter): 46–56.

Ross, Alex. 1994. "The Eccentrics Who Declared Independence for America." *New York Times* (May 22).

Rossiter, Frank R. 1970. "Charles Ives and American Culture: The Process of Development, 1874–1921." PhD diss., Princeton University.

Rossiter, Frank R. 1977. "Charles Ives: Good American and Isolated Artist." In *An Ives Celebration*, 16–26. Edited by H. Wiley Hitchcock and Vivian Perlis. Urbana: University of Illinois Press.

Rossiter, Frank. R. 1975. *Charles Ives and His America*. New York: Liveright.

Rourke, Constance. 1942. *The Roots of American Culture and Other Essays*. Edited by Van Wyck Brooks. New York: Harcourt, Brace, and Company.

Rubin, Joan Shelley. 1980. "Culture." In *Constance Rourke and American Culture*, 62–99. Chapel Hill: University of North Carolina Press.

Rubin, Joan Shelley. 1992. *The Making of Middlebrow Culture*. Chapel Hill: University of North Carolina Press.

Ruland, Richard. 1967. *The Rediscovery of American Literature: Premises of Critical Taste, 1900–1940*. Cambridge: Harvard University Press.

Rutkoff, Peter M., and William B. Scott. 1986. *New School: A History of the New School for Social Research*. New York: Free Press.

Sabin, Robert. 1951. "Bernstein Conducts Ives Symphony No. 2." *Musical America* 71, no. 4 (March): 32–33.

Salzman, Eric. 1967. *Twentieth-Century Music: An Introduction*. Englewood Cliffs, N.J.: Prentice Hall.

Salzman, Eric. 1968. "Charles Ives, American." *Commentary* 46, no. 2 (August): 37–43.

Salzman, Eric. 2009. Email to author, October 22.

Samson, Jim. 2001. "Reception." In *Grove Music Online*, *Oxford Music Online*. http://www.oxfordmusiconline.com/subscriber/article/grove/music/40600. Accessed September 12, 2011.

Santayana, George. 2001. "The Genteel Tradition in American Philosophy." In *The American Intellectual Tradition: A Sourcebook*. 4th ed. Vol. 2, 93–105. Edited by David A. Hollinger and Charles Capper. New York: Oxford University Press.

Sargeant, Winthrop P. 1958. "Musical Events: Saluting Mr. Ives." *New Yorker* 34 (October 11): 170.

Saunders, Frances. 1999. *The Cultural Cold War: The CIA and the World of Arts and Letters*. New York: The New Press.

Schiff, David. 2009. "Ives's Ears." *Nation* 288, no. 1 (January 5): 30–33.

Schonberg, Harold C. 1961. "A Complex Score Is Ives' No. 4." *New York Times* (April 25).

Schonberg, Harold C. 1961. "Stubborn Yankee." *New York Times* (March 5).

Schonberg, Harold C. 1965. "Music: Stokowski Conducts Ives's Fourth Symphony in World Premiere after 50 Years." *New York Times* (April 27).

Schonberg, Harold C. 1973. "Music: A Concert Fuss." *New York Times* (January 20).

Schonberg, Harold C. 1974. "Music: The Pulse of America Beats in the Music of Ives." *New York Times* (October 6).

Schrade, Leo. 1955. "Charles E. Ives: 1874–1954." *Yale Review* 44 (Summer): 535–545.

Sherwood, Gayle. 1994. "Questions and Veracities: Reassessing the Chronology of Ives's Choral Works." *Musical Quarterly* 78, no. 3 (Autumn): 429–447.

Sherwood, Gayle. 1995. "The Choral Works of Charles Ives: Chronology, Style, Reception." PhD diss., Yale University.

Sherwood, Gayle. 1999. "'Buds the Infant Mind': Charles Ives's *The Celestial Country* and American Protestant Choral Traditions." *19th-Century Music* 23, no. 2 (Fall): 163–189.

Sherwood, Gayle. 2001. "Charles Ives and 'Our National Malady.'" *Journal of the American Musicological Society* 54, no. 3 (Fall): 555–584.

Sherwood, Gayle. 2001. "Ives and Neurasthenia: A Response to Stuart Feder." *Journal of the American Musicological Society* 54, no. 3 (Fall): 641–643.

Shirley, Wayne D., comp. 1976. *Modern Music, Published by the League of Composers, 1924–1946: An Analytic Index*. Edited by William and Carolyn Lichtenwanger. New York: AMS Press.

Sinclair, James B. 1999. *A Descriptive Catalogue of the Music of Charles Ives*. New Haven: Yale University Press.

Singal, Daniel Joseph. 1984. "Beyond Consensus: Richard Hofstadter and American Historiography." *American Historical Review* 89, no. 4 (October): 976–1004.

Sklar, Robert. 1972. Review of *From Self to Society* by Robert M. Crunden. *Journal of American History* 59, no. 3 (December): 761–762.

Slonimsky, Nicolas. 1948. "Bringing Ives Alive." *Saturday Review of Literature* 31, no. 35 (August 28): 45–49.

Slonimsky, Nicolas. 1952. "Sur la musique Américaine." In *L'Oeuvre du XXe siècle*, 29. Paris: Congress for Cultural Freedom.

Slonimsky, Nicolas. 1953. "Musical Rebel." *Américas* 5, no. 9 (September): 6–8, 41–42.

Slonimsky, Nicolas. 2002. *Perfect Pitch*. Edited by Electra Slonimsky Yourke. New York: Schirmer Trade Books.

Smith, Henry Nash. 1950. *Virgin Land: The American West as Symbol and Myth*. Cambridge: Harvard University Press.

Soliday, Gerald L. 2009. Interview by author, January 19.

Solie, Ruth, ed. 1993. *Musicology and Difference: Gender and Sexuality in Musical Scholarship*. Berkeley: University of California Press.

Solomon, Maynard. 1977. *Beethoven*. New York: Schirmer Books.

Solomon, Maynard. 1987. "Charles Ives: Some Questions of Veracity." *Journal of the American Musicological Society* 40, no. 3 (Autumn): 443–470.

Solomon, Maynard. 1989. Letter to the editor. *Journal of the American Musicological Society* 42, no. 1 (Spring): 209–218.

Sonneck, Oscar. 1929. "The Future of Musicology in America." *Musical Quarterly* 15, no. 3 (July): 317–321.

Spengler, Oswald. 1932. *The Decline of the West: Complete in One Volume*. Translated by Charles Francis Atkinson. New York: Alfred A. Knopf.

Starr, Larry. 1977. "Charles Ives: The Next Hundred Years—Towards a Method of Analyzing the Music." *Music Review* 38, no. 2 (May): 101–111.

Starr, Larry. 1977. "Style and Substance: 'Ann Street' by Charles Ives." *Perspectives of New Music* 15, no. 2 (Spring-Summer): 23–33.

Starr, Larry. 1983. "The Early Styles of Charles Ives." *19th-Century Music* 7, no. 1 (Summer): 71–80.

Starr, Larry. 1992. *A Union of Diversities: Style in the Music of Charles Ives*. New York: Schirmer Books.

Starr, Larry. 2010. Interview by author, November 4.

Steinberg, Michael. 2006. "My Father Knew Charles Ives (2003)." In *The John Adams Reader: Essential Writings on an American Composer*, 205–208. Edited by Thomas May. Pompton Plains, N.J.: Amadeus Press.

Sterne, Colin. 1971. "The Quotations in Charles Ives's Second Symphony." *Music and Letters* 52, no. 1 (January): 39–45.

Stevenson, Robert. 1978. "American Musical Scholarship: Parker to Thayer." *19th-Century Music* 1, no. 3 (March): 191–210.

Stocking Jr., George W. 1968. "Franz Boas and the Culture Concept in the Historical Perspective." In *Race, Culture, and Evolution: Essays in the History of Anthropology*, 195–233. New York: Free Press.

Stokowski, Leopold. Papers. Mss. 381. Rare Book and Manuscript Library, University of Pennsylvania. Philadelphia.

Strauss, Noel. 1946. "Symphony by Ives in World Premiere." *New York Times* (April 6).

Stringham, Edwin J. 1921. "Ives Puzzles Critics with His Cubistic Sonata and 'Essays.'" *Rocky Mountain News* (July 31).

Subotnik, Rose Rosengard. 1991. *Developing Variations: Style and Ideology in Western Music*. Minneapolis: University of Minnesota Press.

Susman, Warren I. 1984. "'Personality' and Twentieth-Century Culture." In *Culture as History*, 271–285. New York: Pantheon Books.

Swafford, Jan. 1996. *Charles Ives: A Life with Music*. New York: W. W. Norton.

Swartz, Anne. 1987. Review of *Charles Ives: The Ideas behind the Music* by J. Peter Burkholder. *American Music* 5, no. 2 (Summer): 222–223.

Taruskin, Richard. 1975. Letter to the editor. *Current Musicology* 20 (1975): 33–40.

Taruskin, Richard. 1977. "Glinka's Ambiguous Legacy and the Birth Pangs of Russian Opera." *19th-Century Music* 1, no. 2 (November): 142–162.

Taruskin, Richard. 2000. "Corralling a Herd of Musical Mavericks." *New York Times* (July 23).

Taruskin, Richard. 2001. "Nationalism." In *The New Grove Dictionary of Music and Musicians*. 2nd ed., 689–706. New York: Oxford University Press.

Taruskin, Richard. 2004. "Underneath the Dissonance Beats a Brahmsian Heart." *New York Times* (May 16).

Taubman, Howard. 1948. "Records: Ives Sonata." *New York Times* (July 18).

Taubman, Howard. 1949. "Posterity Catches Up with Charles Ives." *New York Times Magazine* (October 23): 15, 34–36.

Teichgraeber III, Richard F. 2010. "'More than Luther of These Modern Days': The Social Construction of Emerson's Posthumous Reputation, 1882–1903." In *Building Culture: Studies in the Intellectual History of Industrializing America, 1867–1910*, 48–74. Columbia: University of South Carolina Press.

Thomas, Michael Tilson. 1982. Liner notes for *Symphony No. 2* by Charles Ives. Concertgebouw Orchestra. Michael Tilson Thomas. Columbia IM 37300 (1982).

Thomas, Michael Tilson, dir. 1970. *Three Places in New England*, by Charles Ives. *Suntreader*, by Carl Ruggles. Boston Symphony Orchestra. Deutsche Grammophon 2530 048.

Thomson, Virgil. 1970. "The Ives Case." *New York Review of Books* 14, no. 10 (May 21): 9–11.

Tick, Judith. 1973. "Women as Professional Musicians in the United States, 1870–1900." *Annaurio* 9: 95–133.

Tick, Judith. 1974. "Ragtime and the Music of Charles Ives." *Current Musicology* 18: 105–113.

Tick, Judith. 1993. "Charles Ives and Gender Ideology." In *Musicology and Difference: Gender and Sexuality in Music Scholarship*, 83–106. Edited by Ruth A. Solie. Berkeley: University of California Press.

Tick, Judith. 1997. "Charles Ives and the Politics of Direct Democracy." In *Ives Studies*, 133–162. Edited by Philip Lambert. Cambridge: Cambridge University Press.

Tick, Judith. 1997. *Ruth Crawford Seeger: A Composer's Search for American Music*. New York: Oxford University Press.

Tick, Judith. 2010. Interview by author, November 21.

Tick, Judith. 2012. Email to author, March 4.

Tomassini, Anthony, Allan Kozinn, Jeremy Eichler, Anne Midgette, and James R. Oestreich. 2004. "A Radical in a Suit and Tie: The One and Only Charles Ives." *New York Times* (May 7).

Townsend, Kim. 1987. *Sherwood Anderson*. Boston: Houghton Mifflin Company.

Treitler, Leo. 1969. "The Present as History." *Perspectives of New Music* 7, no. 2 (Spring-Summer): 1–58.

Treitler, Leo. 1974. "Methods, Style, Analysis." In *Report of the Eleventh Congress Copenhagen 1972*. Vol. 1, 61–70. Edited by Henrik Glahn, Søren Sørensen, and Peter Ryom. Copenhagen: Edition Wilhelm Hansen.

Trent, William P. 1903. *A History of American Literature, 1607–1865*. New York: Appleton.

Tryon, Winthrop P. 1924. "Folk Song and Hymn Tunes of America." *Christian Science Monitor* (November 29).

Tryon, Winthrop P. 1924. "'Freischütz' at the Metropolitan—Other Music of a New York Week." *Christian Science Monitor* (March 24).

Tryon, Winthrop P. 1927. "Of Ives and Others." *Christian Science Monitor* (February 3).

Tueville, Howard. 1974. "Festival in Ives Country." *Clavier* 13, no. 7 (October): 12–13.

Ulrich, Homer, and Paul A. Pisk. 1963. *A History of Music and Musical Style*. New York: Harcourt, Brace, and World.

Van de Vate, Nancy. 1975. "The American Woman Composer: Some Sour Notes." *High Fidelity/Musical America* (June): MA 18–19.

Veysey, Laurence. 1979. "Intellectual History and the New Social History." In *New Directions in American Intellectual History*, 3–26. Edited by John Higham and Paul K. Conkin. Baltimore: John Hopkins University Press.

Veysey, Laurence. 1979. "The New Social History in the Context of American Historical Writing." *Reviews in American History* 7, no. 1 (March): 1–12.

Von Glahn, Denise. 2003. "From Country to City in the Music of Charles Ives." In *The Sounds of Place: Music and the American Cultural Landscape*, 64–109. Boston: Northeastern University Press.

Wakin, Daniel J. 2007. "Newspapers Trimming Classical Critics." *New York Times* (June 9).

Wallach, Lawrence. 1975. "The Ives Conference: A Word from the Floor." *Current Musicology* 19 (1975): 32–36.

Ward, Charles Wilson. 1974. "Charles Ives: The Relationship between Aesthetic Theories and Compositional Processes." PhD diss., University of Texas, Austin.

Warren, Richard. 1972. *Charles E. Ives: Discography*. New Haven: Historical Sound Recordings, Yale University Library.

Weisgall, Hugo. 1959. "Music of Henry Cowell." *Musical Quarterly* 45, no. 4 (October): 484–507.

Whitmer, T. Carl. 1929. "New Music." *Musical Forecast* (March): 5–6.

Wiecki, Ronald V. 1992. "Two Musical Idealists—Charles E. Ives and E. Robert Schmitz: A Friendship Reconsidered." *American Music* 10, no. 1 (Spring): 1–19.

Wilson, Edmund. 1948. "Paul Rosenfeld: Three Phases." In *Paul Rosenfeld: Voyager in the Arts*, 3–19. Edited by Jerome Mellquist and Lucie Wiese. New York: Creative Age Press.

Wise, Gene. 1999. "'Paradigm Dramas' in American Studies: A Cultural and Institutional History of the Movement." In *Locating American Studies: The Evolution of a Discipline*, 166–214. Edited by Lucy Maddox. Baltimore: John Hopkins University Press.

Yates, Peter. 1944. "Charles Ives." *Arts and Architecture* 61, no. 9 (September): 20, 40.

Yates, Peter. 1950. "Charles Ives." *Arts and Architecture* 67, no. 2 (February): 13–17.

Yates, Peter. 1961. "Charles Ives: The Transcendental American Venture." Parts 1–3. *Arts and Architecture* 78, no. 2 (February): 6–8; no. 3 (March): 4, 8, 10–11; no. 5 (May): 6–8, 30–31.

Yates, Peter. 1967. *Twentieth-Century Music*. New York: Pantheon Books.

Yates, Peter. 1975. "Charles Ives: An American Composer." *Parnassus* 3, no. 2 (Spring/Summer): 318–328.

Yellin, Victor Fell. 1974. Review of *The Celestial Country*. *Musical Quarterly* 60, no. 3 (July): 500–508.

Zaher, Noel. 1990. Letter to the editor. *Perspectives of New Music* 28, no. 2 (Summer): 331–332.

Index

DAVID C. PAUL is an associate professor of musicology and theory at the University of California, Santa Barbara.

MUSIC IN AMERICAN LIFE

The University of Illinois Press
is a founding member of the
Association of American University Presses.

University of Illinois Press
1325 South Oak Street
Champaign, IL 61820-6903
www.press.uillinois.edu